African Agency in China's Tea Trade

African Social Studies Series

VOLUME 43

The titles published in this series are listed at *brill.com/afss*

African Agency in China's Tea Trade

Commercial Networks, Brand Creation and Intellectual Property

By

Ute Röschenthaler

BRILL

LEIDEN | BOSTON

Cover illustration: Examples of tea packages, photo by author.

Library of Congress Cataloging-in-Publication Data

Names: Röschenthaler, Ute, author.
Title: African agency in China's tea trade : commercial networks, brand creation and intellectual property / by Ute Röschenthaler.
Description: Leiden ; Boston : Brill, [2022] | Series: African social studies series, 1568-1203 ; volume 43 | Includes bibliographical references and index.
Identifiers: LCCN 2021059595 (print) | LCCN 2021059596 (ebook) | ISBN 9789004505681 (paperback ; alk. paper) | ISBN 9789004505698 (ebook)
Subjects: LCSH: Tea trade–China. | Tea trade–Africa, West. | China–Commerce–Africa, West. | Africa, West–Commerce–China.
Classification: LCC HD9198.C52 R67 2022 (print) | LCC HD9198.C52 (ebook) | DDC 338.1/73720951–dc23/20220104
LC record available at https://lccn.loc.gov/2021059595
LC ebook record available at https://lccn.loc.gov/2021059596

Typeface for the Latin, Greek, and Cyrillic scripts: "Brill". See and download: brill.com/brill-typeface.

ISSN 1568-1203
ISBN 978-90-04-50568-1 (paperback)
ISBN 978-90-04-50569-8 (e-book)

This book is printed on acid-free paper and produced in a sustainable manner.

Contents

Preface

When I wrote the first chapters of this book as a fellow of the African Studies Centre Leiden in February 2019, it was the time when China was fighting against the Corona crisis and large parts of its economy were slowed down. I wondered whether this had resulted in a shortage of green tea in Mali. The quantities they imported were considerable and a lack of tea could easily provoke withdrawal symptoms and social unrest. But in a conversation by telephone, my Malian assistant, Madou Keïta, reassured me that – despite the outbreak in China – the tea supply was sufficient and no shortage happened. It had not noticeably affected the tea sector.

During the 2012 political crisis, when the former Malian president was chased from his office, Malians indeed feared about a lack of tea when many importers of Saharan origin disappeared from the capital, Bamako, to the northern part of the country, anticipating public unrest directed against people from the north. Other Saharan importers remained. They continued to import tea and prevented a shortage of Mali's national drink. Times of crisis bring to mind what it could mean for the population when their national drink that is almost completely imported – including much of the sugar that sweetens the beverage and the equipment that is used for its preparation – would suddenly be no longer available. Its availability is to a large extent owed to the agency of Malian importers, being the patrons of the Chinese tea trade to Africa.

My interest in green tea began many years earlier, in 2005, during my first trip to Mali, with Mamadou Diawara and a group of students from Goethe University Frankfurt. We co-supervised their field schools that they carried out with their Malian research partners at Point Sud, Research Center for Local Knowledge, at Bamako. This was also the time when the tea brands began to multiply and green tea was about to become Mali's national drink. I was immediately fascinated by the tea packages with their amazing names and colourful images emblazoned upon them. But by then, I knew nothing yet about the importance of the beverage for Malians and that the importers travelled themselves to China to select the type of tea and designed their tea packages.

Soon, I began a collection of tea packages, enlarging it with every visit to Mali and to other African countries. The collection meanwhile comprises 163 brands, including 237 different packages because many brands are available in various types and varieties. The collection continues to grow with the assistance of friends and colleagues who send me tea packages from their journeys to West Africa. Parts of the collection were displayed at an exhibition at Schule des Sehens, Johannes Gutenberg University Mainz, Germany, from February to April 2019. On that occasion I also launched an online museum in which the collection can be visited and the tea brand design studied more permanently, at www.virtualgreenteamuseum.de.

Initially, I had intended to publish my research findings all together in one book. But it quickly became clear that such a study would have been too extensive. My findings have been developed into two books: this first volume about entrepreneurship and brand creation examines the landscape of the tea packages and the traders' agency to import and distribute Chinese green tea on African markets. It demonstrates how the major Malian merchants managed to cooperate with their Chinese partners and still succeeded in dominating the tea business. The second volume entitled *A History of Mali's National Drink: Following the Tea Ritual from China to West Africa* deals with the historical journey of green tea from China to Mali, its ritualised preparation and consumption, the equipment employed for this and the social importance Malians attribute to the beverage (Röschenthaler forthc.).

Acknowledgements

My heartfelt thanks are due to my assistant Madou Simbo Keïta in Bamako, without whose help this research on tea would not have been possible in this efficient and fruitful manner that we were able to carry it out. On his motorbike, we explored the city and reached our interview partners much faster than it would have ever been possible with a car. He made wonderful efforts to explain what anthropological research was about, for which purpose it was made and why I had to ask all these questions and details. Nearly all tea importers were open-minded, generous with their time, with gifts of tea and interested in exchanging information. I got to know Madou through Point Sud, Research Center on Local Knowledge, in Bamako, founded by Mamadou Diawara, professor for the anthropology of Africa at Goethe University Frankfurt, for which I want to express my gratitude.

I am grateful to Malian scholars, including Birama Diakon, Amadou Djikoroni, Issa Fofana, Bakary Kamian, Ramata Konaté, Seydou Badian Kouyaté, Malick Sidibe, Drissa Tangara, Daouda Tounkara as well as all the tea traders, importers, consumers, artists, media specialists, critics and officials who were ready to share their knowledge, experiences and business histories. Among these were Alain Achcar, Kalifa Ataher, Ayu, Habib Ben Baba, Abdoulaye Bonde, Abdoulaye Coulibaly, Mamadou Coulibaly, Oumar Diaby, Ramatoulaye and Mohamed Diallo, Ibrahima Diakité, Tahirou Diakité, Boureima Diarra, Moussa Diarra, Lobo Dramera, Mbaye Dramera, Dembele Famallon, Mariko Fofana, Moussa Fofana, Oumar Ag Hadraka, Amadou Haidara, Moulaye Haidara, Moussa Keïta, Dramane Konaté, Birama Koné, Mamadou Kouma, Almoctar Kounta, Hamane Koutam, Moulaye Koutam, Hathie Lah, Ousmane Lah, Mohamend Lamine, members of Sky Negoce, Bakary Sacko, Hamidou Sangare, Ibrahim Saramou, Sambou Sidibe, Oumar Sheik Sissoko, Mody Sylla, Boubacar Tambadou, Boubacar Tandia, Aly Traoré, Moussa Traoré, Ousmane Traoré, Mahamar Touré, Abderahmane Touré, Ibrahim Yara, Kalilou Yara, Mamadou Yatassaye, Yu Min and the Wafa representative in Bamako. I also discussed the topic with Malians in Germany, namely Soumaila Coulibaly at the Frobenius Institute and with Hamet Diop and his *grin* in Frankfurt and with Patrice Kamogne, Bono Armand, Antoine Socpa, Patrick Chena, and Mohamed Nsangu in Yaounde; AK Lee and many other Chinese brokers in Guangzhou and Zhejiang, and Malian merchants and brokers in Guangzhou, Shanghai and Hong Kong.

My thanks are also due to Mamadou Diawara for his insights from his Malian home town; with him I wrote a first article about Chinese green tea (Diawara and Röschenthaler 2012). For the explanation of Chinese words, I am grateful to Luo Li and Sarah Hanisch. Particular thanks are due to Clement Takang who created the virtual green tea museum. I thank Armand Bono who assisted me patiently and constructively with my tea research in Yaounde and Olivier Zongo for his help in finding tea shops on the market in Ouagadougou. I also thank Melanie Gärtner, Matthias Gruber and Ines Neubauer who accompanied me during travels to China and to Martine Nkou who came with me to visit tea factories in Zhejiang; to Li Anshan at Peking University and his Moroccan doctoral student who made the first contacts with tea factories. I thank Kim Glück for spending time in the Library of Congress in Washington to check the volumes of the *Bulletin Officiel de la Propriété Intellectuelle* (BOPI) on those issues that were missing in Bamako. My thanks are due to anthropologists and friends for their moral support and interest in the topic: Bärbel Küster offered inspiring discussion and new insights in the iconographic interpretation of tea packages; Valerie Hänisch told me what she knew about tea from her research in Niger; Soumaila Coulibaly discussed with me the tea ritual and brands; others collected tea packages for me: Bono Armand, Bärbel Küster, Soumaila Coulibaly, Kathrin Knodel, Hauke Dorsch, Kristin Kastner, Abdoulaye Sounaye and Olivier Zongo.

My findings on tea brands and the journey of tea from China to West Africa were presented in lectures and conferences at IFK in Vienna in 2019, Jinan University in Guangzhou in 2018, the University of Vienna 2017; Brunel University, London, 2017, Johannes Gutenberg University Mainz 2017 and 2019, Goethe University Frankfurt 2014, 2016 and 2021, Peking University 2014, University of Bayreuth 2012, at the ASA in Montreal 2011, the ECAS in Uppsala 2011, and the universities of Leipzig in 2010, Birmingham in 2010 and Oxford in 2008. To all the audiences at these events I am grateful for comments and inspiration.

Research on the topic was carried out with the generous help of many organisations and foundations: the four student field schools in 2005, 2007, 2010 and 2012 were supported by the Vereinigung der Freunde und Förderer der Goethe-Universität, the Stiftung zur Förderung der internationalen Beziehungen, the International Office and the Centre for Interdisciplinary African Studies, all at Goethe University Frankfurt; other research trips to Mali in 2011, 2013, 2016, to Cameroon in 2008, 2013, 2014, and to China in 2013, 2014, 2016 were supported by the cluster of excellence 'The Formation of Normative Orders', financed by the German Research Foundation (DFG), and the project 'Africa's Asian Options' (AFRASO), financed by the Federal Ministry of Education and Research (BMBF), and 2018 by Jinan University. I am grateful to the African Studies Centre, Leiden, for providing me with an ideal environment for the completion of this manuscript. I am also grateful to anonymous reviewers for their extremely helpful comments and to Martina Henn and Ralph Cook for their invaluable help in editing the manuscript.

Figures, Graphs and Table

Figures

All photographs are taken by the author, except when mentioned otherwise (permission has been obtained)

Graphs

Table

Introduction

Every month several thousand tons of green tea travel from China to West Africa in a movement that largely thrives beyond the attention of Western observers. Before consumers drink it, green tea has made a long journey. In this movement, that forms part of a growing South-South trade, Malian importers assumed a central role. They trade the growing quantities of green tea from China across half the globe to West African ports, from where they are transported to landlocked Mali. Presently, numerous entrepreneurial African (and some Chinese) traders import containers full of tea from China, placing their orders with the Chinese factories, paying for it and transporting the product to Africa.

Malian importers travel to China for tea – at the latest – since the early 2000s. They travel at their own expense, visiting the family gardens and plantations where the tea is produced, and the factories, which process and package the product for their customers. Several dozen Chinese tea factories have specialised their production to serve African markets. Importing tea requires substantial capital. One container of tea costs at least 65 million francs CFA (about 100,000 Euro) gross and successful importers each ship in at least five forty-foot containers of green tea every month. There are about thirteen such tea importers in Bamako and many more who import container loads of tea in less regular intervals.

Bamako, Mali's capital, has become a major distribution centre for Chinese green tea (Figure 1). The green tea importers bring increasing quantities of tea from China to Mali, distributing it within and beyond the country across their commercial networks, which extend from the cities to the countryside and connect Mali with neighbouring countries and regions. The tea trade provides work opportunities for many economic actors.

In the section called Dabanani on Bamako's largest market, the Grand Marché, more than a hundred different tea brands can be found (Figure 2). Most of the tea packages have been created by Malian merchants in cooperation with their Chinese suppliers. The packages have colourful, often eye-catching designs, with images and brand names such as *Gazelle*, *Tombouctou*, *Cinquantenaire*, *Africable*, or *Obama* (Figures 3a–e).[1] Smaller than cigarette boxes, these 25g packages feature and commemorate the strength of desert

1 The tea brand names and local translations of Chinese tea varieties are in italics, starting with capital letters, to distinguish them from the items (objects, places, people) that the names refer to.

 | DOI:10.1163/9789004505698_002

FIGURE 1 Part of Bamako's Grand Marché, note the piles of tea cartons on the left side of the street, 2013

FIGURE 2 Piled tea packages on the market, Bamako, 2012

FIGURES 3A–E Examples of tea packages: *Tombouctou*, *Africable*, *Askia*, *Cinquantenaire*, *Obama*

animals, the fading glory of trading places, the excitement of social events and the accomplishments of admired politicians. With the creation of the tea brands and their growing popularity, the question of intellectual property became a critical issue as numerous copies of the original tea packages appeared on the market.

Tea is a globalised product available in all corners of the world in many varieties. Among the various teas globally available, Malian consumers favour a particular type of green tea that is produced in China. It first arrived in Mali's north in the early nineteenth century where it was consumed by Saharan traders (Röschenthaler forthc.). After independence, Malians' awareness of the beverage grew, following the government's establishment of a tea plantation. From then on, growing acquaintance with green tea led to an increasing number of Malians starting to make tea drinking a habit and eventually the emergence of Bamako's present-day bustling tea market. In the 2000s, green tea consumption became so popular that it was considered Mali's national drink. Malians prepare their green tea in particular equipment and consume it, sweetened with generous amounts of sugar, in a ritual that can last several hours (for details see Röschenthaler forthc.) (Figure 4). The country has also become a strong centre for the distribution of green tea to adjacent countries.

This study provides new insights into the thriving West African tea culture. It tells the story of the present-day tea traders by whose agency green tea makes its journey from China to West Africa. It discusses their distribution networks and the knowledge and skills required for this trade. It also examines how the tea importers embrace the opportunities that the media and other institutions offer to advertise their products and defend their intellectual property rights in regard to tea brands. It intends to carve out some of the contradictions in which tea importers find themselves entangled: they participate in the neoliberal system of trade and intellectual property with its bureaucratic apparatus and are concomitantly bound to a moral economy of social relationships in

FIGURE 4 Session of young men's tea *grin*, Bamako, 2018
PHOTO BY ADAMA KEÏTA

the more socially responsible but not necessarily less stressful handling of economic goods.

With its focus on the agency of economic actors, the study connects approaches to trade networks and branding with the entrepreneurial activities of individuals who have dynamised West African consumption landscapes. It illustrates that this development is not necessarily dependent on predictable evolutions of the market but is the consequence of achievements of individuals spotting opportunities and invest appropriately. With some luck, grounded local knowledge and extensive social networks that have often grown over generations, some of them have become successful traders, importers and entrepreneurs. Many others, however, have tried to emulate their success, invested all their savings but their tea did not sell quickly enough to secure profits. These local merchants very successfully provided Malian consumers with the ingredients of a beverage that over the course of the 2000s became their favourite drink. The boom in Chinese green tea, the African importers travelling to China, their establishing distribution networks to adjacent countries and even beyond, the creation of their own tea brands and coping with brand piracy in West Africa are phenomena that have so far rarely been explored.

The study contributes to the understanding of African agency and entrepreneurship in South-South contexts and the opportunities and challenges that the introduction of the regulatory instruments of branding, advertising and intellectual property provided for the merchants. These issues pertaining to the development and daily practice of the tea business in Mali will now be addressed in more detail by being divided into four central and interrelated themes. These themes concern the tea trade, trade networks and entrepreneurship; the agency of economic actors in the South-South trade; the ownership, meaning and publicity of tea brands; and the value of brands, intellectual property and piracy.

1 The Current Green Tea Business: Trade Networks, Brokerage and Entrepreneurship

Scholarly attention focused mainly on the tea trade between Europe and Asia, especially India and China. Much has been written, mainly from a European perspective, on the history of tea in China (Hinsch 2016; Van Driem 2019) and its trade to Europe. Beginning in the late sixteenth century with the Portuguese (Van Dyke 2005), trade increased in the seventeenth century with the Dutch (Liu 2007) and other European traders (Hodacs 2016). The British played a prominent part in this trade in the eighteenth century (Ellis, Coulton and Mauder 2015; Krieger 2009) before they began to produce tea in India (Chatterjee 2001; Sharma 2011) and subsequently introduce it to East Africa (Houtkamp and van der Laan 1993).

Interestingly, however, scholarly attention on tea largely ended in Europe and North America. Less is known about the history of the beverage in North Africa (Raji 2003; the books in Arabic language by Damani 2013; and Lakhsassi and Sebti 2012; see also Huetz de Lemps 2001; Leriche 1953; Miège 1957, 1961, 1981; Sebti 1999). Almost nothing is known about green tea in West Africa, where it has only been described occasionally in the context of groups of tea drinking young men (Bondaz 2013; Diawara and Röschenthaler 2012; Kieffer 2006; Masquelier 2013). Concerning green tea in Mali there are only dispersed sources, including some local newspaper articles (see also Bondaz 2013, note 3; Röschenthaler forthc.).

The trade in green tea from China to West Africa is carried out predominantly by Malian merchants. Whilst trade as such is not to be considered entrepreneurship (Schumpeter 1934), as will be shown, some of the green tea merchants can be regarded as entrepreneurs, taking risks and investing their profits in the acquisition of new trade goods, in property and means of production. Until the 1980s, studies on African entrepreneurship have considered the creation of African companies through the lens of the performance of Western firms, noting with irritation that these did not follow the preconceived model. Meanwhile, there are a number of studies by anthropologists and historians on African entrepreneurship, which highlight the successes, inventive strategies and manifold forms of entrepreneurship in different sectors in African societies (Akinyoade, Dietz and Uche 2017; Ellis and Fauré 1995; Giese and Marfaing 2018; Grégoire and Labazée 1993; Hopkins 1988; Röschenthaler and Schulz 2016).

One of the few studies about Malian entrepreneurship is by Jean-Loup Amselle (1987) who categorised entrepreneurial traders in the 1980s according to their level of education. This study resonates well with the tea importers in Bamako who with their revenues from trade were able to send their children to school and university before they took over the parental tea business, thus – as can be added – combining local knowledge with formal education. As the study will show, local knowledge, apprenticeship in the parental business and formal education are of decisive advantage for becoming successful entrepreneurs (chapter 4). An important component of this local knowledge is the awareness of the importance of extensive and well-organised trade or distribution networks.

As far as the organisation of trade and traders' distribution networks are concerned, two types of network studies prevail. Firstly, the structural approaches to networks and their functioning using a general natural science picture (Castells 1996), which refrains from depicting what economic actors are doing in their daily work. The second approach considers existing family or ethnic networks and their organisation of trade. Among these are the so-called trading diasporas which form networks of related representatives or broker-entrepreneurs in trading towns along a trade route that permit the safe transport of goods across large geographical distances, as Jean-Loup Amselle (1977), Abner Cohen (1971), Philip Curtin (1984), Paul Lovejoy (1980), Marie Perinbam (1973) and others documented in nineteenth- and early twentieth-century (West) Africa. Continuities in taking care of customers by African and Chinese brokers have been observed in the tea trade in China (Röschenthaler 2021).[2] The study shows that a combined examination of the work of traders, merchants

2 For African brokerage in China, see also Haugen (2018), Marfaing and Thiel (2015), and Mathews (2015); for a recent overview on brokerage more generally, see Bräuchler, Knodel and Röschenthaler (2021).

and brokers provides valuable insights in the ongoing intersection of the various economic actors in the value chain.[3]

Other anthropologists and historians of Africa have described existing transnational family networks such as those of Senegalese and Ghanaians in Europe and Asia (Marfaing and Thiel 2015), of Lebanese in West Africa (Arsan 2014), trading networks inside the Sahara (Scheele 2012a) and of Indians in East Africa and beyond (Oonk 2013; 2017). These communities are dynamic, flexible and heterogenous, connecting members in a globalising world. They share the same patterns of permanent circulation, constituting what Abner Cohen (1971: 266–281) called a 'moral community'. To some extent these characteristics are also found in the Sino-Malian tea trade but, as will be shown, the Malian traders use strategies that differ for procurement and for distribution of their products when they try to reduce the number of brokers for purchase but eagerly work with brokers for distribution (chapter 5).

For an understanding of the global movement of tea, Arjun Appadurai's (1990) concept of the overlapping deterritorialised 'scapes' has been helpful, serving as a counterpoint to the various local and national tea cultures. In the previously mentioned study on green tea history (Röschenthaler forthc.), the 'teascape' provides a persuasive concept to illustrate the connectedness of the otherwise local or national tea cultures into one larger coherent space enabling an understanding of the commonalities of the different tea cultures. In combination, these two aspects of the dissemination and appropriation of the tea ritual can be understood in terms of 'cultural mobility', i.e. the traceable movement of a social practice, or object through time and space into different cultural, political, social, historical and religious contexts (Röschenthaler 2020a). Such an approach replaces the older concept of diffusion and refers to concrete movements rather than abstract models. These movements include things in their material form as well as the immaterial aspects attached to them. 'Cultural mobility' and '(tea)scape' are analytical concepts to depict the movement of a commodity and associated cultural practices and meanings into an overlapping dynamic cultural space encompassing these practices and meanings in their diversity and local variance. Ultimately both are the result of the agency of merchants trading these commodities and distributing them to the various places and people who embrace and identify with them and integrate them in their daily lives.

3 For a study on a small-scale value chain for the importation of Chinese jewellery to Ghana, see Haugen 2017.

2 The Agency of Economic Actors in Studies on South-South Trade

Tea has reached the remotest regions of the globe but little is still known about the numerous economic actors moving green tea from China to Mali in West Africa and beyond. These are individuals who finance the trade, import the tea, create and own tea brands (together with their Chinese suppliers, chapters 5, 7), and if successful, take the profits and reinvest them in further assets. Most often, currently but also in the past, not much has been detailed about the individual economic actors responsible for the global movement of products; for instance, the historical caravan trade across the Sahara has largely been described in generic terms – we know of the important roles of caravan leaders and landlord-brokers, but less about the individual histories of such people. Of the Sahara and savannah traders, only the ethnonyms are documented such as the Moors, Dyula, Soninke, Hausa, Marka or Djokoramé whereas traders' identities are only rarely mentioned (for exceptions, see Lydon 2009; Scheele 2012a). This is different in Morocco for the Jewish traders, some of whose biographies have been documented (Lévy 1995; Waterbury 1972). In the sub-Saharan context this is rarely the case.

Scholars on globalisation often take the movement of trade goods as given. Their intention is to discuss general questions and criticise particular ideologies and power inequalities. They tend to illustrate their statements with metaphors for these processes that are taken from nature, or from natural sciences. 'Diffusion' is such a concept, as are terms such as 'waves' and 'flows' that show the dimension of movement but veil individual action. African markets are often described as being 'flooded', or 'swamped' with cheap Chinese commodities. Such metaphors are found when precise knowledge or interest in details is lacking. In her study on global FlipFlops, Caroline Knowles (2014: 12) noted that studies of globalisation are 'conceptually over-theorised and empirically understudied' and mainly interested in the macro perspective. She observed that well-known scholars of globalisation, such as Anthony Giddens (2002), David Held (2004) and Saskia Sassen (2007) developed their theories without considering the agency of particular individuals (Knowles 2014: 6), i.e. they discuss agency as being the counterpoint to structural constraints, and less as the achievements of particular individual agents. Approaches on value chains (Gereffi 2018; Gereffi et al. 2005) and on the trade between China and Africa (Alden 2008; Shinn and Eisenman 2012) also often follow an approach which lacks mention of concrete economic actors. They depict movements in generalizing models, subsumed national action and statistics whose abstract figures tell nothing about individual activity which is considered merely anecdotal evidence. Statistics conceal who takes the initiative, places the orders, pays the bills and distributes the products. These studies use different methodological approaches from those of anthropologists and historians when they focus on the macro perspective, on governments and international organisations. Conversely, anthropologists have not taken much interest in the study of business. Scott Taylor (2012: 12) rightly remarked that '"big business" does not easily fit into our dominant Africa narratives'. Anthropologists were mainly interested in farmers, rural markets, small traders, street sellers and market women (Clarke 1994; Nwankwo 2019; Narotzky & Besnier 2014; Valenciano-Mañé 2019). Those who studied business were often interested in the ethnic trades of migrant minorities (Arsan 2014; Jalloh 2002).

The widespread use of statistics to depict economic activity has also contributed to the rather negative image of African economies. One reason is that much economic activity in African countries simply does not enter official statistics, as Janet MacGaffey (1987, 1991) illustrated in DR Congo where she portrayed considerable economic activity, despite political instability and low statistical visibility. She demonstrated that entrepreneurs even took over responsibilities of government, providing infrastructure, such as bridges, enabling the transport of trade goods. This phenomenon has been termed 'informal economy' (Hart 2006) – a term that meanwhile has been widely discussed (for example, Meagher 2010) – or 'shadow economy' (Nordström 2007), and in the context of transnational trade 'globalisation from below' (first used by Brecher, Child and Cutler 1993; for a discussion see Röschenthaler and Jedlowski 2017). Gordon Mathews and Alba Vega define globalisation from below 'as the transnational flow of people and goods with relatively small amounts of capital and informal, often semi-legal or illegal transactions, often associated with the developing world, but in fact apparent across the globe' (2012: 1).

The studies on globalisation from below divert attention from global big business to the universe of small transnational economic actors but they tend to reinforce the impression that particularly African business is predominantly informal and illegitimate, if not outright illegal. This is often true, however, not only for small African actors; the big Western transnational companies also reach out into this realm to secure profits (Ribeiro 2012). Furthermore, dichotomies such as 'globalisation from below' versus 'globalisation from above' amplify the impression that there is only a choice between suitcase trade and superbrands. As this study will show, the Malian green tea trade is not about superbrands nor is it about suitcase and micro-level trade. Tea traders are viable economic actors with registered companies (Röschenthaler 2020a); they travel to China and import green tea from there in considerable quantities to Mali and beyond.

The trade in green tea is part of South-South trade that differs markedly from the North-South trade in black tea with its strong exploitative connotations (Sharma 2011; Vries 2009: 90). Green tea is produced in fragmented or decentralised Chinese family gardens and small plantations from where it is shipped to West Africa without any Western involvement. The production of black tea, in contrast, has been integrated from the nineteenth century into the capitalist plantation economy, which Sven Beckert (2014) calls 'war capitalism'. It was produced with cheap labour in Southern countries to be exported for consumption in the North (see also Mintz 1985). 'Globalisation from below' and the South-South concept can be seen as an important tool for criticising such market-oriented interests generally associated with the North or West (Röschenthaler and Jedlowski 2017). However, the concept of the Global South also does not capture the complexities of movement and the trajectories of those individuals who do not limit their activities to the countries of the South (Marfaing and Thiel 2017). African importers travel not only to China but to various continents and countries for the procurement of commodities, shaping markets and consumption habits through their agency.

Agency has been defined by Sherry Ortner as the capacity to affect things, concomitantly considering the cultural context and the power structures that may shape this agency (Ortner 2006: 137). The roots of debates about agency and the limits of individual capacities to act independently of structural constraints are found in Emile Durkheim who was convinced that the actions of human beings were shaped by social conventions and Max Weber who was interested in human action and its free choices in particular social and economic circumstances (Brettel 2002; Clough 2020; Rapport and Overing 2000).

As earlier mentioned, investigating the concept of agency obviously does not necessarily imply the study of actual individual activity observed in the field. For long, the debate was held mostly on a theoretical level (Giddens 1984, Bourdieu 1977) without examining individual daily action and its social or political constraints (as noted by Archer 2000; Barnard 2000). The objective of the debate was highlighting the entrepreneurial capacities of the poor (Lindell 2010: 1). Drawing from these insights, Clough (2020) differentiates between weak agency (Bourdieu 1977) and strong agency (Evens 2008). Weak agency refers to the restraining influence of the habitus, whilst strong agency is the capacity to get beyond this imprint (Clough 2020). Other scholars (Archer 1995, Bork-Hüffer et al. 2016; Lindell 2010) have distinguished between the agency of individuals and of collectives that have an aggregate effect when individuals with similar intentions are organised in groups and work towards common goals. Whilst merchants usually work independently, such synergetic moments of collective merchant agency can at times be observed to impact the tea landscape in Mali, as will become obvious in the course of the study.

Agency manifests itself not only with merchants and traders but also with the consumers of their products. Still in 2017, Bianca Murillo (2017: 17; see also Trentmann and Otero-Cleves 2017) noted that Africans were rarely studied as consumers. Anthropological studies on individual consumption began with Mary Douglas and Baron Isherwood (1978); they argued that consumers actively used goods to project an impression of their social status and not because they were victims of the marketing industry in favour of the large companies and their brands. Douglas (1992) rather understood commodities as non-verbal mediums of communication. Following her lead, scholars began to examine African consumption in the colonial context and highlighted the important role of consumers in influencing European traders' supply on African markets and local understandings of the imported products (Burke 1996a; Fieldhouse 1994; Guyer 2004; Prestholdt 2008; Van den Bersselaar 2005, 2007).

More recent work focuses on African individual agency, mostly of consumers (Burke 1996a, 1996b; Hahn 2012; Prestholdt 2008; Van den Bersselaar 2005), and to a lesser extent of traders (Lydon 2009; Steiner 1985; Sylvanus 2008). Agency is less central in Timothy Burke's (1996a) work that examines marketing and consumption in colonial Zimbabwe, but Jeremy Prestholdt (2008) highlights the role of African consumers who only accepted trade goods that met their expectations whilst ignoring the rest. Similar observations have been made about consumers in other parts of Africa, and of African traders who had to teach their European and Chinese suppliers how the goods for sale in a particular country had to look like (Steiner 1985; Sylvanus 2008; Van den Bersselaar 2005). The same can be observed in the tea trade (chapter 2). African consumers and traders actively shape the tea supply on the market furthering quality, the majority of them rejecting cheap green tea and black tea.

More recently, especially in the context of Sino-African trade, scholars examined the activities of individual African traders (Axelsson 2012; Bertoncello and Bredeloup 2007; Bredeloup 2012; Bork-Hüffer et al. 2016; Castillo 2015; Cissé 2015; Haugen 2018; Le Bail 2008; Müller and Wehrhahn 2013; Marfaing and Thiel 2015; Sylvanus 2008; and many more) and their engagement as agents in commodity chains (Haugen 2017). In the tea trade,

Malian merchants have successfully emerged in dominating the importation of green tea to West Africa and to control its marketing. The trade activities and the traders' agency are guided and influenced by both culturally learned and embodied behaviours. These might be seen as constraints but in the tea trade they rather appear as enablers and assets providing valuable local knowledge required to successfully survive in the complex tea market. As far as constraints are concerned, Malian importers suggested that their government needed to be more supportive instead of considering them as rivals, even though this issue is in Mali less virulent than in other African countries (see also Grégoire and Labazée 1993: 28–29; Socpa 2016). They also noted that bilateral agreements and policies could be more favourable for traders, above all in China, but this was a concern of smaller traders; the major tea importers rarely mentioned such issues (see also Röschenthaler 2016 for Cameroon). They highlighted the knowledge that was necessary to cope with the uncertainties in the tea trade, be aware of the most recent trends on the market and maintain their position in the 'arena' (Bierschenk 2008) of competing traders' and other stakeholders' agencies. Thus, in the case of the tea trade, the 'arena approach' has proven more promising than the binary of agency and structure.

3 Anthropological Perspectives on Consumption, Branding and Advertisement

From the 1990s, anthropological studies on consumption, brands and advertisement began to increase, including Daniel Miller's (1987) work on consumer behaviour in everyday life. Closely connected to studies of consumption are brands and advertisement that have also for long been viewed rather critically. Anthropological studies of brands are few in number and of recent origin (Foster 2008; Wengrow 2010). Non-anthropological studies are more numerous, for example on brand history (Wadle 1997) and especially on global brands (Manning 2010). Brands are supposed to distinguish the industrially-made commodities of various producers, whilst advertisement is considered to promote products and the image of brands (Hellmann 2003: 25). Criticising the fashion industry, scholars noted that consumers would carry out unpaid advertisement when they wore brand-named apparel (Arvidsson 2005; Foster 2008). Tea consumers can also be considered most efficient promoters of tea brands when they engage in mouth-to-mouth recommendation and leave the empty tea packages on the ground for their friends to see, representing their 'absent producer' (Nakassis 2013: 115) or, in this case, the importer.

The anthropological study of advertisement is still very young, starting with ethnographies on advertising agencies in Asia (Mazarella 2003, Moeran 1996). Only a few studies on African advertisement exist (Alozie 2005; Finsterhölzl 2015; Kalusa and Phiri 2013; Röschenthaler 2009; Wendl 2002). Anthropologists such as Brian Moeran (1996) and William Mazarella (2003) who researched advertising agencies in Asia established that successful advertisements were those which combined local components and global ideas in their images. They applied to publicity what in the context of understanding the integration of global products into local practices has been termed 'glocalisation' (Robertson 1995), 'creolisation' (Hannerz 1992: 264–6), 'vernacularisation' (Appadurai 1996), or 'hybridisation' (Pieterse 1995) and which – considering the local perspective – has been termed cultural appropriation (Hahn 2012; Rao and Ziff 1997). As Giulianotti and Robertson (2006: 173) put it, 'each of these concepts registers the agency of quotidian social actors in critically engaging with and transforming global cultural phenomena in accordance with perceived local cultural needs as well as values and beliefs' (see also Habibul Khondker 2005).

The study of the tea brands and publicity will touch many of these issues. It establishes that, for their advertisement, tea importers focus on local themes that reflect the very local rootedness of tea consumption, whilst the foreign multinational companies use the opposite approach when they advertise transnational black tea brands with images that Malian consumers associate with Westernised life styles, targeting only the middle class (see also Van den Bersselaar 2005, Burke 1996b). In contrast, in the designs of their green tea brands local importers applied much more closely the idea of combining local and global elements into a montage rather than fusing it into a glocalised or better hybridised image. As chapter 6 also reveals. these brands communicate much more than status and voluntary advertisement; they also achieve more than merely adding value through branding, publicity and package design. The tea brands recall memories of past trading towns, the provenance of the product, landscapes and symbols from the inhabited natural environment, social happenings and global events that have no direct connection to tea as a product. The study sheds light upon this social, historical and political commemoration culture through brands that suggest they work differently from brands in other market economies. Such a brand culture is rather unusual and, so far, has not been discussed by scholars.

4 Studies on Brand Value, Intellectual Property and Piracy in Africa

The tea trade, the product and the brands that are created and attached to them, all relate to values of different kinds. Value can concern the price of the tea, of its brand and the symbolic and social values that are attached to its consumption in the tea ritual. Whereas economists study value (price systems), anthropologists study values in the plural form. Alternative to David Graeber's (2001) grounded study of value in the singular, Brian Moeran and Christina Garsten (2013: 1; see also Guyer 2009) are interested in an anthropology of values that focusses 'on (e)valuation as it occurs in social practices, and not inside the mind of an individual', an approach that will be followed in this study.

In the tea trade, it is important to understand the price system but also how this is motivated by the ideas and practices of tea importers. These ideas and practices are then confronted with the intellectual property system that has been promoted as a necessary tool for economic development (WIPO 1999). Intellectual property law is supposed to protect the artistic creations of an individual and the immaterial values attached to trademarks and brands against the exploitation by other economic interests. This is because their creators and owners have arguably invested time, creativity, energy and money in their creations, art work and brands (Altbach 1986; Du Bois 2018; Coombe 1998; Röschenthaler and Diawara 2016).

Intellectual property has been discussed by scholars in different ways. Some advocate that art work and local knowledge have to be protected against piracy (Brush and Stabisky 1996; Ouma 2006). Others take a critical view of intellectual property systems because they restrain the free use of immaterial cultural goods (McLeod 2005; Rowlands 2004). Still others have, in the case of African countries, advocated that international intellectual property law does not work for African creations as owners cannot be clearly identified and privileging an individual as an exclusive owner could be considered unjust as their creations build on the work of past generations (Boateng 2011; for a discussion of the different positions see Röschenthaler and Diawara 2016). There is much scholarly literature on piracy most of which clings to the usefulness of the intellectual property framework and fervently searches for ways to combat piracy. A few scholars analyse intellectual property and piracy as historical developments (Johns 2009) and as phenomena that always appear together (Sundaram 2010) and relativise the pervasiveness of piracy as a practice that has been observed at all times and places (Jones 1994).

Trademarks and brand value have been discussed together with piracy in Asia (Chang 2004; Philip 2005), however, anthropologists of Africa have hardly ever studied brands in the context of intellectual property regimes (Comaroff and Comaroff 2009). Hence it is exciting to ask in which way the tea traders understand their tea brands, the value of these brands, and intellectual property. To what extent do they find it helpful to protect their tea brands and file a lawsuit with the commercial tribunal? How do they understand the interplay of government policies and authorities, intellectual property and their role in society and with their fellow traders? Do they see alternatives to the intellectual property system? A number of studies have discussed alternative ways of understanding and dealing with immaterial cultural goods (Altbach 1986; Frith 1993; Hirsch and Strathern 2004; Röschenthaler and Diawara 2016) and documented local regimes of rights in immaterial cultural expressions (Harrison 1993; Lowie 1928; Röschenthaler 2011), which attribute ownership to other owners than those conceptualised in the international intellectual property regime that might be grasped with the notion of shared ownership (Aguilar 2018; Belderbos et al. 2014, for patents). This study contributes to these issues by highlighting the frictions between various national rights regimes, or diverging understandings of the international conventions that occur and easily produce even unintended trademark infringements related to the present-day Sino-Malian tea trade.

5 Research Methodology

This study is based on ethnographic field research in Mali between 2005 and 2016, encompassing seven field trips that totalled more than ten months. Throughout these years I worked with a Malian research assistant, Madou Keïta. As mentioned earlier, his communication skills enabled him to introduce my project to the tea traders and convey the purpose of my scholarly research that have greatly enhanced their understanding of the objectives of my project.

We made numerous excursions to the tea market in Bamako, to wholesale and retail shops and talked to tea consumers. We spoke to several Chinese importers in Mali and to officials about the workings of their institutions, including the Malian office for the registration of trademarks (CEMAPI) and the commercial court. Newspaper articles greatly contributed to my understanding of the topic, in particular the national daily, *Essor*. We discovered and analysed billboards, wall paintings, sign boards, commercials, the tea package designs, and the *Bulletin Officiel de la Propriété Intellectuelle* (BOPI) in which the trademarks registered in the OAPI zone are published. In the BOPI I found a total of 304 green tea brands that were registered between 1998 and 2018 and owned by 178 importers of various nationalities. Another sample forms my collection of 237 tea packages as well as numerous photographs of tea brands in the market collected between 2005 and 2016, added by images that my assistant sent to me electronically later on. Together, they are an important corpus of materials that will be analysed in this study.

As mentioned above, anthropologists have been interested in studying small traders, especially in Africa, but also concerning Africans in China. In contrast, this study focuses on the successful importers, those who have been most influential in the Sino-Malian tea trade and bring Malians' national drink to the country (for a discussion of studying up, see Gusterson 1997; Shore and Durão 2010). The reason for studying them was my fascination of the tea packages and that I wanted to find out how and by whom they arrived in Mali. We found some indications of their names on the tea packages and asked the wholesalers in the market about the whereabouts of their offices. We interviewed the 13 largest Malian tea importers and 6 occasional importers in Bamako. All these importers have visited China to view tea plantations and factories, to select Chinese suppliers and choose the quality of tea they wished to import. Most of the big tea importers, especially those who also sell other packaged food products, travel several times a year to China as well as to other countries around the globe to visit trade fairs and investigate novelties on the market. Many of the Chinese commodities for the African market can also be transported in suitcases or by air, but entry into the tea business is more demanding: an entire container has to be ordered because connected to this is the creation of the importer's tea brand and the printing of the package design (chapter 2).

When we arrived at their office for an interview, the traders always first questioned whether I wanted to import tea (*Tu veux importer du thé*?). Then they asked whether I had anything to do with the Malian authorities, or with an NGO. Sometimes my assistant's explanations as to the nature of scholarly research and its purpose for the sake of science, without any economic, political or other strategic reasons, took some time.[4] Even then, it was difficult to appreciate why I wanted to know the details of their company and trade activity. The larger the importers' businesses, the friendlier and loquacious they were. The smaller traders were rather more suspicious and hesitant. Once they understood, most of the importers were cordial, hospitable and often presented us with generous gifts of packages of tea or even an entire carton, glasses or plastic bags emblazoned with their

4 Grégoire and Labazée (1993: 9) also noted that researching entrepreneurs was not an easy task.

logo. Repeat visits built greater confidence and complicated issues became comprehensible.

The importers and wholesalers took great care to avoid saying anything that might annoy another tea trader. In their newspaper articles, journalists were much less considerate, naming problems directly. Issues to which importers merely hinted at, were more openly stated in newspapers. One of the importers explained:

> Because you will write something in your book, which can annoy other people, and I do not want to make them angry. When you go and research among these other people, they will not talk and that is the reason. Do you understand? I do not know what you are going to write in your book. … The tea will not make the problems but the money creates the problems. INTERVIEW, BAMAKO, 2013

Initial suspicions normally dissipated as it became clear that I left them to do the talking, letting them decide how much and what they wanted to tell me. Afterwards many were grateful, thanking me for making them reflect upon so many things. Some talked non-stop for many hours so I hardly needed to ask questions at all. Importers tended to be diplomatic in their speech, at least at first. This is understandable because the Chinese traders often visited their offices to enquire about the market. They conducted market research; Malian traders knew that they wanted to get into the tea business and that they would try to be competitive. They had to trust me that I would not try to do the same. For that reason, in this study, I will provide space for the traders' voices but their perspectives will be anonymous. Similarly, to maintain confidentiality, I will present the company histories in less detail than I would prefer.

The conversations were usually held in French as the tea importers were proficient in that language. My assistant then occasionally explained complex ideas and idioms that I did not immediately understand. Many wholesalers and retailers spoke French, too. For those who did not, my assistant translated on the spot from Bámanankan, Mali's trade language, enabling me to pursue further questions. When possible, I recorded the interviews and conversations, listening to them later again and transcribing them and if necessary, obtain further translations and explanations from my assistant, and the trader. The quotations from the interviews are translated into English (with idioms in French or Bámanankan in brackets).

My research was multi-sited. In addition to Bamako, where I carried out most of my work, I also travelled to Morocco (2010, 2015) – through which green tea arrived in Mali from the early nineteenth until the mid-twentieth century; I also visited several West African countries: Burkina Faso (2012, 2013), Ghana (2013), Senegal (2006) and Cameroon (2008, 2010, 2014) where these particular tea packages are found as well. My research also led me to China (2013, 2014, 2016, 2018) to investigate tea production and packaging in factories. I spoke with tea sellers, specialised on the African market, at the famous trade fair in Canton. Additionally, I visited Malaysia (2014, 2017), Vietnam (2017) and India (2017) for comparative purposes, as well as some European cities (Paris, Marseille, Brussels, Frankfurt) which have a large proportion of North African residents but there only the Chinese green teas that Moroccans prefer are found.

6 The Organisation of the Book

Following this introduction, the study is presented in nine chapters that can be divided in three parts: the emergence of the Malian tea market; the agents and their strategies in the Sino-African tea trade; and the legal frameworks of intellectual property and bureaucracy with which the tea importers have to come to terms.

The first part provides background information on the tea trade between China and West Africa; the role of traders in Malian society; the evolution of tea brands on the market in Mali, including their price, brand value, publicity and popularity among consumers.

Chapter 1 summarises the major steps in the Malian tea history from its arrival in the nineteenth century, the creation of the Malian tea plantation to the economic reforms allowing for private trade. It introduces the traders and their place in Malian society, local terms and concepts, the ritualised consumption of tea, its social meanings and its status as the national drink of Mali. It outlines the Malian tea traders' agency in distributing tea, supplying consumers and migrants from the Mande World with the type of Chinese green tea that suits Malian tastes. The chapter also shows that once there is a sufficiently large number of migrants in the countries to which they had migrated, Malian importers begin supplying them with green tea.

Chapter 2 discusses the evolution, the chronology and the longevity of some of the most popular tea brands on the Malian market. It examines the types of green tea that arrived in West Africa historically and at present, looking at the development and sizes of packaging and explaining some of the reasons for the large number of brands, which have multiplied to an unprecedented extent since the 2000s. Whilst at the beginning ownership in the brands was diverse, including many Chinese traders, with time, Malian importers, mostly of Saharan origin, were able to dominate the trade and decide on the types of tea to be imported, thus successfully shaping the tastes of Malian consumers and their ideas about tea quality.

Chapter 3 explores the value of tea both as a product and a brand, and the tea importers' appreciation of these values. The chapter discusses the costs of importing tea; it also looks at the value added by packaging, branding and advertising. It analyses the themes and ideas that are taken up by advertisement, which greatly differ from the images and brand names appearing on most packages, and discusses the production of publicity and the services of advertisement agencies to show to which extent importers make use of these measures to promote their brands. The chapter demonstrates that both consumers and traders contribute with their agency to the brand value: consumers by their insistence on a particular taste that they require tea to have and traders by managing price, purchase and brand communication. Advertisement expands the agency of importers as a visible or audible symbol into the public space.

The second part of the study presents the different types of traders in the Malian tea market, their strategies and distribution networks; how they create their tea brands in collaboration with their Chinese business partners and what meanings are attributed to these tea package designs.

Chapter 4 portrays the economic actors in the tea trade. It is about the individuals, who import green tea, their companies and their trade ventures. The chapter outlines the different categories of traders in the tea business and their interactions, revealing the majority to be Malians rather than Chinese (or even Europeans). The more important ones are descendants of Saharan and savannah traders whose families were involved with the earlier caravan trade. Numerous other traders tried their luck, importing tea from China but ultimately only about a dozen importers proved in the long run to be successful and came to dominate the market.

Chapter 5 examines the traders' distribution networks, their strategies and collaboration with their Chinese suppliers. In this chapter, tea traders explain the dynamics of brands as they grow in popularity, creating a crisis in the supply of good quality tea. Essential for successful tea trade is also to understand what Malian merchants call the 'work of tea' which includes assessing risks, keeping track of things, being informed about customs formalities at the various ports and offering trust to trading partners. Trusting each other seems to be one of the most complicated issues in the collaboration between Chinese and African traders. The chapter also illustrates how in their attempts to expand their markets, Malian traders wish to get closer to the tea production centres, whereas Chinese traders feel driven to get closer to the consumers.

Chapter 6 analyses the designs, names and meanings of the brands. The names and designs employed refer to the product's origin in China, the trade routes undertaken through the desert, and to historical and current trading locations and personalities. They also represent a lively practice of commemoration, taking up not only historical but also political and social events of national and international importance. These tea brands convey part of the significance that tea has assumed in Mali and are integrated in tea groups' conversations about the quality of their tea. This chapter analyses the different elements that appear on the packages: the designs, colours, names and meanings of the brands. This reveals that tea brand designs express a lively remembrance culture, exemplifying global connectivity by commemorating events of social and political significance. It also reveals to which extent their combined creativity brings forward a design that can be considered glocalised.

Finally, the last three chapters discuss the role of intellectual property in tea brands, the various rights regimes regulating intangible goods, the copying of brands and the traders' interaction with the legal regulations.

Chapter 7 explains how the investment in design and marketing the brand entitle brand owners to claim it their exclusive intellectual property which others may only use with their permission. The purchase of a brand-named product involves traders and consumers acquire ownership of the material components of a product – the package and its contents – but not the immaterial aspects – the package design, brand name and trademark. This chapter discusses how these ideas have been implemented and received in Mali and the geographical reach out of brand protection. It presents the organisations that protect intellectual property and reflects on how useful the importers find these institutions. The chapter also discusses alternative ways of understanding and managing immaterial cultural goods by various rights regimes, including China's approach to intellectual property and how Chinese and Malian partnerships work together within this framework. Finally, with relevance to Mali, the chapter looks at the various possibilities with regard to the management of intellectual property in brands and in particular how it relates to Islam, given that the majority of Malians are Muslims.

Chapter 8 discusses the copying of popular tea brands from the perspective of the conceptual challenges of intellectual property, which are related to questions of similarity and singularity, originality or uniqueness of a brand image. It shows that in the landscape of tea brands some of the successful designs served as models for numerous other brands that imitate them in one way or the other. It is about the question of how different designs and names need to be in order to be considered a new and singular creation and at what point brands might be declared a copy that is apt to be persecuted as trademark infringement and unfair competition. The examples of two biographies of tea brands illustrate the brands' 'social lives', the many copies they provoked and how these copies can be understood. It also points to some complexities in the registration policy of the intellectual property organisation for the Francophone Africa (OAPI) and whether these copies might be better understood as collage and montage rather than as either legal or pirated, thus paying homage to local concepts of the immaterial that acknowledge the fragmented character of creation.

Chapter 9 sheds light on the legal implications of piracy and some of the bureaucratic and social challenges involved in the tea trade. It examines tea brands as the importers' intellectual property and the degree of usefulness they attribute to the available institutions for protecting their brand names and designs. The chapter examines three lawsuits related to brand piracy and discusses how Malians deal with brand pirates, preferring not to sue them but to clarify such issues among themselves. Only if this is not successful, they file a lawsuit but tend to withdraw it before enforcement. In addition to proliferating copying activities are other undocumented practices as well as fears about tax collectors and customs officials all of which have an impact on the validity of statistics, on the profits that importers can make in the tea trade and complicate the connection between intellectual property law, piracy and the working of the state.

The conclusion summarises the most important findings of the study, which intends to expose the complexities behind often abstract descriptions of trade through a focus on the economic actors' agency, their fields of action and the overlapping activities of merchants and entrepreneurs. The findings highlight how the Malian importers managed to prevail over their Chinese counterparts in the importation of Chinese green tea and the ease with which Malian merchants travel to China and establish themselves as transnational traders. They also distribute green tea to those parts of Africa to where a sufficient number of migrants from the Mande World has migrated. The study also shows the prominence of Malian economic actors in defining the quality of tea on the expanding market and tracks down reasons for the existence of so many tea importers and brands. It presents the tea brands as a platform for the culture of commemoration and the engagement of consumers and importers in making sense of the value of the tea, the added value of the package, branding and publicity. Since the 1990s, local merchants have to cope with a range of new instruments (branding, advertising, exclusive rights in intangible property) and their complexities in regard to tea brands. These complexities are partly due to diverging rights regimes that also contribute to the frequent trademark infringements. Finally, in spite of their dominance in the tea trade, Malian and Chinese traders have to collaborate in the production of tea brands, engage in co-creating brand designs, share ownership in their brands' intellectual property and above all learn to invest in mutual trust.

CHAPTER 1

The Emergence of the Malian Tea Importers

This chapter provides the backdrop for understanding the current circumstances in which Malian tea importers have become the major agents in the trade of Chinese green tea to Africa and have, together with their Chinese suppliers, created their own tea brands. The chapter begins with an outline of the present tea market before reviewing the history of tea in Mali, the ethnic identity of the traders, local concepts and terms concerning the tea trade, the Malian tea traders' distribution networks in the country and abroad to where people from the Mande World migrated to find work. This outline provides the historical background for explaining how Malian merchants became important agents in the green tea trade with China.

1 The Tea Market, Its Brands and the Malian Tea Plantation

The immense popularity of green tea is reflected in the countless tea brands on the Malian market. All the numerous tea packages contain Chinese green tea, Gunpowder and Chunmee, according to the package descriptions. They are predominantly imported by Malian merchants from China, where many tea companies have specialised in the African market, making their products suitable for it and work for their African customers.

Next to the Grand Marché, Bamako's largest market place, an entire section is reserved for green tea. That there are no equivalent sections for black tea and coffee, illustrates the particular importance of green tea. From the 1990s onwards, this tea section grew to acquire an entire street, the Rue Gouraud,[1] that is now occupied by numerous wholesale tea boutiques (Figure 5). Dozens of differently branded tea cartons are piled up in front of the shop doors, leaving only small gangways to the interior (Figure 6). Until 2002, the number of different tea brands could be counted on the fingers of one hand, as I was told, but in 2007, I counted over sixty in that section of the Grand Marché (Figure 7). The number of tea brands constantly increased as new ones were added, some

1 Henri Gouraud (1867–1946) was a French officer who arrived in Mali in 1894. He sympathised with the local population and stayed in West Africa until 1902. Later he commanded armies in Tchad, Morocco, the Levante and Syria. He wrote a book *Souvenirs d'un Africain* about his African experiences (www.lyceefr.org, 7 August 2017).

 | DOI:10.1163/9789004505698_003

FIGURE 5 People jostling through the Rue Gouraud, Bamako, 2010

FIGURE 6 Piles of tea cartons in front of a wholesale boutique, Bamako, 2011

FIGURE 7 Tea packets in a wholesale shop. Bamako, 2016

persisting for more than ten years, whilst some others quickly vanished from the market.

The importation of increasing quantities of affordable Chinese green tea from 1990s onwards attracted growing numbers of tea consumers who made the tea ritual part of their daily lives. It also invited more and more traders who intended to make tea their business. Some of the present tea traders, or Dyula, had moved to Bamako during colonial time but most of them arrived from the 1960s onwards and began to sell at first tea from the state-owned Société malienne d'importation et d'exportation (SOMIEX), among other products, as private traders were officially disallowed from importing particular trade goods such as tea during post-colonial time. Traders of Saharan origin were also in Bamako before colonial time. But particularly from the 1990s onwards, more of them moved south to the capital. Most of the Malian tea importers have their headquarters in Bamako, a few others remained in Mopti and further down the River Niger, in Gao, or moved to Nouakchott.

1991 was a turning point for the tea trade. Between 1960, Mali's political independence from France, and 1991, when the military regime of Moussa Traoré was ended and democratisation began with reforms of the economy and the media sectors, the state acted as the only entrepreneur of sugar, tea and some other products. With the 1991 reforms, most of the state-owned companies were dissolved and private importation permitted. From then on, various private traders began importing green tea.

Today, everybody in Mali knows that green tea comes from China. Thé vert de Chine – China green tea – is also a legend written on each tea package. Until independence, however, Malian tea importers and consumers had very little idea as to the origin of tea and the long journey it had taken to reach them. Little did they know it grew in family gardens in China (Gardella 1994; Van Dyke 2005) nor that the British had traded it to Europe (Ellis, Coulton and Mauder 2015; Krieger 2009) and gave some of it as a gift to the Sultan of Morocco in the early eighteenth century (Leriche 1953; Miège 1957; Sebti 1999), from where it arrived on camel back across the Sahara in the early nineteenth century, when René Caillé (1996) described the impressive tea ritual Timbuktu and Djenné in 1828 (Lydon 2009).

Throughout the nineteenth century and during French colonial rule, tea was brought to Sahel trading towns by camel caravans from Morocco. Until Mali's independence in 1960, green tea remained largely a beverage of the Saharan traders, except for a few local chiefs and pastoralists (Röschenthaler forthc.).

After independence, in an endeavour to reduce the country's dependence on foreign imports, the Malian government under Modibo Keïta, its first president, decided upon a socialist programme, creating a state-owned import-export company (SOMIEX) through which it imported tea directly from China. It prohibited all private trade, including caravan traders from importing staple and luxury goods, except for dried fish, kola nuts and cattle (Amselle 1977: 264–268). It was no longer legal to bring tea and sugar across the Sahara and along the Senegal River. The state became the only legal importer. Traders could purchase products from the outlets of SOMIEX and distribute them within the country.

The Keïta government also created, with Chinese assistance, a small tea plantation in Mali's hilly south. This plantation produced green tea but as it was not in sufficient quantities to satisfy the growing demand; the government had to import additional tea from China. Henceforth, the Malian government imported tea directly from China to the port of Dakar from where it was transported by rail to Bamako. This tea was blended with the Malian-grown tea to make it suitable for Malian palates used to the taste of Chinese tea and the modifications that it had assumed during its long journey. Whilst Malians were not particularly fond of the tea grown on the Malian plantation, its existence raised awareness of tea in the country and beyond and contributed to ensuring Mali became a centre of tea distribution in the following decades. Consumers were now also the civil servants employed throughout the country. Henceforward, civil servants were the social group that others desired to emulate and from them increasing numbers of people learned how to drink tea.

In the 1980s, after the structural adjustment programmes had been implemented, unemployment among young diploma holders increased as a career in the civil service was drastically reduced due to the reforms. The young men began adopting the practice of holding tea sessions and the *grins* that had emerged around independence – at the time when political parties were created – to discuss politics now began to drink tea. However, they, as most Malians, only possessed the means to buy tea regularly following the 1991 reforms, when private tea importers were permitted to import ever larger quantities of tea at affordable prices (Diawara and Röschenthaler 2012; Röschenthaler forthc.).

At first, these importers purchased tea in West African coastal cities, then in Hong Kong and other Asian cities. There, they contacted Chinese brokers who had travelled to these places following China's gradual economic liberalisation from 1978 onwards. But only when China had signed the WTO agreement in 2001 and opened its economy to foreign traders could Malians travel to China to buy tea directly from there.

The increasing imports by private traders soon presented a challenge for the small national tea plantation, for it was unable to produce tea at a competitive price let alone at a comparable quality. This sparked criticism of the tea importers whose commercial activities, it was alleged, were competing with the national tea plantation and hence they were blamed for causing its problems. Among the factual reasons for Farako's decline were mismanagement, political neglect and the failure to renew the technology. As the costs of production outstripped the proceeds from the sales of its product, the Farako plantation faced a crisis. Although the Chinese tea had to be transported halfway across the globe, it proved less expensive than the home-grown tea. Growing tea consumption more generally sparked off criticism and tea became associated with youth unemployment, laziness and corruption that in actual fact were results of the implementation of the structural adjustment programmes of the 1980s (for more details see Röschenthaler forthc.).

In an attempt to divert such accusations, the major tea importers and wholesalers formed an association, the Association des Investisseurs du Thé Farako. The association announced that it intended contributing cash towards supporting the Farako tea plantation. At first, there were perhaps sixty, some say thirty members, but in the end when it came to contributing actual cash, the number was just thirteen. Six members each gave 30 million francs CFA, and the remaining seven members each gave 20 million francs CFA, producing a total of 320 million francs CFA (about 487,800 Euro). This investment would have made them, alongside the government, stakeholders in the Farako plantation. But in the event, nothing happened and it is unclear where the money went.

The tea importers also assisted the government on other occasions. For example, after the political crisis of 2012, during which President Amadou Toumani Touré was hounded from office, as an act of philanthropy, they distributed tea and other goods to the population to help the interim government (Röschenthaler 2020b). During large public gatherings promoting an importers' tea brands, they also regularly gave generous gifts to consumers (see chapter 3). Before continuing with the tea importers' influence on the tea market and the emergence of transnational importers it is necessary to briefly outline the tea ritual, its interpretation by Malian consumers and their consideration of it as national drink in order to understand the significance of tea on the Malian market.

2 The Tea Ritual, Tea as National Drink and the Ambiguous Meanings of the Beverage

In Mali, Chinese green tea is treated differently from other hot beverages such as black tea and coffee, which are also available. In contrast to coffee and black tea, however, green tea is normally not consumed casually but requires ritualised preparation that makes it a particular medium of communication and sociability.

Malians rarely consume green tea alone but prefer to share the beverage with friends. Its preparation takes time and follows a prescribed procedure. It is prepared in the open air of the courtyard or more recently, by groups of young men, also on the sidewalk in front of the compound. One of the participants is assigned to act as the master of ceremony. He heats the water in one of the two teapots on a mobile charcoal stove, throws the tea leaves in the teapot and boils them for a while. He throws sugar in the other pot, and pours the liquid over the sugar. One glass is set aside for the next round. Then he pours the liquid carefully from the teapot into a glass and back again until it has the right taste, viscosity and temperature and a fine foam appears on the surface. Then the tea is poured from the teapot into small shot glasses before being served from the tray to the guests according to seniority. The eldest participant receives the first glass of tea, then the next until all have had their first serving (Figure 8). Immediately afterwards, the second round is prepared from the same tea leaves but with fresh water. The second serving is sweeter than the first but to make it taste better the glass put aside earlier is added to the liquid. Then the third serving is prepared, which is less strong still, as the tea leaves have lost further strength. After the third serving has been consumed, the participants leave.

FIGURE 8 Master of ceremonies, serving Chinese green tea to his *grin* of watchmen, Bamako, 2016

The entire ritual can take several hours, depending on how lively the conversation and how much time the host is prepared to dedicate to his guests. All participants stay together during the ritual and it is very impolite to leave before the third serving has been consumed. Tea groups or *grins*, as Malians call them, are mostly male gatherings involving men and their friends who usually possess similar age and status. More recently, women have also begun to hold their tea *grins*, however, these will be held in the inner courtyard, or on the shaded rooftop, where they are less visible to the public (Figure 9).

Green tea became the popular drink of large parts of the Malian population from the 1990s onwards when it became affordable following the market reforms. The tea business flourished and increasing numbers of people consumed tea regularly, tea becoming an important part of their daily lives. Tea consumption continued to grow throughout the 2000s. It was lauded by a majority as a medicine, a welcoming drink, an energiser and socialiser, a medium of communication that brought people together to talk and further solidarity. It soon became a focus of reflection and people began to consider drinking it a tradition and even raising it to the status of Mali's national drink.

The widespread consumption of the beverage, however, also led to concerns about the consequences of this development. Its critics argued that tea would

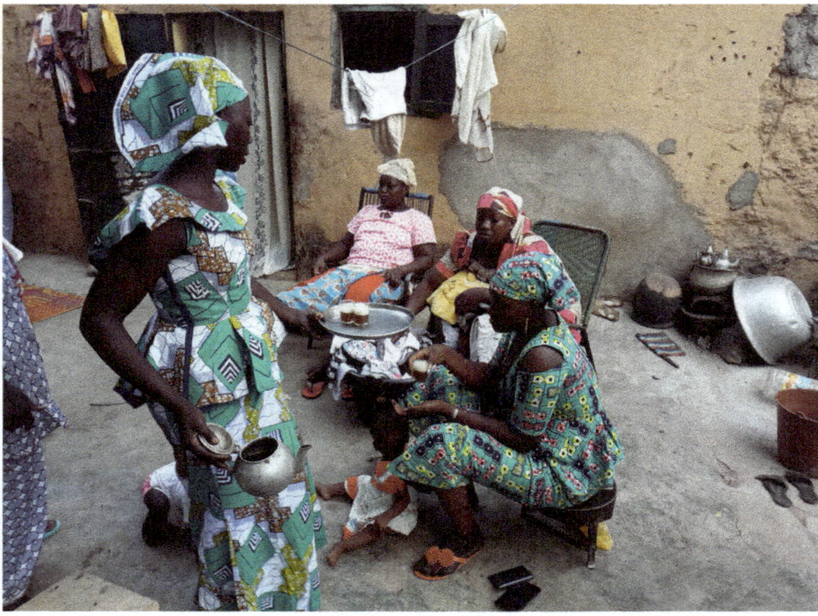

FIGURE 9 Women's tea *grin*, Bamako, 2018
PHOTO BY ADAMA KEÏTA

prevent people from working, and explained the high unemployment rate among young people. Tea would seduce them into idleness as they consumed it with too much sugar while sitting the whole day around the teapot chatting rather than looking for work. In short, critics considered it a waste of time responsible for the downfall of society and its values (Röschenthaler forthc.).

Its critics implied tea was responsible not only for unemployment but also for peoples' laziness and corruption in political life. Indeed, the time during which tea became the beverage of the masses followed the implementation of the structural adjustment programmes imposed by the World Bank in the 1980s, which greatly reduced the opportunities of young diploma holders to find work in the civil service. People projected national problems such as youth unemployment, corruption and the decline of social values on green tea. It would not have occurred to anyone to discuss such issues with regard to black tea or coffee. Consideration of green tea as Mali's national drink is an expression of this ambivalence.

Tea is considered both a medium of communication and sociability and also presents a social challenge, influencing peoples' perceptions of themselves as a nation and their projection of national concerns fell upon the beverage (Röschenthaler forthc.; see also Lakhsassi and Sebti 2012 about Morocco and

Fromer 2008 about Britain). Chinese green tea became so influential in Mali that it replaced other welcome gifts that had previously been imperative. Tea packages have largely replaced kola nuts as a welcome and a marriage gift. Both tea and kola nuts are energisers but originated from different geographical regions: kola nuts from the forested areas south of Mali (Amselle 1977), Chinese green tea from north across the Sahara. Today, kola nuts are only given symbolically in reminiscence of earlier times. Instead, packages, or even entire 5kg cartons of tea and sugar are provided at a marriage.

Malian consumers and traders have played important roles in making tea the main marriage gift and the country's national drink. In order to understand how the tea traders were able to bring the ingredient for the national drink from China to Mali, I will in the following section situate the tea merchants in their social and cultural setting and focus on the identity of the economic actors who were and are involved in this trade.

3 The Changing Role of Local Traders and the Emergence of the Global Importers

Numerous individuals were involved in the commercial nodes during the long journey that tea travelled in the nineteenth century from China to Mali. Among these individuals were different categories of traders, merchants and brokers. Almost all the major Malian tea importers are descendants of families who were once active in the caravan trade. A brief outline of their position in Malian society, the local typology of traders and terms in use will provide helpful insights to understand the current roles of economic actors in the tea trade.

3.1 *Malian Traders' Ethnic and Social Identities*

Unlike today, in pre-colonial times not everyone could become a trader. Societies belonging to the Mande World, which include Mali, eastern Senegal, northern Cote d'Ivoire, western Burkina-Faso and north-eastern Guinea were and to a certain extent still are, socially stratified. The social fabric of these societies consisted of three hierarchically arranged social groups: the aristocracy, i.e. the political elite (royal families and warriors); the free farmers; and the formerly enslaved people who worked for the aristocracy. Then there were the social categories of the artisans (black smiths, carvers, potters, leather workers) and musicians or praise singers (*jèliw*, whom the French called griots) which were largely endogamous groups who interacted closely with the aristocratic families (Diawara 2003; Hoffman 2000; Schulz 2001). The traders formed another social category, often inter-marrying among each other, forming extensive trade networks and holding trading posts and property in many places (Amselle 1977; Perinbam 1973).

The traders were very mobile and moved with their trade goods between the aristocratic groups in various places (Manchuelle 1997: 9–40). The traders, being somewhat outside the established social hierarchy, were considered ambiguous because they earned their living from profit rather than from hard work or privileges – a characterisation that resonates with Simmel's (1950) findings on traders in Europe. Many of the Malian traders, especially those who were from beyond the Sahel, were Muslim scholars and possessed powerful amulets and medicines. In Arabic countries, the role of traders was much more appreciated than in Mali, considered a fully legitimate profession and perfectly compatible with Islam (Lydon 2009). As an aside, the social standing of the traders in Mali does not seem to have been as reduced as that of Chinese traders: there, farming was also the norm but traders were considered to be the lowest social group after the political elite, farmers and artisans (Mann 1984).

Malians make further distinctions between those people who came from the north – the Algerian and Moroccan Sahara – and have lived in Mali since the late sixteenth century, when the Moroccan sultan conquered the Songhay Empire. Other Saharans came from various oases and travelled to the trading towns in the Sahel and the savannah, where they settled acting as landlord-brokers, received caravans and mediated their business (Amselle 1977: 193; Grégoire and Labazée 1993: 13). Bamana often called them variously Songhay, Touareg, *maures*, Arabes, Berbers and *súraka* (light-skinned people) with the generalizing meaning of 'people from the north' but the Touareg in northern Mali call them *laram,* as tea importers explained (interviews, Bamako, 2013; see also Gardi 1985; Röschenthaler forthc.). More specifically, Songhay (farmers) and Tuareg (pastoralists), however, have inhabited the area called the Azawad for far longer than those people to whom the terms *maures*, Arabs, Berbers, *laram* and *súraka* refer who came from Morocco and the Saharan oases to the trading towns. Such collective terms are often found in the scholarly literature, where people from the Sahara are also called 'Moors' or 'Arab-Berbers'. To avoid particular unintended meanings, I will refer to them all as Saharan traders.

By contrast, the traders from the sub-Saharan Sahel and savannah regions are most often referred to as Dyula, meaning simply 'traders' (Curtin 1984: 25; Perinbam 1973). Dyula have often been associated with the Soninke – or Sarakole, the Wolof term for Soninke that came into use among the French – known as influential traders in Mali. These trading groups have been dispersed throughout the Mande World. Victor Azarya (1980: 246) quoting Nehemia Levtzion (1968: 11) gives some idea of how these groups of traders can be understood:

> The caravan trade across the Sahara was carried out mostly by Berbers or North Africans, while the more regional trade in Saharan West Africa was conducted mostly by Muslim Black Africans, called Dyula or Marka in this area. … [T]hey met Sudanese traders, members of the great family of Mande tribes, who brought the gold from the interior. Through their trade base, Mande traders became detached from the agricultural … ways of life. … Under the influence of the North Africans, they adopted Islam, and in their wanderings found hospitality and a sense of community among Muslims in the new trading centres which developed along the trade routes … In this way a new social group distinguished by trade and Islam was dispersed throughout the Sudan.

These various, largely endogamous groups of Muslim traders were known by diverse names in the various ethnic groups. The Malinke of the Upper Niger called them 'Dyula', the Bamana in the region of Segou and Djenné 'Marka', the people in the bend of the Upper Black Volta River 'Dafing' and the people who speak Mole Dagbane languages called them 'Yarse' (of Soninke origin). In the Arabic sources, among the Fulbe and Hausa, these traders are known as 'Wangara' (Brégand 1998; Lovejoy 1978; Massing 2000). Other traders around Mopti and Bamako are called 'Diawambe' or 'Djokoramé' (Gardi 1985). Trading in close association with the Fulbe, they acted at first as the Fulbe's cattle traders, a business the Fulbe would not perform themselves, before becoming well-known traders in Mali. Azarya (1980) suggests that the Diawambe were a mixture of Soninke and Saharan traders, speaking Fulfulde but they were not of Fulbe origin, whereas the Marka or Maraka speak Bámanankan but are not Bamana (Gardi 1985; interviews, Bamako, 2007). All these had trading posts in the large towns along the Niger. In the nineteenth century, the Marka were mainly in Djenné and Dya, the Saharan traders mostly in Timbuktu. The populations of Djenné and Timbuktu were in fact quite heterogeneous and many families had branches established in both cities, facilitating communication between them (Azarya 1980).

The various Dyula in the savannah also established trading diasporas with landlord-brokers who hosted them, their porting animals and trade goods in the trading towns. In the towns bordering the Sahara, they took trade goods from the Saharan camel caravans. Their generation-long profession as traders can be read from their family names. The families with the *jàmu* (clan name) Lah, Dramera, Yara, Bathily, Yattassaye and others are all Djokoramé or Diawambe. These traders of the Mande World travelled across the savannah regions as far south as the forests beyond which they could not go with their porting animals. From there, other traders moved the trade goods with canoes or human carriers to and from the coast. Economic anthropologists have documented how such ethnic or sub-ethnic groups were able to dominate trade with certain products (Cohen 1971) and how particular goods influence the type of markets (Applbaum 2005; Schwimmer 1979, Trager 1981).

These groups of traders covered the entire West African region with specialised overlapping trade networks. As outlined above, the network of the Dyula was interconnected with that of the Saharan traders whose networks in turn were overlapping with those of the Jewish merchants in Morocco and other North African countries and also southern and western Europe – through which tea, sugar and cloth reached Mali in the nineteenth century. The interconnection took place in the trading towns, which hosted traders according to their ethnic origin in particular sections of the town. Here, they found their landlord-brokers who mediated between them, the local rulers and the other itinerant traders. In the nineteenth century, Saharan traders, for example, were to be found in Ndar (Saint Louis), Nioro, Timbuktu, Djenné and savannah towns such as Sansanding, Yamina and Bamako. They also operated northwards via the salt mines of Taoudeni and Ijil, the watering place of Arawane and the oases of the Tidikelt and Tuat.

Judith Scheele noted that some of these traders who came from Tuat and the Tidikelt in Algeria, founded the trading towns of Kidal and Tessalit in what is now northern Mali. They had invested the profits of their trade extensively in palm gardens and livestock, left in the care of their wives' families or that of the Kel (a Tuareg clan) of Tuat. Scheele continues that one of these is the influential Ferjani family of traders from Wad Suf near the Tunisian border who had settled in Aoulef in the Tidikelt in the early twentieth century. They now own houses and shops in Gao, Agadez and Niamey and 'they transformed Aoulef into a showcase of family wealth' (it is no longer a dusty village) and In Salah became the main commercial centre of the Tidikelt (Scheele 2012b: 292). This is of interest because members of this family are important present-day tea importers in Mopti and Bamako, and intermarried with other families of tea importers. The sphere of influence of these traders of Saharan origin extends to cities such as Bamako and as far west as Nouakchott, where many tea brands are registered as well as other West African port cities (chapter 2). Having grown up with and being part of such extended trade networks shape the entrepreneurial vision of traders and are of invaluable advantage for becoming a successful tea importer.

3.2 *Local Terms, Hierarchies and Interaction of Traders*

Independent of their ethnic identity, each of the trading communities has social hierarchies in which the different traders, brokers and merchants manage a volume of trade and a network of social contacts. Traders also differ according to their entrepreneurial activity, depending on experience, capital and standing. I will first explain the local terms that are in use in Bámanankan, and then relate some of them to similar terms in adjacent regions.

The term in Bámanankan for trader, *jàgòkəla* (someone who does *jàgò*, 'commerce'), encompasses petty traders, merchants and caravan traders. Malians also use the French term *commerçant*, which has roughly the same meaning locally. The tea traders, wholesalers, retailers and importers all see themselves as *commerçants* or *jàgòkəlaw* (plural of *jàgòkəla*).[2] The importers and the wholesalers have not used the term entrepreneur to describe their profession. Only one of them who had invested his profits in industrial production saw himself as entrepreneur. He was the owner of a pasta factory whilst the other traders mainly moved goods. But the differences between these terms are not clear cut as most tea importers invest their profit in property, lorries and warehouses and some also in animal farming. They would not even say that they earn their living from the profits of trade but rather insist that they make a living from serious 'work'. According to them, it was necessary to understand this 'work' well as it was risky, required experience, far-sightedness and courage – qualities that entrepreneurs are said to have (Hopkins 1988; Schumpeter 1934; Röschenthaler and Schulz 2016). They often talked of *té báara* or *travail du thé*, the 'work of tea', which includes everything from importing, transporting and distributing the product, but there is no term for entrepreneur in Bámanankan.

Among all these *commerçants*, the traders have differentiated between *vrai commerçants, jùlabá,* 'big traders' or 'merchants', who are influential wholesalers and importers, no longer selling to individual consumers themselves but only distributing their products to other traders, and the *jùlani*, the 'small traders' or *bàanàbāna* (*buyam-sellam* in Anglophone countries). The term *jùlabá* includes both wholesalers and importers. A real *jàgòkəla* is someone who procures goods and redistributes them, whereas the *bàanàbāna* are small retailers who sell to individual consumers. A *bàanàbāna* can be a retailer who has a small shop or a street vendor. Often, they are mobile street vendors lacking (yet) any standing in the business.[3]

2 *Jàgo* means 'trade', *ke* means 'to do' and *la* is a so-called *nomina agentis*, referring to a person doing a specific activity. In combination with *jàgo* it means a person doing trade, i.e. a trader. I am grateful to Holger Troebs for some of the explanations of Bámanankan.

3 *Bàanàbāna* is a term, widely in use in Mali, but taken from Wolof, which refers to a small or ambulant trader (Bondaz 2013: 71, note 22).

Then there are the *coxeurs*,[4] the intermediaries or small brokers, who mediate between the wholesalers and the importers for a commission. In earlier times, an intermediary received only a gift, but today *coxeurs* receive a more fixed rate – the *prix coxeur* – as a commission for their work. The commission will be paid by the wholesaler who engages the *coxeur* to work for him. A clever *coxeur* can gain several times. In addition to his commission, he may add for himself a percentage on the price of the tea he proposes to the wholesaler. He may also obtain an additional gift from the importer which helps to create trust between them and is intended to ensure that the *coxeur* does not mix pirated packages in the cargo offered to a wholesaler (chapter 4).

The small brokers working in the market, mediating between wholesaler and importer (or patron) are quite different from the big brokers, or landlord-brokers, who live in a different town or abroad and host itinerant traders from their home region. In Bamanakan, these brokers are called *jàtigi;* they also receive a commission for their services. Such landlord-brokers have been observed in the trans-Saharan trade (Amselle 1977; Perinbam 1973), as mentioned earlier. More recently, such brokers also offer their services to Malian traders in China (Röschenthaler 2020b). What in the Saharan trade was a requirement for survival has with digital technology and globalisation become far more easy to master but has not disappeared.

Jean-Loup Amselle described the interaction of economic actors in Mali in the 1970s. He notes that the *jùlabá* supervises the trade from home; the *jùladén* (*den* means 'child') who are his sons or apprentices, work as itinerant traders, transporting the goods from the home to the place of exchange, where they are received by the *jàtigi*, who may also be a member of the extended family; he mediates between the itinerant traders from his home region, the local authorities and other local and itinerant traders (Amselle 1977: 193–194; Grégoire and Labazée 1993).

Distinctions between big and small traders and landlord-brokers and small brokers are also to be found in other parts of Africa, for example, in Cameroon (Röschenthaler 2016), in the Maghreb (Schroeter 1988: 21–22), and the Swahili Coast (Middleton 2001). The Arabic term *tajīr* (plural: *tujār*) – derived from

4 The term *coxeur* is a French neologism and related to the verb 'se faire coxer', which means 'being trapped' or 'persuaded into something'. The word is derived from the English 'to coax' or 'persuade gradually' or 'by flattering to do something' (Oxford Dictionary Thesaurus, 2001). Gardi (1985: 75–77) describes the work of the *coxeurs* at the port of Mopti where they mediate between the women who bring dried fish from the inner Niger Delta in their boats and the merchants who buy and distribute the fish in the country with trucks. The term 'coaxer' has been in use in the nineteenth-century Atlantic trade where coaxers served as intermediaries between European and African traders (Brooks 1972: 92–93).

the root t-j-r 'to trade' – refers to someone who is more than mere subsistence trading. A shopkeeper or a small-scale merchant who accumulates stocks is never a *tajīr* but an *atār* or *baqqal* (Lakhsassi and Sebti 2012: 45), or what Malians would call *bàanàbāna*. There were also the privileged traders, the *tujār as-sultān* in Morroco, to whom the sultan had granted the privilege of conducting import and export trade. Daniel Schroeter (1988: 21–23) compares them to the court jews of central Europe in the seventeenth and eighteenth centuries. They were assisted by the *simsar*, small brokers, and the itinerant traders were received by the *dillal* or landlord-brokers (Daniel Schroeter, pers. comm. 2019), all playing a role in the nineteenth-century tea trade in Morocco.

John Middleton (2001: 509) highlights a similar difference between merchants and traders. According to him, the merchants at the Swahili Coast are settled; unlike the traders, they do not move the trade goods themselves. They mediate between foreign traders and the local traders arriving from the interior. These merchants are members of business houses and act as 'commercial middlemen' and 'intercontinental cultural brokers' (2001: 512–513). They meet Asian and African traders separately and negotiate exchanges in the privacy of their houses rather than in the markets (2001: 516). Middleton compares them with the landlord-brokers whom Curtin (1984) had described and also with the nineteenth-century Kalabari and Efik merchants who interacted with European traders and traders from the interior (Forde 1956; Middleton 2001: 522).

Similar constellations of traders and brokers are found in the Malian tea trade. Importers and the major wholesalers are merchants who have their sons and other apprentices in their company and work with small brokers, the *coxeurs*, whereas the *bàanàbāna*, the small traders, have not yet accumulated much capital, buy and sell small-scale. They aspire to have a permanent shop, be retailers and wholesalers, save their profits and invest in trade goods until they eventually become wholesalers, or even importers who have capital at their disposal; entrepreneurial, they invest their profits in further trade goods, property and occasionally production. When combining commerce and brokerage, the *coxeurs* dream of becoming respected in the business as wholesalers, importers, or *jàtigi*.

3.3 *From Caravan Trader to Wholesaler, Importer and Entrepreneur*

Some descendants of former caravan traders and landlord-brokers outlined above are currently tea wholesalers and importers who have become global travellers and entrepreneurs. In pre-colonial times, landlord-brokers were crucial for the safe organisation of long-distance trade. Caravans only travelled between places where resided landlord-brokers from their home region. In a town like Timbuktu, traders arrived with gold from the regions in the southwest, with kola nuts from the forested areas of the south and with fabrics, tea and sugar from Morocco in the north and sometimes from Tuat and Ghadames in the northeast (Perinbam 1973, Lydon 2009). Landlord-brokers from one region stayed in particular sections of a town. Caillé (1996: 232) noted that in trading towns like Timbuktu and Djenné, the Saharan traders (*les maures*) – whom he observed drinking tea – lived as trade agents and landlord-brokers for about four years, after which they returned home with their accumulated fortunes, which may have included many slaves. Then another family member would replace them.

Whilst European initiatives during French colonial times weakened the caravan trade, it did continue until Mali's independence. New national borders complicated the movement of goods. In the early twentieth century, after Bamako became the administrative capital of Mali, numerous traders, especially from the northern part of the country, settled there. Malian long-distance traders, however, found the colonial administration made it difficult to obtain trading licences (Amadou Djikoroni, interview, Bamako, 2016); the administration favoured Lebanese traders. However, as Judith Scheele (2012b) observed, the trade across the Sahara did not come to an end during colonial and post-colonial times, it was merely reorganised, trade goods being distributed in the Sahara itself. It appears, however, that small quantities of tea and sugar still travelled across the Sahara.

Scholars described the organisation of this trade and the role of the landlord-brokers in the Sahara and the Sahel (Perinbam 1973) but they did not mention traders' names. However, in eighteenth and nineteenth century Morocco, some Soussi and Jewish merchants' names have been documented (Lévy 1995; Schroeter 1988; Waterbury 1972). It is rare for a caravan leader's name to be remembered. One of the wholesalers from the Timbuktu region recalled that during the time when they still lived there, i.e. before 1960s, tea came from Mauritania and Morocco: one of the Saharan traders, called Sirti, was better known by the name *Arageigei* – a name that I have also encountered in Morocco – after the tea he brought (interview, Bamako, 2013).

Many stories recounted by Malian tea traders began with their moving to Bamako from the north. Most mentioned a town or village around Timbuktu from which they, their parents or their grandparents had left. Some arrived as early as the 1930s, others in the 1960s. Saharan traders had been in Bamako since pre-colonial times (Meillassoux 1963), but then increasing numbers of other traders had come from the north to find work in the growing capital. Most Saharan traders who had moved north after the introduction of the state monopoly in the 1960s, returned to Bamako after the 1990s.

One of the contemporaries of Mali's first president, Modibo Keïta (Amadou Djikoroni; Bamako, 2016), argued that the notion of 'modern traders' followed independence because traders could then acquire a licence allowing them to work officially. He pointed to the tremendous changes of the economic system that colonialism and independence had brought, explaining that a 'modern trader' was someone 'who has registered his company, who purchased his licence which permits to import and export … because before independence there was not a single capitalist in our country'. Nevertheless, even today, many aspects of cooperation and the organisation of the trade have not changed.

Jean-Loup Amselle (1987) who studied the development of trade in Mali in the 1970s and 1980s, observed three types of traders who by the time had licences. First, there were those who continued as before and who, whilst they could not read or write, sent their children to school. Second, were those who had attended school and followed their parents into business, and third, were newcomers whose parents had not previously been traders. Amselle also noted that the merchant, the *jùlabá*, taught his sons and apprentices the basics of the trade. In due course, he would provide them with the capital firstly to get married and then with *mánankun*, the capital to start their own business. If an apprentice was unsuccessful, he would return to his *jùlabá* and denied another opportunity. A successful apprentice would continue working alongside his *jùlabá* on a more equal footing, pooling their capital until sufficiently prosperous to trade independently (Amselle 1977: 180–185). This is true for the tea market as well.

The tea trade was dynamised by the market reforms following the 1991 revolution. After the dissolution of SOMIEX, as mentioned earlier, private traders organised the importation of tea at first from West African coastal cities, then from Asian capitals and finally from China itself. Whilst some Malian wholesalers imported the same tea that SOMIEX had sold, others sought their own type of tea and Chinese traders sold cheap Gunpowder tea. Previously, semi-wholesalers and retailers procured their products from SOMIEX, subsequently, tea wholesalers emerged, buying tea directly from the importers and selling it on to retailers. Soon after, more Saharan traders, the *súraka*, returned from the Saharan towns and Timbuktu, Gao and Kidal to open companies and import Chinese green tea. Firstly, they established themselves in Mopti, then Bamako; a few operated from Gao. Most of them belong to families who had been traders for many generations. Descendants of Dyula, too, especially the Djokoramé, began to import after arriving in Bamako. Other importers were newcomers, of Bamana and other ethnic identities (chapter 5). The tea trade expanded as did the number of importers, wholesalers, retailers, *coxeurs*, *bàanàbāna* who made a living from the green tea trade. European and Asian companies also tried to sell black tea, but that was obviously less rewarding because Malians craved for green tea.

Following China's entry into the WTO in 2001, it opened the country for private trade, privatising most of its state-owned tea companies. Until then, China had four state-owned tea companies, each with its own tea brand: *Temple du Ciel* (Shanghai), *Chameau*, *Imperial*, and *Evergreen*. Following the privatisation these companies continued to sell tea. From 2004 onwards, other companies were permitted and many large and also small companies began to operate, creating their own brands. Soon Saharan and Djokoramé wholesalers began to seek their preferred tea sold earlier by SOMIEX. Their successes inspired other newcomers to try importing tea, and increasing quantities of good tea became available on the market in Bamako. From all these merchants who engaged in the tea trade during the last twenty years, at least a dozen Malian importers became well established in the tea business. They invested their profits in the trade, in warehouses, transport systems, property and some also in industrial production. They diversified their product offers and may be considered to be not just traders and merchants but also entrepreneurs (chapter 4).

The tea boom was slowed down a little in January 2012, after militant groups attacked the Malian military in the north-east of the country and three months later, controlled most of the north of Mali (Hagberg and Körling 2012). The Malian army managed to oust the president from office without much difficulty but proved unable to conclude the war. Ibrahim Boubacar Keïta became the new president but the situation continued to be highly insecure with the rebels threatening to conquer the south. During spring 2015, François Hollande, the former French president, launched a military action to liberate the north, called Serval, which ended without having reached Kidal, Mali's most north-eastern town. Nevertheless, the rebellion hardly impacted upon the tea trade, having little effect on availability and in subsequent years the importation of green tea further increased (chapter 2). The political situation continues to be highly insecure.

4 The Migrants' Role in Distributing the Green Tea Ritual

As mentioned earlier, the dissemination of the tea ritual in Mali began in the nineteenth century from the trading towns in the western Sahel, situated in present-day northern Mali, Mauritania and Niger. From there, the tea ritual spread further south with Saharan and savannah traders, pastoralists and Muslim scholars. For example, the tea ritual was first introduced to Brikama, southern Gambia, between the 1960s and the early 1980s by a Mauritanian marabout residing there who prescribed Chinese green tea as a medicine. The population adopted the tea ritual gradually in subsequent decades.[5] In Nioro de Sahel, people had observed the Saharan traders drinking tea with curiosity, but became interested in the drink only after they saw the pastoralists whom they did not regard as foreigners adopting the habit (Diawara and Röschenthaler 2012). Following independence, civil servants throughout the country were emulated by family elders and eventually the younger generation (Röschenthaler forthc.). Awareness of tea among Mali's population was also aided by the national Farako plantation and contributed eventually to Mali becoming a centre of green tea distribution.[6] Through their widespread commercial networks, the established Malian tea merchants began distributing Chinese green tea throughout the city of Bamako, to other Malian towns, the rural areas and to adjacent countries.

4.1 *Travelling Traders Transport Green Tea to Migrants at the Atlantic Coast*

Consumption of Chinese green tea is particularly high in big cities and towns like Bamako, Kayes, Nouakchott, Mopti and Niamey. These cities have attracted young people from rural areas in search of work and there they also got to know the tea ritual. Labour migrants from the Western Sahel (Niger, Senegal, Mauritania, Mali) distributed the ritual of drinking Chinese green tea further when they moved to other countries and regions. Large numbers of migrants from the Mande World sought work in the plantation and mining areas and coastal cities such as Accra, Conakry, Lomé, Abidjan, Cotonou and Banjul. Some Sahelian labour migrants also moved to Cameroon, Gabon, Equatorial Africa, Congo-Brazzaville, Angola, to other mining areas in Central Africa and to Mozambique. Many Malian migrants also dwell in Europe and, more recently, in Asian cities such as Hong Kong, Jakarta, Bangkok, or Guangzhou (Bertoncello and Bredeloup 2007).

It is, however, important to note that migration to West African countries and Congo-Brazzaville already had begun in the late nineteenth century (Manchuelle 1997: 119–123), before the tea ritual became widespread in Mali

5 I am grateful for this information to Hauke Dorsch, who carried out research in Gambia and interviewed the grandson of Alhadj Bai Konte, assumedly the first tea consumer in Brikama, in March 2019. He died in 1983.

6 In West Africa, Mali is the only country which established a tea plantation for domestic consumption. Morocco had also established a similarly small royal tea plantation near Larache, with Chinese help. Central and East African countries are major exporters of tea, but have almost exclusively specialised in black tea. Only recently, they began producing small quantities of green tea destined for export to Europe (Houtkamp and van der Laan 1993).

and only very few Malians were aware of the beverage. It is unlikely that migrants carried tea leaves and equipment to these places before the 2000s. Whilst tea drinking was not unknown in the regions south of the Sahel trading towns during post-colonial times, the 1990s invention of the small 25g boxes greatly enhanced its dissemination. As they were invented and produced specifically for the Malian market (as will be explained in chapter 2), wherever 25g tea packages are found, there will be a connection to the Mande World. At first, migrants from the Mande World take tea packages and equipment with them for their own use. Migrants working abroad then ask other Malians returning home to bring a supply of tea in their luggage as gifts or for sale to other migrants. Eventually, travelling traders will establish a more stable supply. In the cities of Europe, for example, only the larger packages (250g–1kg) containing mostly Chinese Gunpowder tea may be found in Moroccan stores, as the number of Malian migrants, compared to that of North African migrants, is small. Here Malians have to rely on travelling friends and traders to bring the popular tea brands.

This is different in the cities of the Atlantic coast, where small tea packages may be found in a few kiosks, indicating that there are migrants from the Mande World who perform the tea ritual. Chinese green tea frequently travels great distances and long detours before being drunk in such places. For example, near Tudu market, in Accra in 2012, Tuareg brothers from Niger sold such packages of Chinese green tea. Some of these brands (*Flecha*, *Azawad*, white AAA) had arrived at the port of Cotonou, from where they were transported first to Niger and from there again to the coast in Accra; others (AAA, *Sahara*) had arrived from Nouakchott, via Niger to Accra and still others (*Gazelle*, yellow AAA) travelled via Bamako (Figure 10). The brothers were selling tea to Sahelian migrants in Accra but had previously been working in Libya, before, due to the crisis returning to Niger in 2011 (Nigerien traders, interview, Accra, 2012). The few green tea packages that I encountered in Kumasi all had arrived via Bamako.

Where the number of migrants is sufficient to support it, Malian merchants will import entire containers of tea destined for the place, and/or local importers may also import their own tea brands. There are enough people from the Mande World in Western Burkina Faso, especially in Bobo Dioulasso, to support the importation of whole containers of several tea brands. Imported mostly by Malian merchants, they arrive via the port of Lomé. Burkinabé traders also travel to Bamako to get tea from there. One told us, he takes an order and the payment from the wholesalers, then travels to Bamako by bus; there he purchases *colis* (four 5kg cartons tied together) of the various tea brands from wholesalers and transports them on a rented lorry back for distribution to the

FIGURE 10 Nigerien traders selling tea from Bamako in Accra, 2012

wholesalers at Bobo Dioulasso (interview, Bobo Dioulasso, 2012). Some of this tea is distributed to northern Ghana, where migrants, as mentioned earlier, from the Mande World work and still smaller quantities of tea are supplied to the migrants from the north in Kumasi and Accra (observation, 2012). Similar happened in Côte d'Ivoire and other West African port cities like Conakry (interviews, Bamako, 2013 and Guangzhou, 2016).

In Equatorial Guinea, Gabon, Cameroon and especially in Congo-Brazzaville and Mozambique large numbers of Malian and other Sahelian migrants live and work. When their population becomes large enough, Malian tea importers begin sending entire containers to the location. The importer of *Achoura*, for example, sends one container per month of the brand to Congo-Brazzaville and one to Mozambique. A Senegalese trader also sells *Flecha* in Congo and Gabon. The Malian importer explained that he only sends a container to countries in which the number of consumers is sufficient, otherwise it takes too long to sell the tea. Should selling one container take more than three months, as in Gabon and Cameroon, then he considered it not worth the trouble (interview, Bamako, 2013).

In Cameroon, Chinese green tea arrives via three different trade routes. In the northern part of the country, tea is imported lose in wooden boxes from the north, probably from Kano in northeast Nigeria or from Tripoli in Libya. The tea imported in wooden boxes has been traded in northern Cameroon since before Malian migrants arrived. In Niger, at least, wooden boxes of tea were imported via Kano where British trading posts have been created in the nineteenth century (Grégoire 1999: 80, note 3). In the 2010s, in rural areas in Niger, the cheaper tea, called the 'tea of the silversmiths' – considered to be poor – came from Kano, whilst the more expensive tea in small packages was imported to cities such as Niamey, or Tahoua, probably via the port of Lomé (Valerie Hänisch, pers. comm., 2016).

Secondly, Malian migrants and traders bring it in the small packages directly from Mali or Niger on the land route. In the early 2010s, these were the most popular tea brands in Mali, including *Gazelle*, *Flecha*, *Arawane* and *Azawad*, sold in Yaounde and in Douala. Thirdly, Cameroonian (and perhaps Chinese) importers order containers of green tea to arrive at the coastal port of Douala. Noting the demand for Chinese green tea, one big Bamileke wholesaler created his own green tea brands, which he sells in Douala and Yaounde to migrants from the Sahel (interview, Yaounde, 2014). Some of these brands are imitations of the popular West African brands whilst others are new brand names and still others are Chinese-owned brands such as the cheaper Gunpowder brands *Chameau* and *Temple du Ciel*. Some Chinese green tea also arrives via Douala from Equatorial Guinea with Cameroonian importers and traders.

Malian migrants in Cameroon consume the best tea in their tea rituals after work in the evening. This is the tea that arrives overland from Mali. Some Malian migrants sell Chinese green tea to passers-by from thermos flasks at the street corner, or from small tables in a market street near the area where the Malian migrants stay. This is the cheap Gunpowder variety of tea, which they mix with herbs and ginger juice and sell to their Cameroonian and other customers (Figure 11). By these means, new consumers gradually have adopted Chinese green tea. They take it when the occasion arises, although in 2014, non-Muslim Cameroonians did not prepare it themselves.

Cameroon is one of the Central African black tea producers that grows tea on four plantations in the hilly Grassfields and the Southwest Region. As in Mali, black tea, however, is consumed differently: infused in larger cups and with milk and sugar, by the rising middle class. They would drink green tea occasionally for health reasons, purchasing it in tea bags found in Chinese stores, which sell about fifty varieties of such teas for any type of health problem; but migrants from the Mande World and Muslims from the north of the country prefer to consume the strong Chinese green tea in a ritualised way as Malians do.

4.2 *Chinese Green Tea Arrives via Bamako in China*

More recently, the 25g tea packages are also available in Hong Kong and Guangzhou where Malians have settled down for trade. Malian migrants have

FIGURE 11 Malian migrant selling tea to passers-by in Yaounde, 2013

worked in Hong Kong since the 1990s, if not earlier (Bertoncello and Bredeloup 2007). In the 2000s, some of the Malian traders began distributing packages of tea to members of the Malian association and to Malian restaurants in the Chungking Mansions in Hong Kong and in the Tianxiu building in Guangzhou. Since the 2010s, they began commissioning a few Chinese kiosks to sell tea to Malian migrants for them. In 2016, the most popular tea brands in Bamako – called *Achoura*, *Flecha*, *Koutam*, *Niger* and *Azawad* – were available in three Chinese groceries in the Tianxiu building. In one of them, also other, less known tea brands were on sale, which Chinese traders unfamiliar with Malian preferences nevertheless wished to sell (Figure 12). Interestingly, when we visited these shops, the Chinese sellers refused to talk about the tea packages, even when I was there with a Chinese-speaking African assistant. However, tea packages of this type were not available in any of the countless Chinese tea outlets and gigantic tea markets (Figure 13).

To reach China, these tea packets make a long journey. The long journey of green tea begins in the Chinese tea gardens, where the leaves are produced, dried and transported to a factory (Figure 14). There the tea leaves are sorted, packaged and transferred into a container, which is transported to a Chinese port such as Hong Kong, Ningbo or Shanghai from where it travels aboard containerships in 45 days to a West African port (interviews, Guangzhou, 2016

FIGURE 12 Malian-owned tea in a kiosk in Xiaobei, Guangzhou, 2016

and Hong Kong, 2016; chapter 5). On arrival, the container is loaded onto a lorry or rail fright transporter and delivered to the importers' warehouses in Mali. From there, the tea is distributed with the help of *coxeurs* (local brokers) to the wholesalers, or with itinerant traders to rural areas and adjacent countries.

FIGURE 13 Tea cakes in a Chinese tea market, Guangzhou, 2016

FIGURE 14 Tea garden at LongJing near Hangzhou, 2014

When a Malian trader – those I know who do this are not tea importers – is preparing for a trip to China, he will purchase packages of the popular tea brands from a wholesaler in Bamako, and carry them in his suitcases by airplane back to China – as if there was not enough green tea there – but this type of tea is not found on Chinese markets. These traders then sell the tea to Malian friends, restaurants and a few small Chinese shops frequented by West Africans. It has to travel twice around half the globe so that Malians can consume in China the tea they know from home (Figure 15).

Obviously, it does not make sense to send an entire container of green tea to Hong Kong and Guangzhou, although in 2014, for example, at least 10,000 Malian traders travelled to China for business, staying there for several weeks, according to the president of the Malian association (interview, Guangzhou, 2016).[7] Most Malians in China work as brokers facilitating the business of African importers. Only a few of them have specialised in bringing green tea to Mali. Some Malian importers I met operated a family business selling Chinese products, where one brother resides and works in China with others in one or several African countries where they sell the Chinese products, including tea (interview, Bamako, 2013). Most of the Malians residing in China trade in other commodities such as building materials, textiles, apparel, shoes and sports equipment (interview, Guangzhou, 2014). This resonates with my findings in Bamako that the popular brands are, with a few exceptions, all imported by Malians with headquarters in Mali (chapter 5).

When they travel to China, the Malian tea importers can employ the services of a China-based Malian broker to orient themselves in the giant Chinese cities (Figure 16). However, most of them do this only on their first trip. One importer, having worked with such a broker noted, that a few Malians based in Guangzhou had the necessary contacts as they are more specialised in other commodities (interview, Bamako, 2013). Once Malian traders have found their Chinese supplier, the factory will send its own Chinese broker who conveys the importers from the airport to the factory and translates for them. Malian importers preferred this as they can then purchase their tea directly from the factory without the involvement of too many intermediaries (chapter 5).

This short summary of the history of tea in Mali provides the background for understanding the present-day tea trade, the traders' renewed agency after the reforms of the 1990s and the gradual emergence of tea brands that

---

7 They purchased trade goods valuing over USD 100 million. The president of the Malian association in Guangzhou received this information from the foreign ministry of Guangdong. It is however difficult to make out the exact number of Africans residing in China, as there is persistent fluctuation and many visa overstayers (Bodomo and Pajancic 2015).

FIGURE 15 Malian trader residing in DRC prepares tea in Guangzhou, 2016

are owned by Malian importers and some Chinese brokers. During the time of the trans-Saharan caravan trade, agency in the trade was fragmented in the hands of various (Chinese, British, Jewish, Saharan, Dyula) merchants. Then the Malian government became the dominant agent managing the import of most stable foods and luxury goods. This changed again with the 1991 reforms

FIGURE 16 View from Malian restaurant, Guangzhou, 2016

and the advent of private trade. Among the various private traders who were active in the 1990s and early 2000s, in the long run, Malian merchants, particularly those from established trading families managed to become the leading importers who dominated the tea trade, as will become clear in the following chapters. They were the most influential actors to mediate between the consumers and the suppliers, selecting the tea and distributing it to places all over Africa where a sufficient number of migrants from the Mande World were residing. To understand these instances of agency, first the development of the tea brands has to be examined.

CHAPTER 2

The Evolution of the Green Tea Brands

From the 1990s onwards, private importers began to import green tea from China. Soon, tea was no longer sold lose from wooden boxes but in various smaller package sizes. The 25g packages were created and the importers began to have their own tea brands (chapter 1). Since then, the tea brands have multiplied significantly. Easily counted until the early 2000s, in the following years an estimated over one hundred could be found in the section for green tea on Bamako's Grand Marché. However, so dynamic is the trade that their true number cannot be ascertained: new tea brands are frequently created whilst others disappear.

This chapter explores the evolution, multiplication and ownership of the tea brands to explain their great number, the success of the small package size, and the identity of the individuals who contributed to shaping consumers' ideas about taste and tea quality. To understand these issues, the chapter begins by examining the types of tea that were traded to West Africa historically and at present. It also looks at the packaging, including circumstances that led to the 25g packages. The second part provides a chronology of the most important tea brands, examining why some lasted longer than others. An evaluation of the tea brands that are registered in the BOPI provides insights in the ownership of the brands, the ethnic identity of the traders, the increase in tea brands and the changing preferences for particular varieties. Not all green tea brands sold in Bamako were created in Mali. Some of them arrived from other West African countries. These creations will be included because they illustrate the development of particular varieties of tea, the increase and diffusion of the green tea consumption in the region and the importance of Malian, mostly Saharan traders in these activities. These importers – and a few Chinese traders – created the most popular tea brands with the longest life-spans.

1 Types of Tea and Forms of Packaging

Asked for their criteria for choosing a particular tea brand, Malian consumers always mentioned taste and quality as being most important. They trusted the judgement of Malian importers, in particular, the Saharan traders whom they considered eminent connoisseurs of tea. In order to better understand the development of the tea brands, the particular Malian taste for tea and how

 | DOI:10.1163/9789004505698_004

Malian importers shaped this taste, it is important to consider what types of Chinese tea possibly arrived with the camel caravans from Morocco via Europe in the nineteenth century.

1.1 *Types of Chinese Green Teas Sold to Europe*

For centuries, in China the best, rarest and most expensive types of tea were reserved as tribute teas for the emperor, his entourage and the political elite. The second-best quality tea was available to the ordinary Chinese people, with only the remaining tea being exported abroad (Krieger 2009: 52–55; Liu 2007: 71). Quality depended on when it was harvested, the size of the leaves and the production region, or *terroir* (Trubek 2005). In the Ming period (1368–1644), precise standards of tea quality had been elaborated in order to determine whether a particular tea was appropriate for consumption at the imperial court. Some of these standards designating production area (Anhui, Zhejiang, etc.), type of processing (degree of fermentation and preservation such as green, black and pressed or brick tea), harvest time (spring, summer, before the rain) and the size of the leaves were then also applied in the tea trade with Europeans.

By 1682, five leaf sizes were available on the Chinese market, among which small leaves were the most valuable (Krieger 2009: 51–56). The market developed quickly, and from 1730 onwards, exporting tea companies were created in China selling tea from Anhui and the West Lake (LongJing) (Gardella 1994; Liu 2007). The majority of these were green teas. Only as demand increased were the less expensive black teas specifically for export to Europe produced, especially in Fujian (Gardella 1994). It is interesting to note that some of the more expensive green teas were traded on to Morocco – and to Mali – whilst the cheaper black teas were distributed to Europe (for more on this, Ellis, Coulton and Mauder 2015; Krieger 2009; Röschenthaler forthc.).

Until the second half of the nineteenth century, the names for the different teas identified in broad categories of green and black tea, types of each (Gunpowder, Hyson) with subtypes (SowMee, Chunmee) were still easily understood. Each type was available in three variations: superior, fine and extra-fine. After 1849, teas were blended (especially those from India, which do not concern us here) and had particular names that could refer to the region of production, the time of harvest and the form of the leaves (Krieger 2009: 56, 140).

Among the Chinese green teas that reached Europe in the nineteenth century were Hyswen, a simple type of tea; Songlo, unsorted, hardly rolled leaves from the last harvest; Hyson, fine well processed leaves; Gunpowder, rolled into little balls; Pearl tea, a carefully rolled Hyson; and Bing or Imperial, a very fine leaf (Krieger 2009: 52–55). The present tea standards continue to use criteria around production region, type of processing, harvest time and leaf size, expressed by names, numbers, A's, stars (1 to 5) and further attributes (special, extra fine, etc.). More knowledge on the Chinese numbering system has still to be acquired. A chart from the 2010s that can be seen in the LongJing Tea Museum near Hangzhou illustrates that most of China's tea production involves green tea (70%); the remaining teas are 12% oolong tea, 7% black tea and 11% other teas (observation in 2014, 2016). In 2018, China produced 1,722,000 tons of green tea, of which it exported 309,800 tons worldwide (daxueconsulting.com 2020; UN Comtrade 2021).

Green tea is dried immediately after harvest, rolled and roasted in big pans at low temperature to stop its fermentation. Pan-firing deactivates the enzymes and preserves the tea's green colour. In the nineteenth century, the leaf teas were carefully packed in wooden boxes the corners of which were re-enforced with metal strips. At the port of Canton, the tea was carefully packed and sealed in these boxes which prevented the leaves from acquiring odours on the long journey in the bellies of the European ships. In London, some boxes would be opened and the quality checked before they were offered for sale in the famous London auction (Houtkamp and Van der Laan 1993; Ellis, Coulton and Mauger 2015). There, Jewish merchants purchased some loads of these green teas for re-export to Morocco. In Essaouira some of the wooden boxes were loaded onto donkeys who carried them to Guelmin in southern Morocco where they were then transferred to camels, as mentioned in chapter 1 (Lydon 2009; Schroeter 2002). One camel could carry six wooden boxes of approximately 30kg each, three on each side (interview, Bamako, 2013; see also Caratini 1989, vol.2, 134–135; Damani 2013: 67–68). To protect them from sand, the boxes were wrapped in blankets. Other camels carried loaves of sugar weighing 2kg – from the Caribbean – which would be consumed with the tea, and also fabrics and other European products.

The journey undertaken by tea from its production sites in China to Timbuktu might take several years which had an impact on its taste as the tea ripened with time and temperature (Röschenthaler forthc.; see also Zhang 2014).[1] The journey from Essaouira across the Sahara to Timbuktu alone required between 65 and 80 days (Miège 1961, vol.2: 146–149). As I observed in the tea factories in Zhejiang, even today, tea for some destinations is packed in such wooden boxes (Figure 17). These destinations include the Middle East and eastern North Africa from where it continues further to northern Nigeria, eastern Niger and Cameroon (chapter 1).

1 Jinghong Zhang (2014) noted that unfermented green tea cakes changed their taste on the far shorter journey from Yunnan to Hong Kong and Taiwan.

FIGURE 17 Wooden boxes in a Chinese tea factory, Zhejiang, 2014

1.2 *The Types of Tea That Arrived in Morocco and Northern Mali*

It cannot be surely ascertained which type of green tea was traded to northern Mali in these boxes, however, it was a Chinese green leaf tea, not brick tea or tea cakes. Most early sources discuss tea in a general way; some mentioning it was green tea without specifying the type. Miège (1957: 379) gives some useful indications. By the end of the nineteenth century, tea was imported to Morocco directly from England and sometimes also from Hamburg, and this was largely Hyson, Young Hyson and Gunpowder. These teas were delivered in chests and half-chests whose weight varied according to the type of tea. A chest of Hyson was 70 pounds, a half-chest 46 pounds, a chest of Young Hyson 55 pounds, and a chest of Gunpowder 82 pounds. Damani (2013: 195) clarified that different measurements existed and that Miège (1957) referred to the Moroccan pound, locally named *ratl*. The Moroccan pound was 540g, the French 500g and the British 485g. Hence, the chests containing Hyson had a weight of 31.7 kg, with a half-chest weighing 20.8 kg; a chest of Young Hyson weighed 24.9 kg and Gunpowder weighed 39.7 kg. Young Hyson was less expensive, of medium quality and sold in the countryside. Hyson was superior and more expensive; both Hyson and Gunpowder came from Anhui and Formosa (Miège 1957: 389; see also Damani 2013: 195; Raji 2003: 178–185).

Some of the Jewish traders who imported this tea into southern Morocco were so closely associated with the product that it became associated with their names. There was *Ataï Afriat* or *Ataï Souiri*, which, according to the Moroccan historian Omar Lakhdar, was a kind of Sowmee (a subgroup of Hyson). *Ataï Afriat* refers to the Jewish Afriat family and *Ataï Souiri* to Essaouira, the Moroccan port, from where the Afriats obtained the tea (2002; pers. comm. 11 January 2016; see also Damani 2013: 197–198; Lévy 1995).

In 1924, a report of the French colonial administration lists five types of green tea that were imported to Morocco. This report is cited by Miège (1957) and subsequently by all other sources on the topic (Damani 2013: 195–196; Lakhsassi and Sebti 2012: 409; Raji 2003: 180). These five types of green tea are Chunmee, Sowmee, Gunpowder, Fungmee, and Young Hyson. Tonkay, the cheapest green tea from China, sold to Europe, is not mentioned. Fungmee and Young Hyson were less widespread in Morocco. These green teas are all subtypes of Hyson (or *Hay-Shan*, 'spring flower'). In Morocco, Chunmee was called *Al Maftoul* or *Chaara* (hair), consisting of complete, longish grey-green leaves and were identified with the number 3971. It was consumed around Casablanca, El Jadida, Rabat and by the Sahraouis, and less often in Fez and Meknes. Sowmee, called *An-Nomeili*, was green or grey in colour, lighter than Chunmee and ascribed the number 8117. It was consumed around Fes, Tadla and Beni-Mellal.

Gunpowder, which was called *As-Souiri* (coming from Essaouira), *Schay al Barūd*, or *Mqrqeb* (*Muqerqeb*) was identified by the number 3505 with its leaves rolled into spheres; it was consumed around Essaouira, Safi, Marrakech, Fes, Meknes, in southern and eastern Morocco. Later, in the 1950s, it became the chief tea of the national import-export society ONTS of Morocco and made up 80% of the tea consumed in the country. Fungmee was not widespread and only consumed in the region of Casablanca and Rabat. Young Hyson, identified by the number 8147, was mainly consumed in the area of Casablanca (Damani 2013: 195–196; Lakhsassi and Sebti 2012: 409; Raji 2003: 182). Each of these green teas is sub-divided into as many as ten subcategories, defined by numbers, stars and A's (Lakhsassi and Sebti 2012: 401–419). Some of the Hyson teas of the first harvest were accorded the numbers 9377 and 9417 (less refined). The most expensive type of Hyson had the highest weight (Damani 2013: 196, note 4 and 5, Miège 1957).

The report cited above appeared shortly after tea was no longer imported to Morocco via London but came instead directly from Shanghai via Marseille (Damani 2013: 199). The importers – Jewish merchants such as the Tulidano (Waterbury 1972) – took great care to ensure they sold the same teas as they had done previously. They also sold Young Hyson Evergreen (G 501); Special Gunpowder, or *Lémkárkáp* (G 601, G 602, G 603, G 604); and Evergreen Hyson (9375), equivalent to the type G 812 and G 813. There was a Hyson called

Imperial, which looked like Gunpowder but consisted of larger balls (Damani 2013: 195, 197). Some of these teas are still to be found both in Morocco and Mali. Amongst the Baydān, i.e. the southern Moroccans and western Saharans, Chunmee or *Maftūl*, was the most appreciated, especially number 9371, followed by 9370 and the slightly lower quality 3008. Also liked was Evergreen Special Chunmee with its number G101 and the types 4011 and 41022. The second-best tea was *Al Muqerqeb*, a strong Gunpowder; Sowmee or *Al Nomeili* was less appreciated (Damani 2013: 199–200). As will become clear below, some of these teas were traded on to Mali.

In the 1910s, tea was not only imported from Morocco across the Sahara but also via Dakar along the Senegal River to the western Sahara by the Senegalese trader Pèdre Alassane, known as 'le roi du thé' (Robinson 2004). By 1891, the French had established trading posts in Nioro and in 1894 in Timbuktu. From there, they traded sugar and it is possible that also some green tea had been brought there by traders from the coastal port of Dakar but at the time it would only have been consumed by a few Saharan landlord-brokers (Lydon 2009: 332) who rather preferred to obtain it from their trading partners in Morocco (chapter 1). In the 1950s, the ports of Dakar and Nouakchott were connected with French ports via Las Palmas; they gained growing significance in the import of green tea throughout French colonial times.

The Canary Islands, especially their capital Las Palmas, were a free-market zone and became an important trading centre in the region for the importation of foreign products such as tea, fabrics, perfumes, and blankets in the region. In the 1970s, between Wad Noun in southern Morocco and Tan Tan, Tarfaya, Saqi al Hamra and Wadi Dahab in West Sahara, occupied by the Spanish at the time, smuggling these products was commonplace. The town of Al Ayoune – a present-day tea brand is named after it – played a particular role as it is situated directly opposite Las Palmas. Some of the Sahraoui traders greatly profited by importing tea from France and Las Palmas to West Sahara – occupied by Morocco since 1973 – and from there to Mauritania. The port of Al Ayoune also connected the Maghreb to Hong Kong, Singapore and Paris.

In the 1970s, green teas were packed in paper cartons of between 250g and 1kg. Their brand names gave rise to a new trading vocabulary. The green teas were again given names not only of influential trading families but also of individuals and *kabilas* (tribal groups), objects, *wadis* and regions reflecting life in the desert (Damani 2013: 70–73). In the Malian Sahel at the time, tea was just named *ataya* (tea), or in Arabic, *schay al ahdar* (green tea).

In short, during the nineteenth century, including large parts of the twentieth century, some of these green teas, especially Chunmee and a little Gunpowder, arrived in northern Mali via Morocco and during the post-colonial times, green tea from Las Palmas was smuggled into Mali via Mauritania. Chunmee was the type of tea that also the Malian independent government imported and which Malian importers were seeking, following the opening of the market to private trade in 1991. The types of tea that arrived in the nineteenth century shaped the taste for tea in Mali. Present-day teas continue to have the same numbers as those mentioned above.

2 The Tea Varieties in Mali and the Chinese Tea Standards

The Malian tea importers were aware of the differing varieties and tastes of the teas produced in China's various regions and thus understood why the tea produced on Mali's Farako plantation would not possess the same taste as that of teas imported from China. The soil, altitude, intensity of sunlight, degree of humidity, time of harvest, processing and the blending all contributed to the taste of the tea, which again could change during the long journey from its place of production to the final destination (interviews, Bamako, 2013; Zhang 2014). This partly explains why both Moroccans and Malians rejected the tea produced at their domestic plantations.

When Malians spoke about the varieties of tea, they always used the term 'quality' (*qualité de thé*). Whilst variety denotes the quality or state of being different or diverse, the way Malians used the term 'quality' seemed to imply a hierarchy, designating improvement or decrease. They combined two meanings of quality: the actual standard of a tea (its variety) and its place in the hierarchy of varieties sorted according to their 'good taste' and fineness. In this hierarchy Gunpowder teas always ranged lower than Chunmee teas and among these 41022 was higher than 4100. Thus, following the tea traders, the term 'quality' is used with this meaning.

2.1 *Tea Varieties in Mali, 1960–1991, and the Introduction of Small Tea Packages in the 1990s*

Between Mali's independence in 1960 and the economic reforms of 1991, SOMIEX imported Chinese green tea in addition to the small quantities that the Malian tea plantation produced at Farako (chapter 1). As Malian importers recounted, the tea produced on the Farako plantation was not easily fitted into the Chinese tea categories, being neither Chunmee nor Gunpowder but simply 'Farako tea' (interview, Bamako, 2013). The locally produced green tea was mixed with Chunmee tea that SOMIEX imported from China. The crates from China arrived at the port of Dakar from where they were transported to Mali by rail. This mixture was sold in four qualities identified as 4011 (the best) and 4012; later in the 1970s, also 4013 and 4014 were available. These teas were of first, second, third and least quality, sold lose from wooden boxes.

A document from the Farako tea plantation (Anon. 1970: 56) states that the rolling and drying of the crude tea and the subsequent refinement resulted in differences in the richness in alkaloids leading to the different qualities. The plantation produced the above-mentioned four qualities: the first sold for 2,250 million Malian francs per ton, the second for 2,150 million, the third for 1,950 million and the fourth for 1,660 million Malian francs per ton. Later, plastic sachets of 10 × 20 × 5 cm were filled with tea and packed in boxes of 30kg. One tea importer who collaborated with the Farako plantation reported that if the ratio of the home-grown tea mixed with the Chinese tea was increased beyond 1%, Malians would not drink it. Even if Farako would be able to increase its production, this ratio had to be maintained (interview, Bamako, 2016).

Before the 1990s, consumers knew their tea by the numbers not by the variety (i.e. Chunmee or Gunpowder). Even if they were illiterate, they would memorise the tea numbers, as for example *Quatre-mille-once*, which thus became like names for the tea qualities (Diawara and Röschenthaler 2012). It seems that at this time, only Chunmee teas were available. One of the older importers recalled:

> These teas were of good quality and without added colours. The tea had a good taste, and people ate the used tea leaves. But these days, you can no longer eat the tea leaves. You can only give them to your animals. There was also tea that changed the colour once it was thrown in water. But the real good tea would not change its colour. Compared to the teas available today, Thé Farako was really good. INTERVIEW, BAMAKO, 2013

Another tea importer explained the relation between the tea sold by SOMIEX and the Chinese numbering system:

> At that time [after independence when he moved to Bamako], SOMIEX imported and sold the tea. There was *Thé Once* [4011], there was *Thé Douze*, and *Thé Treize* and there was *Thé Quatorze*. *Thé Once* was equivalent to *Thé Neuf-mille-trois-cent-soixante-once* [9371, Special Chunmee]. *Thé Douze* was equivalent to *Thé Neuf-mille-trois-cent-soixante-dix* [9370, Special Chunmee II]. *Thé Treize* was like *Neuf-mille-trois-cent-soixante-neuf* [9369], and *Thé Quatorze* was like *Neuf-mille-trois-cent-soixante-treize* or *-quartorze* [9373 or 9374]. These were the tea qualities that were available. … And the real tea connoisseurs took the quality *Onze*. This was the best. It was the supreme quality that people preferred to consume. INTERVIEW, BAMAKO, 2013

4011 designates a fine Chunmee, one of the subcategories of Hyson. Another tea importer confirmed this explanation, saying that

> Earlier on, the *Thé Neuf-mille-trois-cent-soixante once* [9371] and the *Quatre-mille-once* [4011] were the same; but at present, there is also *Quatre-mille-once deux A, trois A,* etc., which are better than the 9371 and the simple 4011. The quality of the tea depends on the region of production and the appellation. And there is still another quality, that we call *Huit-mille-quarante-sept* [8047], which is very near to 9371. But also the best *Quatre-mille-once trois A* [4011 AAA] and so on is less good than the tea that people now [2013] prefer and this is *Quarant-et-un-zero-vingt-deux* [41022]. INTERVIEW, BAMAKO, 2013

As mentioned earlier, these numbers correspond to the numbers of the teas that were introduced from Morocco earlier on (Figures 18a–d)

The importers also remembered the differing weights of the wooden boxes, corresponding with the weight of the various teas. One of the oldest importers explained it most precisely:

> At that time, the *Thé Once* arrived in boxes of 40kg, *Thé Douze* came in boxes of 32 to 35kg, *Thé Treize* came in boxes of 25 to 20kg and *Thé Quartorze,* too. Meanwhile things have changed and boxes of 5kg were introduced around 1984, or 1985. The Chinese exchanged the bigger boxes by the smaller ones of 5kg. And then, 1988, SOMIEX also began to import and sell tea in boxes of 5kg. INTERVIEW, BAMAKO, 2013

FIGURES 18A–D Numbers on the tea packages indicate the varieties of tea: *Dogon* 3505, *Razele* 8147, *Mami Wata* 4011, *Tropical* 41022

Morocco, like Mali, nationalised the tea trade after independence in 1958. The ONTS imported the familiar teas, blended them with the domestic production and rebranded them by giving them local names, such as *La Caravane* evoking Moroccan cultural connotations. The ONTS imported the more popular Gunpowder tea, whereas in Mali the preferred tea was Chunmee. As both governments had prohibited all private imports to support the domestic economy and tea consumers in southern Morocco and northern Mali were craving for the taste of the tea that they knew from before, tea was being smuggled into both countries from Las Palmas via the Spanish West Sahara and Mauritania. The tea smuggled into Mali also came from Gambia and Senegal and from Burkina Faso in the east to where it probably reached from Nigeria. This tea was already packed in paper cartons at that time.

China had also created a state-monopoly on tea processing and export during the twentieth century, however, tea continued to be produced on family farms and small plantations. They delivered their tea to the state-owned factories, especially the Zhejiang Tea Import and Export Company, which had developed brand names for export such as *Chameau* (*Camel*) and *Temple du Ciel* (*Temple of Heaven*).

These brand names given to the cheaper varieties of Gunpowder existed already in the 1970s and were sold in packages of 100 and 125g, as can be concluded from an invoice from Dakar that Damani (2013: 206) discovered in an archive. There was also the better quality Chunmee. One of the Malian tea importers recalled that

> In China, too, there was a monopoly of tea. One company had the authority to sell tea to Africa, and this was the Zhejiang Tea Import and Export Company. They are in Hangzhou. They make the *Chameau* brand. They commercialised their tea and opened their market from the 1990s [actually this began in 1978] onwards, and then it became possible to create private companies in China. From 1992, 93, 94 onwards, the Chinese companies began to sell their own tea brands. You could see several qualities of tea … and importers chose the quality they wanted, whether they want it more bitter or more expensive. And most Malian importers wanted to have 4011. INTERVIEW, BAMAKO, 2013

This was after the market was opened in 1991, as Mali underwent major political and economic changes, including the devaluation of the CFA in early 1994. From that time large quantities of cheap tea arrived on the market, especially Gunpowder. The opening of the market for private importers increased competition and lowered prices. Henceforth, everybody could afford to purchase and drink tea, in spite of the weakened purchasing power due to the devaluation. The downside of this was a decrease in the quality of the tea. Malians who appreciated good tea had difficulties finding Chunmee of at least 4011 quality. The cheaper types attracted negative comments, such as in Bámanankan, the tea was *nyèbere-bò*, 'the droppings of cockroaches'. Soon, Malian importers began to seek the Chunmee tea they prized, and in the 2010s, the superior Chunmee 41022 was preferentially consumed in Bamako.

The Chinese tea standard numbers identify the quality of the tea. One of the tea importers explained how he understood the system:

> Those who are the real tea connoisseurs take the superior qualities of tea. This means that their tea has the grade *Quarant-et-un-zero-vingt-deux* [41022]. This Chinese appellation refers to the new harvest. There is another a little less good quality, which is *Quatre-mille-once*. Its leaf has a 41-grade. If you take *Quarant-et-un-zero-vingt-deux*, you can be sure that you have an opportunity [to make profit], and now you have it additionally with A, two A, three A, five A. At present we have five A. The A's represent different qualities too. [...]. It is about quality and the buds (*tiges*) are longer. If you mention these numbers in China, all the Chinese factories know what quality you are talking about. INTERVIEW, BAMAKO, 2013

Another importer noted that 'All the green teas for the African market are mixed or blended; *Gazelle* is mixed, and also *Super Gaza* is blended. It is not pure. The Chinese make the melange, and each factory has its secrets, which depend on how it [the leaf] is roasted, how oxidation is stopped and how they mix the tea leaves' (interview, Bamako, 2011). The numbering system represents these blends (Figure 19).

One importer worried that 'most of the tea we take here is not 100% pure tea. If it was pure green tea, then the drink would be light and without much colour'. He added that Malians would prefer stronger and darker tea and with lots of froth, encouraging the Chinese to blend it, often adding a colourant to give the beverage a darker hue. He continued:

> What exactly they add, only the Chinese will know. The really good quality green teas do not sell here because they do not get very dark, but this will soon change ... We began with Gunpowder, then came 4011 and 4071, and slowly, slowly the tea assumes a taste that you will not forget. Once you tasted good tea, you will no longer want bad tea. But it takes time [until consumers understand]. INTERVIEW, BAMAKO, 2013

FIGURE 19 Poster at Canton Trade Fair showing numbers of Chunmee teas available, Guangzhou, 2018

The problem of adulterated tea, as many importers note, has been pervasive and it is only over recent years that consumers seem to have developed an understanding of good or pure quality tea.

3 The Emergence and Multiplication of Tea Brands

The first private importers were not very discriminating about the quality of the tea they sold but the more significant Malian tea importers began to acquire the same varieties of tea previously purchased by SOMIEX. At first this tea was imported in wooden boxes of 30kg, later in *colis* of four cartons weighing 5kg each – the size and unit still in use today. The packaging of the contents of the 5kg cartons changed from loose leaves via large packages to small 25g packages.

3.1 *From Ataya to the Tea Brands*

Since the first appearance of tea in the nineteenth century, the package units have gradually become smaller. The large wooden boxes of 20 to 40 kg, depending on the weight of specific types of tea, were replaced by boxes of 10kg, followed by cartons of 5 kg; ultimately, however, the unit, the *colis*, remained. The *colis* became standardised at 20kg and subdivided into four cartons of 5kg, independently of the quality and type of tea. Each of these 5kg cartons could contain either 10 packages of 500g, 20 of 250g, 40 of 125g, 50 of 100g or 200 packages of 25g (Figure 20). The measurements have been adapted in order

FIGURE 20 Tea package sizes, photograph taken at the exhibition 'Ataya – Chinesischer Grüntee in Mali', Mainz, 2019

to precisely fit a standard 5kg carton. In this process, the loosely sold *ataya* became a standardised brand-named product.

The conjunction of the geographic dimension, i.e. the specific route of importation, with the time dimension, i.e. fast transport in less than two months and the gradual modification of the type of packaging, are important because this green tea product is – with the exception of *Thé Farako* – entirely produced and packaged in China. The leaves together with their printed package are imported to Mali as a finished product. The packaging in sachets and cartons brought about the manufacture of the packages with names, colours and images, signifying the birth of the tea brands.

Prior to the creation of tea brands, people consumed *ataya*, as tea is called in the northern part of Mali with its Moroccan-Arabic name, or *duté,* derived from French *thé* in the rest of Mali. After the brands had emerged, they consumed *Baro*, *Cheval*, *Chameau*, or *Obama*. One of the tea importers recalled that when he was young in Timbuktu, his father would just send him to obtain *ataya* for his tea ritual (interview, Bamako, 2013). Another importer remembered that his grandfather displayed his products in the sand at the front door of his compound in Timbuktu. He sold tea lose from the box for 25 Malian francs (interview, Bamako, 2016). At the time, tea might be named after the trader who imported it, such as *Atay Afriat* or *Arageigei*, as already mentioned. In the 1970s, there was little choice as there were few varieties of tea; there were the four qualities from SOMIEX and perhaps sometimes some smuggled 250g tea packages.

Several tea importers were aware that in rural areas there were still consumers who only wanted *ataya* or 'tea', irrespective of quality and for whom brands did not (yet) matter. I also remember a long discussion we had in one of Bamako's wholesale boutiques about whether *Quatre-mille-once* was a type of tea or a brand name. The wholesaler argued that it was not a brand but a 'quality', however, many of his customers insisted that it was not just *ataya* but rather like a brand. For them the qualities had become a brand. The opportunity to choose between several brands – *Gazelle*, *Obama*, *Saddam* – however, only became available in the late 1990s and early 2000s.

As will be shown in the next section, at first, the 25g tea packages were only available in Mali but were soon after also adopted in Senegal, Niger and Mauritania. A few years later, they could be found in other countries to which Malians had migrated and where tea consumption had become popular (chapter 1).

3.2 *The First Green Tea Brands in Mali and the Success of the 25g Packages*

Between 1993 and 1994, green tea packaging experienced an innovation. A Malian of Lebanese origin began to experiment with filling plastic sachets with tea.[2] He owned a company that produced washing powder and a packaging system for filling the powder in sachets. He carried out market research which involved visiting many tea groups in Bamako to discover the appropriate quantity of tea needed for one tea ritual. He settled on producing 25g sachets, filled with Gunpowder tea, which he named *Thé Baro*, meaning 'conversation' in Bámanankan, a reference to the conversations of the young in their tea *grins*. He also collaborated with the Farako plantation and packaged *Thé Farako* in sachets for them.

His next task was to persuade consumers that tea in sachets was an improvement on lose tea from boxes. His main point was that the tea in sachets already contained the exact amount for one tea ritual and only needed to be dropped into the teapot without the need to touch it; thus, it was more hygienic, did not contain sand or other dirt, and excellently conserved the aroma (interview, Bamako, 2016). The sachets easily found adherents and became a huge success.

The next innovation was packaging the 25g sachets in cartons. The importer who began this practice in 1994 or 1995 was Punjabi, a Hong Kong Chinese of Indian origin. He sold his green tea brand, *Cheval*, in packages of 62.5g. As did the Malian of Lebanese origin, he also experimented with different package sizes. He produced packages of 12.5g, but these were insufficient for a single tea ritual. There were also packages of 30g but eventually he too settled on 25g (interviews, Bamako, 2013).

As Punjabi did not have his own facility for filling his sachets, he enlisted the services of the mainland Chinese tea factories. At first, they argued that this would be too expensive and unlikely to sell. The importer insisted on the idea and it became a big success. Since then, all tea importers have adopted this package size and also packaged their tea in 25g sachets inside cartons (interview, Bamako, 2013). A few sachets without carton were still sold in 2016 (*Deux Girafe* [*sic*], *Tilimsi*, sitting *Gazelle*, etc.).

Thé Baro in sachets sold well until about 2004 which saw competition from the increasing number of importers who packaged their tea brands in sachets inside cartons in China. When the Malian of Lebanese origin noticed that consumers were switching to Chunmee, he also began to package the sachets in cartons to create *Thé Baro Super 11*, a 4011 tea (interviews, Bamako, 2016); in 2006, he registered it with the trademark office in Bamako (Figure 21).

In addition to the 25g packages there are also larger packages such as Punjabi's 62.5g, and others of 100g, 125g, 250g or 500g but these are more popular in the northern part of the country and in Mauritania. In Morocco, where also

2 In Britain, mechanical packaging of tea was invented by the Horniman's tea company in 1826 (Butel 2007: 180).

FIGURE 21 Mural of *Thé Baro*, Bamako, 2011

the teapots are larger, only packages of 250g and more are available at all. The larger packages existed before the 1980s, as the documents that Damani (2013) found indicate; however, importers were officially permitted to import them to Mali only in the 1990s (chapter 1). In the late 1990s, the brands *Chameau* and *Temple du Ciel* of the Chinese Zhejiang Tea Import and Export Company were sold in 250g packages containing Gunpowder tea. By 2013, they are no longer available in Mali but can still be found in Burkina Faso, in Cameroon and were on display at the Canton Trade Fair in 2018 (Figure 22).

The larger package sizes of various brands are available in southern Mali as well but appear to be more expensive and less popular. To purchase a package of 250g, one had to have at least 500 francs CFA available, but (in the late 1990s) a 25g package – enough for one tea ritual – cost only 50 or 75 francs (about 0.07 or 0.11 Euro). The small packages also enhanced tea consumption because 75 francs were always affordable (interview, Bamako, 2013). In Bamako, the 25g packages quickly became the most popular, as they did throughout Mali and adjacent countries.

The obvious advantage to the 25g packages is indeed that they are hygienic but a disadvantage is that consumers can no longer see the tea leaves before the purchase and the packages produce more waste. Evidently, the packages would be more expensive but for consumers, the small quantity and the

FIGURE 22 *Thé Chameau* at the stall of Zhejiang Tea Company, Canton Trade Fair, 2016

corresponding small price conveniently allowed everybody to purchase tea on a daily basis. Hence, cheaper tea and the creation of the 25g packages served to democratise the consumption of green tea.

3.3 *The Multiplication of Tea Brands from the 2000s Onwards*

The first tea brand that I found in the BOPI was *Thé Saddam la Force*, registered in 1998, during the Iraq war (chapter 6). It was the first tea sold in 25g packages to be registered and was owned by Senico Sarl, a company based in Dakar that would in the 2000s play a role in selling the widely appreciated *Flecha* brand. *Thé Saddam la Force* was available in Mali as well. *Thé Saddam* was a Gunpowder tea, not particularly good quality but very strong and consisting of very small bullets, almost as fine as powder. The brand name inspired other importers to emulate the idea with, for example, *Warga Touba Super Saddam* being registered in 2002 by another company in Dakar. Many current importers who at the time were still wholesalers, also recalled selling *Thé Saddam*, *Chameau*, *Temple du Ciel*, *Cheval* and *Elephant*, all Gunpowder teas, as well as a good Chunmee tea with the number G101 in packages of 100g.

One of the earliest Saharan importers was Ahmed Abderahmane Abdi (from Tuat in Algeria) who created the brand *AAA* in 1996 or 1997. On each package he printed the initials of his name, AAA, and sold the tea in packages of 250g, 500g and 1kg in Algeria, Niger and northern Mali. In the early 2000s, he also supplied 25g packages (interviews, Bamako, 2013). From the outset, he sold only high quality Chunmee. *AAA* is one of the more popular brands and still existed in 2018 (Graph 6).

While the Saharan importer of *AAA* was selling high quality 4011 Chunmee, or even 41022 Super Chunmee right from the outset, other importers, among whom were Malian, Chinese and the Indian traders, were importing cheap Gunpowder. Malian tea connoisseurs and importers whose parents had already been tea traders lamented the poor quality of these teas and began to seek for better teas in China. They imported 4011 Chunmee and in the 2010s as that became popular with consumers, Gunpowder sales plummeted. Today, *Cheval* and *Baro* are only rarely seen and both Punjabi and the Malian of Lebanese origin gave up importing tea to Mali. *Elephant*, *Chameau* and *Temple du Ciel* of the two Chinese companies (Amsua Trading and Zhejiang Tea Import and Export Company), no longer supply the quality that Malians like to consume.

Until 2002, tea brands were easily counted but by 2007, there were more than sixty brands to be found on the Bamako tea market. New brands emerged every day and others vanished. A few were long-running successes but many others were rather short-lived. From 2002, increasing numbers of tea brands were registered in the Centre Malien de Promotion de la Propriété Industrielle (CEMAPI), the Malian office for the registration of trademarks.

CEMAPI is a member of the Organisation Africaine de la Propriété Intellectuelle (OAPI) with headquarters in Yaounde, Cameroon (chapter 7). Registered brands are published in the *Bulletin Officiel de la Propriété Intellectuelle* (BOPI). After registration and checking by OAPI, a brand is published in the BOPI about 6 month later. The BOPI gives the name and address of the brand owner, provides an image of the brand and some other specifications (see chapter 7). Although CEMAPI was created in 1983, the first green tea brands were only registered in 1998.

My own research findings regarding the brand chronology are partly corroborated by the publication of the newly created brands in the BOPI. However, until today, many importers do not register their brands or they wait until they are sure of the new brand's success. Hence the occasional disparity between the date of creation and the date of registration and publication. Brands such as *Mona* and *Gazelle* were created in Bamako in 2002 and 2003, but *Mona* is not mentioned in the BOPI and *Gazelle* was registered as late as 2006. As will be shown in chapter 7, importers were not unanimous in seeing the advantages of registering their brands. In addition to the documenting of tea brands in the BOPI, which includes more than 300 green tea brands, registered between 1998 and 2018, my collection of 237 brand-named tea packages as well as numerous photographs of tea brands from the market help me establish a rough chronology of tea brand development in West Africa.

4 Twenty Years: A Chronology of the Green Tea Brands 1998–2018

As mentioned earlier, *Thé Saddam la Force* was in 1998 the first brand to be registered; *Chameau* followed later in the same year; *Thé Baro* was registered only in 2006. I have not found *Cheval*, *Elephant* and AAA in the BOPI (Figures 23a–e). They were either not registered or I was unable to find them

FIGURES 23A–E Examples of early tea brands: *Saddam La Force, Chameau, Baro, Cheval, Elephant*

because some issues of the BOPI are missing on the shelf of CEMAPI. Nor were they to be found in the Library of Congress, which is the only library outside the OAPI zone which holds the series.

4.1 *The Evolution of the Tea Brands*

It was a few years before further brands were to be registered with OAPI not just in Mali but also in the other West African member countries (chapter 7). Between 1998 and 2018, I have found registered a total of 304 green tea brands in the BOPI. These will serve as my sample. There may well be a few more, due to the missing issues of the BOPI at CEMAPI and some green tea brands may not be identifiable in BOPI as such. Some of the green tea brands that are sold on the market in Bamako have been registered in other West African countries but are also consumed in Mali. Therefore, these brands are included in this sample.

After the *Thé Saddam la Force* and *Chameau* brands had been registered in 1998, brand registrations increased: there were 6 new ones in 2002, 12 in 2003, 5 in 2004, 17 in 2005, 24 in 2006, 13 in 2007, 10 in 2008, 16 in 2009, 14 in 2010, 8 in 2011, 19 in 2012, 23 in 2013, 19 in 2014, 35 in 2015, 25 in 2016, 29 in 2017, and 27 in 2018. This amazing increase over the last two decades in tea brands is illustrated in Graph 1. It includes the green tea brands registered by importers in all the OAPI member countries. The graph reveals that the number of registered brands owned by African importers (red line) is considerably higher than the number owned by Chinese brokers (grey line). It also demonstrates that increasingly company names conceal the origin of their owners, hence it becomes more complicated to identify their owners' ethnic origin (orange line).

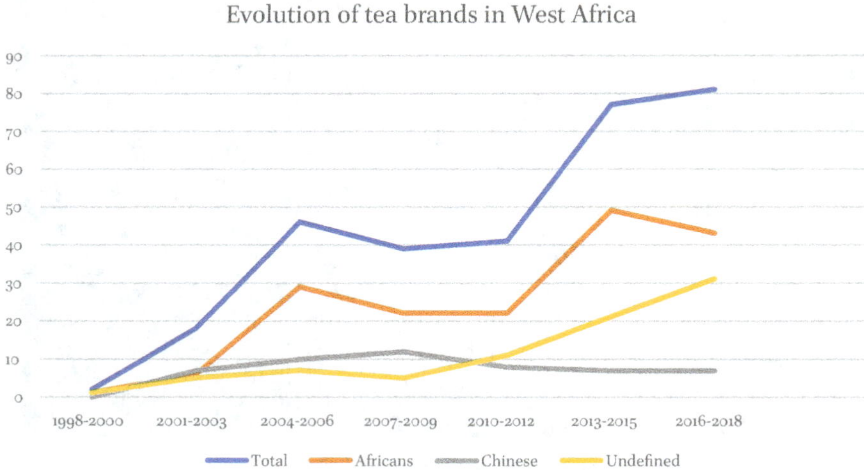

GRAPH 1 Evolution of tea brands in West Africa

Graph 2 depicts the OAPI registration by the cities in which their companies are located. It illustrates the development of tea brands in the region. Of the 403 brands that were registered between 1998 and 2018, 112 were based in Bamako and 15 in other Malian towns (5 in Mopti, 5 in Gao, 3 Koulikoro, 1 Koutiala, 1 Timbuktu); 89 in Nouakchott; 22 in Niamey and 2 Tahoua; 22 in Dakar and 1 Thiès; 6 in Abidjan; 13 in Conakry; 1 Lomé; 2 Cotonou; 1 in Banjul; 1 in Ouagadougou; 1 in Libreville; 1 Brazzaville; 1 in Bisau; 1 in Las Palmas; 1 in Cairo; 4 in Paris and 1 in Levallois; 1 in Geneve; 1 in Brussels; 1 in Colombo; 2 in Hangzhou; and 2 could not be clearly defined. Until about 2016, most of the brands were registered by companies in OAPI member states but more recently, foreign importers have registered with the address of their company headquarters in other countries. Thus, those from outside the OAPI zone are recent registrations.

Graph 2 depicts the gradual increase in the number of importers. At first, importers of Saharan origin were more active in Nouakchott but then Bamako became a centre of tea distribution. Next in importance are Niger and Senegal, whereas there are only a few importers in other countries in and outside of the OAPI zone. The last couple of years show a slight decrease but this does not necessarily mean less tea is consumed but rather that there are more popular brands having a larger number of consumers. The graph also shows importation of tea has increased in recent years in countries that host large communities of migrant labourers from the Mande World. There are importers of various ethnic origin or nationality in a member country of OAPI. For example, Chinese traders may have a company in Mali and register their brands with OAPI but more recently, they have also registered them with a Chinese address.

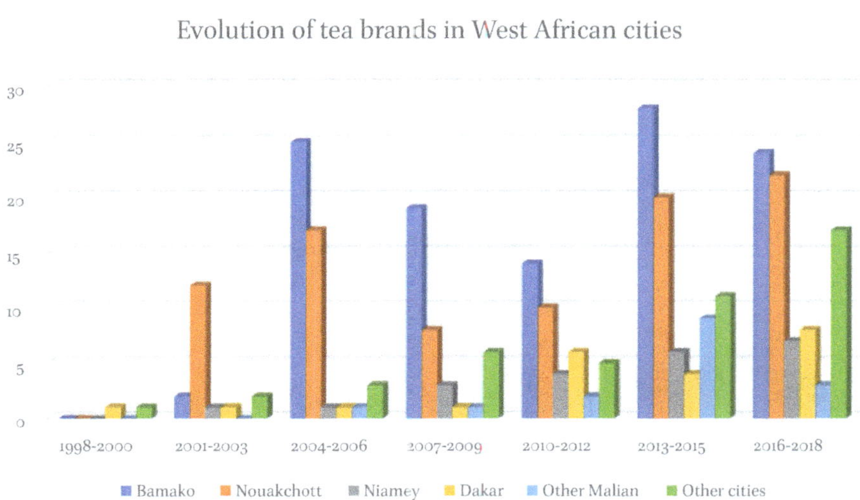

GRAPH 2 Evolution of tea brands in West African cities

Traders of Saharan origin may have a company in Mauritania, Niger, or Mali. Especially Saharan traders with their large distribution networks will relocate their company according to the opportunities available in a country. Political crises, import taxes, customs formalities (free trade zones) may influence where importers have their company and thus register their brands.

A large number of the importers who registered brands in the different towns shown in graph 2 are of Saharan origin. This is revealed in graph 3 which depicts the percentage of importers according to their ethnic identities. The 304 brands registered between 1998 and 2018 are owned by 178 importers. 101 brands are owned by traders of Saharan origin in various countries (Mali, Mauritania, Niger), 48 by other Malians (16 Djokoramé, 6 Soninke, 26 Bamana and others), 5 by Guineans (3 of them Fulbe), 3 by Ivorians, 8 by Senegalese, 7 by Nigeriens (Hausa), 51 by Chinese and 81 by owners of undefined identity. Undefined means their ethnicity – whether Chinese, of Saharan origin or other sub-Saharan Africans – cannot be established from their names alone. This tendency has increased in recent years as importers no longer register under their personal names but under the names of their companies. I suspect that a large percentage of the undefined importers are of Saharan origin and perhaps to a lesser extent Chinese.

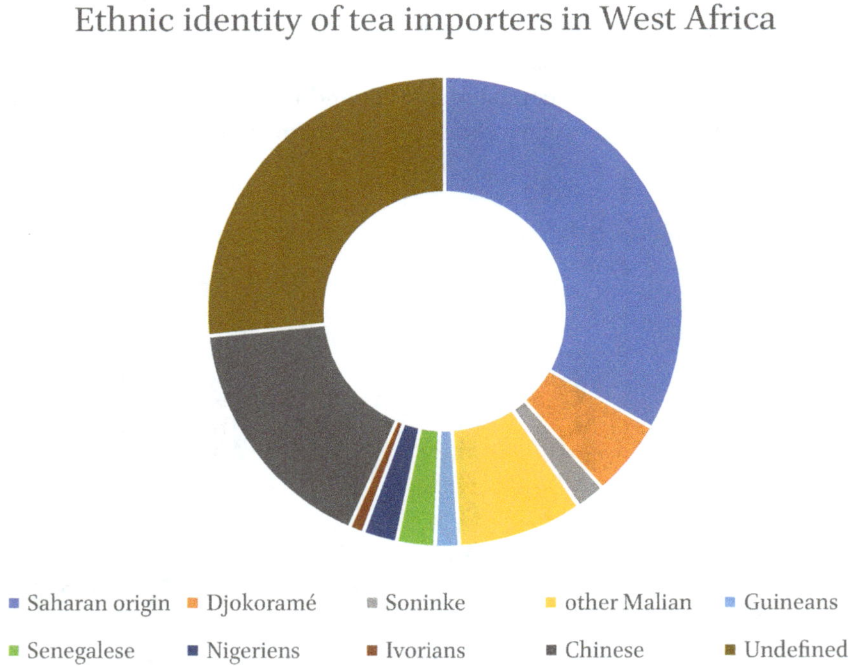

GRAPH 3 Ethnic identity of tea importers 1998–2018

Looking at the increase in the registration of tea brands just in Mali, depicted in graph 4, the shifting importance of traders of different ethnic identity can be read. The graph shows the ethnic identity of the importers who registered their brands in Bamako and other Malian cities. Beginning in 2002 when the first tea brand was registered in Mali, the number of registrations gradually increased from 1 or 2 per year to 14 and 10 in 2005 and 2006. The tea boom slowed down a bit in the following years until it increased to 10 in 2010 and 17 in 2015, after which increase ceased. The 123 importers registering tea brands in Mali may be divided into five major groups: 40 are Malians of Saharan origin, 16 Djokoramé and 6 Soninke (Dyula), 29 Chinese, 20 other Malians such as Bamana – newcomers in the tea trade – and 12 where their ethnic identity could not be verified.

Graph 4 shows that Djokoramé and Chinese importers were prominent at first in registering tea brands but, however, over time they lost their position to importers of Saharan origin, who began registering brands from 2007 onwards (the reasons will be explained in chapter 5). The increase in brands by Saharan traders coincides with their gradual moving from the Sahara further south to Mopti and Bamako and west to Nouakchott in the 2000s (graph 2). The number of brands registered by other Malians remained stable albeit low. Graph 4 also reflects a tendency that I have observed myself in the market as well.

There are at least two issues that should be considered when interpreting this graph. Firstly, the number of registered brands does not reveal anything about the quantities of tea imported under the brands (see chapter 4) and secondly, many importers have not registered their brands. Thus, these statistics only provide an imperfect impression of green tea ownership in Mali. For

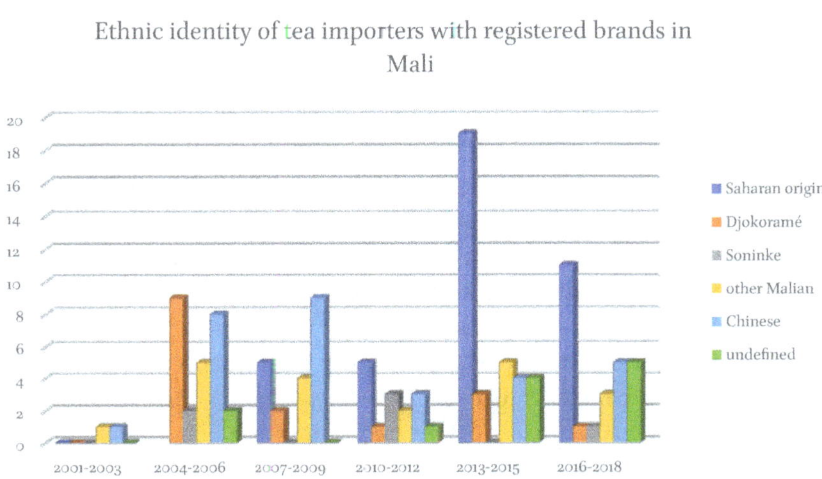

GRAPH 4 Ethnic identity of tea importers with registered brands in Mali

example, of 163 tea brands in my collection 91 (56%) are unregistered. Additionally, 20 brands that I have recorded photographically are also unregistered. It seems, however, that the big tea importers register more brands than the small ones.

In the 2000s, a number of paired registrations between Malian and their Chinese supplier or broker can be observed. Either the Chinese broker and their partner, the Malian importer, each registered a brand in the same year, or in consecutive years and in the same city or different cities, when they have their companies in different countries. For example, in 2004 the Chinese Wang Xiaofeng, who worked as a broker for Dapeng, a Chinese tea factory, registered Askia. A year later, the Malian wholesalers who sold his brands, registered their own short-lived tea brand MOB. Another example is the importer of Hassane Ousmane who registered the brand in 2005; in the same year, his Chinese partner registered her brand Bon MaMa in Nouakchott. In 2006, Bon MaMa was registered again in Banjul by another company (S & S Trading General Merchants). A Chinese registered the Canal brand in 2003 and the Canal typeface in 2004 in Bamako. In 2005, his Malian partner registered 6 brands under his own name and the Chinese partner registered 2 more brands. Thus, in 2005, 8 of the 13 brands registered in Bamako were registered by these two importers alone. By the end of 2005, they again registered some of these brand names, enabling them to use them for additional products. Thus, a sudden increase in registrations can also simply be due to a few importers registering several brands in one year, as happened in Bamako in 2005 and again in Nouakchott in 2013.

Most importers of Saharan origin and some Djokoramé, however, did not work as closely with their Chinese suppliers. They only sold their own tea brands rather than selling for a Chinese broker as well. I will now have a look at the types of tea that these importers were selling.

4.2 *The Evolution of the Types of Teas and Qualities*

As mentioned in chapter 1, the packaged tea that is used for the tea ritual in Mali and the adjacent West African countries is Chinese green tea of two types: Gunpowder and Chunmee. At the time of SOMIEX, Chunmee was sold in four different qualities, which fitted to a certain degree into the Chinese numbering system. In the 1990s, cheap Gunpowder tea brands appeared on the market, many of which were short-lived due to their poor quality. For example, there were only a few container loads of *Thé Maiga, Dogon, Cana Punta, Toucan, Luxe* imported and afterwards they were never seen again. One importer remembered: 'The Gunpowder, at that time, was zero quality. Today, you hardly see Gunpowder (*gros grain*) anymore on Bamako's market' (interview, Bamako,

2013). From 2004 onwards, green tea quality gradually improved and more of the 4011 Chunmee came on the market (Graph 5).

In the second half of the 2000s, many importers offered their tea brand in four (or more) varieties, generally including two types of Chunmee and two types of Gunpowder. All four varieties had the same brand name and package design, differentiated by colour and price. For example, Punjabi sold his tea brand *Cheval* in 25g packages in five qualities: three Chunmee and two Gunpowder teas. The Chunmees were 4011 in red, 9371 in green and 8147 in a different green. The others were Extra Gunpowder 3503 in white and Special Gunpowder G601 in blue package (Figure 24). He also indicated type and price clearly on his billboard. In 2006, he even displayed six teas on a highway near Dakar, all packaged in different colours.

The Chinese importer of *Askia* also offered five varieties of tea: Special Gunpowder 3505 in a blue package, simple Gunpowder 3505 in red, Chunmee 9371 AAA in green, Special Chunmee 41022 with 7 stars in rose, and another undefined Chunmee. This trend began with the Chinese brands but many Malian importers followed suit, although mostly without indicating price or quality. These importers each arranged the four qualities in colours according to their own ideas. Other importers only offered two varieties of tea in differently-coloured packages. One tea importer explained:

> The different colours of the tea packages indicate different qualities, at the beginning at least, and still today to some extent, because they are meant for different regions ... There are different consumers in different regions who want different tea qualities. In the Sikasso region, they have no idea of tea, they just take tea; the main thing is, it is less expensive.
> INTERVIEW, BAMAKO, 2013

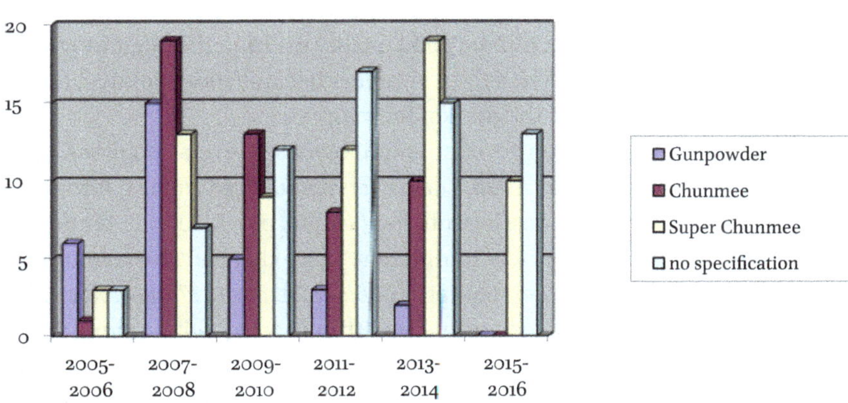

GRAPH 5 Shifting popularity of the green tea types, 2005–2016

FIGURE 24 Billboard with varieties of *Thé Cheval*, Bamako, 2007

In northern Mali – Timbuktu, Kidal and Gao – people preferred Chunmee teas of 9371 whilst 8547 was preferred in Kayes. Among the several varieties that were offered under one brand name, good quality Chunmees 4011 (or 9371) and Super Chunmees 41022 were available from early on. In the 2000s, however, several Malian importers in Bamako complained that their Super Chunmees had been too expensive and for that reason did not sell. Because they proved too expensive for consumers, their sales were low. Profits were easier to accumulate from the cheaper products such as the Gunpowder and Chunmee teas of lower quality. However, AAA offered good quality tea from the beginning and it sold well in northern Mali. When the Chunmees became more popular, these brands remained available on the market for many years.

Up to 2009, it was common to offer simultaneously several qualities of a brand (as did the brands *Cheval*, *Askia*, *Canal*, *Haquiqua*, *Niger*, *Hamza*, *Arawane*, *Hayat*). Only tea importers possessing sufficient capital provided their brands in four qualities. Other brand owners in different years changed the colour and some aspects of the design of their packages (*Obama*, *Azawad*, *Flecha*). Notwithstanding this, many brands proved successful with only one quality. Among these were teas from the lowest up to the highest quality, the latter available only in 250g metal boxes. The successful brand owners offered their brands in the quality most popular at a time: *Gazelle*, *Gaza Super*, *Antilope No.1* and *Taoudeni* were only available in one quality. Also, the super qualities such as *Rocki*, *Achoura*, *Sancho* and *Koutam*, which appeared in the early 2010s were offered in just one quality because it was the best option at the time (Figures 25a–e).

FIGURES 25A–E Examples of popular teas in the late 2000s: AAA, *Niger*, *Azawad*, *Taoudeni*, *Super Gaza*

Apart from the most common varieties, there were also tea packages with irregular numbers such as 550 (*Sonikara* in 2007), 505 AAA (*Tropical* in 2009), 202 (*Joli* red and white) and 777 (*Al Najah* in 2011). There were also the sachets of Farako tea, branded as *Tige* 100. Added to these numbers were further quality indications such as superior, excellent, special, a certain number of stars and A's (chapter 1) (Figures 26a–d).

FIGURES 26A–D Examples of teas with unusual numbers: *Farako Tige* 100, *Sonikara* 550, *Joli* 202, *Al Najah* 777

One importer explained:

> At the beginning, in 2003, 2004, there was not much good tea on Bamako's market. There was only Gunpowder (*gros grain*), which was too strong, too black, too coarse (*gros*). It was not at all fine. And when Gazelle arrived on the market, there was no other tea that was better at that time. It had a very good taste, was highly aromatic and had nice leaves that people

> liked a lot. The consumers bought it and it went very well. Then in 2006, 2007, competitors arrived on the market, first *Super*, then *Antilope*, and then also *Taoudeni*, with the same quality. [Later] ... the taste of Malian consumers changed and the quality of tea changed, too. [Before these] there were other teas on the market, they have been completely forgotten meanwhile, for example *Cheval*, *Canal* and *Golden*, which all went very well earlier on. Nobody wastes a thought again about them. [...] Thirty of them will disappear, and fifty new ones will arrive on the market instead.
> INTERVIEW, BAMAKO, 2013

This is certainly an exaggeration but serves to confirm the general impression of traders and consumers. The same importer continued: 'Tea has seen many evolutions. [...] From 2010 onwards, tea has changed its taste [again]. Now the super qualities have arrived'. He enumerated some of the brands, including *Sancho*, *Flecha*, *Azawad*, *Koutam*, *Ayoune* and *Raissa*:

> These are the super qualities and the teas that people like most. ... The super qualities are different from the quality of *Gazelle* and *Taoudeni*, and the other teas like them. ... There is now also a new type of *Gazelle* with super quality on the market: *Gazelle Rouge* (the *Gazelle* in the red package). INTERVIEW, BAMAKO, 2013

With the emergence of the Super Chunmees 41022 in Bamako from approximately the 2010s onwards, the four varieties became obsolete, as no one wanted to drink Gunpowder and Chunmees of mediocre quality again. Of these, only 4011 was still available in the mid-2010s. There was another cause contributing to the disappearance of the four varieties: each of them was charged a different price but with the appearance of the Super Chunmee teas only one price – 100 francs CFA (about 0.15 Euro) – for all 25g packages remained. There must have been perhaps an agreement between the tea traders to sell all teas for the same price, making the 41022 Chunmee become affordable for consumers. But none of the importers were clear when they mentioned this change to me. One of them hinted at it:

> You will find various qualities on the market. [In some places, tea can be had] for 50, 75, 100 and even 115 francs CFA [...] But here, in Bamako, all tea brands, the super qualities, too, are sold for 100 francs CFA. But these teas [the super qualities] are expensive to purchase [for the importer] and they are different from the hundreds of other qualities that are found on the market. If you ask me, I will prefer to buy super quality for 100

> francs CFA than to buy a simple tea for 100 francs CFA. This is the reason why the super qualities could take off at the market. INTERVIEW, BAMAKO, 2013.

Graph 5 illustrates this change. Consumers henceforth preferred high quality, as one importer stated:

> At present, people no longer consume the *Quatre-mille-once* [4011], they prefer the *Quarante-et-un-zero-vingt-deux* [41022], and of this, there are more than ten different types, like with one A, two A, three A etc. INTERVIEW, BAMAKO, 2013

Traders had differing ideas about the meanings of stars and A's. One wholesaler explained that 'when there are seven stars, then it is very strong; but if there are less stars, it is less strong'. Another importer added: 'If you want to promote your tea well, you must take three A's'. The more stars and A's it has the higher the quality ought to be (interviews, Bamako, 2011).

In 2016, there were still 4011, 9371 and 8147 Chunmees on the market, but most tea brands were indeed 41022 Chunmees. Several tea importers started with one tea brand of average quality acquiring another brand as they progressed to higher qualities. The appearance of the brands *Rocki, Sancho, Koutam, Gazelle Rouge* and *Achoura* reflect this pattern.

Graph 5 shows the popularity of the different types and qualities of tea – Gunpowder (3505), Chunmee (4011, 8147, 9371) und Super Chunmee (41022) – in Bamako between 2005 and 2016, during which most of my collection was assembled. It depicts the qualities, as they are indicated on the packages, of 215 tea brands. Hence, as many brands were available in different qualities of Gunpowder and Chunmee, one brand may have entered the graph several times. The year of assessment is the year they were registered or collected from the market.

The sample consists of 13 brands in 2005–2006, 54 in 2007–2008, 39 in 2009–2010, 40 in 2011–2012, 46 in 2013–2014, and 23 in 2015–2016. In this sample are 31 Gunpowder teas, of which 17 have the number 3505, 2 the number 3503 and 12 are without a number, only specified as Special, Extra, Super Special Gunpowder, or Gros Grain. 51 are simple Chunmee teas, of which 14 have the number 8147, 6 the number 9371, 18 the number 4011, and 13 are without a number. There are 66 Super Chunmees of the quality 41022, of which 61 indicate this explicitly on the package and 5 note only 'diamond quality'. A comparably large number (67 packages) have no specification of any type or variety. Whilst this may imply low quality tea, frequently and interestingly it also means high quality tea (in 15 examples). In this case, the importers relied upon the consumers' trust in their brand's quality, which thus did not require specification.

As already mentioned, at least since 2005, the 4011 Chunmees and the 41022 Super Chunmees were on the market but were considered expensive. From 2005 onwards, the 4011 Chunmees increased and from 2007 the number of Super Chunmees also gradually grew, until they overtook the 4011s. Their number continued to grow such that by 2016, a tea that was not a 41022 Chunmee no longer sold in viable quantities. The low number of tea brands shown in graph 5 for 2016 may be explained in two ways. One is that I might have collected and documented fewer tea packages. A more significant reason may be that the number of brands had fallen due to the growth of the 41022 brands and that the very popular brands captured a growing percentage of consumers. This should not be taken to imply that less tea was consumed, on the contrary, new consumers began drinking tea in Bamako. But when most consumers drink *Achoura*, *Koutam*, *Sancho* and *Flecha*, fewer people are consuming other brands and the number of brands reduces. However, this needs further verification.

5 The Popularity and Longevity of Brands in Different Regions

Consumers and traders agreed without exception that what ensured that a tea became and remained popular was its quality and taste. Whilst individual taste may be difficult to communicate (Peynaud 2005), people claimed on tasting a tea it became immediately obvious whether it was of good quality or not. Consumers explained the changing popularity of a brand by saying many teas possessed good quality at the outset (during post-colonial time) but quality declined over time (in the 1990s), encouraging them to search for alternatives. They eagerly tried new teas, which might taste better than their previous choice. Should the novelties prove unconvincing, consumers would return to their previous favourite brand.

I will now examine the shifting popularity of tea brands. A tea can be termed popular when a certain amount of it can be sold per month in a place. In the 2010s, a popular brand will sell at a rate of five containers per month, and frequently more. In the 2010s, These popular brands were all sold as 25g packages and owned by the fifteen largest tea importers. Any teas selling less than five containers a month, are not deemed popular. What is defined as popular varies in time, as before the 2010s, even successful importers sold less than 5 containers.

In the 1990s, the popular brands were *Baro*, *Cheval* and *Saddam*. These were among the first teas available in 25g packets. Among the Gunpowder teas of the time, they were the better option. *Chameau* and *Temple du Ciel* were much less in demand. In the early 2000s, diversity of tea qualities increased with availability of brands in four qualities: there were, for example, *Elephant*, *Askia*, *Lucky Bird* and *AAA*. One importer explained that *Lucky Bird* was 'made by one of the big tea companies in China. After Zhejiang tea (*Chameau*), this brand became big in African countries. It was available in small packages and in a metal box' (interview, Bamako, 2013). I met the Chinese broker of Korean origin, who had sold *Lucky Bird* in West Africa, in Yaounde in 2014, where he by then owned a Chinese restaurant. He told me he had sold *Lucky Bird* for many years until at some point as it became no longer worth selling, he abandoned the tea trade altogether (interview, Yaounde, 2014). With the exception of *Askia*, which continued for some time and *AAA*, these brands confronted difficult times when *Canal* came on the market in 2003. In the second half of the 2000s, the number of brands eventually increased to 80, but of these only a few were really popular – in 2007, these were *Canal*, *Lobo*, *AAA*, *Al Farouk*, *Arawane*, *Azawad*, *Diamant*, *Le Nord*, *Rass al Khaima* and *Touareg*.

In 2007, a student of sociology told me that she – as did many students – would not personally consume green tea but all the people in her compound drank green tea:

> They consume *Thé Canal*. They say that *Thé Canal* is the best at the moment. Before, they took *Thé Cheval*. And when *Canal* came out, they said, this is better than *Cheval*. They say, there are two qualities of *Thé Canal*, there is the blue *Canal* and the grey *Canal*, and of the two, the grey is best. INTERVIEW, BAMAKO, 2007

The longevity of a tea brand is difficult to measure but Table 1 gives an idea of the interpolated 'lifespans' of some tea brands. If a brand can be seen on the market for several years, this may mean it is not selling quickly or, conversely that it is selling well and new containers are being imported. The popularity of some brands was confirmed by the wholesalers in light of their turnover: *Baro* and *Cheval* were popular for about ten years, *Askia* and *Lobo* for six or so, and *Canal*, *Mona*, *Rass al Khaima*, *Diamant* for five years.

In 2009, there was a further shift in preference with the brand *Gazelle* setting the standard for years to come. Similar in taste and popularity were *Golden*, *Gaza Super*, *Antilope*, the early *Flecha* and especially *Taoudeni*, all good quality Chunmees. Other brands like *Touareg*, *Al Farouk*, were in favour for only about four years, while *AAA*, *Azawad*, *Arawane* were still selling in 2016.

TABLE 1 The life span of selected popular tea brands (the colours' intensity reflects greater popularity).

Brand/ Year	**1998–2000**	**2001–2003**	**2004–2006**	**2007–2009**	**2010–2012**	**2013–2015**	**2016–2018**
Baro							
Cheval							
AAA							
Askia							
Azawad							
Canal							
Lawal							
Lobo							
Gazelle							
Hassane							
Ousmane							
Niger							
Touareg							
Le Nord							
Taoudeni							
Gaza							
Flecha							=>
Achoura							=>
Koutam							=>
Sancho							=>

Many of the less popular tea brands remained on the market. I purchased sets of ten of these for my collection. On tasting the remaining packages, my assistant and his friends complained that these teas were of very poor quality, the second serving with more sugar only tasting marginally better. They stated that even *Lawal* was *nyèbere-bò*, 'droppings of cockroaches', and no one wanted to drink it again nor *Thé Canal* either.

When I returned to Mali in 2011, six 4011 teas were in vogue: *Gazelle*, *Super Gaza*, *Taoudeni*, *Arawane*, *Touareg*, *Le Nord*, as one of the tea importers confirmed (interview, Bamako, 2011). This was also obvious by the tea consumed at the tea *grins*. Everyone suggested that of all these brands, *Gazelle* had an estimated share of the market of about 80%. Everywhere in the Rue Gouraud on the Grand Marché, young men carried cartons of *Gazelle* or pushed them on carts through the crowds (Figure 27). One of the importers observed that

FIGURE 27 Pushing cartons of *Gazelle* through the Rue Gouraud, Bamako, 2013

'*Gazelle*, it is there since long, it was on the market very successful, even before it became really a success; it sold twenty containers per month' (interview, Bamako, 2013).

In 2013, the new trend became visible. *Gazelle*, *Super Gaza*, *Arawane* and *Taoudeni* lost popularity and were overtaken by the Super Chunmees. Among them were *Sancho*, *Rocki*, *Ayoune*, *Al Baraka*, *Koutam*, *Hassane Ousmane*, *Achoura* and *Flecha*. The 4011 version of *Flecha* in a brown package was replaced by 41022 Super Chunmee in white and green. Young people from my assistant's compound said *Sancho* was about to replace *Gazelle* because 'the quality of *Gazelle* has changed; it is no longer good. Only in the village they still take *Touareg* and *Gazelle*'. It is uncertain as to whether the quality really has changed, more likely it seems peoples' taste preferences have changed in favour of the Super Chunmees that now were affordable.

By 2016, this trend became very clear with only four brands most popular: *Achoura*, *Koutam*, *Simida* and *Flecha*. Of these, *Simida* and *Flecha* belonged to Chinese brokers. Wholesalers and importers noted that Chinese brands increased in popularity only when a Chinese trader passed his brand to an influential Malian wholesaler, which was the case with *Simida* and *Flecha* , and *Gazelle* at first (chapter 5). One of the wholesalers agreed that *Simida* was a good quality tea, and the third most popular in 2016 (interview, Bamako, 2016). In 2017 and 2018, the trend for Super Chunmees continued, confirmed by my assistant with accompanying photographs. By then, *Flecha*, *Sancho*, *Achoura* and *Koutam* were the most popular teas in Bamako but *Simida* had almost disappeared. Packages of *Sancho* and *Koutam* had changed colours and their tea certainly had more A's (Figure 28).

Whilst consumers have been sure of their capacity to detect good quality, taste is subjective and cannot be standardised (Peynaud 2005; Trubek 2005). For example, in 2016, a wholesaler gave us some *Thé Rajah*, a Chunmee, telling us it was of very good quality with a fine and pleasant aroma and properly rolled leaves. We tasted it in the compound that evening. It was not bitter, having a rather light flavour. The members of the *grin* were not very convinced. My assistant explained to our guests that this tea was of excellent quality and also very expensive, adding that the tea importer had informed us that people would now prefer this lighter, infused (uncooked) tea. However, just a few days earlier, we had tasted *Simida* in the compound, and on that occasion my assistant had explained that a tea needed to be bitter to be considered good quality. In 2016, everyone stated that *Simida* was a good tea, but I found it bitter, flat and lacking flavour. Tea importers confirmed that some people preferred a bitter taste before they considered a tea to be good, whilst others required a full aroma. One importer speaking of Malians drinking so much tea said 'it is a bit like the Arabs and the Europeans. They prefer to drink coffee, but we here, our coffee is the tea … and some drink it stronger, others lighter, some boil it, others infuse it' (interview, Bamako, 2011). For our guests at the compound tea *grin,* the expensive *Rajah* was not (yet) convincing. It was a light and less bitter beverage, whilst *Taoudeni* which, at the time, everyone claimed possessed good taste was much stronger and more bitter.

However, what was true for Bamako, might not apply to the entire country. In 2016, *Achoura* was the most popular tea in Bamako, but in the countryside,

FIGURE 28 Examples of Super Chunmees, popular in the mid-2000s: *Hassane Ousmane*, *Ayoune*, *Achoura*, *Sancho*, *Rocki*

Taoudeni was still the bestseller. One importer explained: 'If you go to the market in Mopti, you will see that *Taoudeni* is more popular there than *Achoura*, and the Fulani overthere will tell you that they drink *Taoudeni* because its quality has never changed' (interview, Bamako, 2016). Nevertheless, the capital leads as taste maker and trendsetter for the countryside, just as Mali is for the entire region. The tea popular in Bamako some years ago, is today widespread in the countryside and in the countries adjacent to Mali, whereas people in the capital are already drinking other types of tea. In 2012, my assistant noted that meanwhile even in the rural areas, people no longer drank just any tea but had begun to seek particular brands such as *Arawane* and *Gazelle*. Thus, trends established in the capital take a few years to spread to the villages and neighbouring countries.

There are also differences between the countryside in the north and in the south of Mali. In the northern Malian towns, more consumers were acquainted with the beverage earlier than Bamako. They were very aware of quality, however, this is less the case in rural areas in southern Mali, where consumers first had to acquire knowledge about tea before they learned about varieties and brands and perceived differences between them. At the outset, rural people could only afford the cheaper teas but ideas about taste gradually altered when all 25g package brands were sold at the same price (of 100 francs CFA). One importer noted that 'the south of Mali, around Sikasso, is a region where people consume tea but they have no idea of the quality'. Another importer noted that 'now people begin to drink green tea also in Burkina Faso and Cote d'Ivoire, and it [the habit of drinking green tea] is gradually moving southwards' (interviews, Bamako, 2011, 2013). In 2012, in Bobo Dioulasso as well, the popular brands were *Baro*, *Cheval*, *Arawane* and *Gazelle*, brands that (with the exception of *Gazelle*) were Gunpowders that consumers in Bamako had discarded long ago. There, such tea could still be sold for 50 or 75 francs CFA. My assistant immediately noticed that fewer people drank tea in Bobo than in Bamako, i.e. in the periphery of the teascape, tea consumers were still less numerous. Still another importer gave some examples for this trend:

> *Cheval*, for example, was popular in Bamako in the 2000s, and now it is popular in Burkina Faso; *Arawane* was popular in Bamako in 2009 and 2010 and now it is popular in Bouaké. ... If you go to Ouaga now, the Mosh [Mossi] begin to drink tea and they want the tea that the Malians have abandoned ten years ago, namely Gunpowder, and they want to see the flies [tea leaves] in the tea glass, otherwise they don't find it nice to look at. INTERVIEW, BAMAKO, 2016

The taste for tea may vary between the generations, the sexes, urban and rural areas and also between the Malian migrants in the various regions. Additionally, new consumers are continuously recruited. Earlier in Bamako, women were not drinking tea but more recently, this has changed and women are now having their own tea rituals. In contrast, other people, above all the educated students from the rising middle class, in order to distinguish themselves from the majority are refraining from drinking green tea.

Gunpowder teas continued to be sold in southern Mali and adjacent countries. Another importer stated: 'Each tea has its own population. Here in Bamako, people drink *Koutam*, but *Gaza Super* is presently much more drunk in the countries adjacent to Mali such as in Côte d'Ivoire, Burkina Faso and Guinea-Conakry' (interview, Bamako, 2016). People in different regions may have particular taste preferences, however, popular brands nevertheless are disseminated across the countryside from the cities and into less affluent countries with a Mande population or where Mande migrants have settled for work. In Burkina Faso, northern Côte d'Ivoire, Guinea and eastern Senegal, people from the Mande World mostly drink green tea, but gradually also other young people from the popular neighbourhoods begin to have their tea *grins,* or *fadas,* as they called in Burkina Faso and Niger (Kieffer 2006; Masquelier 2013).

Gunpowder and Chunmee teas such as *Arawane*, *Cheval*, *Flecha* and *Gazelle* were available in Ouagadougou, Wa, Kumasi, Accra, Dakar, in Douala and Yaounde, in Gabon and Congo-Brazaville and migrants also took them to China on their travels, as mentioned in chapter 1. In the 2010s, *Chameau*, *Temple du Ciel*, *Baro* and *Cheval* were no longer available in Bamako but I saw them in Yaounde in the mid-2010s, where Malian migrants sold the cheap *Chameau* tea to passers-by in a market street but for themselves they prepared more expensive teas from Mali such as *Gazelle*, *Flecha* and *Achoura*, during a proper tea ritual. After work local people may join them, sit with the migrants in front of their compounds drinking tea with them and learn to appreciate a new beverage.

6 Why so Many Tea Brands?

Among the large number of tea brands, only about a dozen are popular. The others have either lower, the same or even higher quality. If the quality of a tea is too high, the tea will not sell because it is too expensive for wholesalers and retailers to buy. If the quality is the same than the popular brands, it may not sell because of lacking appeal and distribution networks (chapter 5). The largest part is made of brands of low quality. Traders still import cheap quality green teas despite the growing concern for its quality and the popularity of some brands. One of the importers wondered that

> there are people here, who come and risk their whole money with bad tea. Look at this trademark here [he points to a package of *Capitaine* from my sample], I do not know it, I have never seen it, I would not buy it, and I would never produce such a tea. People do not buy such tea. INTERVIEW, BAMAKO, 2013

Many of the numerous brands on the market are low quality, imported by traders who lack a good understanding of the 'work of tea', or the capital to purchase acceptable quality. They believe there is an insufficient supply of tea on the market and want to sell their own. As mentioned earlier, they witness others making substantial profits and believe they can emulate these successful tea importers. I was informed that some importers when in China buy any cheap tea surplus from overproduction making additional profits through its sale without damaging the reputation of their own brands. Obviously, every tea sells sooner or later but often for many importers not quickly enough to enable the recovery of their investment, not to talk about profit and popularity. There are also the pirated teas (chapter 9) whose importers take advantage of the value of existing brands. All these factors contribute to the high number of tea brands.

To better understand this, Graph 6 depicts the number of brands owned by different companies, revealing that the high number of brands is due to many importers owning one brand rather than a few owning many. Of the 178 companies that have registered green tea brands between 1998 and 2018 the great majority (134) has only one brand; 18 importers have 2 brands, 11 have 3 and 5 have 4 brands. Only a minority has more than 5 brands. Both African and Chinese importers own sometimes a few and sometimes several brands. Most big tea importers have 2 to 5 brands, very few own more than 5. The graph however, does not include unregistered brands and those of which ownership was not identifiable.

As a newly created company entitles its owner to reduced taxes, many importers register brands under different company names (chapter 6), thus the figure of 178 companies mentioned above is greater than the actual number of importers. Some tea importers owned many brands because they felt it was useful to diversify their supply and in the event that one brand failed, they would still have other brands to fall back on. Many successful importers. however, rather preferred not to have too many tea brands.

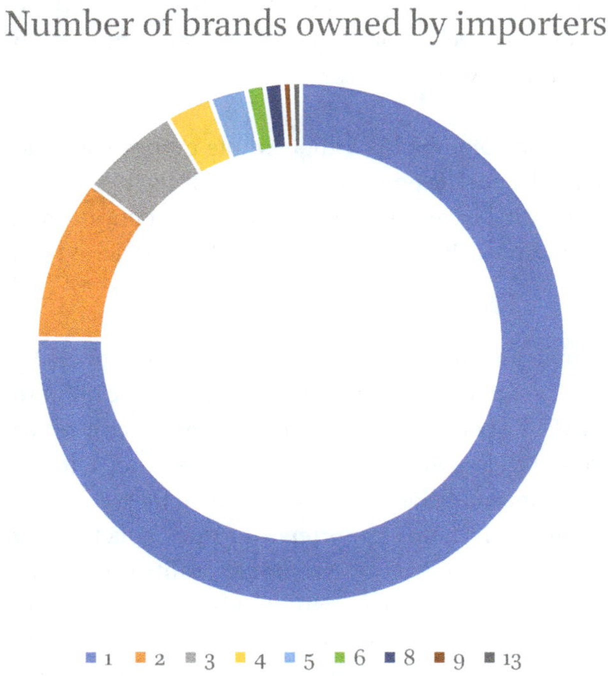

GRAPH 6
Number of brands owned by importers

It should also be considered that owning one or two brands may mean several things. In most cases it suggests brands were short-lived, the importer unable to sell their container of tea rapidly enough. In other cases, it meant the importer decided to work with just one brand, develop it well and ensure its quality remained stable over a long period. Having more than 5 brands demonstrates that the importer is viable by being able to import that much tea but it does not mean they can sell the tea quickly (chapter 4). As one importer explained:

> If I have ten brands, then I cannot sell much of all these brands, but only little. But if I concentrate on one brand that sells well, then I can sell much higher quantities of it, which is more rewarding ... The importer who has fifteen brands, has to sell fifteen containers of different teas. But if you want to work with something seriously, then you will concentrate on this and do it well and then this brand will stay for many years, if the quality remains the same. It is better to sell 15 containers per month of one well-going brand than fifteen containers of fifteen different brands of which not all really go well, and you will not be able to sell one container of it each month. INTERVIEW, BAMAKO, 2013

This importer also argued that 'here in Bamako, there are so many tea brands, but there are no wholesalers who can buy several containers [from an importer] and distribute them. They [the wholesalers in Bamako] purchase 200 or 300 *colis* every week. But if you are over there in Mopti, for example, there are two or three wholesalers who can buy two or three containers at once because they know all the villages, which are dispersed [in the inner Niger Delta] and who all want to take this one choice [*Thé Taoudeni*]'.

In this densely populated rural area, it was possible to sell large quantities of one brand. With fewer brands available, there was less competition than is faced in Bamako and fewer importers. In Bamako, in contrast, there are numerous importers, many wholesalers testing the opportunities with their own brands and consumers who have a great diversity of tastes. These are circumstances which do not lend themselves to the easy selling of large quantities of a single brand of tea. The most obvious reason that explains the large number of tea brands is the success of the influential tea importers, who have inspired many other wholesalers to try their luck in the tea business. Only a few made profits; many others lost their investments.

Ultimately, the tea brands that are popular for a longer period of time are all owned by big tea importers, people who have only a few brands and a good understanding of the 'work of tea', the obvious prerequisite for generating the popularity of a brand. The process began in the late 1990s and early 2000s, when the registered brands were owned by a few foreign and Malian companies. From the second half of the 2000s, more Malian merchants began to own and register brands.

The examination of the types of tea, the package sizes, the creation and multiplication of tea brands have revealed general tendencies in the ownership and agency of Malian tea importers. The graphs only provide a rough idea of this process, because many traders did not register their brands and because statistics often do not grasp the complexity of daily economic practice. However, they clearly depict that the number of Chinese traders who have registered tea brands is far lower than that of Malian importers. Convinced that Africans have little money, Chinese brokers tended to sell cheap Gunpowder tea in Bamako, which worked in the late 1990s when the purchasing power was weak due to the devaluation of the franc CFA and only few affordable teas were available. From the mid-2000s onwards, however, Djokoramé and increasingly Saharan importers found suppliers in China who sold them better tea qualities. They replaced the four (or more) different qualities of tea by only selling one good quality tea. They also adopted the designs of the 25g packages, providing the quantity required for one Malian tea ritual in collaboration with their suppliers.

As outlined in chapter 1, the structural frameworks cannot alone explain the multiplication of tea brands and the successes of the Malian tea importers. Especially those traders whose parents and grandparents had been active as long-distance traders in former times became influential in the current tea trade. Their implicit knowledge has long historical roots and is important for understanding their agency and expertise in the work of tea. In the long run, with their strategies, networks and experience they were able to dominate the Sino-African tea trade and defend it against other Malian and Chinese competitors. As the next chapter will show, mastering the 'work of tea' well includes knowledge about the requirements of importation, the quality of the product and the additional value created by branding and employing particular forms of advertising.

CHAPTER 3

Tea Prices, Brand Value and Publicity

Whilst tea was sold loosely from wooden boxes, the product was considered *ataya*, *duté*, or named after their variety (chapter 2). After tea was packaged and branded with printed images and names, wholesalers became vendors or representatives of brands, which had owners who were different people than the sellers and the producers. The path from tea sold loose to a branded product sold in standardised packages accords with the pattern outlined by Fanselow (2009), from bazaar economy (Geertz 1963) to market or brand economy. Fanselow presented the case that in bazaar economies consumers could not be assured of the quality of a product; adulteration was easily accomplished and market monopolies were hidden from consumers. In contrast, brand economies offered quality of which consumers could be certain, goods were standardised and exchangeable one for another; in short, a brand economy rendered everything transparent (see also Wengrow 2010). Knowledge about brands and quality was expected to create confidence in consumers (Fanselow 2009). This distinction might be analytically useful however bazaar and brand economies are not mutually exclusive. Both forms of markets, in every society, offer unbranded products and packaged brand-named products, often in the same market place.

A second point is particularly clear with green tea in Mali. The introduction of trademarks and brand names on products created awareness of different qualities and brands of the same product. As was shown in chapter 2, consumers accepted that packaged tea was more hygienic, appeared more sophisticated and lent more prestige than unbranded tea sold loosely. However, it was not the brand name or the design that motivated consumers to buy a particular tea. Consumers hesitated to trust the packages and the text that appeared on them, fearing that importers might misrepresent the product, at least to some degree. Rather than as suggested in Fanselow's and Wengrow's assessment, Malian consumers felt packaged products would not protect them from inferior quality or adulteration. Brands as such did not directly promise superior quality in a simple format. Consumers seemed confirmed by the discussion of piracy by government and the media, and by the unstable quality of most tea brands (chapter 2).

Thus, brands require a high amount of trust on the side of consumers; they have to believe that the promise offered by the brand can be relied upon (Applbaum 2005). Packaged and sealed content prevents consumers from seeing

 | DOI:10.1163/9789004505698_005

and experiencing through smelling and touching it. They are therefore unable to check the quality before they purchase. A few of the tea packages include a transparent cellophane 'window' in the carton allowing at least visual inspection (Figure 26b).[1] Many consumers trust the advice of their wholesalers and retailers more than the package inscriptions and advertisement, not to mention the Chinese producers.

This chapter adds further insights to the issue of quality and brand value shedding light on the relationship between the different values attached to the product. Firstly, it considers the price of tea, i.e. its monetary value, the costs of its importation and price politics. Secondly, it reflects on the creation of brand value and the role advertisement plays in adding value to tea brands. Brand value is protected by the legal construction of trademark law (chapter 7) but, as Arvidsson (2005: 238) observed, the literature is remarkably unclear about who and what produces these assets, i.e. whether it is advertisement or consumption as immaterial labour. The chapter demonstrates that both consumers and traders contribute with their agency to the brand value: consumers by their insistence on a particular taste that they require tea to have and traders by managing price, purchase and brand communication. Advertisement helps importers to extend their agency with visible and audible symbols into the public space.

1 The Value of Tea Leaves and Tea Packages

Before the 1990s, when tea still arrived in wooden boxes, tea and sugar were sold together for 100 Malian francs, and this combination was called *thé complet*. The practice was observed in the mid-nineteenth century, as Heinrich Barth (1965, vol.3: 346) noted, when reporting that he was unable to buy tea and sugar separately. Some prices of tea (and sugar) are documented from that time in the Sahara (Damani 2013: 204; Leriche 1953: 736) and Morocco (Hémadinquer 1962: 1150; Huetz de Lemps 2001; Miège 1957: 390) but the values are complicated to compare due to the many differing currencies and weights used. With inflation following Mali's independence, tea prices increased and the *thé complet* cost 150 Malian francs (100 for the tea and 50 for the sugar as before) and shortly afterwards it was 200 Malian francs. After the Malian franc

1 Moroccan supermarkets that sold Chinese green tea had a corner where of each brand a carton box was placed open on the floor so that consumers could see the tea leaves, smell and touch them (Observation in Rabat, 2015).

was devalued by 100% and integrated into the franc CFA zone in 1984, the *thé complet* of Chunmee 4011 was 100 francs CFA.

Damani (2013: 206) unearthed a document showing that in 1978, the company NOSETEX in Dakar imported from Las Palmas 75 tons of tea (3,750 *colis* of 20kg with a value of 112,500,000 francs CFA to declare at customs). This also means that in 1978, a *colis* of tea – the variety is not specified in the document – had a value of 30,000 francs CFA and a ton was 1,500,000 francs CFA (i.e. 1kg tea was 1,500 francs CFA). In 2016, some forty years later, a *colis* had a value of 60,000–80,000 francs CFA.

In 1992 in Mali, tea and sugar were still sold together but the price had risen to 175 francs CFA (Bamba Kiabou 1992); this was brought to an end in the 2000s, with the advent of branded tea. At first, tea brands were available in different varieties, and at various prices. Towards the end of the 2000s, the vast majority of the 25g packages in Bamako were priced 100 francs CFA (chapter 2). This is surprising, as the contents of the packages obviously contained various varieties of tea, yet the price was the same irrespective of whether it was Gunpowder, Chunmee 4011, or Super Chunmee 41022. The tea importers confirmed this finding (interviews, Bamako, 2013). In very exceptional cases, a tea could be 115 francs CFA and tea of extremely poor quality might be sold for 50, or 75 francs CFA. In rural areas, due to the lack of cash income amongst the local population, cheaper teas were still available. In the 2010s, in Timia in Niger, for example, tea could still be bought loose from wooden boxes: some was sold for 75 francs CFA per glass – the quantity required for one tea ritual was measured with the help of a tea glass, as earlier on in Mali – and tea of less strong quality could be purchased for 100 francs CFA per three glasses. It was sold for additional 50 francs CFA with three little sugar bags – as in the time of Heinrich Barth – for the three servings (Valerie Hänisch, pers. comm., 2016).

One importer noted that

> Each social environment and Malian region has its own mode of tea consumption because not all regions are wealthy. There are people for whom 100 francs is a lot of money. There you will market tea for 50 or 75 francs. This will be necessary [if you want to sell tea there]. ... Look at the tea brand *La Vache*, with the cow on the package. This is tea that cannot sell in the capital. Its quality is too poor; these days such tea no longer sells here. INTERVIEW, BAMAKO, 2016

In the early 2010s in the adjacent Burkina Faso, where purchasing power was low, mostly cheap Gunpowder tea was sold; for instance, in Bobo Dioulasso, the price for a small package had just been raised from 50 to 75 francs CFA (wholesaler, Bobo Dioulasso, 2012). In wealthier countries, however, tea might be more expensive than 100 francs CFA; in Côte d'Ivoire it can be sold for 125 francs CFA, in Senegal it might even cost 150 francs. Cameroon and Congo tea can be 200 to 250 francs CFA because fewer people consume it. The importers were certain, however, that 25g packages of tea would not sell for more than 100 francs CFA in Mali because there consumers could not afford more for their daily tea ritual.

One importer explained this further:

> The problem in Mali, and Africa in general, is that it is poor. People do not have means but the consumers, despite their poverty, are ready to take quality, at least sometimes. It is the consumers who are presently imposing the quality and giving more value to all the teas. Take *Flecha*, it is a first quality tea, it is selling sometimes at 1400 francs [the 250g package] and at the same time you can find it for 700. Look, this is the difference. You discover when you consume. But if you want first quality [you take the expensive one, which is not pirated] ... Consumers find all the different qualities on the Malian market, the lower classes, the middle ones, and those which are first class. But other people do not even know, they just want to have whatever tea (laughing). INTERVIEW, BAMAKO, 2013

Another importer explained that when a tea has a poor reputation, then 'people will no longer consume such a bad tea because they already have known the taste of excellence' (interview, Bamako, 2016). Since the 2010s, an excellent tea in a 25g package has the same price than a poor tea. A third importer told me the same but emphasised:

> Now, everybody wants good quality. But the quality should not be too good either. If it is too good, it is too expensive, then people [wholesalers] will not buy it. But if it is a little less expensive, they buy. You can sell a *colis* for 65,000 francs CFA [about 100 Euro], that will work. INTERVIEW, BAMAKO, 2013

Other importers gave similar indications. This raises the question of how the prices are calculated and fixed when in China the various varieties have different prices and also how the tea importers secure their profits. In Mali, the price of a tea package is constrained to no more than 100 francs CFA by consumers' perception of affordability. This means that good tea will be expensive to purchase in China and the importers' profit margin less high than for a cheaper tea. Importers can only earn sufficient profit when they sell larger quantities of the expensive tea to enable the many intermediaries such as wholesalers, retailers and *coxeurs* to make a living as well. Thus, in much a similar way as Ulf Vierke (2006: 439) concluded from his research on bead traders in Tanzania, 'profit is made when purchasing, not selling'.

In the small grocery shops, single 25g packages are sold but on the wholesale market, only sets of ten such packages, entire cartons of 5kg or *colis* of 20kg are available. The 25g packages are 100 francs CFA each but there are variations in the sale prices of sets of ten 25g packages that reflect their higher or lower purchasing prices, at least in theory. Prices for sets of ten packages range from 400 to 1100 francs CFA. Some examples from 2013 illustrate this. All the prices are in francs CFA: *Mabrouka* was 400, *Savane* 450, *François Hollande* 650, *Hayat* and *Yasmina* 700, *Dambé, Sava* and the yellow-green *Askia* 750, *Rocki, Super Thé, Lawal* (the *Flecha* imitation) and *Taaj* 800, *Koutam, Ayoune, Achifa, Jamal Sahara*, the green-black *Raissa, Hassane Ousmane*, sitting *Gazelle* and *Elosra* 900, and *Desert* 1000, *Flecha* 1100 and *Elrosa* 1100, and *Azawad* 1250. Some of the higher prices were probably 'tailor-made' for me, 'the white researcher', by the wholesaler. He could not have presented such high prices to a retailer because the retailer could not make a profit on them. When he sells the 25g packages for 100 francs each, he cannot purchase a set of ten 25g packages for more than 950.

Similar considerations apply to cartons and *colis*. A carton contains 200 25g packages. When the wholesaler sells a carton for 20,000 francs or more, a retailer can make no profit. A *colis* consisting in 4 cartons, would also result in no profit for a wholesaler if the importer sold it for 80,000 francs or more. Sets of ten, a carton or a *colis* can of course be sold to an individual prepared to buy it for the price that the wholesaler asks, but a retailer, mindful of his need to generate a profit would not buy it.

It appears only the best-selling teas – which differ from one place to another – are sold individually in kiosks around town. When a *colis* is sold for 65,000 francs CFA, then the wholesaler, *coxeur* and one or several retailers will be able to share a profit of 15,000 francs per *colis* or 25 francs per 25g packet. If this is the profit margin required to enable traders to make a living, it explains why Malian traders are so critical about their Chinese peers who are reputed to ignore this organisational arrangement by selling various quantities of tea at wholesale prices (chapter 6). They ignored the local moral economy that secured livelihood of the various types of traders in the value chain (see also Valenciano-Mañé 2019, for a similar argument about imported commodities in Equatorial Guinea).

The earlier-mentioned example of *Simida*, which failed to sell at first, began to sell very well only after its Chinese owner gave it to one of the well-known wholesalers from whom then many other wholesalers and retailers purchased it. One importer recalled:

> As soon as the lorry arrived [from the port], he [the Chinese] did not even have to wait until the tea had been brought to his warehouse, it was already sold. Notwithstanding, this is a simple quality [meaning probably 4011 in 2016], but the people liked it. As I told you, often it is not really the ingredients, the quality only, that matter. [When the tea begins to sell, the price of] this tea can go up to 75,000 [francs CFA per *colis*] and [at first] he [the Chinese] gave it to the wholesalers for 64 or even 63,000 and then he increased the price again to 64, 65, 66, 67 and now it is at 68. He might continue to raise it but from a commercial point of view it would be important that he stays [with his price] there, because there are also teas that go up to 70,000 per *colis*, the four cartons [but then wholesalers will refuse to take it]. INTERVIEW, BAMAKO, 2016

The Malian importer of *Gazelle* and *Raissa* sells her *colis* for an amount between 60,000 and 75,000 francs. Depending on the purchased quantity, the white *Raissa* is sold to wholesalers for 64,000 francs per *colis*, the yellow-green *Gazelle* for 66,000, the red *Gazelle* for 70,000 and *Raissa* super for 75,000 francs per *colis*. In a retail shop all the individual 25g packages will be sold for 100 francs CFA, which means the purchase price for the teas of lower qualities will be lower but yield a higher profit margin than that secured on a better-quality tea, the purchase price of which is higher. The distributive chain from importer to retailer secures small profits for all the intermediate traders, although the amounts decrease the further along the chain they sit.[2] Should the importer sell a *colis* for 80,000 francs, at 100 francs per 25g package there will be no profit margin.

I have not observed any negotiation over prices in the wholesale shops. *Colis,* cartons and sets of ten packages are quickly purchased and transported by the retailers; I have watched as sometimes a wholesaler opened a carton and replaced some sets of ten with others of different brands and makes a calculation on a machine, whilst the customer is trying to hand him money. This all happens very fast; there is no time to lose. Prices are seemingly already known to the two parties, perhaps due to the frequent prior interaction or otherwise have been previously negotiated over the mobile phone or by the *coxeur*.

2 See also Heidi Haugen (2017) who studied the profits in a small-scale value chain between China and Ghana, where Ghanaian traders imported Chinese-made jewellery in their suitcases.

Sales of larger package sizes do not follow the same logic. Only few retailers sell them. The prices of the larger packets do not all have the same prices. Larger packages might even be more expensive than the 25g sets of ten of the same variety and brand because fewer of them are sold. Their prices sometimes seem quite arbitrary. A 250g package can be more, or less expensive than a set of ten, of the same brand. There are 250g tin boxes of *Al Baraka*, possessing a deer image, at 1,500 francs CFA and even 200g boxes of *Al Baraka* of the highest quality for 3,000 francs. Highest qualities may not be the best-sellers and are more often sold in prestigious tin boxes than in 25g packages. Farako tea is sold at 1,250 francs CFA for a sachet of 250g from the Farako representative's outlet in Bamako, rather than by wholesalers. It is expensive because the Farako plantation has difficulties competing with the imports from China, as discussed earlier.

25g packages are the most commonly sold and from them the tea importers secure the highest profits. To enable this, the importers must accurately calculate the purchase price of the tea, the expected profit margins for all the intermediaries and to do so within the framework of a cash yield of just 100 francs CFA per 25g package. This means, the importer has to begin his calculations from the 100 francs, and reductions of the price always fall on profits made by the higher-level traders. If the importer can sell the *colis* to wholesalers for 65,000 francs, then the wholesaler will be able to sell one carton to the retailer for 12,000 rather than for 15,000 francs.

By selling cheaper tea, importers can secure higher profits than by selling high quality tea, however, higher quality tea sells faster if it is a popular brand. Therefore, because importers accepted lower profit margins, the availability of good quality teas has increased in recent years. One importer stated 'I will try to buy good quality tea to please myself. You see, today, you are obliged to circulate and put superior quality on the market' for which consumers have not had to spend more (interview, Bamako, 2016). No doubt, importers could accommodate reduced profits because sales increased considerably with the growing demand for good tea over a short period of time. A 'copier' or 'brand pirate' could also make huge profits but only until he had ruined the brand of its legal owner.

2 The Costs of Importing Tea

I admit, I have been unable to comprehend all the issues around the generation of profit from tea importation. Understandably, importers were reluctant to disclose how much profit they made on the importation of a container of tea but my assessment is that it is likely to be substantial. On their websites, Chinese tea factories indicate their prices in US dollars per kg. Prices vary according to type and quality of tea. The websites also indicate a factory's production capacity for each type of tea and display the minimum quantities that must be ordered (usually a 40-foot container or half container of 20 foot). Prices given in the tea factory include the printing of the package design and costs of transport and customs in China and Africa must be added.

Calculated from the Malian perspective, one *colis* of 800 25g packages can be sold to wholesalers for 60,000 to 75,000 francs, let us assume an average 65,000 francs CFA. One 20-foot container can transport 500 *colis* à 20kg each or 400,000 small 25g packages, amounting to 10 tons of tea. Most importers use 40-foot containers, which contain 20 tons of tea, i.e. 1,000 *colis* or 800,000 25g packages.

After distributing the contents of a 40-foot container of 1000 *colis* for 65,000 francs each to wholesalers, the importer collects 65,000,000 francs CFA (about 100,000 Euro). This income includes the importer's profit, the price of the tea, the packaging, transportation costs with ship, lorry, or rail, the customs levy in China, the tax and the customs levy in Mali – formerly 3 million francs CFA (about 4.500 Euro) and from 2013, 6 million francs CFA per container. It may also include any registration fees for the company and the tea brand.

Thus, following its sale, a container has a value of at least 65 million francs. One of the major tea importers said one of his containers redeemed 75 million francs CFA at sale (interviews, Bamako, 2013, 2016), and another had a value of 80 million francs (about 120,000 Euro). He added that one container would provide 14 million, which may have been his profit but he did not explain this in more detail. Another importer stated two years earlier that one container 'was' 5 million francs CFA (interview, Bamako, 2011) (which seems underestimated, except that their tea was more expensive than the average, for example, as high as with the Chinese internet platform Alibaba). Successful traders importing substantial quantities of tea are able to obtain discounts on the tea, transport and customs (interviews, Bamako, 2013 and Shenzhou, 2014).

The amount of profit an importer can realise on the contents of one container very much depends on the purchasing price in China. The price for 4011 green tea from a company near Shenzhou that I visited in 2014, was 4 USD per kg, for 41022 3A 4.21 USD and a very good 41022 5A was 5.36 USD per kg in the 25g packages. I was given similar prices in another factory near Shenzhou in 2014. If we take 4 USD per kg, then a ton would be 4,000 USD and 20 tons 80,000 USD (about 70,000 Euro) to which transport, tax, customs fees must be added. When this sum is subtracted from 100,000 Euro, 30,000 Euro remains. From this figure, an estimated 6,000 Euro for transport and 9,000 Euro for tax and customs – a total of 15,000 Euro – must be further deducted remain, leaving 15,000 Euro as profit margin. The purchasing price in dollar will reduce if an importer buys directly from a tea factory, as the successful importers do (at least none seemed to buy with Alibaba). It will be further reduced if they import larger quantities, meaning several containers each month, as do all the big importers. Then the profit margin will be considerably higher. This also means an importer needs capital investment of at least 48 million francs CFA (about at least 70,000 Euro) for bringing each container from China to Mali.

Being able to sell several containers peer month is a criterium of a successful importer, as one of them remarked: 'If you can sell a container every three or four months, one can say that you have a foot in the tea business. Most of the tea importers work like that. It is a minority that sells ten or twenty containers, and once you can do that "then you are deep in the tea (*et puis toi, tu es dans le thé*)"' (interview, Bamako, 2013). Another importer put it this way: 'If you can sell five containers per month, then your business is going, but only when you sell more than five containers, then you can say your business is really going well' (interview, Bamako, 2011). One of the importers even stated that he would import 20 containers each month to Mali, 10 containers to Niger, 3 to 6 containers to Burkina Faso, 3 or 4 to Mauritania, 1 to Senegal, half a container (a 20-foot container) to Gambia, half a container to Congo-Brazzaville and Equatorial Guinea, and 1 container to Morocco (if not to Algeria) (interview, Bamako, 2013). Taken together, this would be 45 containers of Chinese green tea, which would make a turnover of almost 3 billion francs CFA (about 4.6 million Euro) per month. In 2018, he was also selling to Mozambique (according to his website).

The same importer who ships most of his tea to Mali via Lomé and Burkina Faso also mentioned that he can sell at a lower price than other importers:

> Just to give an example: if you buy your tea for 10 francs and you can sell it for 50 francs, your profit is high [but it will not last]. Someone else buys his tea for 10 francs but can only sell it for 30 francs, his profit is less, and someone who buys his tea for 30 francs and can sell it for 50 francs, also earns not very much [but it will be more sustainable]. INTERVIEW, BAMAKO, 2013

With this, he wanted to say that it was unwise to focus on immediate profit; better was to consider the longer-term, and it was also important to manage copiers and strategically protect one's brands (chapter 5).

Because he purchases large quantities, this importer is able to buy quality tea for a reasonable price. Whilst his product is expensive, he purchases it for a good price and attracts a healthy profit through the sales of large quantities in many countries. He explained: 'If someone would tell me in 2008 or 2009 that he imports 15 containers, I would say that this is a lot. But if you tell me today, that you sell 80 containers, I say that it might be possible' (interview, Bamako, 2016). Apparently, an exaggeration, it illustrates the dimensions the trade can assume. In 2016, roughly a dozen big tea importers each sold more than 5 containers per month, a few of them achieved sales of more than 15.

3 The Creation of Added Value through Branding

Following the examination of the pecuniary value of tea and the peculiarities of the Malian tea market, I will now look at how the brand affects the value of tea and consumers' perceptions of it. Although the small packages are more expensive compared to larger packets, requiring more packaging material and resources, they are very successful. However, it is not the mere pecuniary value of the tea and the package that determine their market value. An identical tea presented in a similar package may have a completely different market value. The brand itself represents an added value, termed the 'brand value', and this complex value creation can be only partly planned.

Brand value is difficult to define and fluctuates. Consumers' perceptions of the success, or decline of brands revolve around quality. So, for instance, some claimed that the decline in the reputation of *Canal* followed decrease in quality. They suggested: 'he [the importer] pirated himself (*il s'est piraté soi-même*)' or that 'it is due to counterfeiting (*les gens disent ce n'est plus de la qualité*)'. Other consumers stated that 'the taste of the *Taoudeni* brand had now assumed the taste of *Gazelle* (*le goût de* Gazelle *est maintenant le goût de* Taoudeni)'. Rumours may also contribute to the rise or decline of a brand's fortunes (Coombe 1997), as one importer noted: 'the other tea companies might try to criticise your company and it [your brand] loses in value' (interview, Bamako, 2013). Therefore, importers took great care to avoid annoying other importers.

Consumers' agency is reflected in their ability to contribute to a brand's success, or failure merely by circulating rumours, or criticisms (Coombe 1997). Consumers may appreciate a particular green tea brand for a time, but they are always ready to try new teas, comparing quality. Thus, few brands are able to survive on the market for more than ten years (Graph 6). What prevails over time is the enchantment of the tea ritual, which outlasts any particular brand of tea. In their valuation of brands, consumers tend to trust Malian tea connoisseurs far more than Chinese producers and traders.

Even when importers sell tea of similar quality, some teas sell better than others such as *Gazelle* and *Taoudeni* earlier, followed by *Flecha, Koutam, Sancho* and *Achoura*. Whilst consumers argue in terms of quality and taste, it is nevertheless obvious that the brand 'adds value to the product' (Moeran and Garsten 2013). As outlined above, some scholars interpret this added value as originating in the marketing strategies employed, others see it arising from the consumers and their agency (Arvidsson 2005; Foster 2008). When a product such as green tea has been confiscated and its package – together with its branding – are destroyed, it can be sold but, independent of its quality and in the absence of package and brand image, only very cheaply. This demonstrates that the trademark and the brand image projected, are detachable from the commodity (Nakassis 2013: 115). The value is created with several components: quality, package, the brand name, advertisement, the strategy of the importer, knowledge of 'the work of tea' and the wholesalers' and consumers' appreciation. However, in the case of tea in Mali, what exactly the brand value depends upon cannot be easily identified, at least not as clearly as suggested by some scholarship.

Some scholars differentiate between brand and trademark. The British 1875 Act of trademarks defined a trademark as a distinctive device, a mark, a name of an individual, or a firm printed in some particular manner; a written signature or copy of a signature of an individual or a firm, or a distinctive label or ticket (Bently 2008). Since then, the meanings encompassing trademarks have expanded. A trademark may be a name, word, phrase, logo, symbol, design, image, or a combination of these elements. Trademarks have to be distinctive and non-descriptive; they indicate source and serve as a badge of origin. Thus, each trademark is unique and easily registered (Jamar 1992). The best and most successful brands are immediately recognisable by their trademarks, may have immense emotional content and will inspire loyalty (Tan 2010: 202). Nakassis (2013) develops this further, stating that basically everything can become a trademark as long as it has the capacity of abstract distinction and can be graphically represented (except for marks based on sound and smell).

However, a brand is more than a trademark. A 'brand is a set of associations linked to a name, mark, or symbol associated with a product or service, and the interaction of customers with brands is important as they create associations' (Calkins 2005, quoted from Tan 2010: 202). Brands function as capital, as consumers create brand value through their agency, often unintentionally (Arvidsson 2005: 237–238). This value is created through the willingness of consumers to pay for a product and results from the cooperation between producers – in the case of tea, the traders – and consumers. It emerges from a company being able to connect to the world's passions (Foster 2007: 708, 715–716). Brands are a regime of value (Appadurai 1986; Nakassis 2013: 111; Röschenthaler 2020c) that makes a commodity more than its use and exchange value (Nakassis 2013: 114).

Brands are thought to be surrogates of an absent producer (Nakassis 2013: 115) and are supposed to create trust between owner and consumers. They aim at replacing the consultation with the seller (Hellmann 2003: 11, 20). The brand owner vouches for the quality of the brand, relocating trust from the retailer to the producer. From the outset, the names of producers and importers appeared on the tea packages but eventually this practice was abandoned; henceforward consumers connected the product with its brand name. The advertising of tea did not pick up ideas of the brand names but concerned the context of consumption – most often the tea *grin* – as will be shown below.

More generally, brands or marks were first connected to producers of a product, and supposed to enable consumers to easily distinguish between similar products created by other producers. Brands, or better still trademarks, are about sealing, labelling and marking. They are attached to a product from which they can usually be separated (Wengrow 2010: 15). Brands distinguish almost equivalent commodities from one another and differentiate between authorised and counterfeited goods (Coombe 1997). Increasing mass production has brought changes to the uses of trademarks and brands, with the latter increasingly referring to a commodity's meaning, and currently to the context of consumption associated with a product (Arvidsson 2005: 243–244). Arvidsson is primarily concerned with global super brands to which particular emotions and an image are attached through advertisement.

Although 'brand' might have a different meaning in Mali from that applied in other market contexts, I will use the term here to refer to the added value of the tea packaging. The brand is not merely the name appearing on the package or even the trademark that may sometimes be found. It includes the complete design printed on the carton. In the tea trade, this is more complicated; the consultation with the retailer is not necessarily replaced, and the producer is in most cases not the brand owner but completely unknown to consumers. The consumers might be aware of the importer as the brand owner, but if the brand owner happens to be a Chinese trader, the identification does not work well in favour of the tea brand, as explained in chapter 2. Alexander Peukert rightly noted that many products bearing trademarks are no longer sold by producers but by traders, and trademarks have also become subject to trade (Peukert 2016b; see also Hellmann 2003; Wadle 1997). In the case of tea, too, the brand is not necessarily owned by the manufacturer, but by the trader, or importer, especially as the product is not sold in the country of origin. In Mali, only a few brands were owned by the producers, i.e. the Chinese factories. Tea brands either belonged to Chinese brokers working in Mali or, more often, to Malian importers (chapter 2). The brand rather represents the importer and his skill in selecting a good quality tea.

This brand value is enhanced by consumers' imagination, inspired by the design of the printed package as much as the actual brand name and consumers' ideas of quality. Brands build on the immaterial labour of consumers. Through productive communication and their agency, consumers create the value of brands (Arvidsson 2005: 237). Thus, the value of tea is also politically relevant. Reflecting on how brands and adverts work, a senior member of staff at the national advertising agency, the Agence Malienne de Presse et de Publicité (AMAP) concluded: 'As soon as, if ever, you [with your brand] have arrived in the memory of people, the money is flowing' (interview, Bamako, 2007). Having the flow of money in mind, one of the importers confirmed in a low voice: 'There is a whole lot of money in the tea' (interview, Bamako, 2013). Appreciating all this renders it understandable that brands are a considerable capital worth defending.

When consumers buy a package of tea, they also 'buy' the brand, or its attraction and emotional associations, not just its content. As David Tan (2010: 203) notes and as will be shown below, this attraction may be created through personal experience, word of mouth, media, promotion, packaging, display, and even the attitudes of the retail staff. From a combination of these components a brand acquires a life of its own, making a statement about quality, reputation and sometimes even of perceiving life itself. The advertising also draws on these imaginations, relating them to the consumers' activities and thinking.

4 Types and Themes of Malian Green Tea Publicity

Advertisement transforms a product into a brand (Hellmann 2003: 25). In promoting a brand, it adds further value to the product by connecting it with particular emotions, ideas and lifestyles (Moeran 1996: 276–296). As will be shown in this section, the tea advertisements in Mali only partly correspond to these characterisations of Western brands. They do not sell primarily a lifestyle but showcase the product, adopting contexts of green tea consumption. Both brand owners and consumers were sure that lifestyle advertisement would not work with green tea in Mali (for a similar statement regarding alcoholic drinks in Nigeria, see Van den Bersselaar 2005).

Billboards advertising green tea brands are few when compared with the multitude of tea brands available on Bamako's Grand Marché and to the number of billboards advertising other products such as milk, cars, banks, and property. Billboard advertising promotes at least as many brands of black tea and instant coffee as green tea.[3] This is the case also for commercials on radio and television. Nevertheless, green tea sells in Mali. Despite persistent advertising, black tea and coffee brands are far less numerous and have fewer adherents. I have not found any advertisement for tea prior to 1991 in Malian newspapers.[4] Until the mid-2000s, most tea publicity in the Malian public media almost exclusively promoted black tea.

To make themselves heard and pronounce their intentions, advertisers use various forms of media (Mazarella 2004). I will examine the various media employed to publicise green tea, before considering the attitudes of consumers and tea importers towards advertising and the ideas presented in it.

The media reform of 1991, encouraged by the World Bank, entailed the obligation that Office de Radio et Télévision du Mali (ORTM) – the public media – sign a contract requiring the sale of advertising space to private businesses (Diakon and Röschenthaler 2017). The independent media that proliferated following the reforms obviously had to finance themselves by advertisement, or through foreign donor institutions, churches and political parties. Foreign companies used the opportunity to advertise, especially in the public media, but local companies were quite hesitant to invest in commercial publicity. Nevertheless, a few green tea importers explored the opportunities from the 2000s onwards. Thus, commercial advertisement by private businesses is at least as recent as the tea brands themselves, only becoming relevant for Malian consumers during the last couple of decades.

4.1 *Types of Green Tea Publicity*

Most commonly seen are self-adhesive A2 or A3 posters stuck to office, shop or warehouse doors, delivery vans and still more informally to lantern posts and kerbs. Importers also distribute such posters to wholesalers and other potential customers. I saw tea brands advertised by this means on the delivery vans of all the well-known tea importers (Figure 29). Some just attached posters to their vehicles whilst others commissioned professional or amateur artists to paint the adverts by hand or with templates. Those importers owning lorries

3 During the 2000s and 2010s, billboards were used to advertise several tea-bagged black tea brands such as *Lipton, Dilmah, Chaya, Aloysie* and *O'Linda*.

4 This seems to have been different in Morocco, where before the closing of the national society for tea and sugar, which previously distributed these items, the pages of the most popular newspapers, radio and television were full of advertisements for tea produced in the country. Lakhsassi and Sebti (2012: 27–28) and Raji (2003: 73–74) write that Moroccans were used to see advertisements for coffee, but found it strange that tea was advertised which they already knew much better themselves and which only had different names now. The state also used tea and sugar in its propaganda.

FIGURE 29 Painted delivery van of *Thé Haquiqua*, Bamako, 2007

also had their brands painted on them (Figure 30). Importers also commissioned artists to paint images of their brands on their office doors, roofs and external walls of their warehouses, or otherwise paid fees to a property owner, or commune, permitting them to paint representations of their products on walls that, for example, surrounded a football field, or faced a public street.

Agence Malienne de Presse et de Publicité (AMAP) – responsible for advertisement in the public realm – offers three sizes of billboards: small, medium and large and long, which may be sited alongside busy tarmac roads. In the 2000s, many billboards were painted, especially those for green tea. The *Mona* and *Canal* tea brands had several painted billboards in 2007. Those advertising *Canal* were located at strategic places in town, such as near the big mosque and the Chinese embassy. Chinese importers and their Malian partners used printed billboards as early as the 2000s; for example, there were billboards of *Cheval*, *Hamza* and *Askia*. In 2013, there were printed billboards for *Hamza* and *Mubarak* on one side of the poster and *Bon MaMa* and *Hassane Ousmane* at the other side, and for *Aly Cherif* and *Mon Village* on one side and *Ciwara* and *Golden* on the other side, commissioned by a Chinese broker and her Malian partner (Figure 31). In 2013, billboards for *Askia*, and one for *Thé Imperial*, remained in place, although these teas no longer sold well. It seems that from the outset, it was mostly the Chinese suppliers who financed the printed advertisement for green tea.

FIGURE 30 Painted Canal lorry at the warehouse, Bamako, 2007

FIGURE 31 Billboard of tea owned by a Chinese broker, Bamako, 2011

Billboards, especially painted ones, remain in place for several years, persistently reminding consumers of a brands' existence. In the 2000s, several importers chose to employ painted billboards. Importers selling several products in addition to tea, often advertised them on billboards and walls as well. In 2010, there were several artistically-painted billboards for Spaghetti *Santa Lucia*, with *Mona* tomato sauce, *Sahel* milk and *Belle Mona Lait* as well as *Thé Mona* and *Thé Lobo*. The importer of these branded products told us that he preferred painted billboards because if quality paint was used, they lasted several years, whereas a printed billboard was far more expensive and deteriorated within three or four weeks (interview, Bamako, 2007). For the fiftieth anniversary of Mali's independence, he commissioned a fabric bearing images of his products, his logo and Mali's anniversary logo as promotional gifts for valued customers who would commission a tailor to make a dress from it (for an image see Röschenthaler 2015: 709). However, the fabric did not reference his tea brands because it was meant for female customers who would identify with the other food products rather than with tea brands.

Other importers felt right away that the printed billboards were much nicer than the painted ones: 'printed posters are easier, more precise, and more attractive than painted billboards' (interview, Bamako, 2007). In the 2010s, when painted billboards began to be abandoned, the tea importers advertised their products on their vehicles, on the radio and television and via social media. They advertised all their products (green tea, black tea, rice, pasta etc.) each having its own publicity arrangements. In 2016, hardly anymore painted billboards were to be seen.

All importers distributed gifts to valued customers, among them single tea packages, sets of ten and even entire cartons. They commissioned small posters for doors and company cars, caps, tea glasses, T-shirts and plastic bags with the brand image as gifts for regular customers to whom they sold *colis* of tea. Some gave away calendars bearing images of tea packages, or winning options – gifts that participants could possibly win – and slogans such as 'Buvez le Thé Niger avec le fruit de longévité, c'est pour une santé fer (Drink Thé Niger for a long life and a sound health)'. Traders considered it important 'to give some small gifts and things that please people' (interview, Bamako, 2011). One importer noted:

> These things are seen in the city or in other towns when people walk around with them, and everybody can see them; and the small posters can be attached to walls in markets and submarkets, on cars, everywhere, you will suddenly see people carrying your brand. When people see the image, it may encourage them to ask for this tea in the shop. The billboard, in contrast, is stable, it is not mobile, it always stays where it is'.
> INTERVIEW, BAMAKO, 2013

These forms of mobile publicity carry tea images across the city, even to rural areas, covering large space with their messages.

Tombolas are a very popular form of advertisement, often used by importers to bring their new tea brand to public attention. Tombolas are held in stadia, attended by huge crowds attracted to the event by the promise of music and entertainment; they can buy a potentially winning ticket and, if lucky, may win a valuable prize such as a motorbike, television set, computer or even a holiday in Paris, if less fortunate, they will have to be satisfied with merely tea, cap or T-shirt emblazoned with the printed brand logo.

Some tea importers attend the international trade fair, FEBAK, at Bamako. In 2009, for example, I saw stalls promoting *Arawane, Touareg, Niger, Arrami, Canal* and *Confo*. Excepting the big companies that owned *Arawane* and *Niger*, all were Chinese-owned brands. The students hired to staff the stalls were unaware of the nationality of the owners of these tea brands. The stalls were decorated with fabrics conveying printed images of the different tea brands on show. The major importers also increasingly have websites informing potential consumers about their products, extending their agency into the virtual global space.

Most tea importers placed commercials on television but comparably few used billboards to promote their brands, especially this was true for the most successful teas in the early 2010s, including *Gazelle, Gaza Super, Taoudeni* and *Achoura*. They placed commercials on the national television, ORTM, on the private television station Africable and in some of the numerous private radio stations. It is interesting to note that green tea is not only advertised in the media but in some cases, tea brands also promote and advertise popular media outlets, such as Africable, Canal+ and Horizon and the mobile phone provider Ikatel. These companies represent innovation and serve to open doors to the wider world by informing people about what is going on globally (chapter 6). Naming tea after them creates a platform for praise, of honour and respect that concomitantly makes these media stations a topic of discussion by attendees at tea *grins*. Praise, honour and respect are important concepts in Malian society (Charry 2000; Diawara 2003; Schulz 2001). Providing praise for their patrons was one of the tasks of griots and griottes while patrons themselves would not perform praises in public. Thus, an importer advertising his own products has been a strange idea at first and met with reluctance (Diawara and Röschenthaler 2013). Consumers being willing to promote the tea of importers was the preferred option and resonates well with local ideas about praise. Even more beneficial was the rare case that a tea became the theme of a popular song. An example is 'Thé Achoura' by the Malian rapper El Brune on the record *El Brune Star*, with videos on YouTube.

In the late 2010s, a new trend appeared, begun by a campaign for the *Flecha* brand. It employed billboards of the largest possible size, depicting a man in a white shirt and suit jacket holding a tea glass. New to the genre, it carried a slogan: 'Pour les amateurs du thé de premier choix'. A few weeks later, *Koutam* displayed their new tea in a red package on a billboard; two nicely-dressed young men were depicted drinking tea together. Their slogan was 'Un amour de thé' (Figure 32). Then *Sancho* also used a billboard upon which a couple

FIGURE 32 Billboard for Thé *Koutam*, Bamako, 2018
PHOTO BY MADOU KEÏTA

was portrayed, between them a table bearing a tray of tea. This billboard announced a tombola with which consumers could register and possibly win damask cloths, mobile phones, a refrigerator, a motorbike and a car. All these items were illustrated on the billboard.

Soon after *Flecha* announced its own tombola: 'Jouez et gagnez' (play and win), where consumers could win damask cloth, wax cloth, a refrigerator, a flatscreen television, motorbikes and a ram (Figure 33). A year later, in

FIGURE 33 Billboard announcing the tombola of *Thé Flecha*, Bamako, 2018
PHOTO BY MADOU KEÏTA

December 2019, *Flecha* announced another tombola to run alongside popular entertainment, featuring the Malian rapper Iba One. Consumers might win not only the usual flat-screen TVs of different sizes, Jakarta motorbikes, refrigerators and, of course, cartons of tea but also the attractive proposition of title to property, land on which they might build a house. In December 2019, a new tea arrived on the market, *Thé Faguibine*, named after the dam west of Bamako. Its billboard advert portrays an elegant lady pouring tea into glasses behind the renowned Malian singer Salif Keïta who praises the tea with his arm raised; the slogan is 'intensement agréable' (highly pleasant).

This recent series of billboards adopted a new approach to promotion, no longer depicting just the product and its quality but using slogans and also images of fashionable people and celebrities in the act of consuming tea. These had something very Malian about them, concomitantly connected to the consumers' aspiration to participate in global consumption – something that Mazarella (2003) and Moeran (1996) in their research on advertising agencies defined as constituting successful advertisement. Such images were much easier to create through digital printing than with hand-painted billboards.

4.2 *Consumers' and Importers' Expectations of Advertisement*

The big tea importers all ran commercials on radio and television from time to time and also displayed small posters. Some of them only did this, it seems, because other importers did it; others felt it was right to occasionally support the media and also were aware of the advantage accrued by investing in informing the public about a new brand. A student of sociology explained: 'on television, people see new tea brands in commercials, and because they are curious … they buy this tea to find out whether it is different from other teas'. A similar idea was mentioned by one of the importers who explained that advertisement 'makes consumers know that your tea exists, or reminds them that your tea is still on the market' . He even added 'many importers advertise their tea once, and think when it is going well, they no longer need to advertise it' (interview, Bamako, 2007). Another importer whose brand had been selling well for years shared a similar opinion, saying:

> We place commercials on television and radio [ORTM, Radio Liberté and Radio Klédu] from time to time, not just to advertise our brand, but to remind people of the spirit of the brand (*l'esprit de la marque*), that *Gazelle* still exists, because other people [importers] tend to think that if a product is selling, publicity is no longer necessary. They then stop advertising because the product is selling well. INTERVIEW, BAMAKO, 2013

Such assessments suggest some tea importers are in agreement with the policies of many brand owners and advertising agencies in other parts of the world. They emphasise the need to constantly refresh brands in consumers' minds (Malefyt and Morais 2012: 37), as positive change creates values (Appadurai 1996).

Despite these views and the advertising activities they were engaged in, importers and local companies had also other reasons for their reluctance to advertise. Some feared because generally only the larger western companies had the resources to constantly advertise, that if they advertised that in fact might draw the attention of the authorities to their company, believing they were successful and wealthy. Others knew the public were unimpressed by advertisement and simply ignored it. The prevailing opinion among consumers and even business people was that if a product required advertising, it must be of low quality; in short, high quality products sold themselves. Suspicion of advertisement may also derive from previous experiences of political propaganda for which people were sensitised during colonial times and later by post-colonial governments. Indeed, the word for advertisement is in many European languages closely associated with propaganda. Until the early twentieth century, in Germany, for example, all advertisement was called 'propaganda'. In Spanish, 'propaganda' is still the word for advertisement; and, in Italian, for proselytism (see for example, Röschenthaler 2009).

All my interviewees were of the opinion that the best and most effective publicity for any product was word of mouth recommendation. They considered the opinion of friends far more trustworthy than conventional forms of advertisement and particularly influential in young people's tea groups. Tea groups were very fluid, participants often attending the *grins* of other groups and by this means information about tea brands spread quickly across the city. For the *grins*, it was always of interest to know which tea other *grins* were drinking. Unintentionally, by littering the area around the stove with the empty tea packages, or attaching them to the handle of a teapot to protect their hands from the heat, grins served to advertise the brand of tea they consumed (Figure 34).

The names of tea brands provided a good topic for beginning a conversation, as participants assessed and evaluated the taste and quality of teas. Should a group drink low quality tea, it would be ridiculed and potential guests would shun them. So a group needed to consume a popular tea to ensure respect in the neighbourhood. Tea *grins* are about prestige and good taste and thus they contribute to the value of a brand when they consider it top quality. As tea brands were all priced the same, prestige was not determined by financial capacity but quality and connoisseurship. In this respect, in Mali, green tea differed from, for example, beer, where prestige was generated from conspicious

FIGURE 34 A *Gazelle* tea package attached to the handle of a teapot, Bamako, 2011

consumption by those wealthy enough to afford the strongest and most expensive brands (Röschenthaler 2019; Van den Bersselaar 2007). As with beer drinkers, the tea *grins* could be said to operate competitive brand communities (Muniz and O'Guinn 2001; Nakassis 2013) conveying their status in society through the tea they choose to drink (Burke 1996b; Douglas and Isherwood 1978; Trentmann and Otero-Cleves 2017).

Criticizing capitalist market economy, Arvidsson (2005: 237) indicated that brand value was created through the agency of consumers: 'Brands build on the immaterial [unpaid] labour of consumers through productive communication'. This resonates well with the practices of tea *grins* who speak a great deal about the taste of tea and their discussions shape opinions about the beverage. Here the 'work' of providing the most efficient form of publicity – word of mouth 'propaganda' between tea friends – is carried out. Friends take news about tasty new brands to their own tea groups, which will be curious to taste and discuss any new tea. Drinking tea of a certain brand in the public or semi-public space is also considered by importers the most effective advertisement of tea brands. Such forms of advertisement are deeply rooted in social life; commercial advertisers have been jealous of these efficient forms of voluntary publicity because it is unpaid work that makes a brand sell (Arvidsson 2005; Foster 2008).

In the nineteenth century, Saharan traders had a similar model role when impressing their guests by performing the tea ritual. It was, however, rather an exclusive ritual not meant to entice others to imitate it immediately. In Mali it took more than a century before ordinary people were ready to emulate it (Röschenthaler forthc.). Nevertheless, it was the former role of these Saharan traders that shaped the notion that people from northern Mali were the more competent tea connoisseurs and that thanks to this, 'it was sufficient to give your tea to a Saharan trader and money would be earned'. The same importer suggested that for the Bamana it was like that: 'if the Arab [Saharan] traders sell tea, that is as if you [the importer] already have 25% of the profit in your pocket. But a Chinese cannot sell the tea' (interview, Bamako, 2013). The mere involvement of a particular type of person in selling to consumers an importer's tea brand enhanced the value of their tea.

In addition, the wholesalers' influence also contributes to whether a tea will sell or not. A wholesaler might persuade a retailer to invest in a particular tea and promote it among their customers (chapter 5). They may guide the retailer with their knowledge, suggesting which teas might interest consumers and by this means influence the range of teas sold in shops. For the importers, a wholesaler's recommendations are the best advertisement for their products. Upon their involvement and narratives might depend the success or failure of a tea brand. For example, in February 2011, just before the start of a football match and during peak-time evening viewing, I saw a nice commercial in ORTM for *Thé Baro*. The following day, we attempted to buy this tea in the Grand Marché, asking for it in several dozen wholesale boutiques. The tea was unavailable and none of the wholesalers even knew that it had been advertised the day before. They knew only that this brand of tea had been popular in the past but that currently consumers no longer drank it. Apparently we were also the only people who had recently asked about the tea. The wholesalers obviously did not promote this tea.

Malian consumers told me that even though the design on a package might be nice, that did not mean they would buy it. As one of the importers explained: 'You can not say that the tea sells because of the image on the package; it sells because of the taste of the tea' (interview, Bamako, 2013). Consumers, too, insisted that what counted was the content of the package i.e. the quality and taste of the tea. Several suggested that a good package design ought to emphasise the virtues of the tea and stated the best promotion was to sell good quality at an affordable price. Checking the quality and providing advice about tea consumption to the population they believed was a role of government (young men, Bamako, 2013).

Even though the young men in Bamako suggested the package design was important for marketing, one added that only those with little knowledge about tea would consider the package design when buying tea; the others only bought tea that they knew possessed a good taste. They insisted only the taste mattered. Even though consumers told me they ignored advertisement and did not buy the tea because of the package, the package did have some importance, as they would reject tea that was not contained in such a package but rather a transparent plastic bag. They felt they could not offer such a tea at their tea *grin*. These examples illustrate the complexity of value creation that unfolds in an interplay of being informed about a brand, its being presented in an attractive packaging, and consumers' opinion fed through various forms of publicity.

4.3 *Themes in Malian Tea Advertisement*

In contrast to the way, tea is advertised in countries through which tea was imported to Mali, Malian images selected to publicise Chinese green tea are quite uniform, involving the product itself and its current consumption, especially at tea *grins*. To point out its specificity, I will briefly discuss tea adverts in other countries along the tea trade route.

In earlier times, the consumption of tea in Europe was linked with the trade in silk, with china or porcelain and the 'Enchanted Orient' evoking exotic stories about India and China. During the nineteenth century, in Britain, these images were closely connected to British identity and its Empire (Lakhsassi and Sebti 2012; Fromer 2008; Ukers 1935, vol.2, chapter on the history of tea advertising) and they also appeared on advertisement for tea. These adverts connected exotic images with superior national identity. This was different in Morocco and Mali.

In Morocco, two images strongly associated with Moroccan national identity appear repeatedly in tea advertisement: the first of these conveys the idea that drinking tea ennobles the consumer; it references the partaking of the royal tea ceremony by the royal court, evoking impressions of the 'royalty of tea' through its association with the sultan. The second image, epitomised by depictions of nomads in the desert sitting at the entrance to their tents, drinking tea, highlights impressions of the traditional tea ritual as it is conducted in rural areas and the desert. Raji (2003: 73–74) explains that successful advertising follows these ideas, focusing on 'the valuation of the Moroccanity of tea, its conviviality and its rootedness in popular Moroccan culture'.

That images of present-day tea *grins* are central in today's Malian green tea advertising is probably largely due to commercial advertising being a rather recent introduction. It does not work with the image of royalty, and despite tea being the national drink, there is no nationality in tea advertisement. Whilst most will agree that northern Malians are the true tea connoisseurs, they do only rarely figure in commercials and on billboard advertisements. Missing from adverts is the diversity of ideas, represented by caravans, names and images on the tea packages which may be due to the limitations of advertising budgets which precludes complicated cinematography. Advertising is thus all about ordinary Malian people drinking tea. China does not figure prominently in tea advertising (except on some of the Chinese-designed billboards), reflecting Malian opinion that Chinese traders cannot successfully sell tea.[5]

Commercials and billboards suggest drinking green tea is something of ordinary people, rather than of the wealthy. Usually, they depict young men who assemble in tea *grins* to indulge in consuming it. This sets green tea advertising apart from that of black tea, mostly by foreign companies, which portrays young middle-class consumers, distinguished by their clothing, the place of consumption, and the manner by which they drink tea; for example, depicting a young couple smiling at each other which refers to the western concept of how couples consuming together. A typical example is a billboard of *Dilmah* black tea from tea bags (Figure 35). Young consumers argued that the tea adverts should focus on the product, present its virtues, depict the package and perhaps someone drinking tea with evident satisfaction rather than focus on life styles that were not their own (interview, Bamako, 2005).

Most billboard advertisements (and also small posters) for green tea depict the product and sometimes a person enjoying a drink of tea. Early billboards in particular focused on information about the product. They were illustrated with branded tea packages in different colours, sometimes with indications of quality and price, but without slogans. One very prominent billboard was that of *Canal* tea, which showed a well-known actor from national television, portrayed sitting on a chair, surrounded by various *Canal* tea packages; he brings a full glass of tea to his pointed lips (Figure 36).

The preparation of tea at a *grin* is the most popular theme in tea commercials. The individuals appearing in commercials are predominantly young, reflecting the age of the men in tea *grins*; all had the complexion of the majority population of southern Mali; Chinese and Saharan traders are not normally represented. Of twelve commercials for green tea that I have examined only one involved people from northern Mali, in this case, Tuareg, i.e. people with blue turbans drinking and

5 The image of China seems to change among the young people. They all know that China is not only a rising economic power and the main producer of green tea but also a country of important scholarship. One young man stated that 'China with its high population numbers is a creating and producing country … it stabilizes the youths because it produces their tea' (young man, Bamako, 2013). Such positive opinions about China reflect its growing media presence and image enhancement among Africans (Diakon and Röschenthaler 2017).

FIGURE 35 Billboard for *Dilmah* black tea, showing couple drinking tea together, Bamako, 2007

FIGURE 36 Billboard for *Canal* tea with well-known Malian actor, Bamako, 2007

praising *Thé Tombouctou.*[6] In commercials for *La Main à Main*, *Baro* and *Gazelle et ses Petites* an actor presents the tea, explaining as they do so how good it tastes. A smiling young woman prepares tea next to her husband who slurps it with delight in a commercial for *Thé Canal.* For a *Serval* commercial, friends walking along a street, meet a tea group and praise the tea for its taste and provision of energy.

A variation of this story appears in a *Lawal* commercial: a man surrounded by his friends has just finished preparing the tea, when other friends happen by and ask what brand of tea he is serving. Upon hearing his answer, they laugh and depart, saying they will go to where they can get *Lawal*, their favourite tea. In a *Flecha* commercial, a stressed patron steps out of the house, is asked by the doorkeepers what ails him before they offer him some tea. The man drinks, smiles and asks for another glass, before taking the package in his arm as if it were a baby and feeling relaxed returns with it to his house.

Women are frequent topics for discussion at tea *grins*, and also occasionally appear in commercials. An *Achoura* commercial shows some friends preparing tea at a small street. They joke, laugh and chat until an attractive young woman passes by. The men stare at her, one tries to impress her but she makes known that she thinks his behaviour ridiculous; the friends laugh at him. In another *Flecha* commercial, a husband is searching his neighbourhood for his wife, when he discovers her, she is preparing tea for her lover, thus alluding to the sexual connotations of female tea consumption (Röschenthaler forthc.). In 2017, *Flecha, Sancho, Achoura, Koutam*, the most popular brands, launched their tombolas not only on billboards but also in commercials on TV, announcing the goods that participants could win.

5 The Production of Advertisements

As mentioned earlier, some importers were convinced that wholesalers and consumers were the better promoters of their tea than commercial advertising. One recent importer explained her approach:

> You have to launch your product, you make publicity and all that, consumers do not arrive by themselves. You have to reach out to them to make your product known to them. This means you have to spend money to do this. So, we made publicity on the radio, on television and we had launching events, and we distributed the tea in the Regions of Mali.
> INTERVIEW, BAMAKO, 2013

6 These were commercials for *La Main à Main, Askia, Tombouctou, Canal, Lawal, Gazelle et ses Petites, Baro, Serval, Achoura, Sancho*, and two for *Flecha*.

Another occasional importer explained that normally importers would first distribute some tea among the wholesalers and single packages to individual consumers:

> When they appreciate your tea, you can continue, and if the tea is not going well, you just give it another name the next time you import, or you stop importing it. When it begins to go well, you can register your brand and then you can make advertisements. INTERVIEW, BAMAKO, 2007

But his tea failed to sell, and he did not create publicity, or even make small posters.

5.1 *Producing Commercials*

When they want to advertise on television, tea importers can choose between the national ORTM or the private television station Africable. In the following, I discuss the production of commercials broadcast in ORTM, using the example of the *Canal* brand.

Merchants have the choice as to whether they want to produce commercials themselves – although ORTM will insist on certain quality standards – or better still commission a private advertising agency, or AMAP, to provide actors and organise the filming. The latter approach has the advantage that the audience will already know the actors, which might serve to enhance the credibility of the commercial. All the actors employed by ORTM have studied theatre and are well-known professionals. They work as commentators, present awareness campaigns on television and most rate highly with the population in terms of credibility, which is transferred to the products they advertise. Actors are not normally employed to advertise more than one tea brand in a short period nor would they become involved in advertising poor quality teas for fear of damaging their credibility as a television professional.

The merchant of *Canal* – a brand owned by a Chinese broker and sold by his Malian business partner who also imported his own tea, *Lawal* – followed the above approach. As the tea began to sell, the Malian partner decided to make a TV commercial before then arranging advertisement on several billboards in town. I will consider this example in more detail as it explains the production and the peculiarities of making and broadcasting an ORTM commercial in Mali in the 2000s.

At first, the Malian partner distributed *Thé Canal* to wholesalers and in 2005, after it began to sell, they made their first commercial. To achieve this, the Malian merchant contacted AMAP, the national advertising agency, to inquire about the process of creating a commercial with them. After he and AMAP had agreed on the length and content, he paid AMAP who then commissioned a camera team and mounting. The Malian importer then approached the actor recommended by ORTM, a well-known comedian, explained his ideas for the commercial and paid him. AMAP then commissioned the ORTM team and filmed the commercial.

The actor, a professional who had studied at the National Arts Institute (INA) in Bamako, had performed with the national *kòtèba* group[7] as a comedian, had acted in films, made other commercials for ORTM and was also a technician at the Radio du Mali. In this commercial, he staged a Malian tea ritual, in which Malian social values were combined with the delight of drinking *Canal* tea. The merchant had largely left the conceptualising of the commercial to him, saying that he just wanted the tea to become well-known and to sell well. The merchant allowed the actor to taste his product and as the actor liked it, there was no reason to decline to make the commercial. He did not have to say 'look your tea is not good, if you want me to advertise it, you have to improve it. *Canal* tasted good at the time' (interview, Bamako, 2007).

The commercial is simple and convincing, starting with Malian kora music, the actor's 'wife' prepares tea for her 'husband' in the courtyard of their compound. He watches her as she serves him the tea which he drinks with an audible slurp, his face breaking into a smile before he utters words of appreciation.

For the merchant, the commercial was a success. Subsequently, he commissioned a billboard advert, depicting the actor drinking a full glass of tea. The actor revealed that one day people came to his house requesting tea. They asked him: 'We have seen you on the billboards in town, is this not you?' He remembered the merchant visiting to capture a photographic portrait some time earlier. He had not been asked whether he agreed to his image being portrayed on a billboard. Seeing his portrait on several painted billboards and also on the side of the huge company lorry and the delivery van which toured the city, people recognised him as the well-known actor in ORTM. They took him as their brand pioneer. 'They were thinking I was rich because I was on a billboard but I had to explain to them that it was just a billboard, which was publicity for the Djokoramé [the Malian partner of the Chinese importer]. They were thinking: If this man finds *Thé Canal* good, then there must be some truth in it' (interview, Bamako, 2007).

The actor explained to them that he had no family connection to the merchant, that the merchant was in any case a Djokoramé – a member of particular

7 *Kòtèba* is an entertaining role play and a local form of theatre, popular in Malian (Bamana) villages. The national *kòtèba* theatre group, Kotéba national du Mali, was created in 1969 and combines traditional Malian theatre, staged on the village square, with international repertoires (Meillassoux 1964).

families of traders (chapter 1) – which he himself was not; and there was nothing more than a joking relationship with his family. But when people continued to inquire about his tea, he contacted the merchant and asked him to supply some cartons of tea for him to distribute to his visitors: 'people liked it so much, especially the blue packet'. The importer also organised a tombola, inviting the actor who was given the seat of honour in the first row. He also wanted to gift him a Jakarta motorbike but this he declined because he thought it might encourage people to believe he would also receive money from the Djokoramé merchant (interview, Bamako, 2007).

The actor said: 'If there was only the commercial, people would easily forget this tea, but when they see the billboard, it reminds them of the commercial on television' (interview, Bamako, 2009). The Malian merchant explained: 'We first worked with him [the actor] on the TV commercial and then on the billboard. It is done this way, because the people will know him already from television and can recognise him on the billboard later' (interview, Bamako, 2007). He further explained that the billboard functioned as an aide memoir and amplifier of the message in the commercial. Interestingly, despite the great popularity of the TV actor, not all of the consumers when shown photographs of the billboard recognised him. Some assumed he was a tea seller, others an Arab.

In this case, the credibility of the tea, its good quality and success, were closely connected with the prestige and popularity of the actor and it also illustrates how a brand's value and marketing may be enhanced by a good advertising campaign resonating with Malian social values.

5.2 *Producing Billboards, Wall Paintings and Signboards*

The employment of a well-known actor and his multiple remediations amplified the visibility of a brand, projecting the importer's agency into the public space. During the 2000s, after traders became convinced of the benefits of advertisement, young artists began to offer them services entailing the production of painted advertising signs. Signboards, warehouse walls – or those of other properties – posters, lorries, delivery vans, billboards and anything for which they could be commissioned to decorate would be painted. Signboard artists had existed much earlier but one of the importers remembered that the owner of *Thé Cheval* was the first to commission the painting of tea packages on walls (interview, Bamako, 2007).

In 2007 I spent two months in Mali talking to the numerous painters, working for traders, barber shops, hair dressers, or photo studios in Bamako. Many had migrated from Côte d'Ivoire following the conflict subsequently endeavouring to earn a living in Bamako by painting.

Similar to actors featuring in ORTM commercials, some painters had studied at the Institut national de l'art (INA) or even at the newly created Academy of Arts in Bamako. Most were unable to achieve their ambition to earn a living from their art, as there were too few affluent citizens with the means to enable the purchase of art work. Others had gone through an informal training, with an older brother, or other relative, or another established painter, subsequently becoming self-employed. In the 2000s, some artists had become well established and had set up their own companies, as for example Promo 2000 in Hamdallaye, which painted theatre sets, signboards and billboards – one of which was made for *Thé Sahel* (interview, Bamako, 2007). These artists possessed albums documenting their work which is shown to potential customers and from these we identified some of those who had worked for tea importers.

In 2007, we observed paintings on the wall of a football field in the Nyarela neighbourhood. It was at a time when blue and green colours were popular on tea packages. The wall was freshly painted and displayed various products of the brands *Mona* and *Lobo* as well as a range of other items sold by the company. Adjacent to it, on the same wall, in the same colours and style, were representations of *Canal* and *Lawal* products (Figure 37). Consultations with several importers and with painters revealed that the *Mona* and *Lobo* products were made first, followed sometime later by the *Canal* and *Lawal* products. For the right to display their products on the wall, the importers paid the commune of Nyarela, rather than AMAP, because the wall was on the football property, owned by the commune.

We located the painters, both of whom had studied at INA, engaged in creating a large billboard along the tarmac road leading to the airport. The day before, we had found the billboard at the road side, but it was merely painted

FIGURE 37 Mural with painted *Canal* products, Bamako, 2009

white. Meanwhile, they had completed the reverse side, depicting several packages of *Thé Mona*, before working on the front where a plate with spaghetti *Santa Lucia* and *Mona* tomato paste was emerging (Figure 38).

On another day, they explained that the importer of *Mona* had witnessed them painting one day and approached them. Learning of them from him, the Malian partner of *Canal* commissioned them as well. The two merchants gave the artists samples of their products, to use as models for their work. They were free to use their own discretion in organising how the products on the billboard should be displayed.

These artists have created other billboards, sometimes arranging designs on their computer, enlarging the image and transferring it to the billboard or a vehicle, sometimes they used templates to render the work more precise. These painters had no studio and worked either at home, at their patron's property, or on the roadside. Commissioned by the owner of *Mona*, they first painted his signboards, cars and delivery vans, before he asked them to design and paint the walls of the football field and finally create his billboards. He paid them 500,000 francs CFA for painting the images on the wall and paid a further 700,000 francs CFA to the commune (interview, Bamako, 2007). We visited the two painters – brothers as it turned out – in the courtyard of a warehouse where they painted with a group of other artists, some of whom were

FIGURE 38 Billboard of *Thé Mona*, just completed by the painters, Bamako, 2007

also their brothers and their cousins. They painted cars, lorries and signboards for various patrons, all of whom owned import and export companies and wanted to advertise their products. Painting both sides of a lorry might earn them 100,000 francs CFA. One painter said their customers often complained that their work was too expensive but he explained this was said without considering that advertising in this way represented a long-term investment that could last ten years and provided they paid for high quality paint, would still look good (interview with three artists, Bamako, 2007).

6 Advertising Agencies

Before 1991 and the advent of the media reforms, the only advertising agency in Mali was the state-owned AMAP. Afterwards, numerous private advertising agencies began offering services. AMAP continues to control public advertising space in the city.

6.1 *AMAP: Commercials and the Placement of Billboards in Public Space*

Anyone wanting to advertise in the public realm, which involves the verges alongside roads, or in the national media must contact the national advertising agency, AMAP. Since the decentralisation programme, some of its responsibilities have been relegated to the communes of Bamako, as in the context of the murals mentioned above. AMAP is also responsible for the content of advertisement. It was considered impossible, for example, that AMAP would permit the national brewery to advertise its beer brands in the public space. The rules that are valid in the cities and towns, however, do not apply to the roadsides *between* cities. Hence, billboards advertising beer can be found there, but until 2013 at least, this was not possible on public walls in Bamako. Generally, private space can be freely used by its owners, provided it does not offend public morals. They may also at their own discretion, rent it out to others.

AMAP has several departments: one for billboards and another for radio and television commercials broadcast by ORTM. Commercials last a maximum of one minute and the price at peak viewing time – just before the *feuilleton* (the soap opera, or rather telenovela) – was 232,000 francs CFA; half a minute costs less and five seconds cost 61,000 francs CFA. Prices at other times of the day were about a third less (according to a table dated 2005). Added to these prices is value added tax of 18% (interview, Bamako, 2007). Brand and shop owners organise the production of commercials themselves, although AMAP can assist with finding actors and by providing a camera crew. The importer of *Antilope No.1* showed us a bill, stating payment amounting to 1,400,000 francs CFA for a commercial broadcast eight times over the course of two months, just before the popular show Top Etoile – a performance of well-known griottes and griots – on ORTM in 2011. Brand owners might also wish to advertise in *Essor*, the national newspaper, but to date I have not seen it carry any publicity for tea.[8]

Billboards are only found alongside the tarmac roads connecting neighbourhoods with one another. According to a table from AMAP of 1999, a small billboard of 3 × 2 m was 247,000 francs CFA for one side and it was 309,000 francs CFA for both sides. Therefore, most importers had double-sided billboards of the middle size of 4 × 3 m for 581,000 francs CFA. Some Chinese companies rented the larger double-sided billboards of 5 × 3 m for 721,000 francs CFA. The long billboards of 7 × 2 m that the importers of *Flecha* and *Koutam* used in the late 2010s would have been 735,000 francs CFA. These prices exclude 18% value added tax but include rental of the material construction of the billboard, the selection of its location, its erection and the guarantee of its safety. Second year prices are reduced by half. These prices are for billboards located in an average public space site in the city. A good place, for example, at a road junction or in front of a large mosque, might be twice as much.

AMAP also offered billboard printing services. A print for a 3 × 4 m billboard was 93,000 francs CFA (tables of AMAP from 1999 and 2001). Thus, advertising was an expensive undertaking, another reason why so many Malian tea importers considered the billboards an unnecessary expense. In total, an average-sized billboard could easily cost 400 or 500,000 francs CFA (interview, Bamako, 2007). It would also be possible to arrange much cheaper printing in China. One tea importer who had his printed billboards provided by his Chinese supplier, explained that he paid only USD 75 for his printed poster from China, whereas for a painted billboard he would expect to pay 200,000 francs CFA (roughly 3 times as much). He thought it important to frequently renew the images employed in his adverts. For his first billboard during its first year, he paid 1 million francs CFA to AMAP, and the subsequent year cost him only 500,000 francs CFA. Because of the expense, he rented just one billboard (interview, Bamako, 2007).

6.2 *Private Advertising Agencies*

Since the 1990s, most visibly in the 2000s, numerous advertising agencies, some of which were unproductive, sprung up offering long lists of services. We tried to arrange appointments with some but only a few gave the impression that

---

8 One full page in colour was 500,000 francs CFA, a black-and-white page was half the price, and a quarter of a page in colour was 145,000 francs CFA. To this, a service fee of 25,000 francs CFA and value added tax was charged as well (table from AMAP of 2005).

they were successful or at least carried out any work at all. The likely reason for the failures might have been an over-supply of advertising agencies itself perhaps a result of new companies being entitled to financial assistance (République du Mali 2012). After having arranged some commercials with ORTM, most importers experimented with private advertising agencies; cheaper, having no fixed price list and open to negotiation, they appeared an attractive option.

Commercials made by private advertising agencies could be broadcast with ORTM and Africable, the independent Malian television station with an Africa-wide coverage of Francophone countries. The owner of *Thé Arafat*, for example, commissioned Signature, a private advertising agency, to produce a commercial for his tea, buying broadcast time with Africable and showing the commercial every day for several weeks. This was far cheaper than the ORTM prices. He also worked with CreaCom who made the commercials for his *Thé Sonikara*. CreaCom was owned by a well-educated young man who had several employees and apprentices. He had a network of actors and camera crew and used various creative software with which he produced the commercials.

This chapter considered how package design and various forms of advertisement enhanced the value of tea brands, of which personal support and recommendation by word of mouth via *grins* and wholesalers was considered the most effective and concomitantly the cheapest form of advertising in Bamako. Importers saw commercial advertisement as a means to enhance brand value by informing consumers about the existence of a specific brand of tea. Whilst advertising could be easily commissioned, it was nevertheless expensive often having uncertain outcome. Thus, it was employed more as an amplifier for already successful tea brands.

The best-selling brands were not those who mostly relied on commercial advertisement. It was rather the other way around. Successful brands advertised because their owners had the means to cover the costs because their tea was selling well. In their approaches to advertisement, Malian importers focused on product information, Malian values and consumption in the tea *grin*, which differed from those of Chinese traders who tried to interest consumers in the Chineseness of the tea (Figure 31). When talking about the quality of tea, Malian consumers obviously have different ideas than their Chinese producers and suppliers. To be excellent, Malian tea must be strong, bitter and taken sweetened whilst in China, tea has to be light and pure. In spite of these different approaches to tea, the cooperation between the major Malian tea traders and their Chinese partners seemed to be rather smooth most of the time. Malian importers' encounters with China, their journeys to procure tea and the interaction between those individuals who are involved in the tea trade will be discussed in the next chapter.

CHAPTER 4

The Traders of Mali's National Drink

This chapter examines the agency and interaction between the individuals who trade green tea from China across half the globe to consumers in Mali and how they came to be involved in the tea businesses. Following the liberalisation of the Malian economy in 1991, a new generation of importers travels by air to other continents to visit trade fairs and their suppliers in China (and elsewhere). They bridge larger distances in a shorter time: their parents have only rarely journeyed abroad by air, travelling mostly on land in motor vehicles, whilst their grandparents travelled long-distance on foot with caravans of porting animals (chapter 1).

My elaboration begins at the kiosks and small supermarkets – the endpoints of the value chain – where consumers find Chinese green tea for their daily tea ritual. The owners of these retail outlets acquire the tea from the wholesalers who in turn purchase their supplies from importers with the help of the *coxeurs* (chapter 1). These economic actors in the tea trade may be differentiated according to the quantities of tea they sell. Retailers sell individual tea packages, the wholesalers sell sets of ten 25g packages, larger tea packets, cartons and *colis*, and the importers distribute only *colis*. There are also a few semi-wholesalers who sell the larger packets and sets of ten.

1 The *Butiki Koroboro* and *Súraka*: Where Consumers Buy Their Daily Tea

Consumers in Bamako purchase packages of green tea at the kiosk or 'corner shop'. These retail shops go under the generic description *butiki koroboro*, 'Songhay kiosk', in Bámanankan, because they are run by Songhay (not Tuareg or Saharans) from the northern part of Mali. These *butikis* are numerous being found in Bamako's many neighbourhoods. Single tea packages are also available in small supermarkets, known as *butiki súraka*, or literally 'shop of the light-skinned people', referring to the Saharan traders (in contrast to the shops of the Songhay, or 'dark-skinned people'). These shops usually stock about half a dozen tea brands as individual packages, the owners choosing to stick to the most popular brands, although, as my assistant explained, 'if you do not have that particular brand he is asking for, the customer never comes again' (interview, Bamako, 2016). In 2016, we visited several such *butiki koroboro* and

 | DOI:10.1163/9789004505698_006

Saharan supermarkets (*butiki súraka*) to appreciate where people procure the leaves for their tea ritual, the identities of the sellers and what brands were on offer. Two will serve as examples.

The first is a typical *butiki koroboro*, located in Hamdallaye Plateau in the very street where my assistant has his compound. The small shop which had existed for ten years, was less than eight square metres and had a small entrance area beneath a shady roof where the vendor would take his tea. The delapidated roof was sealed against rain with folded empty 5kg tea cartons (Figure 39). The owner was of Songhay ethnic identity, coming from a village

FIGURE 39 Songhay kiosk, with entrance area, Bamako, 2016

near the town of Timbuktu. He sold sugar from a large bag, anti-moskito coils, sachets of *Barika Tigi* washing powder, mayonnaise, small transparent plastic sachets, bonbons, biscuits, French bread, locally-made soap balls, Malian groundnut cooking oil customers could decant from a large container and four different brands of Chinese green tea. These tea brands were *Sancho, Achoura, Gazelle* and *Koutam*. They were available in packages of 25g for 100 francs CFA each (about 0.15 Euro).

Of the four brands, he told us, his customers first chose *Achoura*, and secondly *Sancho*. He also explained that for him it was more expensive to obtain *Achoura* than *Sancho* and the other two brands. A carton of *Achoura* could be 19,000 francs CFA and one of *Sancho* and the other tea brands 16 to 18,000 francs CFA. At first sight, it appeared he would earn more selling *Sancho* but in fact *Achoura* was the better option as he sold more of this brand (chapter 3). He bought his tea in packages of ten, or 5kg cartons containing 200 packages, from a Malian wholesaler in Hamdallaye who offered the same prices as wholesalers at the Grand Marché. The owner of the kiosk stated that he would acquire those tea brands his customers asked for rather than following the wholesaler's advice.

Later, my assistant explained, that most retailers owning these shops were Songhay originating from rural areas around Timbuktu in northern Mali, where they have their compounds and families. They come alone – not wanting their families to be in the city – to work in the family shop for several months before returning home to administer their business there and look after their farms. A brother, son or cousin would then substitute for them in the shop in Bamako. This reminds of the Saharan traders in Timbuktu of Caillé's (1996 [1830]) time who spent several years in the town and then returned to their families in the Sahara whilst a brother continued the trade in Timbuktu. *Butiki koroboro* had quite some fluidity; some closing whilst others reopened in another street, nearby.

The second shop was a small supermarket located in Hamdalaye ACI 2000, a newly constructed neighbourhood with large villas and office buildings. The shop was owned by traders of Saharan origin from near the Mauritanian border, was about 20 square metres, had existed for two years and had many products for sale, including primarily international brands: large containers of cooking oil (*Dinar* from Côte d'Ivoire, *Afia* from Morocco, *Oleo* from Algeria), cornflakes, black teas in tea bags (*O'Linda, Lipton*), biscuits, large rice bags, bonbons, *Ajax* cleaning powder, *Nido* milk powder, various bottled soft drinks; no bread and or products from open boxes or bags were sold. This shop sold six different brands of green tea: *Achoura, Sancho, Koutam, Gazelle, Tabankort*, and *Tilimsi*, all of which were priced at 100 francs CFA. The vendor explained that *Achoura* was the most popular brand. The last two brands were less popular but their owners were friends of the shop owner.

There were other supermarkets that did not sell the green tea used in the Malian tea ritual. There is no name for these in Bámanankan. Lebanese supermarkets, locally called *supermarchés libanais*, whilst not necessarily larger than the *supermarchés súraka*, sell a different range of supplies. Lebanese supermarkets are thought to attract the more affluent rising middle class, reflected in their stocking of a variety of black teas – in tea bags (called *lipton* or *lipiton*) – rather than Chinese green tea. In contrast, the *butiki koroboro* and the *butiki súraka* are frequented by more ordinary local people from the neighbourhoods, their supply of green teas largely reflects the popularity of the various tea brands at different times.

In addition, there are one or two large, expensive French supermarkets stocking tea that sits with European tastes and budgets. A few Chinese supermarkets exist, selling green teas favoured by the growing Chinese population of Bamako (Diakon and Röschenthaler 2017). Malians would not drink them. There are also a few supermarkets of Malian wholesalers, described as supermarché with the name of their Malian owner added, i.e. *supermarché chez Tandia,* Tandia's supermarket, or *magazin de Diakité*, the shop of Diakité. They sell the popular brands of Chinese green tea for the Malian tea ritual and the lot of other products they import (Figure 40).

FIGURE 40 Supermarché chez Tandia, with painted tea packages of *Le Nord, Tourareg, Sancho*, Bamako, 2013

These retailers are the decisive intersections between the market and consumers, catering for the various social groups of Bamako's inhabitants. As different preferences emerge at different times and places, the supply of tea brands of the popular *butiki koroboro* and *butiki súraka* might differ in Bamako's various neighbourhoods and also in other Malian towns and the surrounding rural areas. The brands offered by the range of shops at particular times depends on word of mouth-advertisement in the tea *grins* (chapter 3) and recommendations by wholesalers. As will become clear in the course of this study – and despite the statement of the seller in the *butiki koroboro* – these wholesalers and the brokers who mediate between wholesalers and importers play a large part in promoting specific tea brands to retailers and possibly even negating promotion of others.

2 The Wholesalers and Their Influence on the Tea Business

A few tea wholesalers had shops in Bamako's neighbourhoods but most worked in the Rue Gouraud at Dabanani near the Grand Marché. All those I met were men. As long as the state had the monopoly on most imports and exports (chapter 1), SOMIEX, the state-owned import and export society, acted as both importer and wholesaler, selling its products to retailers and semi-wholesalers from its outlets. Private tea wholesalers gradually emerged following the dissolution of SOMIEX and the reforms in the early 1990s. Traders remembered that even in the late 1990s, only four or five wholesale boutiques existed in the Rue Gouraud, today known as the 'tea road' (interviews, Bamako, 2013; chapter 1). From the 2000s onwards, numbers of wholesalers constantly increased so that by the 2010s, the entire street and even adjacent side streets, were crammed with tea boutiques, easily recognisable thanks to the piles of colourful tea cartons in front of their entrances, often extending far into the street (Figure 41). Nowhere else in Bamako is there such a density of tea than that seen in the Rue Gouraud in the Dabanani section near the Grand Marché in the ancient Bozola quarter, where the first traders of Saharan origin had settled (Röschenthaler forthc.).

Where the Rue Gouraud begins near the tarmac road, are the smaller semi-wholesalers, selling from tables shaded by umbrellas. Beginners in the tea trade, they sell sets of ten tea packages and also tea in 100g or 250g paper boxes, tea glasses, teapots, batteries and other small commodities (Figure 42). They were happy to talk to me whilst they thought I wanted to buy but reluctance set in when it came to answering questions. My assistant suspected they were selling pirated tea packages (more on piracy in chapters 7 and 8) and feared my

FIGURE 41 Piles of tea cartons near the market, Bamako, 2010

FIGURE 42 Stall of semi-wholesaler at Dabanani, displaying tea packages and teapots, Bamako, 2011

mission was to expose them. More generally, all the smaller traders were rather cautious when compared with the more successful traders.

We visited a wide range of the wholesale boutiques, asked for their owners' opinions about the tea market, tea brands, and, when possible, their shop's history. Whilst all the wholesalers were friendly, they were at the same time generally also wary about my research. I suppose this was because competition between them was rampant, local wisdom suggests it wise to talk less rather than more and they were always busy serving customers.

As mentioned in chapter 1, the wholesalers are locally called *commerçants, jàgókəla* or *jùlabá.* Some wholesalers describe themselves as *boutiquier en gros* or *demi-gros* – wholesalers and semi-wholesalers – which meaning they are selling to customers of different financial capacities. Additional to entire 5kg cartons and *colis*, they sell green tea in sets of ten 25g packages, and paper and tin boxes of different sizes (100g, 125g, 200g, 250g, 500g) from shelves behind the counter (Figure 43). Some wholesalers only offer tea, whilst others also supply milk powder, sugar, rice, bonbons, tomato paste and other condiments.

I will now discuss the stories of six wholesalers of various ages and influence, which sheds light on their agency and interaction with retailers, *coxeurs*, importers and other wholesalers.

FIGURE 43 Inside a tea wholesale boutique, with *coxeurs* on the right side, Bamako, 2013

The first semi-wholesaler I introduce is an older *koroboro* trader from near Timbuktu. One of the biggest tea sellers in Bamako, he sold lose tea from wooden boxes before the 1990s, during the time of SOMIEX. In the late 1990s, just as other traders began importing tea from China, he gave up the tea business. When we talked to him in 2013, he was about 75 years old. Before he began selling tea in Bamako in 1969, he had travelled to Tchad where he traded metal boxes for storing garments, and iron water basins. In 1967, he went to Mecca. On his return, he purchased tea from SOMIEX, which he sold at the trade fairs in Timbuktu and Gao. By 1971, he had saved enough money to open a retail tea boutique in Bamako, from which he sold all four qualities of SOMIEX Chunmee teas: 4011, 4012, 4013 and 4014, i.e. the first, second, third and lowest qualities. After SOMIEX was dissolved in 1991, he decided that the advent of the small tea packages would prevent him making a reasonable profit, so he sold his remaining SOMIEX stock, advertising it on radio. From then onwards, he travelled to Germany and France purchasing bargain fridges (interview, Bamako, 2013).

The reason this tea trader gave up the tea business represented an opportunity for others. A new generation of wholesalers emerged in the 1990s and they gradually began to populate the Rue Gouraud. There was, for instance, the wholesale shop from which my assistant used to buy tea when he needed larger quantities, for example, as a marriage gift. Both in the shop and at its entrance were piled stacks of tea cartons, leaving only a small path for customers to enter and leave, and for the young helpers who conveyed cartons of tea to customers' vehicles. Tea was sold in paper and tin boxes of 100g, 250 and 500g, the 25g packages in sets of ten; they also sold entire 5kg cartons and *colis* and a few other packaged products. We visited their shop many times.

The owner of this boutique was the retired father of a family whose numerous sons had taken over the shop. The eldest was born in the 1950s; all the brothers had attended the Coran school (interviews, Bamako, 2007, 2009, 2011, 2013, 2016). The sons were always very friendly, but as Wahabis did not shake hands with me. Every time we arrived they would ask the reason for my questions. Despite the fact the shop was always full of customers, long and heated discussions often arose with both the sellers and the customers engaged about the objectives of research, or the content of one of my questions. This provided a welcome opportunity for my assistant to demonstrate his rhetorical skills. For example, we discussed when tea brands appeared in Mali and also the attitude of Islam to brand ownership (see chapter 7). These discussions became a kind of advertisement for the shop and customers often stayed to listen, or participate in them, whilst refreshing themselves with soft drinks sold from the shop's fridge. It represented an experience for people and of course I always bought some sets of tea packages for my collection.

Further down the Rue Gouraud, we visited another wholesaler (interview, Bamako, 2011) of Soninke ethnic origin, or more precisely, a Marka trader, who mainly worked as the representative in Bamako of some Mauritanian importers whose tea he sold. Before becoming a wholesaler, he worked for five years in Brazzaville. On returning to Bamako, he began to trade milk powder but in the 1990s, when private importers brought tea from China, he began to sell tea for them. At some point, Chinese traders invited him to sell their tea. He agreed, sold some tea for them and expected them to bring him a few cartons now and again. To his surprise, his Chinese partners ordered an entire container of tea. He declined to take it, explaining that he did not have the capacity to buy and sell a whole container. The Chinese traders offered it to another wholesaler. Since then, he decided to work only with Mauritanians.

The third of my wholesalers was a young man from Sikasso (a town in Mali's south) and a newcomer in the tea business. Together with his elder brother, in 2010, he had just begun to open his wholesale shop at the Grand Marché. In the late 1990s, as a boy he taught himself how to sell tea buying entire cartons of it and selling individual packages to customers. He recalled there being only four or five wholesale tea shops in the Grand Marché. He bought his tea cartons from one of these wholesalers and others from some of the *coxeurs* (brokers) (interview, Bamako, 2013).

The fourth wholesaler was in 2016, according to one of the big tea importers, the most influential wholesaler in Bamako. He told us he never attended school but at a young age began to retail tea packages from a tray on his head. When his father retired, he took over his tea business. His first kiosk in the Rue Gouraud, opened in 2004, was very small and he could hardly stand upright in it. The business was successful and soon he was able to rent a larger shop. We met him for the first time in this boutique in 2013. The business was so successful he did not consider selling anything other than tea. Soon the space became too cluttered and he relocated to a new shop, the size of three shops combined, where we found him again in December 2016. Meanwhile his younger brothers who had finished school began working with him in the shop. As his father had earlier, apart from a few additional small items such as tooth paste, bonbons and the instant coffee of a befriended importer, he only sells tea. His shop is full of tea, a huge shelf along the wall behind the counter displays various tea boxes, other tea packages are piled up on the desk, cartons of diverse tea brands fill the remaining space and empty tea cartons cover the floor (Figure 44). In 2013, among these cartons were the popular brands *Arawane*, *Ayoune*, *Gazelle*, *Koutam*, *Niger*, *Sancho*, *Al Taj*, *Taoudeni*, *Raissa*, besides many others.

The wholesaler keeps samples of all these teas to help monitor sales and compare their quality. Some of his success may arise from his regular reporting

FIGURE 44 A tea wholesale boutique full of tea cartons, Bamako, 2016

to the tea importers, his suppliers, about how well their tea is selling. He felt they listened to him and that those who accepted his advice, appreciated it. He said that some chose not to listen, realising only later that his advice would have been helpful to them. Some importers felt it was sufficient to use their own agents to sell their tea but his advice was to sell it via wholesalers like himself as well. After he sold their tea, they realised the advantages of doing as he suggested.

When the retailers receive complaints from their customers, i.e. ordinary consumers, they pass their complaints on to the wholesaler, and he then has to carefully consider how he raises the issues, if at all, with the importer. As he fears importers may interpret negative comments as an attempt on the part of himself to boycott their tea, or rather more likely, lower the price, he prefers to wait until the importer telephones him to discuss business. This wholesaler believes he provides considerable assistance to the importers in selling their tea but feels they ought to make more efforts to acknowledge his important role in helping their business to thrive. He happily advises retailers from the villages about which tea brands are in vogue in the city and of good quality. By these means, the wholesaler promotes certain tea brands above others. He feels their owners ought to acknowledge this by selling him their tea at a reduced price. He emphasised he owed no debts to any importers as he tends to pay in cash and rarely by instalments (interviews, Bamako, 2013, 2016).

Two brothers feature as my fifth example. They were among the first of the few traders to open a wholesale boutique at the Grand Marché in the late 1990s. One of the more successful tea importers recalled:

> Before he [the fourth wholesaler] became big, they [the two brothers] were the most influential tea wholesaler. Now it is him [the fourth wholesaler], and these two are still the most important tea sellers. And what I like most, is that he makes nothing else than tea, but the others [the two brothers] also sell sugar, milk, soap, as you can see when you come into his boutique. INTERVIEW, BAMAKO, 2013

Whereas the fourth wholesaler is not (yet) an importer, purchasing his tea from other Malian importers the brothers did delve into importing themselves (and thus also belong to the group of importers who had once owned a tea brand, presented in the next section). In their boutique, they stock cartons of the successful Malian importers such as *Thé Raissa*, *Dambé*, *Hassane Ousmane*, *Gazelle*, *Gazelle et ses petites*, *Sancho*, *Flecha*, *Al Najah*, *Rocki*, *Obama* and *Lawal* and they also take a much larger percentage of their teas from Chinese importers, stocking at least as many cartons from Chinese brand owners such as *Al Farouk*, *Ramadane*, *Al Cazar*, *Askia*, *Haquiqua*. They sell, for example, the tea of the Wafa company with brands that are registered by Xiu Xiaomei. The fourth wholesaler also sells a few cartons of Chinese brand owners but he obtains them from the wholesale boutique of the brothers via a *coxeur* not from the Chinese owner.

Another example are several brothers of Saharan origin who some years ago had moved from Gao to Bamako. They ran several companies in various countries – their business cards had addresses in Mali, France, USA and China – and they worked closely together. One brother lived in Shanghai for twenty years. Their wholesale company was the only one, whose office was located in the new market area, rather than near the Grand Marché. They had the exclusive right to sell *Thé Arrami*. This tea was registered by the Chinese company Africasie Internationale Mali Sarl in 2009. I have seen *Thé Arrami* stocked in a number of shops over several years but traders stated it did not sell well because of its superior quality and tea wholesalers preferred not to buy it. Their main business, however, was not tea but rather energy saving light bulbs. They did not seem happy to chat about tea and they have never been mentioned by any of the other tea importers. Their story also illustrates that being a trader of Saharan origin does not automatically mean that they can successfully sell tea.

These brief portraits illustrate wholesalers in different career stages and varying degrees of exercising agency on the tea market. What for some brought to an end their involvement in the tea trade, presented an opportunity for a new generation of wholesalers who became specialists in selling packaged tea. Some of them seem to possess quite some influence in promoting certain tea brands above others and helping to achieve success for tea brands. The most influential were specifically those wholesalers focused only on selling tea and eschewing diversification into other products as had the third and fourth wholesalers described above. Their stories also show that some had travelled widely to other countries before becoming traders or wholesalers in Bamako. That they receive their products from importers or from a representative of an importer, is what all these wholesalers have in common. Importers and wholesalers know each other, and whilst they regularly talk on the mobile phone with each other, they nevertheless prefer to work with the *coxeurs*, the small brokers who act as mediators between wholesalers and importers. A reason could be that wholesalers usually have 'weaker ties' (Stovel and Shaw 2012) with *coxeurs* than with wholesalers who are their colleagues, and often also their friends or even relatives.

3 Mediating between Importers and Wholesalers: The Brokers or *Coxeurs*

On our arrival in December 2013 at the boutique of the fourth wholesaler, we observed how he paid cash for 200 *colis* of *Thé Gazelle*, that is 800 cartons. The wholesaler handed the bundle of notes to the *coxeur* or broker who would then pass it to the *Gazelle* sales manager from whom he purchased the consignment. Wholesalers frequently do not directly negotiate with the importer and brand owner, nor with their representatives but rather the communication, cash and tea are channelled through a *coxeur*. The importer of *Gazelle* distributes containers of tea from China to her four representatives, or agents, at Bamako and many more in the other Regions of Mali. A wholesaler buying his tea from one of these agents, can be certain he is not acquiring pirated tea. This is important to all parties in the exchange because poor quality pirated tea would ruin the brand's reputation and everyone would lose in the long run. If the importer sells a *colis* for about 66,000 francs CFA to a wholesaler, the consignment of 200 *colis* – mentioned in the previous section – must have had a value of 13,200,000 francs CFA (about 20,000 Euro) that the *coxeur* was personally entrusted to pass to the sales manager of *Gazelle*.

The *coxeurs* are young men with an influential role that offers plenty of scope for manipulation. They mediate between wholesalers and importers, or their representatives. As one wholesaler (interview, Bamako, 2013) explained: 'On a normal day, three to four *coxeurs* will come to my shop, but on good market days there can be many more'. The *coxeurs* come on their own initiative, or call on their mobile phones; neither wholesalers nor importers call them. A *coxeur* visits wholesale shops each day to discover whether a wholesaler requires tea. If the reply is affirmative, he will propose a price and the wholesaler will decide bearing in mind that within the next hour another *coxeur* might arrive, perhaps offering a better price, whether he finds the price acceptable. The wholesaler will also bear in mind the price at which he can sell the tea, ensuring it will not be higher than that offered by other wholesalers and of the need to stock as many different brands of tea as may be required to satisfy all his various customers. He also will want to be careful because if the price of the tea is too low, it might be pirated.

The wholesalers need to be confident they can trust the *coxeurs* as indeed also do the importers. *Coxeurs* have to be trusted with cash given to them by the wholesalers which they convey to the importer, assuming the transaction was not conducted by bank transfer. They also have to be trusted to deliver the purchased tea rather than some pirated product. These circumstances make the wholesale boutique a decisive place where action in the exchange and delivery of the product take place. The *coxeurs* were understandably quite wary about my research; they had a hard time imagining I actually engaged in scholarly research rather than be an aspiring future wholesaler, or even a covert government spy (interview, Bamako, 2013).

The *coxeur's* role essentially involves walking from the premises of one tea wholesaler to another in order to establish their requirements. The abovementioned wholesaler continued:

> When a container arrives, he [the *coxeur*] will already know which wholesaler wants this tea brand, and ideally, the container is already sold as soon as it has arrived. He knows everything. He knows all the wholesalers and all the importers and representatives of tea brands. INTERVIEW, BAMAKO, 2013

The *coxeur* will be paid for his work by the trader, normally the wholesaler, who has employed his services. Sometimes an importer may ask him to perform a task, such as announcing the arrival of a container of tea, then the *coxeur* will be paid by him. This commission is called 'le prix du *coxeur*' or 'le pain du *coxeur*', 'the price' or 'bread of the intermediary' (chapter 1). Normally the wholesaler pays the commission who asks the *coxeur* to look for and bring this or that tea brand. In the event, the *coxeur* frequently benefits twice; firstly, by the gift or commission received from the wholesaler and secondly, from the additional value that he puts on the price of the tea set by the importer, about which the wholesaler will not know. A wholesaler could easily negotiate directly with an importer but there are advantages in working with a *coxeur;* some feel they can negotiate better with a *coxeur*; they can also acquire smaller quantities of tea to observe how well they sell, whereas an importer always wishes to sell larger quantities. If the tea sells the wholesaler can then decide to work directly with the importer. Often, however, even with the involvement of the *coxeur*, most payments between importer and wholesaler are conducted by bank transfer, at least officially.

It seems that the roles of wholesalers and *coxeurs* are the most decisive for promoting tea brands: they can ensure a brand's success or cause it to fail by boycotting it. Importers also influence the activities of wholesalers and *coxeurs* when they discuss the workings of the market and the sale of their tea brands with them. Importers of course may and do advertise their tea in the media (chapter 3) but many were of the opinion that wholesalers were the best vehicles by which to market their brands. Taken together, this interplay between the various actors is what makes particular tea brands successful, each party – wholesaler, *coxeur*, importer and consumers (see chapter 6) – plays their part.

4 Malian Importers of Green Tea

Until the 1991 economic reform, the state had been the only legitimate importer but even before then, whilst unable to import, a few large private Malian companies were permitted to function as representatives of foreign brands such as *Lipton*, or *Maggi*. When SOMIEX was dissolved, private companies filled the niche and began importing tea. One of the first was Ba Traoré. One importer recalled: 'He was first, and then all the others began to import as well. Ba Traoré was a big tea importer, he has just died a few months ago. … He imported loose tea in wooden boxes … He did not yet have his own tea brand' (interview, Bamako, 2013). Another tea importer also remembered that at that time, he obtained 30kg boxes from Ba Traoré; after one or two years, the sizes changed and he imported the 5kg boxes, which he sold until about 1995 (interview, Bamako, 2013). These were the same qualities that SOMIEX had previously sold, in addition to Gunpowder. And there were also others who imported tea in wooden boxes and smaller cartons.

During the 1990s, also traders of other nationalities began importing tea. This is when smaller cartons with brand names were introduced. One importer recalled there were Chinese, who knew the tea market and worked in development projects in Mali first. Some of them remained in the country after their contract expired, contacted Malian traders and sold cheap Gunpowder teas to them. Among these were the state-owned Chinese brands *Chameau* and *Temple du Ciel* (interview, Bamako, 2013). Then there were other traders of European and Asian origin selling black tea; as late as 2005, I could see murals, that had not been refurbished for a long time, depicting black tea brands such as *Akbar*. Then tea brands like the earlier mentioned *Thé Saddam* (consisting of tea dust), imported by a Senegalese company appeared in 1998. An importer named Pinchou with a registered brand named *Khaima* was listed under a company address in Paris; Punjabi – the Hong Kong Chinese of Indian origin – sold *Thé Cheval* and the Malian of Lebanese origin also sold his brand *Baro*. Early on, Saharan traders were also involved. AAA and some Djokoramé traders also began importing better quality Chunmee teas from China, as will be elaborated below; there were also Bamana newcomers engaging in the tea trade. Other Chinese followed with the brands *Elephant*, *Lucky Bird*, and *Askia* (chapter 2).

The tea importers in my sample fall into two groups. Firstly, there are the wholesalers who decided at some point to import their own tea brand from China but have only done so irregularly or have since reverted to wholesale again; and secondly the big importers who sell a variety of products or have chosen to specialise only in supplying tea. The majority of the importers were men, but a few women also engaged in tea importation, and one of them became a successful tea importer. I will consider the occasional tea importers first.

There are many wholesalers of some standing in Bamako. Most only focussed on wholesale but there are some who experimented with importing tea themselves. One of the first successful importers was Ba Traoré mentioned above. Another was the fifth wholesaler introduced in the previous section. In 2005, he attempted importing his own tea brand *MOB*, but I have never seen this on the market; in 2015 he imported again two brands, *Nouja* and *Nouza*, but neither sold well. He registered his brands, but his primary business continued to be selling the tea brands of Chinese and other Malian importers. Many wholesalers who tried to break into the importation business, dropped the idea after they recognised the difficulties, they had selling their product. Some returned to wholesale, others continued importing other Chinese, or European products instead. Many who had little or no previous experience in selling tea thought they could emulate those who had profited from the trade. Such traders invented a variety of excuses over the telephone to avoid talking with us at all.

One influential wholesaler was in the early 2000s the owner and importer of a tea brand named *Ikathé*. He had a large shop at Dabanani, crammed with products such as various brands of green tea, large bags of powdered milk, and mayonnaise etc. One of his employees was sat, in an arrangement that I have seen in several Chinese shops in Cameroon, hidden behind products on an artificial leather chair above the floor, so that he could easily survey the entire place. This importer and his brother owned the company, and they had inherited the business from their father, a man, originally from Banamba, who was among the first generation of Soninke traders who came from Mopti to Bamako. In 2001, after seeing others importing tea, they decided to get involved, too. Finding their Chinese supplier on the internet, one of the brothers went to Hangzhou to meet him and also visit the plantation and his factory. The Chinese supplier subsequently reciprocated with a visit to Bamako. The tea sold well for several years, and as a result in 2006 they registered their brand, *Ikathé*. But suddenly, it became unpopular; the importer suspects the Chinese suppliers reduced the quality. Thus, they ceased importing tea and henceforth only stocked products imported by others. *Ikathé* was still available in 2007, and I also saw a delivery van sporting the painted brand design on its side, but by 2009 it had disappeared.

The Malian importers of *Deux Chevaux* were two brothers, one of them explained that one day they agreed to import their own tea. It did not sell very well, thus they decided not to invest in any advertising at all nor register the brand with OAPI because of the expense (interview, Bamako, 2007). Similar stories were related by other wholesalers. Among the earlier ones were the importers of *Thé Dogon, La Théière, Super Lion* and *Maiga* in 2002. *Maiga* was owned by a Chinese company called La Maison du Thé and as late as 2007, I saw a few packages of *Maiga*. Among the more recent short-lived tea brands are *Buffle* and *La Vache* which arrived in only a few containers, different from *Thé Obama* and *Rakim* (same owner as *La Vache*) which remained available for several years but without achieving the profit margins desired.

Another importer, an established Malian wholesaler, sold mostly green tea. We visited his shop of approximately 20 square metres, much of which was jam-packed with cartons of tea, and a few other items; free of stock was only the small space where the owner sat on a comfortable office chair, wearing an embroidered tunica and a fes of the same colour. This importer owned *S.Lere*, a brand he had registered in 2008. Whilst very friendly, he did not reveal many details about his business. He sold his own brand, and tea brands owned by other Malian importers such as *Chaban* of a Djokoramé trader. However, most of the brands he sold (*Mina, Officiel, Konfo, Tombouctou, Haidara, Razèle*) were owned by Chinese brokers. As did another of the influential wholesalers, he worked with several Chinese suppliers, but unlike the brothers who once imported *Ikathé*, he sold little other imported foodstuffs. He did sell some products from Wafa, the Chinese import company. He worked with Wang Xiao Fang, the registered owner of several tea brands: the relatively successful brand *Askia* (2004), *Halal* and *Haidara* (2005), and a nameless brand, the packages of which sported the image of a mosque (2006), *Haquiqua* (2007), *Razèle* and *Golden* (2008).

This importer-wholesaler also worked with Xie Wen Shuai, a Chinese broker from Hangzhou who owned the brands *Wilibali* and *Konfo* – *Konfo* included green tea and a medicinal and anti-mosquito liquid, both registered in 2006. In the same year, he also registered products of the brand name *Wilibali*, but not tea, which had already been registered by Xie Wen Shuai three days earlier. In 2013, he said that he had worked with Xie Wen Shuai for a long time in Bamako but that he had now returned to Hangzhou, from where he organised other businesses (interview, Bamako, 2013). When I was in Hangzhou in 2014, I tried to meet Xie Wen Shuai but he postponed our meeting several times, saying he had to go to Beijing. As I was also going to that city, I suggested meeting him there, but on my arrival, he told me that he was already at the airport and intending to fly to Dakar. He did not explain what his purpose or plans were for going there. During our discussion with the importer-wholesaler, the new broker replacing Xie Wen Shuai arrived in the shop to collect his share of the sale of the tea. The wholesaler handed him a heavy parcel of notes, which the broker counted in our presence without hesitation, not even objecting to being photographed while counting (Figure 45). However, the wholesaler's Malian assistant took care not to appear in the picture. When the broker finished counting, he put the parcel in his bag and strolled away with a broad smile. The wholesaler's main business was the sale of tea for Chinese brokers importing to Mali. His own tea brand, *S.Lere*, was on the market for many years, but was not sold in large quantities.

Chinese green tea promised huge profits, so many wholesalers felt inclined to try their hand importing their own tea brands. For example, the importers of *Thé Cinquantenaire* are a family of Fulbe traders, who had in 1966 migrated from a village near Timbuktu to Bamako, where the head of the family opened a shop selling foodstuffs. They received us in the living room of their compound; from floor to ceiling it was decorated with carpets and cushions to sit on and the windows were darkened to keep the temperature low. The head of the family used to buy his tea in 30kg wooden boxes from SOMIEX and sell it to his customers in quantities measured in a tea glass and then rolled in a newspaper, together with sugar. After the dissolution of SOMIEX, he continued to sell tea imported from China by other traders, starting with Ba Traoré and AAA.

In 2010, whilst Mali prepared for the fiftieth anniversary of its political independence from France, one of his daughters developed the desire to

FIGURE 45 Chinese broker counting money that he received from the Malian wholesaler, Bamako, 2013

own her own tea brand, which she chose to call *Thé Cinquantenaire*. She is a businesswoman, the owner of two bakeries and a shop in which she sells European products. In the spring of that year, she travelled to China and spent two months there. In Guangzhou she worked with a Chinese-speaking Malian intermediary who organised visits for her to several tea factories (interview, Bamako, 2013). The tea factories have their own brokers who collect customers from the airport or railway station, invite them to dinner and take them to the plantations and factories (Röschenthaler 2021). She sent the samples given to her to her father for him to examine, selected what she felt was a quality tea and ordered her first container load. After its arrival at Bamako, via Dakar, she distributed its content to various wholesalers all over the country. Her tea sold well, so she ordered more containers. In 2012, when the political crisis began, her wholesalers, fearing political problems, disappeared with all the money from the sales of her tea and she was only able to recover half her investments (interview, Bamako, 2013). Just recently, in 2019, she again owned a tea brand named after her company and the large dam west of Bamako, *Thé Faguibine*, and advertised it with a large billboard featuring Salif Keïta drinking her tea (chapter 3).

One importer, a young Bamana trader who had mainly sold washing powder, after deciding to import tea, travelled to China in 2013. It was the year after the coup of March 2012, in which French president François Hollande had sent his army to help liberate Mali's north from the rebels. This inspired the naming of the tea brand *Thé François Hollande*. We visited this importer in one of his shops, where he related his experience to us. It had not been long ago that his first container of tea had arrived; *Thé François Hollande* was now to be seen everywhere at Dabanani. He explained: 'It [the brand] is to acknowledge François Hollande because he made an effort to save our country and this has motivated me so much and that is the reason why I am into tea now' (interview, Bamako, 2013).

As a safeguard, he had asked for an appointment at the French embassy to reassure himself that they would have no objections to his plans. Five days later, he received a personal letter from the ambassador, which he read out to us: 'Monsieur, concerning your tea, we give you the permission to call your tea François Hollande. I have the pleasure to inform you about this agreement in the name of the French Republic'. After receiving the permission, he registered the brand and then travelled to China. Working with a Malian translator, he visited some tea factories and selected a good quality tea. Upon its arrival in Bamako via Dakar, he sent two cartons of *Thé François Hollande* to the French president, who acknowledged its reception with compliments. The wholesalers were keen to distribute the new tea and he had many ideas as how to promote it and develop further products under his brand name (interview, Bamako, 2013). At first, *François Hollande* sold well; Malians clearly appreciated the efforts of the French president, however, their enthusiasm waned after it became obvious that French intervention had not resolved the issues; sales of *François Hollande* declined.

This newcomer possessed promising ideas but just as many others had discovered before him, he could not continue importing tea, demonstrating that although the demand for tea is high, selling tea is not an easy task. There are many factors influencing the fortunes of a tea brand. The imagination of traders and consumers about the derivation of good tea – people from northern Mali and the Sahara being tea connoisseurs – is very important but does not automatically ensure a brand's success, as the example of *Thé Arrami* illustrated. A thorough knowledge of the tea business is also important but even wholesalers with considerable experience behind them can fail. Many have given up importing tea after selling just one or two container loads or even after selling tea for a few years. In contrast, others who enjoyed success may have had more perseverance, knowledge, capital, good luck and more extensive networks.

5 The Major Malian Tea Importers

Whilst the occasional importers are many in Bamako, of the major tea importers existed only about fifteen. Except for two, working from northern Mali, we were able to interview all of them, many several times. All the tea importers started like the wholesalers outlined in the previous section but some during the 2000s and 2010s were able to establish themselves as big and successful tea traders, importing over five containers of green tea each month. Among them the most successful are Malians who have concentrated on only Chinese green tea. Some of these importers are more entrepreneurial than others, invest in property and in some cases, in production also. Beginning their businesses in small offices in the Rue Gouraud at Dabanani near the Grand Marché; with improving profitability, most went on to construct larger office and warehouse facilities near the industrial zone where there was more space available. These tea importers all told me repeatedly that there were only about fifteen traders who imported large quantities of tea.

The thirteen big tea importers that I present in this section, sell either just tea or tea and a range of other products, mostly produced in other continents; a few also produce brand name products other than tea. Foreign packaged products appeal particularly because Malian migrants often returned home from France bearing them gifts and thus, they represent the 'good life' in the West, including consumption of mayonnaise, powdered and condensed milk, tinned meat, pasta and tomato paste. The products are procured from foreign companies, for which some of the importers act as trade agents possessing the exclusive right to sell in Mali. Occasionally, they worked with Chinese suppliers in this way as well, but Chinese brokers tend to supply a number of wholesalers with their brands, rather than just one. The biggest tea importers, however, insisted that they preferred to remain loyal to selling just the one product – Chinese green tea – at least at first and concentrate on making this a success. They also preferred to import and sell their own brands of tea. The narratives in the stories of these importers show a clear trajectory toward success despite the fact that some had not even attended school nor learned accounting.

I have categorised these successful tea importers according to the size of their companies and the variety of products imported. Here, I first discuss those traders regularly importing tea of one or more brands and a range of other products; some of them sell these products in their supermarkets, and some are additionally industrialists producing brand-named products themselves (importers of *Baro*, *Kangourou*, *Sancho*). Secondly, importers who have one or several brands of Chinese green tea and are also representatives of foreign companies, importing other products with the exclusive right to sell them in Mali; some of them sell several types of products under the same brand name as their green tea; i.e. they have a portfolio of products under one or several brand names (importers of *Arawane*, *Rocki*, *Niger*, *Lobo*, *Lawal*). Thirdly, I describe tea wholesalers who have turned into big tea importers focusing only on the sale of green tea brands (importers of *Hassane Ousmane*, *Gazelle*, *Gaza*, *Antilope No.1*, *Taoudeni*). Other tea importers, whose companies are located in northern Mali and Mauritania, include those of *Azawad*, *Le Patron* and *AAA*, but only *Azawad* has a representative in Bamako. Among the big importers and the influential wholesalers and occasional tea importers are thirteen founder members of the Association de Thé Farako (chapter 1).[1]

5.1 *Importers of Tea and Other Packaged Products*

The three companies covered here are major tea importers. Whilst Chinese green tea is an important product to them, it is only one of the products that they sell. Some of them (importers of *Baro*, *Kangourou*) are industrialists and produce their own brand-named products, others (importers of *Kangourou* and *Sancho*) have also created supermarkets in which they sell the products they import. The importance of politics to entrepreneurial success is particularly evident in the family history of the importer of *Thé Baro*.

5.1.1 The Importer of *Thé Baro*

Early on, the company was associated with the Malian Farako tea plantation. The importer, a Malian of Lebanese origin, was known for inventing the packaging of tea in 25g plastic sachets, after his Chinese suppliers sold him a packaging machine, enabling him to package his products in Mali. This was a huge success for at least ten years. To understand this development better I will briefly summarise the family history of the Achcars in Mali. In 1924, Emile Achcar (1904–1994), the father of the importer, aged 20, left the Lebanese village of Bait Shabab in 1924 (Arsan 2014: 59; Kamian 2006).[2] He first went to Dakar where he became a trade agent for the French, remaining there until 1930 (Kamian 2006). After losing all his money and commodities in a trade deal in Cairo, he relocated to Bamako and there sold wholesale consignments of manufactured wares, mainly textiles, imported from Europe (Paris, Marseille, Manchester, Liverpool) to Dakar by other Lebanese traders (Arsan

1 The importers of *Achoura*, *Arawane*, *Gazelle*, *Hassane Ousmane*, *Sancho* and *Ikathé* gave 30 million francs CFA each and those of *Gaza*, *Lobo*, *Kangourou*, *Rocki*, *S.Lere* and *Cinquantenaire* gave 20 million each (interviews, Bamako, 2013; chapter 1).

2 In 1918, nineteen adult members of the Achcar family lived in Guinea, others in Kayes and Senegal (Arsan 2014: 55, 59).

2014: 142). Emile Achcar and another Lebanese family, the Watshi, also traded kola nuts, transported by Lebanese traders from Côte d'Ivoire to Bamako. From Bamako – the central point of both Lebanese and African kola networks – the nuts were distributed by lorry or rail through the Soudan and Senegal using networks which, like those that ran between Freetown, Grand Bassam and Dakar, were founded upon ties of kinship: Achcar, for instance, traded with his brother Joseph in Kaolak, Senegal. These trade routes appeared closed to outsiders (Arsan 2014: 147).

Bamako's Lebanese traders were particularly affluent. Eighteen of them possessed working capital of over a million francs at the time (Arsan 2014: 131) and in 1945, Emile Achcar had deposits of almost 2 million francs. Until 1950, Emile Achcar focused entirely on his trading activities. He purchased kola nuts from farmers in Côte d'Ivoire, transporting them by lorry to Bamako and on rail to Dakar. In Dakar he purchased cigarettes, salt, sugar and bicycles, which he transported by rail to Bamako. He also shipped groundnuts to Egypt and Europe. He rented vehicles to transport his products between Côte d'Ivoire, Guinea and Senegal. He was known as 'the king of salt and kola nuts'. No-one talked about tea in Bamako at the time.

From the 1950s onward, Emile Achcar began to diversify and establish industrial production. Thus, he began to compete with the big colonial trading houses (such as SKOA, CFAO, Peyrissac, Chavanal, Compagnie du Niger Francais, Vezia, Buhan & Teisseire, Maurel & Prom). Despite opposition to the industrialisation of the country from the colonial government, Achcar successfully negotiated a quota for sugar and established a confectionery, called La Grande Confiserie du Mali. In 1954, he purchased land in Maniambougou (a neighbourhood in Bamako) from a French citizen and constructed an industrial complex producing ice cream, lemonade, cooking oil, soap, glassware, tin products, bricks and cement, and he had a pigsty. He also became politically active, supporting the independence movement. In the 1940s, three of his children were born in Bamako and in 1950 his youngest son was born in Lebanon. In 1946, Emile's Lebanese wife took the children to Lebanon for schooling (in a Jesuit school). Emile stayed in Bamako, visiting them once a year, all this to permit the education of his children; later, they studied in Europe (Arsan 2014; Kamian 2006).

Following independence, Mali's socialist policies brought trade restrictions and economic life became difficult for the Lebanese traders. The 1964 trade law obligated most European and Lebanese companies to close down and relocate to countries like Côte d'Ivoire, Senegal, or Burkina Faso. Emile Achcar had developed many trade, industry, transport, agriculture, and social projects; he was philanthropic, distributing rice and meat in the poor quarters of Bamako; people came to him for guidance; he helped them find work, lent them money and mediated in their conflicts. Emile Achcar stayed in Bamako, hoping for good relationships with the government but in 1963 his company in Maniambougou was nationalised and around the same time, the sugar company in Kaolack, of which ownership was shared with his brother, went bankrupt just ten years after its creation. In 1964, Emile Achcar considered to leave Mali and asked his eldest son to liquidate his trade and production plants (Kamian 2006).

The son, however, decided to keep the confectionery, the only property of the Achcars that had not been nationalised. From 1969, he managed it with the help of Malians and his two younger brothers. In 1978, their sister and her husband also joined them. In 1984, Emile returned to Lebanon permanently but his children remained in Mali. In 1979, following the droughts, they grew grain and produced flour with American support, in Diré in the region of Timbuktu, and created the Grand Moulin du Mali (GMM) and the Boulangerie Bagami. The eldest son grew rice, producing 80 tons daily. In 1997, the two elder brothers created the Groupe Achcar Mali Industrie (Groupe AMI) when diversifying their company and, henceforth their holdings consisted of four companies: the confiserie with 350 employees, the mill with 350 employees, and GAM transit with 20 employees, and the mineral water production (EMM) branded *Diago*, which was created in 1997 and employed 50 people. In total, their companies provided employment for 770 people. According to a signboard at the company entrance of AMI in 2016, they also bread animals. Their children took over the business in 2006 (Kamian 2006) and the daughter's children started battery production (Kamian 2006; see also Dougoutigui 2010; Fofana 2014). The Achcars' story illustrates the close connection between enterprise with politics and how dependant the survival of companies is on favourable policies (see also Jalloh 2002). However, close relationship with politics can easily bring its own problems as well as lead to accusations (Piel and Tilouine 2015).

In 1990, one of Emile's sons created a company for manufacturing soaps, detergents and cosmetics (SODEMA); he also created an airline (MAE – Mali Air Express) and began importing green tea from China. He presents his products – vegetable oil, powdered milk (the brand *Nono Barkama*), washing powder (*Barika Tigi*) and his brand of Chinese green tea *Thé Baro* in two qualities: Grosgrin [sic] (Gunpowder) and 4011 (Chunmee) – on a website under the company name SAEF (Société Achcar et Fils) and SODEMA.

When we arrived at their company in Bamako's industrial zone in March 2016, one of Emile's grandsons received us in very friendly fashion but as his father was travelling, made arrangements for my assistant to talk to him at a later date. During that meeting, the father explained to my assistant that in the beginning, the idea was to increase the sale of Farako tea but it seems that the consumers did not warm to the idea. They considered this tea too dry and too bitter, so it was blended with tea imported from China. Finally, as a higher percentage of Farako tea was not acceptable to Malian consumers, it was blended at a ratio of just 1% Farako tea with Chinese tea (chapter 1). In order to lend the tea a better taste, the tea plants would need more humidity, requiring new plantations and machinery. But with the structural adjustment programmes and the privatisation in Mali, tea was no longer considered an urgent project on the government's agenda. Interest in tea was revived, however, in 1993 or 1994 when the government of Alpha Konaré asked Emile's son to help them better promote the Farako tea produced at Sikasso (interview, Bamako, 2016).

Emile's son visited the Farako tea factory and subsequently a delegation of the Chinese government approached him on the same matter. Until then, both imported and Malian tea from the Farako plantation was sold from boxes of 20kg. Customers received their tea rolled up in a paper; its taste thus became easily contaminated and the wrapping was unhygienic. As his company was already selling washing powder packaged in small sachets, he developed the idea of packaging tea in similar fashion. After visiting numerous shops to see how tea was sold, he concluded that 25g was the most appropriate quantity to meet the requirements for the three servings of the tea ritual. He developed the small sachets, creating the brands *Thé Baro*, the tea of the *grin* (group of friends) and *Thé Imperial*.

After about six years of preparation, production began and in 1997, his tea had conquered the market. At the time, he had an advantage because the Chinese did not want to sell tea in sachets. They considered sachets too expensive, preferring to sell their tea in 25kg boxes (interview, Bamako, 2016). Emile's son advertised the small sachets on television: the commercial showing a small boy asking the vendor to give him tea in sachets rather than wrapped in newspaper because it was cleaner and better conserved the aroma. Several consumers recalled having watched this commercial.

Selling tea in sachets became a huge success, as people no longer wanted to buy lose tea. Achcar, the only one packaging tea in sachets himself, became one of the largest tea importers. His tea business employed 150 people. He also owned a subsidiary company, the SOFACI (Société du Faso pour le Commerce et l'industrie) which produced plastic containers and soaps in Bobo Dioulasso, Burkina Faso.

In the early 1990s, when Emile's son started the tea business, Mali imported just 700 tons per year; a few years later, in 1998, the tea imports had risen to between 7 and 10,500 tons (UN Comtrade 2021). Emile's son attributed this increase and the high level of green tea consumption to the use of sachets.

Thé Baro and *Imperial* sold very well until 2003 or 2004 after China had signed the agreement with the WTO, liberating the Chinese tea market and numerous other Malian traders began importing and selling tea first in 25g sachets, and then in printed cartons. He did the same (chapter 2). In 2016, Achcar still sold tea, but had ceased importing it because competition between tea importers made it no longer worth the effort. Emile's son concluded that the competition was 'unfair' because many tea importers employed informal approaches in their business dealings whereas he paid all customs and tax due. Laughing, he added, that he managed his company according to strict rules whereas the informal sector was much more powerful in importing tea. He still travels to China, but only in pursuit of his other product interests (interview, Bamako, 2016).

5.1.2 The Importer of *Thé Kangourou*

When we travelled on my assistant's motorbike, several times I saw the legend Capal above the entrance of a small supermarket. One day in late 2013, we stopped to investigate and on approaching the shop we were reassured to notice small posters at the entrance advertising *Thé Kangourou*. In front of the shop, sitting on a bench, was the owner of the supermarket Capal and of the company Société Oumar Negoce and the importer of *Thé Kangourou* (who also sold his brother's brand *Le Palmier*). We had previously seen cartons of *Kangourou* on the Grand Marché and *Le Palmier* I knew from my visit to Burkina Faso a year earlier. We sat beside him on his bench and he recounted his story whilst we were served tea by one of his employees. He had recently been to China and in Paris and had visited the food trade fair (SIAL) in Cologne, Germany.

This importer had already traded tea from SOMIEX. Following SOMIEX's dissolution, he worked with European partners, especially the Swiss company Jiman, which sold Chinese tea. He worked with various Chinese companies whose tea he sold before deciding to create his own tea brand around 2010. He learnt about the existence of Australian kangaroos during a visit to that country. He found them fascinating, so much so that he decided to include kangaroos in the design of his brand. It is an animal of forests, plains, savannahs, and woodlands which occurs only in Australia and Tasmania. He felt African consumers, unfamiliar with Australian wildlife as they generally are, would consider the animal exotic and surprising. He put his idea to his Chinese supplier, sending him images before they discussed which variation would be most impressive. He intends to continue his brand with its kangaroo image but should he start selling tea of another quality, he would simply modify the package colours.

His younger brother, living in Abidjan, the economic capital of Côte d'Ivoire, also created a tea brand, named *Le Palmier*; he has imported it since about 1998 and sells it to migrants from Mali, Mauritania, Niger, Burkina Faso, Côte d'Ivoire and Senegal. *Le Palmier* was registered with OAPI in 2007 by his company Palmier Trading.

The importer sells much of his tea wholesale to other traders as well as in his supermarket. He also imports other products from abroad such as coffee, pasta and rice, which he sells in his supermarket. However, his most recent project was to construct a pasta factory in a suburb of Bamako. Under the brand name *Pasta Roma,* he created a range of pasta products, which he registered a few years ago. He chose the name having worked with Italian companies for some 20 years. Whilst his pasta is made in Mali, the name inspires ideas of the original pasta and its association with Italy. He purchased the pasta machines in Italy – one of his brothers lives near Venice – and the grain (i.e. wheat) to make the flower is imported from Spain. He expressed pride in his ownership of a factory and production site. Apart from Achcar, he was the only tea importer who described himself as an entrepreneur, which he indeed was. On our departure, he gifted us a set of *Kangourou.*

5.1.3 The Importer of *Thé Sancho*

The importer's office and the company's supermarket are situated in the Immeuble Tandia. In 2013, it sold the company's three brands of Chinese green tea (*Touareg, Le Nord, Sancho*) and various other packaged products that the company imported. When we arrived, the importer received us in his office. He was wearing a well-designed, dark velvety suit and on his desk was a large flat screen computer, two mobile phones and other office accoutrements. Behind the desk was a collection of packaged products including *Sancho* tomato paste, the green teas *Sancho* and *Touareg*, sachets of *Thé Farako*, the black teas *Gold Bond, Akouna* and *Victoria, Akouna* tomato paste, *Thé Sava* and *Flecha* and two sachets of Chinese leaf tea and *Café Tropical.*

The company is a family-run enterprise of Soninke traders. The importer inherited the business from his father. Having completed secondary school, the importer began trading. His father first sold tea from the Farako plantation, and sugar and rice from SOMIEX. The importer recalled: 'This was tea of good quality. We were young but we tasted it. It was a 4011 [Chunmee] and consisted of small longish grains'. After SOMIEX closed down, in the 1990s, the importer opened an office at Dabanani and began selling tea such as *Thé Elephant.* However, the quality of the teas available was no longer considered acceptable as private traders began to import diverse teas disregarding their quality. The importer considered how he might bring the quality teas of the earlier times again to Mali.

His friends proposed asking from the Tuareg [actually Saharan traders] who had formerly brought tea to Mali from Morocco and Mauritania. He travelled with Aeroflot to Liberia where all foreign companies had representatives: 'There were Chinese, Taiwanese and Pakistani trading posts. And it was possible to buy goods tax-free in Liberia. Traders came from Burkina Faso, Senegal, Mauritania and Algeria to purchase goods' (interview, Bamako, 2013). He procured tea from the Chinese Amsua Trading company and sold between 50 and 80 other products (blankets, radios, slips, travel bags, thermos flasks) at the time. There, he learnt that tea came from China, and that he could visit the country (at first only Hong Kong).

He decided to travel to Hong Kong where he bought tea from a Hong Kong-based Chinese broker. He recalled:

> The first time I visited Hong Kong was in 1990. China was not yet open. But all the Chinese representatives and the trade agents of the Chinese factories were there at Hong Kong. So, we bought tea from China via Hong Kong … When you arrived, there were other Malians living with their Chinese wives. There were brokerage offices. When they saw an African, they came to talk to you, asking: what are you looking for. You reply you look for tea. There were many brokers: Malians, Nigerians, Pakistanis, Arabs, all of whom knew where the offices [of the Chinese representatives] were. If you arrive at the airport in Hong Kong, some of them [African brokers] wait for you there and they will show you where to go; they receive a commission [for their work]. We follow them, because this way we can be sure to find what we are looking for … And we knew that there is a place called Chungking Mansions, which once you are there, it's is over, you feel at home, you meet a brother, and even if they are from another nationality, they will help you. INTERVIEW, BAMAKO, 2013

Up until today, Chungking Mansions is a central meeting and shopping place for Africans doing business there or moving on to mainland China (Bertoncello and Bredeloup 2007; Mathews 2011).

In 2001, this importer specialised in foodstuffs. Soon after, as soon as China was open, he travelled there with a friend. This friend had a Chinese contact, who subsequently became his supplier, at Hangzhou. His first tea brand he called *Thé Touareg*, in hommage for his Tuareg [Saharan] friends who had advised him on how to import good Chinese tea. The people from northern Mali liked this tea. Following that, his second tea brand, *Le Nord*, was registered with OAPI in 2006; his most recent brand, in 2012, was *Thé Sancho*, a Super Chunmee, named after the cowboy Fernando Sancho.

These three company histories were established by families of traders who at first sold other products before beginning in the 1990s or 2000s to import tea. They are family-run businesses, benefitting from strong tea brands, but also selling, and in the first two cases, also producing other trade goods. The second and the third companies (importers of *Kangourou, Sancho*) are not just wholesalers, as are the companies discussed in the following section, but (except for *Thé Baro*) are retailers also: they have established supermarkets, selling their own products as well as those imported from other companies. The first and the second companies (importers of *Baro, Kangourou*) additionally became industrial entrepreneurs who produced brand-named products in Mali. The first company was at the beginning of the new packaging format of 25g, representing a major step in the history of green tea in Mali (chapter 2).

5.2 *Importers Representing Foreign Companies or Having a Portfolio of Products under One Brand Name*

The five companies have the exclusive right to sell products of a foreign company in Mali and some of them (*Niger, Lawal*) have additionally created portfolios of branded products but also have a strong focus on Chinese green tea. For example, the company that imports the green tea *Lawal*, also imports *Lawal* powdered milk, *Lawal* spaghetti, *Lawal* tomato paste and *Lawal* black tea in tea bags etc. These companies are all family enterprises, in which several brothers took over the wholesale companies of their fathers. The first three companies (importers of *Arawane, Rocki, Niger*) have the greatest diversification with some of the sons having created their own companies but most continue selling tea. In the other two companies (importers of *Lobo, Lawal*) the sons work closely together in one company in which Chinese green tea is an important product. The second and third companies work closely together with a Chinese company, the fifth company worked at the beginning closely with a Chinese company before continuing alone after five years. The first and the fourth companies worked on their own, their Chinese supplier never having had an office in Mali.

5.2.1 The Importer of *Thé Arawane*

Thé Arawane, named after a small town, a former important camel watering place on the trade route across the Sahara, a little north of Timbuktu. Available on the market for more than ten years, it is one of the successful Malian tea brands. Its importer is a son of the company's late founder, Madala Kouma (pronounced Chouma), of a Soninke family that had been traders for centuries. At first, the company supplied tea from SOMIEX, and following its dissolution, they sold tea imported by others such as the brands *Cheval* and *Elephant*. The father himself never drank Gunpowder tea and thus the son travelled to China to investigate importing Chunmee 4011 and to link with a good supplier. In 2006, the company registered its own tea brand which they called *Arawane*. In 2012, when the Super Chunmees became popular, other brands such as *Ayoune* and *Fouta* were added but the company continued to sell *Arawane* mainly in neighbouring countries such as Burkina Faso and Ghana, where it employs agents, in addition to those employed in the regional capitals of Mali. They always worked with the same Chinese supplier.

The company is one of the oldest private Malian companies, being created in the 1980s before the 1991 economic reforms. They import food products and soaps and are the official representative of several international companies such as Nestlé and Unilever. They have the exclusive right to sell *Maggi* cubes, *Calvé* mayonnaise, *Pharmapur* soap and *Lipton* tea in Mali. It is a big company whose premises are situated in Bamako's industrial zone.

The son with whom we spoke is responsible for purchasing and marketing the company's green tea brands. When we arrived at his company office, he told us that he had recently attended the big international trade fair at Düsseldorf, just after returning from a trip to China, to which country he is a frequent visitor. A large part of its tea is consumed within the company itself. In 2013, the entire company drank *Arawane* and during our visit we observed via the glass doors of the importer's office tea being offered to company employees all the time. During the interview tea was also served to us – it carried a handsome cap of froth – several times. The company's new brand is *Ayoune*.

5.2.2 The Importer of *Thé Rocki*

We visited this importer in his office in Bozola, a short distance from the Grand Marché. He had inherited the company from his father, who like his forefathers had been a trader in the town of Banamba, known as a town of traders. Whilst the father was born in Banamba, his family moved to Bamako, where all his own sons were born. They say they are Bamana, but most of the traders of Banamba are of Soninke origin (Girier 1996). The father established the company in Bamako around 1988, at a time when tea was still arriving in boxes of 10kg. At first, the father bought his tea from SOMIEX, subsequently buying *Thé Cheval* from the company of Punjabi, as many other tea traders did. After that, the company began working with Ye Wei, a Chinese supplier, the director of Le Mont Tea & Enterprises Co Ltd at Nouakchott. A Chinese broker visited Bamako to discuss the establishment of formal business arrangements and agree on a partnership that entailed the sale of the Chinese company's tea brand *Rhass al Khaima* in Bamako. The Chinese broker sent some tea cartons to test and having accepted the quality, they ordered more, paying for it by bank transfer. The Malian trader liked the brand image – a tent with tea drinkers on the package – but had no idea of the meaning of the name *Rhass al Khaima* (see chapter 6).

Until 2011, when *Gazelle* became more popular, he sold *Rhass al Khaima* but then, being inspired by the gazelle image, created his own tea brand, named *La Biche*, registered in 2011 but mainly sold in Guinea. Its package depicted a gazelle and sported colours resembling those of the brand *Gazelle*. In 2013, he created another brand, *Rocki*, a Super Chunmee, and in the same year, the Chinese owner registered *Rhass al Khaima* as a brand. In 2013, they were still working with the same Chinese company, which encouraged them to create their own tea brands and also proposed the package designs. For his own brands, the importer travelled to China to check the quality and conduct negotiations. In 2014, his company registered two more brands: *Tamanrasset* whose package had a design similar to that of *Golden*; and *Super Thé* with a design that is reminiscent of that of *Flecha*. The company also continued to purchase products – milk and crevettes, although no longer tea – from Punjabi. The company also sells spaghetti *Pastrani*, produced by a pasta factory in Senegal.

5.2.3 The Importers of *Thé Niger*

One of the sons of this Djokoramé family told us that in the mid-1970s their father moved from Nioro du Sahel near the Mauritanian border to Bamako, opening a boutique in Bamako's Ngolonina neighbourhood, selling SOMIEX tea. After SOMIEX closed, the father became a most successful tea trader, first travelling to the Atlantic coastal towns and bringing tea from there to Bamako. He went to Dakar, Abidjan, Lomé for his tea because at that time, China had yet to open its market although there were Chinese brokers located in these towns. At first, the family sold Zhejiang tea of the *Chameau* brand, and then they began to work with the broker of *Lucky Bird* tea, and, when China opened its market for private importers, they went directly to China themselves.

This son and his several brothers were all born in Bamako and in 2013, five or six of the brothers and their cousins, were involved in the tea business but also sold packaged foods. He said,

> We were born in the tea [business] (*nous sommes nées dans le thé*), and this means that what we are doing, is selling tea. If you search the internet for our company, you will see that most of what we sell is tea.
> INTERVIEW, BAMAKO, 2013

He is director of one of the family's tea companies which he created in 2006; it has 26 full-time employees. He has also recently visited China to check products at the Canton autumn trade fair and to meet tea sellers. With his older brother, he sells *Thé Niger* and *Oiseaux Blanc*; two younger brothers represent the Chinese brand *Hayat*, which in 2013 included two brands of tea and a portfolio of other products such as spaghetti, tomato paste, instant coffee and canned meat; one younger brother had just returned from China; another works in Congo, where he trades electronic gadgets. This family of importers has become one of the big players in the tea business, but have also diversified into other products.

5.2.4 The Importers of *Thé Lobo*

The Malian import-export company combines representing foreign brands such as *Santa Lucia* with importing Chinese green tea and packaged food products from other countries abroad. The owners are a family of Djokoramé traders from the Region of Kayes, now established in Bamako. One of the sons recalled his father creating the company in 1991, at first selling fabrics before specialising in food stuffs. They sold *Thé Cheval* from Punjabi – the Hong Kong Chinese trader of Indian origin – in the mid-1990s but this was not a success. The company's founder travelled to Europe regularly where he met his French and Chinese suppliers at the SIAL food trade fair held in that year in Paris. Since 1997, the company has participated in the international food fairs. They sell rice from India, sugar from the Netherlands, milk from France, instant coffee from Brazil, bottled beverages and other wholesale products. Their French supplier owns the brand *Mona* which includes tomato paste, powdered milk and sweetened condensed milk. They also import *Santa Lucia* Spaghetti from Italy. The company has a ten-year contract with both brands guaranteeing it the exclusive right to sell them in Mali.

In the early 2000s, the company founder began creating his own tea brands. In 2002, he launched his first tea, *Thé Lobo*. The other brands subsequently created by the company contain similar tea, differing only in regard to the package size of 25g, 100g, 200g etc. and include *Mona*, *Bonya*, *Serval*, *Tjernaba* and *Dawla*. We interviewed the father in 2007 at his small office in Dabanani. During the interview, his eldest son just booked a flight to China online and a customer arrived bearing a package of cash – payment for an order of 50 big cartons of sardines – which he handed to the father. The interview was brought to an end at that point so he could count the money and dedicate his energy to the order. The father himself never travelled to China instead sending his eldest son to supervise the ordering of the first containers of tea. Since then, the son has been to Hangzhou many times to visit the tea gardens in the mountains and the processing factories.

In 2004, they created the brand *Sahel*, which does not include tea but concentrated and sweetened milk *Sahel* and mayonnaise *Sahel*. The products were advertised on the company's first billboard, which was sited alongside the tarmac road in Bamako's Torokorobougou neighbourhood on the southern bank of the River Niger. Meanwhile another tea importer had registered *Thé Sahel* whose painted van we saw in August 2007. The company sells its products in all the Regions of Mali where they employ trade agents and in Côte d'Ivoire and Senegal. As we were informed by the sons, most of their trade agents are members of the family, others are close family friends or trusted business partners (interviews, Bamako, 2013, 2016). Their products and a brief history of the company are presented on their website. In 2016, as the company owns a dairy farm near Bamako, it sold fresh milk, named *Tjernaba*. Meanwhile the company relocated its offices to a glass-windowed larger premises and the founder's sons – all of whom have studied, the youngest in the USA – took over most of the company. Every noon, a company cook brings a large plate, stacked with food, which is consumed in the office and shared by the sons with all their employees. The plate is placed on a mat and a table cloth on the floor, around which everyone sits on tiny stools in an empty spot between piles of tea cartons and bags of rice.

5.2.5 The Importers of *Thé Lawal*

The company was created by three brothers whose parents came to Bamako from Nioro du Sahel. The parents lacked the money to send their children to school, only the youngest brother was educated in a Coranic school and the middle brother had taught himself how to read and write. The parents were Djokoramé, traders, and their sons learned from them the skills required for trading and managing a business. These brothers are good examples of people who can be successful in business despite lacking formal education. They grew up in the market and in 1991, they began as street vendors, selling small goods themselves and saving the proceeds until they had sufficient reserves of money to invest in their own trade goods. The sons of the importer of *Thé Lobo* were friends, their father had much more experience than they for he had travelled to Europe. They discussed their ideas about how to start up a business and travelled together to the trade fair at Cologne. The brothers established their company in the mid-1990s and later in that decade they began collaborating with the Chinese broker, Rudolf Shen. They discovered, contacted and invited him via the internet. They formulated with him an agreement to cooperate, drew up a contract and developed the *Canal* brand, selling at first poor quality *Canal* pens.

Then one day, inspired by a documentary screened on television, which highlighted how Malians had begun to import tea from China, they decided to sell tea. One of the brothers visited their Chinese partner in China to learn about importing tea. At that time, not many tea brands existed in Mali, and only *Cheval* and *Askia* were successfully selling. Their partner, Rudolph Shen arrived in Bamako and established a company named Canal Mali Sarl and registered *Thé Canal* in 2003 and the brothers began selling *Canal* products for him. By the end of 2003, the Djokoramé brothers had saved enough money to enable them to buy property in Daoudabougou and to formally register their company.[3] In 2004, by selling tea, they had amassed the largest amount of money in the company's history. They purchased more warehouses and planned to build a large new company building.

In 2004, Shen registered the *Canal* typeface, and in 2005 he registered it again under his personal name Shen Jian Liang; he also registered the tea brands *Toucan* and *Piano*, and *Capitaine* in 2009. The brothers sold his and their own tea brands. In 2005, the brothers began registering their own tea brands, named *Lawal, Africable, Arafat, Badia, Cana Punta* and *Thé Lah*; to these they added in 2007, *Zamzam* and *Sonikara*. In the same year, both the brothers and Rudolph Shen registered some of the brand names again for other products. There was *Lawal* spaghetti, tomato paste, powdered and condensed milk, black tea in sachets, cooking oil, mustard, and other *Lawal* products as well as *Canal* spaghetti, tomato paste, powdered and condensed milk, tooth paste, cooking oil and mayonnaise etc. (Figure 37).

In 2007, when we first met them, the brothers still occupied a small office near the Grand Marché. The company had 24 permanent employees and not only did they collaborate with Shen but also had arrangements with other foreign companies, which had been found using the internet. They procured mayonnaise from the USA and milk powder from the Netherlands. The managing brother regularly travelled to Europe, the USA and China to procure goods, to obtain inspiration from exploring novelties on the market and on trade fairs and to scrutinise the production of the tea they imported. He suggested this was vital as the Chinese tea traders often added colouring agents to their product in order to give it a stronger appearance. He also observed that upon starting to sell his own brands his supplier had sold him poor quality tea.

3 The creation of an enterprise requires several documents: a tax identification number (NIF); a tax document (*patente*) for the current year; and the document showing registration of the enterprise with the commercial court, an outline of the company's management and an outline of contract management (DLC) and payment of an annual registration fee of 500,000 francs CFA (about 760 Euro), according to the Direction nationale du commerce et de la concurrence (interview, Bamako, 2011).

The second eldest brother, who managed the company and travelled to China, was inspired and friendly and only 29 years old. All their company's products were displayed on his desk ready to be shown to potential customers. He gave me his plasticised business card and enjoyed telling me a story about a representative of the tax authority who on visiting the company premises wanted to talk to his boss; the official could not believe that he was the person in charge. As at the time a transit visa was required for travelling to China via France, he described how, on applying for a visa with the French embassy, he had to provide them with the details of his bank account and explain how much money he would be carrying. On his arrival in Paris, he was directed to a routine inspection, the operators of which wanted to inspect his wallet. On seeing the 300,000 USD in the wallet, they considered confiscating the money assuming it was the proceeds of sales of illicit drugs; they found it difficult to believe a young Malian could earn that amount of money from normal trading activities. He insisted on speaking with their superior who eventually accepted his explanations. At the time, it was not yet possible for him to obtain a credit card in Mali. Meanwhile he has a two-year visa for France and a five-year visa for the USA.

By 2007, they had built their office facilities and spacious warehouse in Ngolonina, near to Bamako's industrial zone. It is a large complex, entered via an iron gate, and enclosed within a concrete wall that displays painted images of both theirs and the brands of their Chinese partner. A lorry, sporting an image of the *Canal* brand and of a life size portrait of the actor employed to appear in the company's *Canal* TV commercial (chapter 3) was parked in the courtyard. All pervading in the building was the odour of fresh paint. The office where we conducted our second interview was on the first floor and on its desk were two calculators, desktop and laptop computers, empty boxes for packaging products, biscuits and other product samples. On the wall hung a large mirror with the *Canal* typeface. We were given presents: tea, mayonnaise, water and Coca Cola. The company maintained the office in the Grand Marché for some years, finally closing it around 2011.

We visited the brothers in their new office building more than once over several years. In 2013, the company courtyard was as busy as before but they had changed some of the murals on the wall and added images of new products. Present in the courtyard were a smaller truck and a horse. Two secretaries made us cups of *Lipton* black tea. The desk was laden with a huge flat screen television, large cans of tomato paste and other product samples: spaghetti from Dubai, Egypt and Turkey and *Pasta Masta* made in Ghana, *Arafat* canned sardines, condensed milk from China and several expensive Chinese green teas.

The manager welcomed us, whilst his secretary brought him a charcoal stove and shisha pipe – brought back from a journey – from which he smoked with evident delight. He was very friendly but also somewhat concerned about our visit. He informed us that the company had not renewed its partnership with their former Chinese supplier because the cooperation with them had become rather too complicated. They felt their partner had cheated them. By then they were procuring their green tea from a different Chinese supplier but tea was no longer their primary product. They were also importing from China a variety of other products and yet more from other countries as well. He had just ordered a large consignment of tomato paste from China, and some mayonnaise from France. They primarily imported various food items from Germany and France. He explained their profit margins were much less favourable than when they had been selling tea with their former Chinese partner but the arrangements with their new German partner were far more reliable and the German partner provided very good advice. Meanwhile, it was now the younger brother who travelled to China. Previously, they had imported coffee and mayonnaise from Brazil but this had become too expensive, so now they imported coffee from India. They had also created three companies in order to better manage their various products.

The brothers' success brought them admiration from many people because they were among the first Malians to rapidly make money importing tea. From having almost nothing, within a few years they had acquired property, warehouses, a lorry, and a new office building. The actor commissioned to feature in the *Thé Canal* commercial (chapter 3) acknowledged that he admired the quick advance of the importers, saying 'they have been courageous. I have admired them because of their courage. When I saw him [the middle brother], I thought to myself, I am much older than him, but his courage made me accept his offer. They have courage, they have a mission' (interview, Bamako, 2007). Others were more sceptical, in referring to the brothers having no knowledge of accounting, how to calculate income and expenses (interview, Bamako, 2007).

These five companies illustrate the variety of strategies that the tea importers have adopted. They do not only import Chinese green tea but also other products from various countries and continents, for some of which they had the exclusive right to sell them in Mali, and with others they created entire product portfolios under one brand name.

5.3 *Importers Focussing on Tea Only*

In common with each other, the five tea companies presented in this section, focus wholly or mainly on the green tea business and can be described as the biggest tea importers in Mali. The first importer discussed here is a member of a Djokoramé trading family that relocated to Bamako; one of the sons who created his own company, at first selling veterinary medicines before switching his focus to tea. The subsequent importers of Saharan origin are related to each other, the families have often intermarried and are part of, or related to the Ferjani and/or Mantalamane families whose forebears came from the Tuat in Algeria (chapter 1). Members of this big family live in Niamey, Tahoua, Timbuktu, Arawane, Gao, Nouakchott and further south in countries such as Guinea. The second importer had a large company selling a wide variety of products, including lorries. At a certain time, his company worked alongside a Chinese trader whose brand of tea he sold. Later, he created a tea company in Bamako, appropriating the brand. The third, fourth and fifth companies sold tea at first for the second importer before establishing their own companies and becoming influential independent tea traders.

5.3.1 The Importer of *Thé Hassane Ousmane*

We met this importer in 2007 and again in 2013. In 2007, he had a small office in a building at the Grand Marché. When we arrived, there was a young Chinese woman, his tea broker, at his computer designing posters for his tea. At first, he worked in his uncle's company, the main focus of which was fabrics but it was also involved in the tea trade. His experience here taught him how to recognise the type of tea people liked to drink. He travelled to Dubai and other countries in Asia to identify products for import, i.e. cloth, towels, and other items, as many did at the time. Then, for a few years, he worked with his cousin, portrayed earlier, who collaborated with the Chinese trader owning *Thé Canal*. In 2005, he decided to create his own company and to import tea in his own right. He has specialised in Chinese green tea since then but also continued to sell veterinary medicines to cattle farmers. As do other importers, he occasionally travels to China, Austria, France and Germany, but prefers remaining in Mali to travelling.

Thanks to the internet, he found his French-speaking Chinese broker, and subsequently, in 2005, travelled to China to negotiate. They created *Thé Hamza*, the name he suggested for his first tea brand and 'in twenty minutes it [the design] was put together; they [the Chinese] have all the images [in their computer] and then I took the tea to Mali' (interview, Bamako, 2007). His tea was not at first very popular but after he advertised it on radio, television and on some billboards, 'el hamdulillah, it started to sell. That is how it began'. He explained: 'Hamza was a big Muslim fighter, it is a name that sounds well in Malian ears'. He added that in the event of one brand not selling, he always has several others to fall back on: '*Hamza* is dead now; it was Gunpowder; it no longer sells; and then I sold *Bon Maman*, which went quite well. In Burkina Faso, it was even more popular [than in Mali]. … I also had *Mubarak*, which did not sell either. I really had to struggle hard' (interview, Bamako, 2013). He registered *Hamza* in 2005, and *Mubarak* in 2007. *Bon Maman* was owned by his Chinese supplier. *Hamza* and *Mubarak* came in four different qualities (see chapter 3). Although continuing to sell veterinary products, he has decided to focus on tea, rather than selling a portfolio of other products under the same brand name as other importers do. He then created *Hassane Ousmane*, a Chunmee, that at first proved too expensive for the wholesalers. Eventually, in the 2010s, when the Super Chunmees became popular, he managed to get a foot in the tea business with *Hassane Ousmane*. The tiger head in a medaillon became the company logo and was henceforth to be found on all his tea packages. It was the importers' tenacity that eventually led to his success.

5.3.2 The Importer of *Thé Gazelle*

The history of *Gazelle* begins with a Chinese trader who owned the tea named *Gazelle* and worked in Geneva for Hui Hong, a Chinese company. He met Amar Taleb, in Geneva, a merchant of Saharan origin in Niamey. A contract was agreed for Amar Taleb to sell his tea in Niger. Amar's company, the Société Amar Taleb, was a big import-export company that had existed for many years, importing lorries and cars from Europe and selling them in African countries. In the 1990s, the company had a branch in Guinea which represented the Japanese car manufacturer, Nissan. Some of my interview partners said, Amar Taleb was from Gao, others thought he was Algerian, married to a Malian woman. In 1970, he owned a seventeen-seat airplane and had a foundation, based in Geneva, La Fondation Amar Taleb, so we were informed by his former trade agent (interview, Bamako, 2011).

From 2003 onwards, Amar's contract with the Chinese trader, resulted in containers of *Gazelle* arriving at the port in Togo before being transported by lorries to Niamey, from where Amar Taleb sold the tea in Niger and Algeria. In 2003, wishing to sell *Gazelle* in Mali as well, he created the Société Amar Taleb in Bamako; the company sold only tea. He assigned two of his nephews to sell *Gazelle* in Bamako and they were successful. They also travelled to China to inspect the tea produced by their supplier. After some time, because working for their uncle failed to provide them with sufficient income, they decided to import their own tea brands. The pair each created his own company and their previous experience helped in the creation of *Thé Gaza Super* and *Thé Antilope No.1* (see below), their successful tea brands. They also continued to profit from the brand value of *Gazelle* (more on this brand history in chapter 8). In 2006, following the departure of his nephews from his employ, the merchant employed another young relative who sold *Gazelle* even more successfully. He also travelled to China, accumulated experience in the tea business and before long he had also decided to establish himself as an independent tea importer with the brands *Taoudeni* and *Achoura*. These became popular teas in the 2010s in Mali and beyond.

Meanwhile, in 2015, the merchant died in Niger, aged 92 years old. As he lived in Niger, we never met him, although in 2011, we did meet his trade agent in a small office on the road to Koulikoro. By 2013, however, there was a large new office building in the city centre where we spoke with the sales manager several times. At that time, the deceased importer's daughter was about to take over the tea business having inherited the company. She employed another member of her family as a marketing agent and continued to sell the very popular *Gazelle*. The sales manager's branch of the family had been traders for generations and came from Arawane to sell tea in Timbuktu, which they brought across the Sahara from Morocco on camels (interview, Bamako, 2011).

Alongside *Gazelle*, the daughter also created her own tea company with a new brand, named *Raissa*. From the outset, both companies worked with the same Chinese company which was supplying a stable quality product. The sales manager continued to visit the company's supplier in China to supervise the quality of their tea.

To enable the effective distribution of *Gazelle*, the company has trade agents both throughout Mali and abroad, in Gambia, Côte d'Ivoire, Senegal, Mauritania, Burkina Faso and Niger. Much of the success of *Gazelle* was due to the fact that it arrived on the scene exactly at the right time, in the right quality – good but not too expensive – and remained stable. The sales manager recalled:

> When *Gazelle* arrived in 2003 or 2004, there was not enough good quality tea on the Malian market. There was only Gunpowder, which was too strong, too black, too coarse. It was not at all fine. When *Gazelle* came, there was no better tea on the market. It had good taste, it had a nice aroma and handsome leaves that people liked a lot. ... So, you have to have good quality tea, and if you do not sell good quality, you will be quickly out of the market. INTERVIEW, BAMAKO, 2013

Within a short time, however, *Gazelle* faced competition as other good quality teas arrived in Mali. Hence, the sales manager explained: 'every tea will be sold, but you always have to have in mind that there is competition. If you do not take care, others will quickly take your place' (interview, Bamako, 2013). When the Super Chunmees came along, the company created the red *Gazelle* and the daughter of the late importer the new brand, *Raissa*. According to a newspaper article of 2010, the company owned by Amar Taleb's daughter, Mme Ben Baba Jamila Ferjani, annually imports 50,000 tons of tea, amounting to over 13 billion francs CFA in customs fees and providing employment for 6,000 people (Fall 2010). These figures might be exaggerations but they serve to foster the impression that a great deal of money can be made from tea.

The history of this company illustrates the value of connectivity, i.e. the pan-regional business networks operated by family members and friends who, coming from mobile working traditions, may be employed as trade agents. Previously, for generations they spent years based in a location, investing in property and social relationships there, before moving on to expand their portfolios. Thus, owning property did not prevent geographical mobility, especially in the Sahara (Scheele 2012a). The history of this family also illustrates how former cooperation can deteriorate into competition among and between family members when frictions develop. Over just a few years at least three new companies emerged out of the core business. Advantageous to them have been their apprenticeship, extensive trading networks, and their focus on tea alone. Other family members from time to time may have wanted to import tea as well but not all of them have been successful. From the same family but in the north of Mali, the importers of *Thé Tilimsi* have been in the tea trade with partial success for several years.

5.3.3 The Importers of *Gaza Super*

Whilst we were trying to track down the importer of *Thé Gaza Super* in 2011, we were directed to a neighbourhood near to the Grand Marché. *Gaza Super* employed a representative, a brother of the importer, but did not yet have an office in Bamako, so we were received in his house. We were invited to sit in the reception hall which was comfortably laid out with carpets and cushions. Several family members were already living in Bamako whereas the company headquarters remained in Mopti where their eldest brother resided. The representative told us that his large family – members of which were owners of Hotel Azalaye and Hotel Salam – was a branch of the extensive Mantalamane family that had previously resided in Arawane and Timbuktu (interview, Bamako, 2011).

After ceasing to work with the importer of *Gazelle*, the future importer of *Gaza Super* established his own tea brand and company in 2007. In 2016, we met another family member, acting as representative of the company in a small office near the Grand Marché. He had university education and in 2006 had written his thesis on the history of the tea trade in Bamako. He was also an enthusiastic footballer who had played in the renowned Bamako stadium and later for a Moroccan team whilst he continued his studies in that country.

After graduating he began to work in the tea business. Tea was what he always wanted to do. His father had been a tea trader and his grandfather had brought tea on camelback across the Sahara. The family sold tea before the French came to conquer Timbuktu, where his grandfather, Koutam, displayed his tea alongside rice and millet 'like a sand dune' on a mat in front of his house. At that time, tea was sold for 25 francs. The grandfather – and all the traders in Timbuktu at the time – procured their tea from Morocco, which country they also frequently visited (interview, Bamako, 2016).

The grandsons of Koutam were all born in Timbuktu and have Malian nationality. Some members of the family established themselves in Mopti to sell tea, and others in Bamako. The first representative recalled that the tea was first imported in wooden boxes of 20kg, then of 10kg, then of 5kg and finally arrived the 25g packages. First there were 25g sachets and then the 25g tea packages. They started with the brands *Gaza Super* and *Chameau Super*, then in 2011 came *Nuovo Gaza* and *Salam* (interview, Bamako, 2011). For *Super* the brand design was amended; the gazelle-like design was replaced with a caravan in sand dunes. *Koutam* was introduced, named in honour of their grandfather, and was followed by the brands *Zaine* and *Amar*. All their brands are registered; *Amar* by a branch company (Somia Ferdjani).

The representative in Bamako often travels to China but frequently their female Chinese broker, reciprocates with visits to Bamako, bringing commercial presents, amongst them a poster in Chinese depicting their tea packages, which is displayed on the wall of their Bamako office. All payments between them and their Chinese partner are conducted by bank transfer. The headquarters of the company is still in Mopti, where the elder brother works. They also have representatives in Gao, Kayes and other towns and countries such as Côte d'Ivoire, Burkina Faso, Mauritania, Guinea-Conakry and Senegal (interview, Bamako, 2016).

5.3.4 The Importers of *Thé Antilope No.1*

Whereas the importers of *Gaza Super* enjoyed increasing success with their tea brands – *Koutam* becoming one of the three most successful brands in 2016 – it was not all smooth for the importers of *Antilope No.1*. As did *Gaza*, *Antilope* had the image of a gazelle on a yellow package which resembled the brand design for *Gazelle*; both brands, as well as several others, thus benefited from the success of *Gazelle* (chapter 8). In 2011, we talked to a younger brother of the importer in Bamako in his office in the so-called tea road, Rue Gouraud. Easily recognisable by its yellow door, emblazoned of an antelope (Figure 46). He was very friendly, offering us glasses of *Antilope No.1* to drink as we discussed his story. He told us he held Algerian nationality and used to move between Algeria, Gao and Timbuktu and in the future planned to be in Bamako. My assistant suggested that his relocation to Bamako might have had some connection with the politics around the Accord d'Alger of 2006. This resulted from an aspiration to bring to an end the Tuareg rebellion and encouraged with the incentive of a financial contribution, young people to enter the Malian army, or to engage in business rather than political discords (see also Pezard and Shurkin 2015).

He also told us how he had transported cargo across the Sahara in trucks. He presented this as a risky activity, describing how if they were caught and arrested for any reason, perhaps simply because their truck appeared to be overloaded. One could be consigned to prison, without trial, effectively forever. 'And if someone offers you to get out [of prison], you will accept it whatever that may mean, even if it means [becoming a member of] Al Quaida'. The other tea importers dismissed the company as not being serious in the tea trade. Whatever the reason behind his plans, with his brothers, he created *Antilope No.1* in 2008, registering it in 2009. The company's headquarters were in Bamako as yet they did not employ representatives in other parts of the country. Traders wanting to purchase his tea had to visit his office in Bamako. The company only sold tea and advertised the brand with ORTM.

By early 2012, even before Mali's political crisis began, most Saharan tea importers had closed their offices and disappeared to northern Mali, or to neighbouring countries, fearing an escalation of the political situation in Bamako and being held responsible and persecuted. After the March 2012 coup, when my assistant dialled his mobile phone number, he answered by saying he could not reveal where he was. When we searched for him in December 2013, we found the door to his office locked. Neighbouring traders said that the office was empty and that Interpol had raided the premise, confiscated all tea, closed the shop and conducted a search for him as far as neighbouring Burkina Faso; it seems that he had become a member of the National Movement for the Liberation of Azawad (MNLA) and become involved in the rebellion.

When we discussed these events with the neighbours and I took photographs of the closed shop (Figure 46), more and more people gathered around us, offering their own interpretations of the situation. One suggested I contact Interpol which was still looking for him, another surmised that I wanted to contact the importer because I was white and wanted to support the rebellion; and, a third person theorised that I possibly merely wanted to buy tea. Yet another insinuated that he may have made 'his millions' with the money from the rebellion and from selling drugs. Other people 'knew' that he imported tea to launder money acquired from the sale of drugs and black-market cigarettes. We heard such accusations more than once. Following these events, we continued to see some of the small packages and above all the 250g packages of *Antilope No.1* available but the importer's name on the package had been

FIGURE 46 Locked office door of *Thé Antilope No.1*, Bamako, 2013

changed to Ets Ben Habib Side Boubacar and later to Ahmed et Frères, presumably relatives who continued selling his tea.

5.3.5 The Importer of *Thé Taoudeni*

In 2013, when we met him for the first time in his office in Bamako, he was only 34 years old. Born in northern Mali, he decided to become a tea trader and in 2016, was among the most successful tea importers in Mali. He recounted us his story in several interviews in 2013 and 2016. He attended to a technical high school in Bamako and following graduation from school in the late 1990s, he gained a fellowship from the Malian government to study in Algeria. On returning to Mali, he decided against pursuing a career in an office in favour of becoming a trader. His mother was an import-export trader but she had nothing to do with tea. Starting work with Amar Taleb, possibly a relative, he began to sell the *Gazelle* brand for him in Bamako. He travelled to China to supervise the quality of the tea and collaborated effectively with one of the tea wholesalers who successfully promoted *Gazelle*, thereby gaining valuable experience.

After some time, he decided to have his own tea brand. To be able to do this, he collaborated with a cousin or 'big brother' under whose name he intended to import his tea. The cousin, in 2007, ran an import-export company in Mopti, registered in his name, thus he possessed the relevant documents. Both men had money invested in the company. In 2009, the future importer of *Taoudeni* travelled to China for two months to search for a suitable quality of tea, visiting many tea factories before deciding upon a product possessing similar attributes to *Gazelle*. In the same year, he opened a branch office in Bamako and he registered the brand *Taoudeni*, a fine Chunmee, in the name of his cousin. As he knew this route well, he imported his tea to Mopti via Togo and Burkina Faso. Much of the tea was sold in Mopti and some other consignments went on to Bamako. Within a short while, he was able to sell several containers of tea each month. Over a period of five years, he had saved enough capital with which, morally supported by his cousin, to establish his own company, with headquarters in Mopti, and create a new tea brand in his own name.

In 2010, he again visited China to investigate potential teas for his new brand. Later, he claimed that because he manages all his company alone he no longer had the time to travel, adding: 'when you work well with the Chinese, then it is not even necessary to travel there all the time. You see, they work very well with me' (interview, Bamako, 2013). Being careful not to confuse wholesalers and consumers who might think the tea was pirated, he kept the cousin's name on the packages of *Taoudeni* and waited with the new brand that would bear his own name, until the Super Chunmees became popular. In 2013, was the moment to launch his new brand *Achoura*. He showed us the model design of the new tea brand. 'I made this with my supplier in China. I give him my ideas, we communicate about it, and he makes the design in his office. I have already ordered 5 containers of it, one for Mauritania, one for Niger and three for Mali'. His cousin now works for him, selling his tea in Nouakchott.

In 2013, he was selling at least a total of 20 containers of *Taoudeni* and *Achoura* each month and more were being sold in other countries where Malian migrants were living (chapter 1). In the year of the political crisis (2012), he was able to sell 40 containers per month simply because other importers were fearful, had closed their warehouses and ceased importing tea. The following year, his sales slumped back to pre-crisis levels. His success and volume of his sales attracted many Chinese brokers seeking cooperation but he rejected these advances because he felt he already had a good relationship with a trusted and reliable supplier.

He continued to sell a lot of *Thé Taoudeni* in Mopti, being transported by boats – which can carry up to 10 or 15 tons of tea – to the many small villages, which live from fishing, farming and cattle, in the densely populated inner Niger Delta. Near Mopti, he owns a large warehouse from which his lorries distribute the tea further afield to Gao, Kidal, Timbuktu, Segou and Niger. A call from his trade agent in Niger will instigate the sending of a lorry to Niamey.

Other lorries take tea to villages near the Mauritanian border and other lorries are sent to Ouagadougou, coming directly from Lomé.

Most of his tea (20 containers) is consumed in Mali. He maintains a network of trade agents in the regional capitals and even in the smaller towns, who hold the exclusive right to distribute his tea. He also employs representatives abroad in important towns of other countries: in Niger, Algeria, Burkina Faso, Mauritania, Senegal, Gambia, Equatorial Guinea, Pointe Noir in Congo-Brazzaville, Buaké in Côte d'Ivoire, and in Mozambique. Other employees load and unload the lorries and transport the tea to the warehouses. His agents and employees do not necessarily come from his extended family.

Selling so many containers, requires careful logistics management, for at any one time some containers have to be ordered, will be travelling aboard ships, some will be arriving at their various destinations and others will be in storage at a warehouse. To help manage his numerous transactions, his Chinese supplier provided him a computer programme which helps him monitor, making the entire process very transparent. It lists all his orders and the various steps in the supply chain, showing each container leaving the port of Shanghai and Ningbo and to where it is travelling, when it arrives (45 days later) and when payment for each order is due. Both he and his Chinese business partner update these details every day. Each container and container ship are ascribed a number making it possible to identify at any time the exact location of any container and where it is destined: Lomé or Nouakchott, for example. The programme also details the type of package in the container and provides a proforma invoice.

From the outset, he invested his profits in importing more tea; then investing in the purchase of warehousing and lorries. In order to be independent of transport companies, he purchased vehicles to transport his products from the West African ports of arrival and to distribute to his customers. He recalled having to pay expensive vehicle hire charges, even though tea cannot be considered a heavy cargo, and rent for warehousing at 300,000 francs CFA. In 2012, a bank offered him the opportunity to purchase a warehouse on credit, which he accepted, and subsequently, he has purchased others. He has acquired a warehouse of 35 × 25 m in Bamako and twelve warehouses in Mopti; these are 700 square metres by a hight of 9 metres; they store not only tea but also other products (interview, Bamako, 2016).

Then he considered investing in property as well as other product lines but emphasised the need for caution. Firstly, he said, he feels it is important to enlarge the main business. However, unlike other importers, who after achieving some success, begin thinking they immediately need a big office and to employ secretaries, lose day-to-day hands-on experience of what is happening in their business; this importer manages his business alone, enjoying maximum personal control. He waited for several years, until in 2016, he constructed a big new, glass-walled office building next to the Hotel de l'Amitié (Figure 47). But he said, he wants to maintain his connection to 'where it all started' by keeping his small office at the Grand Marché: 'in Mali we say, this is the source of your good luck, you should respect it and not abandon it' (interview, Bamako, 2016). He has only worked in the tea business for a good ten years and considers himself a newcomer to the trade but his is the only business that sells between 40 and 50 containers of tea each month. He claims, his Chinese supplier sends him the tea without even asking how he will pay it. They give him millions in credit, if he requires it, and do not even bother with preparing paper work. He said he has no time to travel, but wanted to meet his Chinese supplier in Paris during the latter's stop-over between the USA and Shanghai. From Paris the importer intends to travel to the Belgian border to purchase truck heads for Ghana where they would be transformed into lorries for transporting his tea.

In 2019, he announced on his website the sale of *Achoura* condensed milk, a brand that he had registered in 2018. He now also owns a chicken farm, having a fenced area of 5 hectares. He can sell 9,000 chicken each week. In 2016, he had told us that he invested in chicken-rearing just to see whether it would

FIGURE 47 Photograph of the new office building of the owner of *Achoura*, Bamako, 2016

work and to provide employment for Malians, but it seems that this is the beginning of his product diversification.

In summary, the stories of the five importers discussed above who are selling only, or mainly, tea illustrate that setting up of a well-working distribution network is key to successfully selling large quantities of tea. This has been particularly obvious in the last example (*Taoudeni*). The last three, selling *Gaza Super*, *Antilope* and *Taoudeni*, all of which share the same quality with *Gazelle*, a fine Chunmee 4011, had previously successfully sold *Gazelle* for the Nigerien importer of *Gazelle* but after a few years, established their own companies and became market competitors to *Gazelle*. Whereas the first (*Hassane Ousmane*) and the second importer (*Gazelle*) began with different products before focussing their energy on tea, the last three, after a few years of gaining experience, began right away with tea. After having sold Chunmee 4011 of good and stable quality, they all except the fourth (*Antilope*) established a Super Chunmee brand. The fifth importer (*Taoudeni*) has recently begun to enlarge his products offering a brand portfolio, as the importers of the previous section did. Different from them, however, he only began with the portfolio after having achieved the largest share in the tea market.

6 Other African and Chinese Tea Importers

The importers discussed so far are considered the most successful among tea importers. All have their headquarters in Bamako or Mopti. In this section I will briefly mention a few examples of tea importers who have their main office in Mali's north or abroad. A few of them have a trade agent in Bamako (*Azawad* and AAA). The expansion of the tea trade has also encouraged traders to extend the importation of tea to the coastal West and Central African countries. There are also a number of Chinese traders who attempt to establish themselves more or less successfully in the Malian tea market.

6.1 *African Importers with Headquarters in Northern Mali*

Imported by two brothers, one located in Niamey and Gao, the other based in Nouakchott, *Thé Azawad* was registered in 2004. The headquarters of the company, Société Alfatah, is in Gao. Its existence pre-dates the arrival of the 25g packages, when tea was sold from wooden boxes. It also sells many other products. *Thé Azawad* was established in the late 1990s, being sold at first only in Gao. In 2004 it was registered with OAPI and sold in Bamako. By 2013, the brothers had employed a trade agent in Bamako who received us in very friendly fashion in his office, gifting us an entire carton of *Thé Azawad* and some solid tea glasses adorned with the *Azawad* logo provided by his Chinese supplier. The trade agent, a *koroboro* or Songhay, represents the brother in Niamey but is unrelated to their family.

The tea brand AAA is named by the initials of its owner, Ahmed Abderahmane Abdi (chapter 2). He is one of the earliest importers of tea packages, his brand features prominently in the Malian tea market. The owner is a Malian of Saharan origin who began his career as a trader selling dates, moving between Algeria and Gao, and by about 1997 or 1998 had begun importing tea to Gao in paper cartons of 1kg, 500g and 250g. He was one of the first importers to sell good quality tea in carton boxes. In the mid-2000s, his product was the best high-quality tea available in Bamako, a Super Chunmee 41022 (interview, Bamako, 2013). Some say, he had a trade agent in Bamako, however, we have not been able to find him.

The importers of *Tilimsi* or *Tilemsi* (both variations of the name exist on their tea packages) are also Malians of Saharan origin and related to the importers portrayed in the previous section, trading between Gao in Mali, Algeria and Southern Morocco. They named their tea brand – depicting a herd of camels – after a valley, or hill near Gao. According to the package description, the importer is Ben Ahmed and on other packages Tilimsi Distribution Sarl.

The very mobile merchants of Saharan origin are quick to seize opportunities as they occur. Many settled in Nouakchott, the capital of Mauritania, importing tea through its port, at times when customs policies were more favourable than in Mali or Niger (Marfaing 2012). From 2003 onwards, an increase in registrations of tea brands by Saharan traders in Nouakchott can be read from the published details of BOPI (chapter 2). This reflects the general increase in consumption of tea and the rise and fall in customs fees. In 2006, the importer Nezaha registered the popular tea brand *Le Patron*, and the Guinean-Malian Ahid Ould Ahmed registered *Thé Diamant*. Both brands sold successfully in Bamako.

6.2 *Importers and Tea Wholesalers in Other African Countries*

Another brand selling well in Bamako was *Flecha*. Rambazo Moussa in Tahoua, Niger, sells *Flecha* – at first a Chunmee 4011 before becoming a Super Chunmee 41022 – for a Chinese importer. After some time, the *Flecha* brand was also sold by Senico Sarl in Dakar. However, there were no *Flecha* trade agents in the towns where *Flecha* has become as popular as it is in Mali. Traders said that the Chinese supplied *Flecha* to both Rambazo Moussa and Senico, however, others insisted that the quality of the *Flecha* from Niger was slightly better than that of Senico. As neither Rambazo Moussa nor Senico wanted to discuss it, not even briefly at the telephone, it was not possible to verify this. In 2013, we talked with Senico's trade agent in Bamako. Oddly, he insisted the interview was held in a quiet street rather than in a place where we might sit down. A few years later, in 2018 and 2019, my assistant informed me that their office in Bamako was established and the company was organising big advertising campaigns, including tombolas, large billboards and commercials on television. The imports from Senegal were clearly overtaking those of Niger where *Flecha* was not particularly advertised. Senico had an early appearance with tea in 1998, when they introduced one of the first private tea brands – *Thé Saddam La Force* – to the market (more on *Flecha*, chapter 8).

Another Senegalese importer in Dakar is Mamadou Diene, the owner of the popular brand *Al Baraka*, which exists in many varieties, some sold in tin boxes and also flavoured with jasmin. From 2016 onwards, tea brands were increasingly registered by importers, not only in Nouakchott but also Conakry, Abidjan, Accra, Douala, Libreville. Most wholesalers in Bobo Dioulasso, Burkina Faso, bought their tea from Malian importers (interviews, Bobo Dioulasso, 2012 and Bamako, 2013). Based in Abidjan, one brother of the importer of *Kangourou*, imports the tea brand *Le Palmier*, as outlined above. In Yaounde, I discovered several green tea brands in shops near the Marché Central. Among them were the Chinese brand *Chameau* and a brand called *Palais du Ciel* (in imitation of *Temple du Ciel*) as well as other seemingly pirated brands. Some brands were imported by a Cameroonian wholesaler who sold them and his own three brands in his shop in Yaounde. The seller (interview, Yaounde, 2014) explained that they distributed them to different retailers in Douala and Yaounde. They had learned of the green tea brands from Malian migrants in the country and then decided to create their own tea brands. One of the brands clearly reminds of the design of *Gazelle* and a second of *Flecha*.

6.3 *Chinese Importers in Mali*

After 1991, one of the first tea importers was Punjabi, the Hong Kong Chinese of Indian origin, who around 1994 or 1995 – shortly after the Malian of Lebanese origin had begun selling tea in 25g sachets – was first to sell tea in sachets that were placed in small cartons containing 25g of tea (chapter 2). He had his headquarters in Hong Kong, trading his tea to Mali, Senegal and other countries. Beginning with Gunpowder, he later added Chunmee. His brand was named *Cheval* and it came in several qualities, which he sold to tea wholesalers, some of whom eventually also became importers of tea. Malian importers admired Punjabi's impressive offices from which he sold a large variety of products: 'He was a multi-billionaire who made the Chinese factories work for him' (interview, Bamako, 2013). By the 2010s, *Thé Cheval* was rarely seen in Bamako's markets but other products of the *Cheval* brand, for example, condensed milk and tomato paste could be purchased. Further afield, in other countries, especially in Burkina Faso, *Thé Cheval* continued to be sold.

The other early Chinese companies were the state-owned business Zhejiang Highten which sold *Chameau* and *Temple du Ciel*, and Amsua Trading which sold *Lucky Bird* and *Amgro*. The former, earlier-mentioned tea broker of Chinese-Korean origin, sold the brands of Amsua Trading in West African countries before he moved to Cameroon and opened a Chinese restaurant (interview, Yaounde, 2014). He was an impressive character but strangely reluctant to say much about his business story when I met him twice at his restaurant in Yaounde.

As mentioned earlier, the company owned by Rudolph Shen, Canal Sarl, in Bamako sold *Thé Canal* in collaboration with a Djokormé trader. After having made a fortune with *Thé Canal*, he returned to China. The Chinese Wang Xiao Fang registered *Thé Askia* in 2004 and several other tea brands in the course of the following years, which were sold in cooperation with one of the big wholesalers outlined earlier. Other Chinese companies such as Wafa owned by Xu Xiaomei held the brands *Ramadane*, *Al Farouk* and *Jamell Sahara*, selling their tea through the same Malian wholesaler. The Chinese trader Xie Wen Shuai worked with the importer of *Ikathé*, and after their successful cooperation, he returned to China to plan new trading opportunities with Africa. However, Chinese tea brokering companies – owned by as many women as men – were few in number and not very successful unless closely workIng with Malian wholesalers or a Malian business partner. This was especially the case with the owner of *Thé Joli* who had difficulties selling tea on his own.

This chapter illustrated the close interlinking of economic actors in the tea value chain, departing from retailers in kiosks and small supermarkets, to wholesalers and, between them and the importers, the intermediary services of *coxeurs*. Each of these actors employs different skills to assert their place among many other emerging traders and brokers. This entails maintaining their business networks, exchanging and cooperating with other traders, accumulating market knowledge and they will also, in their particular node, try to influence the market with their inventive strategies. The way these traders interact gives the tea market its particular profile. Refusal to cooperate and ignorance of the working of the Malian tea market will soon provoke complications for their business. This has happened not only to Chinese traders but also to Malian newcomers in the trade. Being of Saharan origin is advantageous for becoming a tea trader but no guarantee for success.

Among these economic actors are some who have created their own job patiently learning, experimenting and saving capital, others learned through apprenticeship in a family business. Some of the wholesalers became importers bringing their own tea to Mali from China, thus becoming important actors in the tea trade, others begun their career right away with importing. Whilst Chinese traders operate in the tea business, in this sector, it is Malian merchants who have become dominant and among them especially those who are the descendants of old, well-established trading families (chapter 1). In their attempts to emulate the success of these traders, many 'new' entrants to the business have started importing tea from China. Among all these tea traders only about fifteen have been successful over the long term and among them, those who primarily focus on tea have come to dominate. The next chapter examines the strategies and distribution networks of these Malian importers and their collaboration with Chinese suppliers.

CHAPTER 5

Secrets of Success, Distribution Networks and Sino-Malian Collaboration

Tea became the green gold not only for China (Macfarlane and Macfarlane 2003) and the British (Ellis, Coulton and Mauder 2015; Sharma 2011) but since the 2000s, for many Malian merchants as well. This chapter sheds light on how Malian merchants achieved to become successful importers, how they manage knowledge, risk and capital, organise transport and their distribution networks, and what role trust plays in the cooperation between Malian and Chinese business partners. Essential for successful tea trade, as will be shown, is to understand what Malian merchants call the 'work of tea' which includes being aware of the leaf varieties available and the specificities of the tea trade, assessing risks, keeping track of things, being informed about customs formalities at the various ports and offering trust to trading partners. Trusting each other seems to be one of the most complicated issues in the collaboration between Chinese and African traders (see also Haugen 2017; Rubbers 2009).

1 Money, Knowledge, Risk and the Crisis on the Tea Market

Against the backdrop of the importers' trajectories (chapter 4), this section looks first at the conditions, the risks, the strategies and the prerequisites necessary to becoming a successful tea importer. These include possession of capital, experience, knowledge and intuition. Especially, knowledge and intuition are a requirement to fully appreciate the challenges posed by developing a popular brand of tea and avoid provoking a crisis on the market.

1.1 *Money, Risk and Knowledge in the Tea Trade*

Today, importing tea is no longer the preserve of the Djokoramé and Saharan traders; people from all social categories of the Malian society may become involved in this activity (chapter 1). Newcomers in the tea trade, however, will have to face many obstacles. There are the financial barriers to overcome, including the cost of the government annually renewable import licence,[1] the

1 The licence to import is obtained from the Direction nationale du commerce et de la concurrence in Bamako. It includes the application to import specific goods (*demande d'intention*),

 DOI:10.1163/9789004505698_007

brand registration valid for five years and sufficient capital indispensable to finance the purchase, transport and customs fees attached to at least the first container load of tea (chapters 3, 7–9). Additionally, experience in the tea business is required. One of the influential tea wholesalers replied to my question about the imperatives in ensuring success as a tea trader: 'To establish oneself in the tea business, you first of all have to understand what tea is about (*il faut connaître le thé*)'; another said: 'You have to know the market (*il faut connaître le marché*)'; and a third replied: 'You have to "live the market" to know (*on doit vivre le marché pour savoir*)' (interviews, Bamako, 2013). Reflecting on the successes of some merchants, one of the importers explained:

> Tea entails a lot of money. However, not everyone can sell tea. … It does not go without experience and knowledge of 'the work of tea'. … I can give you a brand that is even better than my tea, but it will not work with you … because you will realise that I have the people, I know where to put my tea; it is not an easy product, you have to fight for your place on the market (*il faut se battre sur le marché*) … because people have understood that it is possible to make so much money with tea, they all want to trade with tea. This goes on until they all have realised that their money is gone. But they do not want to drop the idea. They refuse. They do not want to abandon the tea trade because they think one day it will take off and they will regain all their expenses. This is crazy. They will never regain their money. It is simply impossible. INTERVIEW, BAMAKO, 2016

Importers have to gain experience in *té báara,* the 'work of tea', and understand it very well and they must accumulate their own capital during their training period (chapter 1). One of the aforementioned importers further explained that the investments made and the risks the newcomers were taking were considerable and were undertaken in a state of optimism and with the hope of extraordinary rewards:

> The amount of money involved in the tea trade persuades many to travel to China and import their own tea. But even if the quality is high, it will not be easy for smaller importers to sell their tea because they must master the complex 'work of tea', or all their money will be lost. INTERVIEW, BAMAKO, 2013

---

the proforma invoice, with the FOB (the purchasing value of the goods and packaging), the tax stamp of 1,500 francs CFA and the receipt of the certified cheque (interview, Bamako, 2011).

Many of the successful tea importers were concerned that so many traders only chased the money that might be earned from tea: 'All these people, they are only looking for money ... But me, I am not [only] looking for money. I take my tea trade seriously. It is not [primarily] the money, but tea is my work. If there is money, it is fine, too' (interview, Bamako, 2013). Another importer explained:

> When the newcomers are lucky, they can recover their investments, and only with much experience, they will be able to make profit. Only when an importer is able to sell five containers per month, you can say that the business is going well; when you sell more than fifteen containers, the business has really taken off. Most importers, however, do not get beyond selling one single container, and for that they take several months or even years, and only a few importers are able to keep their brands stable over many years. INTERVIEW, BAMAKO, 2013

The aforementioned importer added:

> There is a lot of money that can be made with tea, a lot, a lot, and you will think, I too will go to China and bring tea. You go to China, you bring tea, and you will see that it does not sell. Because you have to know the 'work of tea'. Tea can destroy your money quickly. You bring five containers and distribute them among the wholesalers. After one year, two years, people still do not want to drink it. Even if you give it to them for free, they do not want it. But if it goes well, it turns like a machine that produces. Perhaps out of twenty people who sell [import] tea only two or three master the 'work of tea'. They will remain on the market; the others will stop it sooner or later. INTERVIEW, BAMAKO, 2013

As the tea importers' short business stories (chapter 4) illustrated, most successful ones were the children of tea wholesalers. Many of these importers and wholesalers grew up with tea; they were introduced to the product by their tea trader parents through whom they received training, experience and knowledge working in their parents' shop. Several of them told me, all using the same phrase: *Nous sommes née dans le thé* (we are born in, or with, tea). One of them compared it with a first love, saying:

> Tea, I will always stay with tea, it is like a first girlfriend, you always remain attached to her; because the tea, after some time you find it out; tea, it is my life, like you make your studies [referring to me], you will continue with it, you cannot just forget about it. INTERVIEW, BAMAKO, 2013

Others began their training later, with an uncle or other relatives, following university studies; and still others acquired experience working alone as street vendors. or as *coxeurs*. They saved money until they could afford to rent a shop, become a retailer and thence, a wholesaler. They had to acquire their knowledge and experience through trial and error. People, whose parents had not been traders encountered the most difficulties understanding the 'work of tea', success at which was largely put down to possessing a feeling for the right quality and price, as well as having extensive trade networks 'inherited' from parents. Networks were a decisive factor in the success of traders able to sell tea in large quantities over a short period of time.

In combination with experience in the tea work and trade connections, education offers another advantage as to the management of the business. My findings suggest that Amselle's (1987) classification of entrepreneurs from the 1980s (chapter 1) is still valid to some extent. These days, most importers have studied economics, finance or accountancy at university, whilst a few others have not even attended school. They have taught themselves to use computers and read and write; and whilst they can count money, they may not necessarily be able to manage an accountancy system and thus they lack an overview of their finances. Although illiteracy among importers has become rare, my observations show that it does not prevent merchants from taking business travels to other continents and be successful importers.

Discussing the current market situation and dynamics with fellow traders and exchanging opinions and gossip is another important strategy. Lacking interest to engage with other traders deprives a person of information which might assist successful competition with other importers on the market. It is rewarding for importers to chat with wholesalers and ensure smooth cooperation with them. As mentioned earlier, wholesalers are influential. One of the importers explained that much of the success of a brand depended on the wholesalers:

> We [the importers] cannot sell the tea; we bring the tea. It is these sellers [wholesalers] over there [in the market] who can make your tea sell. He can make the money and the customers come. He can say, try this one, it is good, it is high quality. Due to this, you [the customer] take it with you, you try it, you see it is true, you come again, you pay; that is how it works.
> INTERVIEW, BAMAKO, 2013

Wholesalers are in the position to promote a brand or make it disappear in a corner. Wholesalers could join to purchase all of a brand but not sell it if they wish to boycott an importer.

It is also important to know what to discuss with whom. When we visited one of the bustling wholesale shops, the owner made a busy impression and was not willing to explain much to us. Lengthy explanations that our questions were only about understanding the history of the tea business did not fully reassure him. His reluctance may have been, on the one hand, due to the many important things that were going on in his boutique and, on the other, that traders, especially Chinese traders, often visited wholesale shops to conduct market research with the objective of establishing themselves in the Malian market. They also told various stories of the purpose of their visit. He simply could not be sure and decided it was wiser to evade explanations, especially since tea was such a complicated and risky business, with much at stake.

1.2 *The Importance of Stable Quality and the Crisis of the Tea Market*

The most difficult task for an importer was to win the trust of consumers, who always talked about quality, the concern being that the quality of the tea might not be consistent. One major tea importer explained: 'Even if the quality is not the best, as with *Taoudeni*, it must always remain the same' (interview, Bamako, 2013). To maintain consistent quality represents considerable challenge. As long as only a few tons of tea are imported, it is not a significant issue. But now with forty-foot containers carrying 20 tons of tea arriving every day, the question arises how are the Chinese suppliers able to satisfy demand, whilst also delivering consistent standards.

Additionally, the quality and taste differ between the various tea-producing regions, and from year to year. Region, soil-type, elevation, climate, harvest time, type of leaf, care during the processing and blending of leaves all influence the quality of the tea and due to the quantities required to meet the growing African demand are almost impossible to guarantee. One tea importer explained:

> The tea that comes from northern China is different from that of southern China. I do not know why, but therefore the quality of tea is never stable. Since the beginning, I get my tea from one factory and I import five containers per month. My supplier explains that sometimes they get the tea from this tea garden, sometimes from another, and that is the reason why the tea cannot always be the same. I noticed that sometimes their tea is good and sometimes not. When the demand is getting too high, they have to procure more tea from another tea garden where the taste of the tea is a bit different. It is the same with carrots and tomatoes. Some gardens are better for them than others. … In certain regions of China, in Zhejiang, the tea is better because the humidity is higher and there are mountains. That is what they tell me. It is a big factory, the third biggest in China and they are good, they have much capacity. INTERVIEW, BAMAKO, 2013

Growing popularity for specific tea brands poses problems not only for suppliers but also for the survival of the brand itself. As one importer explained, 'there is no merchandise in Mali with which you can make more profit than tea, but especially with tea, you can also lose all your money in one day'. He added:

> Sometimes, although it rarely happens, consumers like your tea so much, that suddenly, the demand is higher than the supply, then this means crisis for your brand. This happens especially when the wholesalers pay you before the tea arrived, because they want to secure their share of the delivery before the tea has arrived in your warehouse. In that case the tea brand has much value. The crisis announces itself when the Chinese suppliers cannot ship the supply quickly enough. … The success of your brand can provide some financial security but in such a case, it can also ruin you. INTERVIEW, BAMAKO, 2013

Another importer commented on the same problem:

> And when the importer transfers his money to his supplier in China, he waits [for the container], but nothing happens because the demand has outstripped their ability to deliver. The importer may wait for fifteen or twenty days before the supplier informs him as to when the tea may possibly arrive but then the money has already been transferred and the wholesalers have already paid you. If the container does not arrive, you are unable to supply the tea either because there is not enough of the tea [in China] or tea of a lower quality is delivered. INTERVIEW, BAMAKO, 2016

In the beginning, importers will make great efforts to raise interest in their brands, employing a range of publicity to attract consumers and by persuading wholesalers to promote them. But having raised the profile of the brand, once wholesalers and consumers have accepted it, everyone wants it: traders forward their money to you even though the product is sold out and new consignments have yet to be delivered. The tea is sold already before the container has arrived. It is a criterium for a successful tea brand when orders are placed by retailers and wholesalers in advance of deliveries, but this is also the moment when the exercise of shrewd discretion is necessary. In wanting to satisfy the demand, the importer (or the supplier) may be tempted to lower the quality because they do not want to lose customers and they want to make their profit; because the suppliers are not able to provide more tea in the required quality and have to procure additional tea from somewhere else, the taste of the tea will differ from which was expected.

The lifespan of a tea brand directly depends on its quality, as another tea importer explained:

> If the quality does not change, you can sell your brand for many years, but if the quality changes, this is not good. ... If you think, for example, why not take this other quality, it is a bit less expensive and you bring it, people will notice immediately that you changed the quality. They no longer buy it. It is always the same with the tea; it is a question of quality. INTERVIEW, BAMAKO, 2013

Hence, the success of a tea brand depends first of all on the consistency of its quality. However, it should not be too high, because high qualities are rather too expensive; neither should it be too low because poor quality tea will not satisfy consumers (chapter 2).

It becomes complicated when a tea brand begins to 'take off'. *Thé Canal* is an example, as the aforementioned importer explained:

> Once it takes off, the profit margin is amazing both for the importer and the wholesaler. The wholesaler notices that everybody [his customers] comes [to his shop] and wants to pay for the tea in advance. Demand quickly exceeds supply ... creating the moment of crisis. Traders can then impose their own price on the market. ... This does not happen with products the prices of which are regulated by the government such as for rice, sugar and milk. INTERVIEW, BAMAKO, 2013

The same importer explained the difference between these products:

> I could also sell rice or sugar but it is better to concentrate on something that you really master well. Only then it is not easy for someone else to compete with you because you have a vision of how to do it. When I began, I only supplied the Mopti region, but now I supply the entire Mande World, and even beyond, to Gabon and Congo. ... One should stay with one thing, and not sell whatever comes your way. You never know whether you can continue to make money with that. If you take rice, it is politicised, if you take sugar, politics are in there too. Today, they [the politicians] support it and you sell it, but later on, you cannot know whether they still like you ... and if you look in what they [the other importers] invest, the money they have as profit, you can still invest it in something useful ... [Many of them] immediately think they need to have a large office, a secretary and other employees that they do not have to do the work, but it is better to do these

> jobs yourself, in order to keep yourself informed about how your business is developing. INTERVIEW, BAMAKO, 2016

Another example for the tea crisis issue is provided by the *Flecha* brand, which is owned by a Chinese trader who arranged its sale through a wholesaler based in Niger and another based in Senegal. One importer remarked:

> *Flecha*, too, it is a good tea, it sells well, but what does it do? It constantly creates crises on the market. The people are asking for more *Flecha*. But now there are many people who have put the same quality as *Flecha*, and with them it does not sell because they have no idea how the market works, and if your tea is blocked on the market, you are finished, and you have to lower the price. INTERVIEW, BAMAKO, 2016

Then he continued to explain how the crisis was created:

> *Flecha* is of good quality, and if you tell me that you import more than two containers per month of *Flecha* then you are lying, which means that this cannot be the same good quality. If you work with a good factory in China, they will tell you right away how much they can produce. … The tea needs time to grow, and to be processed.

The quantity a company can produce is mentioned on their website. He continued:

> As tea is a product that is in high demand in Mali, and you need ten containers per month, if you don't bring them, people will break your doors, they come even if the tea has not yet arrived at the sea port. This encourages people [wholesalers] to travel to China themselves. This person [who imports *Flecha* in Niger] knows the business and the tea work, he is serious in his dealings. Obviously, he thinks about the consumers. He imports one container or so, but he does not import more. But then there are traders [he refers to a second company selling *Flecha* from Dakar] who take some of it to Mali and other places. … But as you only have a small quantity, yet people want more of your tea, one day you [decide to] import three or four containers, and then you are obliged to lie. The profit stays with you for a certain time. Then other traders [the copiers of the brand] go to China, they want to get good quality like that but they have taken bad quality, others have taken medium quality but it is not the same as the *Flecha* quality.

To continue building up your brand and to keep it alive, it is important to know how the tea market is working. The same importer explained that it is not just the advertising and quality that ensures a tea sells:

> I can sell ten containers of *Flecha* in a month, but you cannot … you can only sell 1 or 2 containers. … Tea is not a product that you can put on the market and expect to sell easily. You need a lot of good luck with tea, and you can make many errors. … There are many teas, like *Thé Paradis*, for example, [that did not sell and] there are many traders whose tea remains in their warehouses. They can no longer sell it. *Gazelle et ses petites*, at one moment it went well, but it quickly ended. INTERVIEW, BAMAKO, 2013

Tea brands have a dynamic that the importers have to tame. They want their product to sell and see it survive in the marketplace for a long time. To succeed in this, price and quality must match, and consistency in quality must be maintained. The importers' task is to control the demand, be aware how much the supplier can deliver and keep the quality consistent, to avoid creating a crisis, accomplished by importing a tea that is not of too high quality and may be sold for 100 francs CFA, whilst providing sufficient profits for the various traders and the importers themselves. An importer has to be aware of the quality consumers want and how much traders are prepared to pay for it. The aforementioned importer suggested that the Chinese supplier might have to work with several tea gardens and plantations and several factories, in order to be able to provide a large quantity of a popular tea, and jokingly added: 'this means it can be as much as half of what China can produce' (interview, Bamako, 2016).

Importers were aware that green tea was also being produced in other countries but they suggested that all green tea imported into Mali came from China. One importer stated about green tea produced in Sri Lanka: 'this is not interesting for us [the importers]. The only soil that makes good green tea is in China, and even there it is only made in certain provinces' (interview, Bamako, 2013). Thus, turning to another production country would not solve the crisis issue.

A tea crisis does not mean a lack of tea in the country, but rather perhaps a lack of 'good' or popular tea, meanwhile plenty of less desirable tea would languish unsold in warehouses. Importers mentioned three means of coping with such crises: firstly, gradually raising prices until wholesalers reduced the quantity of tea they purchased. They could, for example, gradually raise the price for a *colis* to 75,000 francs CFA, if they increased the price further, a single package would be more than 100 francs CFA and consumers would no longer buy it (as one importer had observed about *Simida* in 2016) (chapter 3). A second strategy was to remove the product from the market for a while and then rebrand it as a more expensive product. Thirdly, the product could be sold in lower quality. This approach was considered short-sighted by many importers and wholesalers, because it provided some quick money but, as consumers would notice the change and cease buying the tea, 'kill' the brand and undermine its value (Röschenthaler 2020b). This is what was meant when importers and consumers said 'they pirated their own tea'.

When a brand 'takes off' it may fall victim to piracy, especially so if demand exceeds supply. Rival importers may then 'jump onto the hype' around the brand. Obviously, this can easily ruin a brand. Should importers recognise their brand has been pirated, if it is registered, they can order to confiscate the pirated products and sue the pirate. The victimised importers can also alert consumers via the media that they should make efforts to identify and purchase the original product and also explain to their friends that the pirated packages containing lower quality was not the importers' fault. Copying brands only became an issue once tea brands had been developed. Branding obviously changed people's perspectives of tea (chapters 7–9). In addition to managing brand popularity, other considerations such as choosing the arrival port, having effective distribution networks and knowledge about China's tea production also played a role.

2 Ports, Market Networks and Tea Distribution

In China tea production is fragmented. Most of the green tea is produced in family tea gardens and small plantations in various provinces of eastern China. There the tea leaves are harvested, rolled, roasted and dried before being rapidly transported to the processing factories, usually located nearby. They are then conveyed to other factories, often located nearer to the coast, in which the tea leaves are sorted, packaged and filled in shipping containers.

Here, the brand design is created (chapter 6), the printing of the cartons and the packaging are carried out. All this is done in China where the cost of the process is much cheaper than it would be in Mali. The factory orders the printed cartons from another supplier who delivers them ready to be unfolded and filled. Small factories package the product manually with teams of three: one person weighs the leaves and fills the sachet, a second seals the sachet, placing it in a carton, the third closes and seals the carton with the cellophane overwraps and bundles the 25g packages into sets of ten before packing them in a 5kg carton. Other factories possess huge machines which weigh the tea, fill and seal the tea packages in sets of ten, pack them in cartons which are bundled in *colis* automatically. Whether a package is filled by machines, or by hand can be detected from the type of sachet. Machines can, for example, only handle plastic and paper sachets, not silver papers. *Gazelle, Taoudeni, Achoura, Hassane Ousmane* and *Koutam*, among others, were all packaged automatically. I have seen two tea factories in Zhejiang which packaged the tea manually (Figure 48) and several tea importers showed me on their computers images of gigantic automatic processing and packing machines in Chinese factories. The importer of *Hassane Ousmane* remarked not without admiration: 'That is how China developed itself' (interview, Bamako, 2016).

An entire supply industry exists in China for the production of packaging materials: folding cartons, sachets of plastic, paper, or silver, cellophane overwraps, glue, plastic cords to bundle the cartons, which are ordered from specialised Chinese manufacturers. Other factories do the printing of the cartons. The supplier is responsible for bringing it all together: materials, the printed cartons, packaging and the provision of export documents, the container and finally the transportation to the Chinese port. Many of these factories are nearer to the ports in China from where the tea leaves for a West African port.

2.1 *Choosing a Port for the Arrival of Cargo*

The 'work of tea' also includes the acquisition of knowledge about the various ports and the customs formalities. Tea is mostly shipped to West Africa

FIGURE 48 Chinese workers packaging tea for the Malian market, Zhejiang, 2014

from Shanghai and Ningbo, and some is sent from the port of Hong Kong. The large containerships can arrive at a West African port within 45 days. Tea for landlocked Mali may arrive variously at Lomé, Tema, Abidjan, Dakar or Nouakchott. The choice of port selected by an importer for their cargo depends on several issues: the formalities involved, customs, and transport fees play a role as does the port's proximity to that part of Mali or another country where the tea is to be sold. Most importers tested several ports, choosing those that suited their needs best.

The decision as to which port to choose requires an understanding of the customs formalities and transport costs, which differ slightly between the various countries. We asked several major Malian importers which ports they used; some shipped tea to several ports: Dakar was named five times, Lomé four, Abidjan three times, and Tema once. One importer, for example, explained that they tried to diversify their containers to Dakar, Abidjan, and Lomé to avoid them all arriving at the same port, in case of crisis in that country. At the port, haulage enterprises may be hired to transport the tea to Bamako, or other destinations. Only a few importers were able to use their own vehicles. From Dakar, importers can take advantage of the railway connection with Bamako, but from the other ports, lorries are the only option. Abidjan is the nearest port to Bamako, but importers were hesitant to use it because of the civil war (2002–2007) and the Ivory Coast's recurrent political instabilities. Lomé was favoured because of its large and safe port that became a free trade zone in 1968, resulting in smuggling products to adjacent countries with less favourable import taxes (Axelsson 2012: 51–69). The import taxes at the ports of Abidjan, Dakar and Nouakchott were higher but lorry transport costs were lower. The customs fees depend on the type, quantity and uniformity of goods, the transport costs on the distance and the road conditions. Ultimately, the overall costs from all the various ports are about the same.

After a lorry has arrived in Mali with its consignment of tea cartons, they travel directly to the importers' warehouses, most of which are large enough for the content of several shipping containers. From there, the tea is distributed to the wholesalers around the country, and to adjacent countries. If an importer intends to sell an entire container in a different country, the container is sent directly from the port to this country rather than via Mali. Because of customs fees, containers ordered by an individual importer are always declared separately according to their final destination. The major merchants import tea from China to be sold in several West and Central African countries and thus arrange for the tea to arrive at an appropriately located port: For example, tea that is to be sold in Côte d'Ivoire, arrives at Abidjan, if being sold in Niger, it will arrive in Lomé and if in Burkina Faso, whilst it will also arrive at Lomé, it will be sent to its destination separately; tea sold in Guinea-Conakry will arrive in Dakar and be transported by lorry to north-east Guinea, where most consumers are to be found; finally, cargo destined for Gabon and Congo-Brazzaville will be delivered to the ports of Libreville and Pointe Noire.

2.2 *Access to Market Networks*

It is also important to sustain an effective distribution network. This begins with connecting to the right wholesalers who appreciate the product and can influence the distribution of tea brands to retailers and kiosks (the *butiki koroboro* and *súraka*) in the city and to traders from other parts of the country and abroad.

Some importers may purchase tea just for consumption in their own company, as did at first the importer of *Thé Arawane*; others may sell their tea to the public through their own supermarket, as did the importers of *Niger* and *Kangourou*. As it may take a while to consume or sell an entire container of tea in that way, importers intending to grow their business will need to distribute their product more widely. They will not only send their tea brands to wholesalers in the city, as explained earlier, but also to other Regions in Mali. This will require to appoint company representatives or trade agents located in these places. All the major importers who successfully sell several containers each month have such trade agents and warehouses located at least in some of Mali's various Regions. These trade agents will receive a salary and housing and be responsible for supervising the warehouse and the distribution of the product to the local wholesalers (interview, Bamako, 2013). Wholesalers may themselves become representatives of a tea brand in exchange for the exclusive right to sell the tea.

The agency of Malian importers does not end at the country's border. Many of the more popular tea brands in Burkina Faso or Ghana belong to Malian importers and brands such as *Gazelle*, *Taoudeni*, *Flecha*, *Arawane*, *Azawad*, *Lobo*, or *Achoura* are sold in these countries and even as far afield as Cameroon, Congo-Brazzaville and Mozambique. To build their distribution network, importers require considerable capital and depend on reliable personnel. One importer explained that wherever he sells tea, he has appointed his own trade agents, even in Congo-Brazzaville: 'I have trade agents everywhere. All of them are Malians. I have sent these people to these places and provide them with housing and salaries' (interview, Bamako, 2016).

The main advantage conferred in managing a large distribution network through reliable trade agents is being better able to control what happens with one's brands. More piracy can be observed where there are no trade agents than in those places where they operate (interviews, Bamako, 2013).

The representatives will know the amount of tea of a certain brand they have received from the importer and may thus be able to detect whether there are brand pirates at work in the Region, seeking to profit from the brands' popularity. Most of the importers' tea has to pass through the hands of these trade agents. In case they notice suspect tea packages, they will question vendors as to its origin.

Just as Malian importers operate networks extending into neighbouring countries, importers from northern Mali, Mauritania, Senegal, or Niger may manage their own trade networks which extend into Mali, especially Bamako. Importers headquartered in another Malian city, for example in Mopti, or Gao, may have a representative distributing tea in Bamako. Here again, the efforts of the trade agents contribute to a tea brand's popularity in any particular region. Often these trade agents are from the importers' extended family, but may also be recruited from among reliable family friends, or business partners. Two tea importers may also share a trade agent (interview, Bamako, 2013).

Where a tea importer has no representative, local traders will procure tea from the nearest representative or travel to the importers' headquarters. In 2012, I have interviewed traders who regularly travel from Bobo Dioulasso to Bamako for certain tea brands. An advantage of this is that it presents the opportunity to purchase also tea brands of other importers in Bamako. A further advantage is that they might negotiate a lower price for the tea than may be obtainable from a trade agent although they of course will need to add their travel costs to the price.

Access to market networks presented a challenge for Chinese importers in Mali. They could not easily sell their tea because they first needed to build up their own networks and secondly because consumers associated the idea of 'good tea' with traders from Mali's north, rather than with Chinese vendors. As mentioned earlier, Chinese traders were successful with their methods of market research and sales of cheap products in other sectors, such as household goods (see Röschenthaler 2016, for Cameroon), but in trading tea they had difficulties competing with Malian traders. In the tea business their strategy did not work. Chinese traders were obliged to pass their brands to Malian wholesalers who, if the quality of the tea was acceptable, would operate the business for them because only they had the necessary distribution networks, without which it was impossible to sell larger quantities of tea. Through cooperation with those Malian wholesalers, prepared to work with them, some Chinese importers became quite influential – but only some and only for a few years. These wholesalers first needed to instruct the Chinese traders what quality Malians wanted to drink. In this way, importers and wholesalers exerted considerable influence on the quality of tea on the Malian market.

3 Collaboration between African Importers and Chinese Tea Suppliers

Collaboration between Malian and Chinese traders took place on several levels. They had to agree upon the tea quality, establish partnerships, find some mutual comprehension and trust to be able to get along and trade with each other.

All nineteen Malian tea importers we interviewed have travelled to China, most several times; many told me they travel there at least every year to negotiate directly with their Chinese suppliers. Some of them travel frequently because they also import other packaged products from China. These importers also travel to other Asian countries, to Europe and to the Americas; indeed, when we visited them, many importers said: 'Oh, I have just returned from China two weeks ago', or 'I just came back from a trade fair in Europe yesterday'. The traders travel using their own money, visit tea plantations and factories and return home with tea samples to select the ones they want to order. Some expressed admiration for China's big cities, their fly-overs, high-rise buildings and their public transport system. Accompanied by their suppliers' brokers, they travelled by car to plantations, factories and ports. Some enjoyed travelling, some not. One of them explained that he preferred to avoid travelling and only does so once every three or four years, if possible. He issues his orders and pays for them online and by phone. 'I don't like travelling', he said, 'China can be very complicated … and there are places where they have not seen someone black like me. … The distances are vast and if you are there during festival period, you cannot purchase a ticket for any train because everyone is travelling' (interview, Bamako, 2013).

One female importer related us details about her first journey to China. This was the occasion she ordered her first container of tea and realised that importers met tea vendors at trade fairs in China:

> These trade fairs are the meeting places of all the entrepreneurs. There you get the contacts; all tea agencies are there; all Chinese tea brokers go to these trade fairs to present their tea. Importers pick up the contact numbers of all the suppliers. These Chinese will call you. Even if you do not want to buy anything from them, they invite you to come to their factory. … They will come and pick you up at the airport, they lodge you, give you food, pay your hotel, until you depart … They tell you the kilo price of tea in dollars. It is expensive but it is the best quality. And you buy it with packaging, transport costs by ship and from the port to Bamako, and the two customs fees. INTERVIEW, BAMAKO, 2013

She also explained how she insisted on checking the quality of the tea she purchased.

> The first time, they placed the tea in the container in front of my eyes and I left only after they had finished with that. They placed it in the container in Ningbo from where it went to Dakar. They also tell you the date the container will leave China and when it will arrive at Dakar. This is … 45 days. They give you the documents, which you will hand to the transport agent. He brings the cargo through the two customs points and delivers it to your warehouse. You have to pay for all this, which is very expensive. I had containers that came via Dakar and other containers that came from Ghana. INTERVIEW, BAMAKO, 2013

She added that at first, she worked alongside a translator whom she knew from the Malian community in China. Another importer explained that 'we who know the region, we can go there on our own, but those who are new in the tea business, they cannot take the risk to go there without any knowledge of French, English or Chinese (interview, Bamako, 2013).

The aforementioned importer met her supplier at the Canton Trade Fair, other importers found their Chinese partners on the internet, had recommendations and contact details from friends, met them at European or other Chinese trade fairs, or through the visit of a Chinese broker to their office. For example, one of the Djokoramé traders made contact with his Chinese supplier over the internet and subsequently, the Chinese broker visited him in Mali. They agreed upon cooperation and signed a contract that defined how much each of them would receive of the profit they made. Then the Djokoramé trader sold the Chinese broker's tea brand for a year, before importing his own brand-named teas with his partner's assistance. Another Malian importer met his Chinese partner at a trade fair in Paris, and subsequently, his son visited the supplier in China to establish the partnership. The son also visited several other Chinese factories to create further brand-named teas that they import to Mali.

A friend supplied another importer with the contact details of his supplier. He telephoned him and from then they began to work together. He explained:

> I have to trust him, when I send him my money. And he has to trust me and give me ten days to send the money. We have worked together for more than ten years now, and most of the time, we have no problems. If the quality does not remain consistent, you also have to understand, that in different seasons, it can be different'. INTERVIEW, BAMAKO, 2013

As part of a strategy to create trust, he regularly visits his supplier near Hangzhou, in China. Whilst in China, at first, he travelled accompanied by a Chinese-speaking Malian intermediary, but he added that these intermediaries can also create problems by mistrusting the Chinese suppliers. Hence, 'more important than the language are trust and money'. When he intends to travel, he phones his Chinese broker to give him his flight number and arrange to be picked up from the airport on arrival, make his hotel reservation, convey him to the hotel and then to the factory (interview, Bamako, 2013).

Once the importers have established contact with their supplier, an African intermediary is no longer required. They communicate directly because in all the tea factories work English- and French-speaking freelance brokers who organise the journey of foreign merchants in China (Röschenthaler 2021). In addition to direct interaction when in China, the Malian importers can negotiate over the phone with them. Later, the brokers will also visit the Malian importer in Bamako, or wherever he works. Frequently, these brokers will not only visit their trading partners but also other traders to whom they propose their tea. One importer explained: 'even this Friday, a Chinese broker from Hangzhou in Zhejiang was here; some of them come regularly, but we also go there to do our own research. We take a close look at each factory to see what it can offer. This is the basis on which we discuss; we check the different qualities, and if we agree [on the tea quality and price], we discuss the conditions, and how the tea will be paid for, and then we can start working' (interview, Bamako, 2013).

The idea of working (*travailler*), as mentioned earlier, was an important local concept in our conversations with tea importers. For example, one importer explained that they chose one of their suppliers after having collected tea samples from several factories in China:

> When you have the choice [of samples] you will know what [tea] exactly you are looking for. Over there [in China] you conduct your own research to find your tea supplier. … You will work with him, and if he works well, then you establish confidence in him and you will remain with him as your partner. INTERVIEW, BAMAKO, 2013

He continued:

> These Chinese will facilitate everything for you. You just go there to check the quality you want and they will organise the rest for you … They can also organise the transport, the customs, depending on which port you prefer. And all depends on which kind of contract you have signed with

> them. They do all this because they want to keep their customers. When the product arrives in Dakar, for example, you go there with your supplier, and either you or your supplier brings it to Bamako.

He added that he had worked with the same Chinese company and experienced few problems since the late 1990s when he began importing tea. Even though this company was a bit pricey, his Chinese partners worked well and were reliable. A competent supplier does not risk losing good customers. Other suppliers might dispatch good quality tea at first but then gradually lower it. Malian tea business newcomers easily fell prey to this behaviour, desirous of hastily emulating the successful traders, they find an unreliable supplier. This importer also asserted that it made little difference whether a Malian importer had a legally binding contract with the supplier, cooperative working would either be successful or not but the outcome of legal action in the event of a breach of contract by someone working in China was rather uncertain.

All Malian tea traders work with Chinese brokers to purchase their cargos of tea from Chinese suppliers. The only question is at which point on the tea trail – in China or Mali – the product changes hands. Some Malian importers work with a Chinese factory directly from which they receive their tea and with whom they create their tea brands, selling the tea in Bamako. Other Malians order their tea from a Chinese trading company; these companies procure the tea from a Chinese factory and convey it to their Malian customer and brand owner. Some Malians establish their own tea brands whilst also acting as the representative of their Chinese supplier or another Chinese trading company in China for whom they sell tea on the Malian market. Other importers cooperate with a Chinese trader who owns a company in Bamako, selling both their own tea and the brands belonging to their Chinese partner. Some initially sell a tea brand owned by a Chinese partner and after a few years, having learnt the 'work of tea' go on to establish their own brands.

Cooperation between Chinese suppliers and Malian importers was sometimes instigated when Chinese traders visited Mali looking for partners to sell tea for them. They agreed an arrangement whereby the Chinese trader imported the tea and his Malian partner handled the product because he was able to sell in Mali more effectively. The partners shared the profits. Some Chinese brokers have attempted to sell tea in Bamako themselves but convinced that Africans have little money, they offered them cheap tea. Whilst this strategy seemingly worked in the late 1990s, when few good teas were on the market, from the mid-2000s onwards, as explained in chapter 2, cheap tea no longer sold.

As my research into the Malian tea market reveals, in all the years the brands of about six Chinese importers partnering with Malian importers, or tea wholesalers have performed successfully. But most Chinese tea traders were only able to succeed for a few years. This was mostly due to a poorly supported distribution network, the influence of wholesalers being able to promote or block brands and mostly because of the conviction of Malian consumers that good tea may only be sold by established Malian traders.

During my visits to Mali on several occasions we saw Chinese men and women working at computers in the offices of Malian importers, installing a programme or creating a design. Interactions between Chinese and Malians, that we observed, were conducted with some jokes but few words. Nevertheless, I met several Chinese traders, or brokers personally but whilst some of them were friendly, meaningful conversations were very difficult to maintain. Their interest in the conversation centred on selling tea only.

One day we phoned the seller of *Thé Joli*. He had placed a Malian name on the package but the Chinese owner answered the phone himself. Without even waiting to hear what we wanted, he explained that *Thé Joli* was finished and that 'you have to wait until there is more coming'. But we, nevertheless, requested a visit to his warehouse located in the Ngolonina neighbourhood where many traders had warehouses. We waited for him sitting on a bench in front of his shop. Arriving on his motorbike, without looking left or right, or greeting anyone, he removed the lock from the door, went inside and phoned us, asking where we were. We walked into the small hall and saw cartons of *Thé Joli* in two qualities of Chunmee, the better of the two, 41022, was obviously sold out. As soon as he understood we were not buying, he urged us to leave. I had the impression we had disturbed him whilst he was cooking, which he wanted to resume. From the beginning, this Chinese trader did not consider that we had any other idea than buying tea.

We met with the owner of the Chinese Wafa company. He lived and worked in a part of a compound he shared with a Malian family but no sign indicated that a company operated from it. However, all the people we asked knew where the Chinese trader lived. He was very friendly but spoke in a mixture of English and French that I found difficult to understand. He summoned a Malian from within the compound to translate my French into a version that he could comprehend. He explained that he had lived in Bamako for ten years and regarded the city as his home. He imported tea from Zhejiang and one of the wholesalers handled its sales for him. The Chinese trader set the price of the tea and they trusted each other. However, in this conversation it was impossible to be sure who owned the tea brands depicted in his brochure (he, the wholesaler, or another Chinese).

4 The Presence of Chinese Tea Traders in Mali and the Issue of Trust

During our interviews, trust between Chinese and Malian trading partners was a recurrent issue. Both Chinese and Malian traders mentioned the great importance of trust in this business. Whereas, for example, Malian merchants in Bamako had confidence in the *coxeurs* and entrusted them to convey large sums of money to another trader (chapter 4), trust was more complicated when Chinese traders were involved.

Malian and Chinese trading partners visited each other to explore whether they were able to work together. They jointly created the package design, learning from each other through their partnership. Many worked together but did not really trust each other. Initial reluctance toward helping my research may also stem from experience with Chinese traders. They were seen walking around the market, mobile phone in hand, asking questions, taking photographs and conducting research before beginning to sell tea themselves. One of the Malian importers explained: 'The Chinese are quite visible here on the Malian market. They come here to carry out market studies to know how the tea business is going here because tea in Mali is a market for the Chinese, too. It is a very big market' (interview, Bamako, 2013). Another importer reported that there were always Chinese traders promoting their tea to you. They send you their samples, and you choose your quality. You will begin with small quantities, and if it is good, then you order larger quantities

> But this always goes by bank transfer, because in case the product does not arrive, there is still the bank, and the bank will return your money. … You need to be very careful in these things. … Some [Malian importers] also go to China with their money, they pay their product and the transport [in cash], but then the risk is much higher that the money might be lost. INTERVIEW, BAMAKO, 2013

The demand for tea in West African Sahel countries like Mali encouraged many Chinese tea companies to specialise in the African export market. These companies work alongside freelance brokers who are paid a percentage commission on the proceeds of each successful transaction of tea as a commission from the factory. The brokers speak English and French and are thus able to communicate with African traders, which the factory owners usually cannot. A Malian merchant trading in Shanghai explained, that those brokers who were successful in their job were also those who could travel to Africa, visit their trading partners and also sought to find new customers (interview, Shanghai, 2014).

One importer was sure that the Chinese were keen to maintain good relationships with their Malian trading partners as well as, whenever possible, ensuring consistent tea quality: 'The Chinese do not cheat people (*Les Chinois ne trompent pas les gens*)' (interview, Bamako, 2011). But this obviously does not apply to all partnerships with Chinese traders. Another importer did not easily trust Chinese traders, saying

> Many importers have met their Chinese supplier here, because they travel to Mali to look for customers and then propose whatever quality of tea and if you work with someone you do not know well and invest your money with them, then you may be sent a lesser quality than the one you ordered and the sample they presented to you. INTERVIEW, BAMAKO, 2013

Several importers informed me that the Chinese traders who visited Mali were not actually employed by a Chinese tea factory. They were freelance brokers working in their own interest, 'looking for money' (interviews, Bamako, 2013). Obviously there have been Chinese brokers who offered tea to everyone and anyone, trader or not, suggesting they sell it for them: 'They make a proposal and want it to go ahead simply because they want the commission from their factory; they are not really interested in building a relationship nor in advertising the brand. They just come and want to bring bad quality' (interview, Bamako, 2016).

Trust is a basic requirement for success in trade, as one of the big tea importers remarked, when he talked about his observation that some of the Djokoramé traders these days began to ask for credit from banks, putting a great deal of effort into winning their trust. But it was more sensible not to take bank credit but to win the trust of trading partners:

> Whatever people will tell you, there is no need to look for the trust of the banks, you better ought to gain the trust of your supplier. You have to demonstrate to him that you are trustworthy and working seriously. Today, the factories give me 5 billion or 10 billion credit, and all that without any document; they are not afraid because they know that I will not 'eat their money'. And I myself know that I don't do that and prefer to get the profit. Because I do not work only for the next two or five years but for the next ten or twenty so that my children can be in the tea business later on as well … They [the Chinese] will not do this with other Malians because they already have met bad people who did not pay. And me, I am not afraid to give my Chinese supplier 10 or 15 million of credit. And it is necessary to communicate. The Chinese here, they do not even

> communicate. You have to be courageous enough to take a bit of a risk. And [make them know that] you cannot easily disappear with my money, because there is a bond between me and you, which guarantees that you do not 'eat' my money. INTERVIEW, BAMAKO, 2016

As mentioned earlier, there are some Chinese traders, settled in Bamako, trying to sell tea, although they generally have difficulties unless they enlist the help of a Malian trader. The aforementioned owners of *Thé Joli* and *Simida* are good examples. One of the wholesalers knew that

> From the day, the Chinese owner of *Simida* gave his tea to a particular wholesaler, the tea was selling so well, that in 2013 it became the third best-selling tea in Bamako, and also other wholesalers began to take *Simida* from him to sell. Like this it can work out that people [traders] buy tea that belongs to a Chinese. INTERVIEW, BAMAKO, 2013

One of the importers confirmed this opinion:

> With the Chinese here, you have the impression that all their teas are sold by Malians … They come here with their samples, but these people have difficulties adapting to the realities, they do not know how things are done here, they do not have access to the networks; these people are very suspicious, they do not trust you. All these are important reasons why they have the impression that things here do not work according to their mindset. INTERVIEW, BAMAKO, 2013

Chinese traders find it easier to sell commodities other than tea for which, as mentioned earlier, low prices are the incentive behind the purchase. Such commodities can be found in Chinese-owned shops, however, Bamako lacks the 'Chinese quarter' or 'street' that exist in some other African countries.[2] Those Chinese traders who sell tea on their own account often irritate Malian traders because they are perceived as not following the Malian trading order which permits each intermediary a little profit (chapter 3), as one of the importers

2 For example, in Dakar (Scheld 2010) and Douala (Racaud 2018). Most Chinese in Mali are working in private enterprises which carry out projects for the Malian government such as the construction of the new bridge across the Niger and the flyovers in the city. Government opens a competition, and the enterprise that wins due to its good prices gets the project. Other Chinese are private individuals who run bars, hotels, restaurants, small supermarkets, sell cars and other equipment, or are in education and media (Bourdarias 2009; Diakon and Röschenthaler 2017).

noted. He complained they ignored the division of tasks between different traders, believing they can do everything themselves from importing the tea, running the wholesale and retail aspects of the trade, and even serving street sellers queuing in front of their shop wanting to purchase a consignment of merely a few packages at wholesale prices (interview, Bamako, 2013; for a similar discussion in Cameroon, see Röschenthaler 2016).

Both Chinese and Malian traders were certain trust was absolutely vital for successful trade (*il faut avoir confiance*). However, several revealed that they 'do not trust each other' and the feeling is mutual (interviews, Bamako, 2013). The Chinese traders, with whom I talked, considered trust to be a problem in Mali; one in Bamako said: 'The market here is not good because it is not possible to establish good relationships with politics' (interview, Bamako, 2013) and the importer of *Thé Joli* insisted that 'trust is a problem in Mali. Malians are reluctant to pay immediately, preferring later. Malian traders are not serious, you cannot trust them' (interview, Bamako, 2013).

To ensure the popularity of a brand, however, Chinese and Malian traders must cooperate and despite all the obstacles learn to trust each other. It is for this reason that Malian importers prefer to travel to China and visit tea plantations and factories themselves. There, they choose from among them the best offers from trustworthy partners who are always brokers. The journey is considered to yield rewards and is thus a worthwhile investment. The practice also serves to guarantee the importer has partners closer to the source of production, can obtain a better price and have fewer intermediaries compared with working with a Chinese broker in Mali.

5 The Interconnection of Malian and Chinese Trade Activities

Both Chinese and Malian traders desire to control the commodity or value chain: Malian traders want to be nearer to the source of production, whilst Chinese brokers seek to be closer to the eventual consumers. Seen from a historical perspective, tea was at first produced and processed in China and sold to Europeans mainly from Canton (Guangzhou). Between the seventeenth and the nineteenth centuries, Chinese tea traders did not travel to Europe or West Africa. The tea was transported aboard European ships to a European destination, mainly Britain, and from there to Morocco, largely under auspices of Jewish traders, and from there southwards to where Tikna and other Saharan traders conveyed it on caravans across the Sahara (chapter 1). Saharans and Dyula had their own trade spheres, extending into circumscribed regions along established trade networks. At that time, West Africans were not in immediate contact with Chinese traders, but in the course of the twentieth century direct cooperation between China and some West African governments – such as that of Mali – was established and straightforward importation became possible, although only on the higher political level rather than between private traders. Post 1991, Malian traders ventured to the West African coast, then to Hong Kong and in the 2000s eventually to China itself, gradually honing in on the centre of tea production.

Conversely, seeking to get closer to foreign tea consumers, Chinese traders at first established agencies in Hong Kong, then in West African port cities before eventually setting up in Mali, where they attempted to sell tea directly to consumers. Whilst both Malians and Chinese sought to trade in tea, as this chapter had shown, each faced both linguistic challenges and culturally specific ideas of how trade had to operate. The interconnection of Malian efforts to get nearer to the source of production and Chinese attempts to reach tea consumers results from the desire of both parties to control the value chain and obtain for themselves better trading conditions. These interconnections extend from Mali into the market networks of adjacent countries, the West African port cities and to Central and even East Africa, to places where migrants from the Mande World went to find work, taking with them their pleasure in drinking tea. Chinese importers may also be found there (chapter 1). Here, Malian migrants often know less about tea qualities than their compatriots at home in Mali. There, cheaper tea qualities may be sold to some of them, which provides opportunities for Chinese importers to enter the market, at least for a while. Chinese companies and brokers are also present in Morocco and in the eastern part of northern Africa, where some tea is still sold in wooden boxes.

Becoming a successful tea importer requires possession of capital, experience and knowledge of the market. Some of these requirements can be learned through formal education, apprenticeship and by trial and error. Entrepreneurial merchants had to take risks, invest their capital wisely, collaborate with a Chinese supplier, create a brand and decide at which port the cargo should arrive and create an efficient distribution network. But that was not all. The importers emphasised that tea is a product with its own specificities and challenges and that therefore one needed to know the 'work of tea', which includes managing a popular brand and avoid provoking a crisis on the market.

Another challenge was deciding when the right time for diversification of brands and products had come and re-investing one's profits wisely in durable assets (property, means of transport, production units, livestock), thus creating employment for Malians and contributing to development. If possible, merchants bought their own warehouses and tried to control the transport of their products from the port by investing in lorries to make them less dependent on renting storage rooms and employing transport companies, as there is only one railway system connecting Mali with the port of Dakar. In Mali the situation is not as complicated as in DRC where entrepreneurs have invested in infrastructure (roads, bridges) in order to be able to carry out trade (MacGaffey 1991). An advantage for developing the intuition of making all these decisions wisely was growing up and learning in a family of established tea traders.

All Malian tea merchants had to collaborate with Chinese suppliers and establish at least a minimum of trust in this cooperation. Both Malian and Chinese traders were aware of this but unsure as to the extent to which to trust each other. Both were of the opinion that one could never be fully sure of one's partner. These apprehensions contrast, however, with the statements of those successful merchants who had put efforts in winning the trust of their Chinese business partners. They knew that their Chinese suppliers – once mutual agreement and trust was established – would be interested in stable relationships and refrain from cheating because they wanted to continue to sell them tea so that both could win. As will be shown in the next chapter, creating a successful tea brand depends on the cooperation and input of both Malian and Chinese business partners and the effort they invested in this collaboration.

CHAPTER 6

The Tea Packet Design, Co-Creation and the Culture of Commemoration

When Malian importers have decided for ordering a consignment of tea, the product is packaged in paper cartons in the Chinese tea factory. These packages are emblazoned with the design, the brand name and other details that the Malian importer wishes to see on the packet. The design is co-created or co-designed by the Malian and Chinese business partners. In a much similar way as Von Pezold and Driessen (2021) following Vilarinho (2019) noted in their studies of textile designs in Mozambique, Malians and Chinese partners collaborate in the creation of the package designs. Malian agency in this collaboration becomes visible in the extent to which Malians follow the propositions of their Chinese partners or otherwise are prepared to offer their own suggestions and images. The approach of Malians slightly differs from that of Chinese brokers and from the close study of the tea package designs can often be read which of the parties has dominated the creation.

It is important to obtain an overview of the different elements that appear on the packages, the colours, logos and brand names in order to understand the design. The following sections describe the material aspects of the tea packages, analyse the designs and the imagery and consider the meanings that lie behind brand names and images. This reveals that tea brand designs express a lively remembrance culture, exemplifying global connectivity by commemorating events of social and political significance. It also reveals to which extent their combined creativity brings forward a design that can be considered 'glocalised', or rather 'hybrid' and 'bricolage'.

1 Collaborative Brand Creation

Firstly, it is important to understand the origin of ideas for the brand names and designs. One of the questions I asked tea importers was, how did they reach decisions regarding the portrayal of their brands. Several means were mentioned. The importer of *Rocki*, who previously sold *Rass al Khaima* on behalf of a Chinese tea broker, explained: 'It was my supplier who created the brand. He proposed the brand to me' (interview, Bamako, 2013). Malian traders

 | DOI:10.1163/9789004505698_008

observed that Chinese brokers, when visiting their African trading partners, conducted their own market research in order to find inspiration for possible new brand names. The importer added:

> They walk around for several weeks and that is how they get their ideas. He [the Chinese broker] wants to know how he can develop his business. They created all these brands, not we. When they create a brand, they make a logo [actually a draft of the design] which they send to you, telling you to have a look and when you agree that it is good, they take that image [to print it on the tea package]. They also make all the errors that you can see on some of the packages. INTERVIEW, BAMAKO, 2013

This importer trusted Chinese broker's intuition as to what might sell in West Africa. The brands owned by this importer were created after suggestions from his Chinese supplier. Sometimes, he proposed a name and the broker put it together with an image found on his computer.

Other tea importers, however, insisted that they always proposed their own ideas to their Chinese brokers rather than expecting suggestions of their supplier. They reached their decisions carefully to ensure their designs did not share unintended similarities with pre-existing brands. Another importer said: 'The Chinese will also make some propositions as to the brand name, and the design, but you explain how you want your brand. You tell them how you want your package to look like. Then they put the design together, enhancing or modifying the colours on their computer. They can show you a great many different designs from which you can choose' (interview, Bamako, 2013). The importer of *Thé Niger* explained:

> I make the propositions; I make my design; look, it is not yet finished [he shows me the design of his new brand on his computer]; I make the first part, then I send it to them [the Chinese supplier], and they also work on it and develop my idea. They have their own design specialists. INTERVIEW, BAMAKO, 2013

To enable them to do this, all the major tea importers have desktop computers in their offices, facilitating online exchange with their suppliers of brand imagery and other information. In this way, the brands are co-created with the Chinese suppliers who produce the final version of the brand design, but how big the part played by the Malian importers is in supplying the initial ideas, depends on their individual decisiveness and creativity. Another importer noted that

> You discuss your tea package prototype (*échantillon*) with your Chinese supplier. They have graphic designers and technicians who identify the quality of tea and tell you 'this is super quality with a certain number of A's' and they even have words in their language for that quality.
> INTERVIEW, BAMAKO, 2013

The various details – including, if desired, the telephone number and address of the supplier and importer – may appear on the package, as required by the importer.

The three statements illustrate different degrees of intensity of co-creation and accordingly Malian agency in shaping the tea brand design. Malians being the patron of the trade, Chinese partners supply them with ideas, or follow their suggestions. The design may be termed a culturally hybrid product, which, as the analysis of the package designs will illustrate, can consist to different proportions of African, Chinese and global design elements and combines Malian and Chinese input to the co-creation.

2 The Design of the Tea Packages

Through the printed image and its design, the package in its material form is intrinsically connected to its immaterial aspects (Miller 2005; Röschenthaler and Diawara 2016). Both have to be looked at as an ensemble. In daily life, when tea packages are sold and change hands, customers purchase the material aspects. The immaterial attributes remain the property of the owner or importer, as will be further discussed in the following chapters.

The package design represents the immaterial aspects, the marks and images, presented on the smooth surface of the printed paper carton. The design comprises several basic distinguishable components; these include colours, decoration, brand name, other written information (type of tea, quality, provenance), logo, and pictures. Some of these components are found on most packets but in various combinations. An examination of the BOPI reveals the green tea package designs tend to convey a specific ambiance and evoke sensory experiences, making them both unique and easily distinguished from designs of other products. I will examine these components and their design and also evaluate my sample of 237 tea packages from my collection mostly acquired in Bamako between 2007 and 2018. I first consider the materiality of the packages, then their dominant colours, the frames, the images and the brand names that often convey a different meaning than the images. Finally, I discuss these design elements as an ensemble and the different approaches to the creation of the designs by Chinese and Malians.

2.1 *The Materiality of the Tea Package: Size and Weight*

A few Chinese green tea brands come in transparent plastic sachets only but most are enclosed within a thin, printed carton. The packages, as mentioned earlier, can be available in the sizes of 25g, 62.2g (only Cheval), 100g, 125g (rare), 250g, 500g (rare) 1kg (very rare in Bamako). In most of Mali, especially in Bamako, the 25g packages are by far the most popular. Their measurements are 4 × 7 × 2 cm – smaller than a cigarette box. In the early years, until 2007, there were also a few 25g packages in the form of cubes (*Tombouctou, Canal*) but then the rectangular version has become the norm. Some of the brands are also available in the 100g, 125g, 250g and 500g packages of the rectangular, or cube form. But the 500g and 1kg packages are normally only found in Morocco. If a brand in a particular quality is available in several packet sizes, then all packages will bear the same design.

Because many people had expressed so much concern about the possibility that they were being cheated by Chinese tea sellers, I decided to weigh the packages in my collection with an electronic letter scale. Without exception all had at least the weight indicated on the package, and often they weighed about 20% more than that (30g instead of 25g, or 280g instead of 250g). The differences do not lie in the weight of the packaging material, for empty 25g cartons weigh less than 1g.

2.2 *The Dominant Colours*

A packages' colours strongly influence its appearance. Designs including sky-blue on the upper part and sandy colours lower down, refer to desert imagery and present a timeless feature on many packets. Others, however, saw changes in colour every few years. Among the first tea packages were the dark green ones from the Chinese state-owned tea factory. But then, every three to four years, the dominant colours seen on the tea market have changed, following a fashion led by a currently successful tea brand. Whilst the trends of blue-green colours (*Askia, Canal*) and by white-green (*Flecha*) were set by Chinese importers, the intermediate trends, inspired by *Gazelle* and *Achoura* brands were determined by Malian importers.

In the mid-2000s, lush greens and brilliant blues were favoured, harmonising with the tea leaves and following the colours of the popular brands *Askia* and *Canal* at the time. *Thé Canal* billboards and wall paintings, which celebrated the blue and green colours (chapter 2) still amplified this impression. *Al Farouk, Hamza, Obama, Razèle, Tombouctou* and *Touareg*, which followed, possessed variants of these colours. Roughly half of these green and blue packages were Gunpowder and the other half Chunmee 4011. At that time, most brands came in four qualities of which usually those in green and blue were the most popular – the others being either of lower quality or more expensive. But, of course, not all importers followed fashion when selecting colours. Once the *Canal* brand became unpopular, colours began to change and a superior tea quality became the new norm.

Around 2009, yellow, brown and light green colours became the model. Beginning with the *Gazelle* brand, numerous other tea brands were inspired to follow suite and used these colours in fine stripes. Among them were variations of the *Gazelle* design (*Antilope, Gaza Super, Super, Gazelle et ses petites, La Biche*, etc.). Aside of the yellow stripes emerged designs with brown stripes and an arrow motif, beginning with the *Flecha* brand. In 2012, these yellowish and brown hues were replaced with a series of white, silvery waves and blueish moss-green motives at the bottom. This began when the *Flecha* brand reinvented its colours and began to sell Super Chunmee tea (41022). This arrangement again inspired numerous imitators who invented a number of more or less similar variants (*Koutam, Lawal, Hayat, Super Thé, Hassane Ousmane, Thé MS*, etc) (more on these in chapter 8). A short while later, new preferences emerged with *Achoura*: strong red and yellow-orange which focussed on tea equipment motifs.

2.3 *Decorative Elements as Part of the Tea Package Design*

There are three framing styles in brand images: floral, oriental and wooden box framings; especially the early packages were decorated in this way.

The earliest of these decorations were the floral garland-like styles used to frame the edges of a package. Prominent are those that resemble design of the state-owned Chinese tea company and its brands *Chameau* and *Temple du Ciel*. Most of the brands, using them are owned by Chinese traders (*La Main en Main*). Geometric designs frame the images carried by other brands (*Arawane*), or a band may be applied around the four corners of the package (*AAA*). The geometric designs might be inspired by Islamic art forms, as there are also designs with decorated oriental archways (*Al Malik*) and stylised arches (*Lobo*).

The third variation in decorative framings presents the carton as an imitation of a wooden box, evoking memories of the original containers in which tea arrived as cargo transported by camel caravans across the Sahara in the nineteenth and the first half of the twentieth centuries. The design even depicts the metal fittings and the nails and clips with which they were attached to each corner of the box and along its edges. Early versions of the brands *Azawad*, *Tombouctou*, OBS and others were based on this motif and displayed a medallion encapsulating the brand name and image at the centre of the design. For example, the first packages of *Azawad* are designed representing a wooden box that bears a medallion and a desert landscape in the middle. The more recent Azawad packages dropped this feature, only showing the desert landscape, including a man leading a camel caravan. *Obama* and *Olala* are less prominent variations of this genre of wooden box stylisation and *Le Patron* has limited the reference to the nails and clips (Figures 49a–e).

FIGURES 49A–E Examples of tea packages with decorative frames: *Hamza, Lawal, Rarhous, Thé du Sahara, Le Patron*

More recent tea packages either employ simple frames around the central image and brand name (*Taoudeni, Ciwara, Lawal*), or they provide no framing at all (*Sancho, Achoura, Gaza Super, Gazelle, Flecha*).

2.4 *Written Information on the Packages*

On all packages is written in French *Thé vert de Chine*, often also in English 'China green tea', in Arabic *Al schay al siniy al ahdar* and in Chinese characters *Dong guo lü chá*. Additionally, there is an indication of the weight in gramme of the product and the country of origin: *Produit de la République Populaire de Chine* or 'Product of the People's Republic of China'. Many packages indicate the type of tea (Gunpowder, Chunmee) and the variety with a number (3505, 4011, 41022) according to the Chinese system of tea standards, as well as further indications such as 'special' or 'extraordinary' etc., with stars and/or A's (chapter 2). Recommendations as to how the tea is to be prepared appear on the side of some packages alongside messages about the health benefits it has. Some may also have a printed bar code on the side; often this is an indication that the brand is owned by a Chinese broker.

Nearly all packages carry an expiry date (month and year) and sometimes also the month and year of harvesting, as well as other indications such as approval and lot numbers on the bottom. Normally, the expiry date is five years after harvest, but the owners of popular brands have decided to reduce it to three years only, and a few others have extended the period to eight years. A few importers also indicate the trademark office registration number and the sanitary proof number on the bottom. According to a senior member of staff at CEMAPI, the approval number identifies the Chinese factory from which the tea came; the lot number identifies the particular charge of tea. In the 2000s, most tea packages displayed the name and address of the importer, their email address and phone number, and quite often. the address of the Chinese supplier. The French words are almost always spelt without accents.

From 2013, increasing health awareness among consumers drove brand owners to mark packages with the legend '100% natural'. At the same time decorative and written elements were reduced and fewer Arabic and Chinese letters appeared on packages. Most brands, especially those belonging to Malian importers, carried straightforward designs, adding nothing superfluous; front and backside as well as the sides portray the same image and design (*Sancho, Taodeni, Gazelle, François Hollande*). The sides may differ slightly in that one side bears the writing in French (*Thé vert de Chine*), the other in Arabic (*Al schay al siniy al ahdar*). Increasingly importers printed the message ostensibly addressed to potential brand pirates that the design was formally registered with OAPI.

In 2016, few importers continued to provide their name and contact details; often even the type of tea would no longer be indicated, for respected tea importers only imported Chunmee 41022 anyway. Some importers printed their details on 5kg cartons, but not on the small packages. If we take 123 brands from my collection, only 76 importers provided their names on the package; 49 indicated nothing. Of the 76, a third gave only their name and phone number, others also had an address, email, or both printed on the packet; among them, 55 were African and 18 were Chinese importers, and of the remaining 3 it is unclear whether the company is African- or Chinese-owned. Of the 49 who did not give an indication of ownership, I identified 27 from my interviews, or by consulting the details held at the BOPI; among these were 16 African and 11 Chinese importers.

Chinese importers seem to be more eager to indicate phone number and address than the African importers, presumably because they were less well-known to *coxeurs* and wholesalers than were Malian importers and would not want to miss out business with potential customers. Malian importers need not indicate their contact details because the *coxeurs* will quickly inform and update any new wholesaler who opens a shop about the activities of all the importers and their brands, as wholesalers are their potential new customers.

This is one reason for the omission of contact details, but there are others. One of the importers explained: 'In the past, my name, my company and my phone number were on every package, but now I told my supplier that I no longer want this, because a lot of people call, and you spend the whole day on the phone' (interview, Bamako, 2013). Also, when a brand owner's information is freely available, it is too easy for the authorities to make contact. Another importer, whose packages sported his details, suggested: 'Many don't print the name of their company, because then the authorities are more likely to visit you because your address is easily accessible. Some probably do not want this' (interview, Bamako, 2013), and another importer said: 'If your name is not there, the packages might easily be believed to come from Mauritania, or elsewhere, but it is also possible that it is because of the tax collectors' (interview, Bamako, 2013).

Hence, certain information has to be given, such as the indication of the type of product, the country of production, the approval and lot numbers and the expiry date, but other information can be handled quite flexibly. And in the course of their learning process, the Malian importers especially decided to only provide such information that was absolutely obligatory. Principally, the Chinese law prescribes the indication of the contact details but many Malian importers convinced their Chinese suppliers that they had reasons why they preferred it differently.

2.5 *The Picture, or Image*

Many tea packages have a picture that blends and resonates with the main colours used in the package design such as the blue of the sky above and the yellow, orange or brown desert landscape below, mentioned earlier. Some brands portray this theme simply as a desert landscape, or with depictions of sand dunes, camel caravans, and people. There are also designs that employ colours, the brand name, another small image in an extra frame, or an image of a wooden box, thus refraining from depicting an eye-catching central image.

The BOPI also provides a rich source for the analysis of tea packages, especially for the early ones before I started collecting. The tea packages that have been registered and published in BCPI, are illustrated in black and white, and for an additional fee, in colour. Early brands, registered between 1998 and 2002 seem quite diverse; many repeatedly use the same images, only adopting different frames and names in the central part of the design. They are often based on the floral motifs of the formerly state-owned Chinese tea factory, which produced *Chameau* with its two-humped camel and *Temple du Ciel* with a Chinese temple as images (both existing in Mali since 1998). *Thé Saddam la Force*, registered 1998 in Dakar, shows a tea glass; *Warga Touba* (2002, Dakar) a ram, which could refer to the popular habit of drinking tea after eating roasted mutton in one of the street restaurants; *Sonipit* a bushfire (2002, Niamey), and *Echakara* a Tuareg bag made of leather used for storing tea equipment (2002, Nouakchott). From 2002 onwards, particular motifs are recurrent.

2.5.1 Tea Equipment

From early on, tea equipment had ubiquitous presence on package designs. At least 35 packages belonging to my sample display elements of the tea set, variously depicting a teapot, decorated copper or brass trays, tea glasses, mint leaves, sugar cubes, tea leaves, or even a samovar. The illustrated teapots include varieties with applicated copper snouts and handles, as they were once beautified by Saharan silversmiths; the typical Moroccan pear-shaped and decorated teapots, often with several feet; round earthenware and flat ironware teapots, reminiscent of Chinese styles; or the popular round metal and coloured enamel pots (Creyaufmüller 1983; Röschenthaler forthc.). On some designs, a Tuareg, or perhaps a *shaykh* is depicted pouring tea in the glasses.

The representations of tea glasses show a similarly large variety: there are large and columnar-shaped glasses in Moroccan style, often colourfully decorated; the smaller and ripped shot glasses used in Mali; others have handles, or a curved form like Turkish tea glasses; some stand on decorated metal saucers (all unusual in present-day Mali). The depicted glasses – between one and twelve, or even more, as is common in Morocco – normally appear full of tea, each topped by a frothy cap. As replacement for glasses, some images portray tiny white porcelain bowls or small cups with handles, sometimes with saucer and cover, others with blue decoration, which refer to the Chinese tea ritual. Some of the cups, as is the case in Europe, are larger and higher-sided, others appear like small, fragile porcelain cups seen in China. Some of these pictures incorporate Chinese imagery such as architecture, a Ginseng root in the tea glass, a tea cup decorated with a dragon; a white porcelain lantern, a tea caddy, a tea session in a green natural environment.

While the illustrations of most teapots and glasses are reproduced from photographs, others are stylised portrayals of teapots, glasses or cups. All this can be arranged in different combinations on the design. My interviews and the analysis of the brands published in BOPI reveals that nearly all the brands depicting Chinese imagery and round earthenware teapots are owned by Chinese brokers, whilst Malian brand owners prefer to choose images that depict tea sets that are more familiar to Malian consumers, i.e. pear-shaped, or round metal teapots and two small shot glasses. The majority of brands depicting Moroccan teapot types are owned by Saharan merchants and a few Chinese brokers. Brands having metallic and enamel globular teapots depicted are owned by both Malians and Chinese importers.

The tea glasses and cups cannot easily be ascribed to either African or Chinese brand owners. This may result from the inclination to imitate the *Flecha* brand which uses as its central element a porcelain tea cup with a handle, recreated with many variations: decorated with a dragon motif, or the number indicating the tea quality, or the cup being replaced by the dragon motif only. Hence, the unfamiliar elements in Mali are most often devices, generally employed by Chinese brand owners, only being copied by Malian or other West African importers in the event that a brand using it becomes popular. An analysis of Chinese landscapes leads to a similar conclusion.

2.5.2 Chinese Landscapes

Waterfalls, tea plantations, tea trees and people plucking tea leaves are prominent features in designs owned by Chinese importers (*Canal, Askia, Paradis, Chunli, Amgro, Ousmane Oumar, Olala, Yasmina, Sahha,* HTA, *Arrami*). Such images are only rarely seen on Malian-owned designs (*Arawane, Obama, Raissa*).

2.5.3 The Tent (*al khaima*, in Arabic)

In 2002 and 2003, six green tea brands bearing the tent motif were registered in BOPI. One of them is registered in Paris and five in Nouakchott. Judging from their owners' names, three are Chinese, two Saharan and the Parisian one, Pinchu, may be connected with Las Palmas. One of these brands (*Rhass al Khaima*) is also distributed in Bamako by the Malian partner of its Chinese owner in Nouakchott. The tent motif was introduced by Chinese traders. Variations of it include lilac or white Tuareg tents, some surrounded by sand dunes, palm trees, dromedaries, or veiled people sitting on a mat, drinking tea. Some of the brand names reflect the tent motif (*khaima*), one depicts a tent but lacks a brand name, and another (*Khaima*) has a brand name referring to the tent but the package depicts a tea-drinking group with camels and a mosque in the background.

2.5.4 Further Desert Landscapes

In my sample, fourteen tea package designs depict desert landscapes with sand dunes and oases, most additionally portray caravans, and people either leading or riding the dromedaries. Some of the images are based on photographs, others are more abstracted and include amended colours. Six of these are registered by Malian, eight by Chinese traders.

2.5.5 Portraits of Individuals and People Drinking Tea

Seven packages depict people drinking tea: in a tea group or *grin* (*Kunawolo*), a couple drinking tea together (*Ikathé*), or someone pouring the tea for a group (*Bon MaMa*). Others depict people wearing veils in a Sahel town (*Nioro du Sahel*), a stylised group (*Les Grins*) or individuals such as a Kungfu fighter (*Konfo*). There are also a few portraits of people: *Le Patron*, with a photograph probably depicting a senior relative of the importer; *Wilibali*, a religious leader represented by a drawing; and *François Hollande*, portraying the former French president.

2.5.6 Animals

Animals provide the central motif for a great number of tea package designs. Some portray strong and admired desert and savannah animals: three employ elephants (*Maiga, Capitaine, Elephant*), ownership of which is unclear; horses are found on four packages: one is owned by a Hong Kong Chinese of Indian origin (*Cheval*), the horse with wings (*Al Farouk*) and a horse rider with a spear (*Ciwara*) are both owned by Chinese traders, and a mule (*S.Lere*), owned by a Malian. Other animals depicted include giraffes (*Deux Girafe* [sic]), fish (*Capitaine*), a lion (*Super Lion*), a tiger (the logo of *Hassane Ousmane*), a wild cat (*Serval*) and a kangaroo (*Kangourou*); the first three probably have a Chinese owner and the last three are owned by Malians merchants.

Then there is the two-humped camel, owned by the former Chinese Zhejiang Tea Import and Export Company, now named Zhejiang Highten; and there are numerous brands with one-humped camels (dromedaries), single or in groups. Some are owned by Malians (*Africable, Tilimsi, Super, Lawal, Tabankort, Tilemsi*), others by Chinese (*Jamell Sahara; Piano*), and ownership is unclear for some (*Hamed Ousmane, Rarhous, Thé du Sahara, Sarama*).

There are many gazelles, most of which are variations of the famous *Gazelle* brand: a sitting gazelle (without name), *Gazelle et ses petites, Antilope No.1, Gaza Super, Nuovo Gaza, La Biche*, a gazelle head (without name), and *Arrami* and *Al Baraka* depicting deer, all owned by Malian or Saharan traders, except for Arrami. Finally, six tea packages have representations of birds: an ostrich (*Ramadane*), a white pigeon (*Oiseau Blanc*), a small pigeon (*Rocki*), a bird with a crested head (*Taaj*), a toucan (*Toucan*), a white bird (*Pintade*) and a stylised bird (*Lucky Bird*). The first four are owned by Malians, and the other three are Chinese-owned.

2.5.7 Depiction of Singular Items

Among the singular items portrayed are salt bars from the Sahara (*Taoudeni*); Dogon masked dancers (*Dogon*); the Jasmin flower (*Al Baraka*); and mosques

(*Haidara, Chaban, Wilibali*); one of the mosques is Al Khūz as-Sharīf, the third holy Muslim place; another is al Masjid el Aqsa behind the dome of the rock in Jerusalem; others depict royal symbols such as the crown (*Wel Taré, Al Taj, Ayoune, Bonya*); the bow and arrow, together with a cup – the Chinese-owned *Flecha* that has been imitated in many guises by Malian and other importers of various nationalities (*Sahara, Hayat, Hassane Ousmane, Lawal, OBS, Super Thé, Flechena*, etc).

Then there is a majestic Baobab tree (*Baobab*), a Baobab tree adjacent to round houses and people (*Baobab*); a stylised tree (*Adoua*); a river (*Niger*); an volcano (*Sancho*); the figure of Mami Wata as snake charmer (*Mami Wata*); a football (*La Main en Main, Askia, Cheval*); and the logo of Mali's fiftieth anniversary celebrations (*Cinquantenaire*).

Some 12 package designs carry no specific picture or central image, their design merely playing with colours, forms and abstract components.

An interim conclusion arising of the study of tea package designs is an apparent tendency for Malian brand owners to rarely adopt Chinese imagery except in respect of the occasional use of images of tea leaves and tea plantations. The other images are variously owned by both Chinese and Malian importers; West African and Arab imagery is creatively applied following market research by Chinese traders during their visits to Malian and Arab partners. The frequent discrepancy between central image and brand name is also striking.

2.6 *The Brand Names*

Almost all these packages have a brand name printed on them, only a few do not. I will sort the brand names according to the themes referred to, before discussing the entire design and how far the names correspond with the images and, as far as information is available, what importers intend to convey with their brand designs. Brand names and images represent a wide range of topics of which some are not at all connected to the beverage. African merchants tend to create more coherent brand designs in which brand name and image refer more closely to each other whereas Chinese traders prefer designs composed of various apparently unrelated components.

2.6.1 Geographical References: Place Names, Trading Towns, Regions

Thé Arawane refers to a formerly important trans-Saharan caravan camel watering town, situated 664 km north of Timbuktu; *Rarhous* to a town in northern Mali; *Nioro du Sahel* is named after a trading town near the Mauritanian border; *Taoudeni* after a settlement in northern Mali where salt was formerly extracted from a dried salt lake by slave labour (see also Lovejoy 1986); and *Tombouctou* (the French spelling of Timbuktu) after the well-known trading town and centre of Muslim scholarship at the boundary between Sahara and Sahel; *Tilimsi* refers to a village, valley and region in northern Mali; *S.Lere* to a commune in the Region of Timbuktu, comprising the town of Lere and seventeen villages. It became known during the northern Mali crisis, but the brand was already registered in 2008. *Agouni Salam* is named after a village group composed of Agouni, the name of a village and seat of the commune of Salam in the Region of Timbuktu; it is also the name of the tea company there. *Azawad* refers to the desert region of that name, including a few oases in northern Mali. Azawad became better known during Mali's crisis following the 2012 coup but the brand had already been registered in the early 2000s.

Other brand names with geographical references are *Niger*, referring to the River Niger which is Mali's most important river, an important transport route, also for tea, especially in its inner delta, as well as a source for fish and provider of water, essential for life in the rather dry Sahel landscape. *Ayoune* is the town in West Sahara – important for trade in tea after World War II – the name literally meaning 'eyes' in Arabic; the brands *Desert*, *Al Sahara* and *Thé du Sahara* quote the dry region between North Africa and the Sahel; *Tenere* refers to a part of the Sahara in Niger; other references to ecological zones are *Le Sahel* and *La Savane*; while *Le Nord* refers to the direction from which tea arrived on first reaching Mali, in the nineteenth century; and finally, *Arrami* is the name of a star.

Whereas some of the place names recall the importance of former trading towns, others are names of villages from where the importer comes, still others commemorate specific event in a place. *Gaza Super* derived from Arabic *ghrazi*, 'the conquerer', refers to the town in Israel or Palestine, 'the invincible city'. The tea brand – registered in 2006 – does not just refer to the city but was intended to commemorate the Gaza conflict, as its owner explained to me (interview, Bamako, 2011). *Tabankort* is a village in the northeast of Mali, near Kidal, at the southern border of the Adrar where Ifoghas and Idnan Tuareg live. Here a confrontation between the rebel groups of MNLA and MAA cost many lives in July 2014. This tea brand, which memorialises the incident was registered in 2015.

2.6.2 Animals

In many cases, where an animal is pictured, the brand name is also that of the animal. Only on 13 packages, name and depiction coincide, on 6 the animals can form part of the environment to which the brand name refers but the majority of these brands (21) has a name referring to something else than the depicted animal. So, for instance, the brand *Gazelle* portrays a gazelle; *Deux Girafe* [sic], two giraffes; *Capitaine*, a fish commonly found in the River Niger;

Oiseau Blanc, a white bird; *Cheval*, a horse; *Kangourou*, a kangaroo; *Serval*, the wild cat of the same name; and *Elephant*, an elephant. There are many more examples.

Some of these animal names have additional connotations of which some people might be aware, others not. *Chameau* depicts a two-humped camel employed to transport tea on the terrestrial Silk Road across Asia to the Middle East, and it is the logo of the formerly state-owned Chinese tea company. There is also *Deux Chameaux*, depicting two camels, and *Jamell Sahara* [sic], an Arabic word meaning 'camel of the desert'; such animals have been employed to carry trade goods, tea and sugar included, across the Sahara. The horse, after which *Cheval* is named, is known in the Sahel and Sahara where horse-riding has been widely practiced and the fantasia – war-like performances – is staged on richly decorated horses; the horse also has great meaning in Asia, where nomadic groups bred horses; Chinese emperors sought to obtain them from Tibetans, for use by his cavalry of war, in exchange for tea (Giersch 2010).

Gazelle is a collective term for several gazelle species. In Arabic there are three words for gazelle: *al ghrabi*, *al ghrazel* and *al ghraim* or *ghrīm*. All begin with the Arabic letter خ, which is pronounced as a guttural r; in Latin letters it is written either with G, R or D. There are several names of tea brands that all refer to one or the other version of 'gazelle'. There is *Gazelle*, *Razèle*, *Chazel*, *Daim*, but also other French words referring to the animal such as *Antilope* and *La Biche*, a female gazelle.[1]

2.6.3 Ethnic References and Nomadic Life

Thé Touareg refers to the ethnic group of Niger and northern Mali, particularly known as tea connoisseurs, second only to Saharan traders. Some Touareg families also dominated the trade in salt from Taoudeni and further east between the Sahara and the Sahel. Another ethnic reference is made by the tea brand *Dogon*. The image on the tea package depicts masked Dogon dancers, however, such masked dancers have no direct connection with tea and the Dogon are rather more reputed to be lovers of millet beer, than of green tea. Another apparent reference to an ethnic group is Sonikara; this brand may cite the Soninke who are known as influential traders. Owned by a Malian trader, the packet design is replete with Chinese themes, including a Chinese-style house. *Rass al Khaima* – literally 'the head (*rass*) of the tent (*khaima*)' in Arabic – refers to a promontory but is also the name of an emirate in Hormuz, as the land extends

1 Incidentally, Abu Dhabi is also derived from the word *ghrabi* or 'gazelle', but this is not a brand-name for tea.

into the sea in a form resembling the shape of a tent. Another brand name reference to nomadic life is *Al Jawal*, 'the traveller.'[2]

2.6.4 Symbols

Thé Ciwara names the carved antelope head-crest, which was part of the dancing costume of the *ciwara* masked dancers, belonging to a Bamana cult association responsible for the supervision of agricultural work (Imperato 1970; Wooten 2000). The head-crest has since become a national symbol of Mali. The head-crest depicted on the package is rather small in comparison to the portrayal of a horse rider, armed with a spear, which is probably inspired by a movie character.

Tjernaba is known as a benevolent bush spirit which appears in the shape of a snake; *Mami Wata* quotes the printed image of an Indian snake charmer that has been copied by West African carvers to represent a female water spirit, which lures people beneath water to participate in her riches, in exchange for their spiritual independence (Drewal 2008; Salmons 1977). In Mali there was a popular song called 'Mami Wata', although its heyday preceded the appearance of the tea brand.

Diamant, on the package also written in Arabic, *El Mās*, refers to 'diamond', a symbol of material and immaterial values; Diamant is not only a brand name but is also seen as an attribute of quality to the Super Chunmees. Then there is *Flecha*, an arrow, depicted on the package, with a bow, recognised as a symbol for the power and direction lent to the arrow by the archer. There is *Piano*, which could allude to the musical instrument but also to the soft play of music, but the image on the package is a dromedary. Other brand names quote royal symbols such as *Taaj*, or sometimes spelled *Taj*, meaning 'crown' in Arabic. Although crowns have appeared on several tea packages, only the brand name *Taaj* or *Taj* actually means 'crown'. On the *Al Taj* package is depicted a crown, but on that of *Taaj*, appears a bird. Another symbolic royal reference is *Al Cazar*, the palace, in Arabic.

2.6.5 The Tea Ritual

A good number of brand names refer to tea, tea equipment and activities connected with tea such as *La Théière*, the teapot; *Thé Mina*, the ensemble of the tea set (*té minən*), *La Menthe*, the mint, in Mali only occasionally added to tea; *Nature*, referring to the naturalness of the tea leaves; *Sinothé*, referring to the

2 There is an album with Sudanese music, released in 2013, called 'Al Jawal', a reflection about nomadic life, in which each song represents another step in the journey, with new cities and people along the way.

origin of tea from China; *Akwaba* is an Arabic word meaning glasses (*akwāb* being the plural of *kūp*, glass); and lastly *Akwaba* is also the name of a once popular salsa dance bar in Bamako.

The names *Baro* and *Les Grins* are closely connected to tea. *Les Grins* refers to the small groups of primarily young men drinking tea and chatting (chapter 1). The *Les Grins* package shows a stylised group of people sitting around a tray and tea equipment. *Baro* means 'chat' or 'conversation'; drinking tea provides an ideal social context for this activity by bringing people together for a period of time. One variety of the *Baro* package design employs the national colours green, yellow and red. The reputed abilities of a good tea are underscored by the slogan written on the package: *Akani* (good) *fari foni* (to unfold the body), which could be translated as 'tea unfolds bodily powers and energy'. The design also displays a caravan of people and a two-humped camel, thus connecting the tea to the company – the Zhejiang Tea Import and Export Company – from which this importer procured his tea.

2.6.6 Social Values

Some of the brand names allude to Malian social values with terms in Bámanankan, the trade language spoken in large parts of (southern) Mali: *Dambé* means 'dignity'; *Kunawolo* means 'the one who brings honour, pride and glory to others'. In the context of tea, it could be the one who brings the package of the right quality, at least the picture of a large group of people taking tea might imply this interpretation; *Bonya* means 'the biggest and strongest' and 'hospitality'; *Dawla* 'beauty, charm and elegance'. *Mon Village* refers to the home place, where one comes from and where one's roots are.

Other brand names are derived from Arabic words and cite values that resonate well in the larger region, including North Africa: there is *Elosra*, from Arabic *el osra* or *usra*, 'the family'; *Sahha*, from Arabic 'health'; *Salam*, from Arabic 'peace'. The name could also refer to the commune Salam in the Region of Timbuktu (as in the tea brand Agouni Salam); *Hayat* is the Arabic word for 'life'; *Mona* is the Arabic word for 'the one hoped for or desired', it is also a female name and a French brand; *Sarama* means in Arabic 'capacity of resistance, decision, force'; *Hamza* is an ancient Arabic name, meaning 'sour (refreshing) in taste' and used as a name synonymous to *sarama*; the owner explained that Hamza was the name of a strong warrior; *Achifa* is derived from Arabic *chifā*, 'recovery, health'; *Al Atik* means 'the ancient, the very old'; *Golden* or *Schay al lathīd* means in Arabic 'the tasteful one'; *Lawal*, is from Arabic *el awal*, 'the prime, the first, the best'. This is also a common personal name in Mali and has been a name in the family of the importer; and *Haquiqua* means in Arabic 'reality, the real, the truth'.

2.6.7 Religious References

A number of brand names refer to the Muslim religion, calendar, the prayer, or are blessed names. *Al Maouloud* is the celebration of Prophet Mohamed's birthday; *Chaban* is the eighth month in the Muslim calendar, the month before the Ramadan; *Ramadane* refers to the ninth month, the month of fasting. *Achoura* is the tenth day in the first month of the Muslim year, on which Husayn ibn Ali, the grandson of the Prophet was martyred in the battle of Karbala in Iraq (it is also the name of an Indian festival).

Arafat is a station of the Hadj on the way to Mecca; *Charifa* refers to al Khūz as-Sharīf, the third holy place of Islam in Jerusalem; *Meka* refers to the holy pilgrimage site and city, Mecca. *Halal*, designates behaviour, food and drink that is allowed, and might refer to early debate as to whether green tea should be considered *halal* or *haram* (Damani 2013; Lakhsassi and Sebti 2012).

Mubarak is a holy word, derived from *baraka*, the blessing, it is also a personal name that means 'the blessed one'. *Mabruka* is the female form of this name; there is also *Al Baraka*, 'the blessing'. *Rakim* or *rahīm* is a Muslim name and is mentioned in the Quran; *El Jihad* is the holy war; *Al Fajr* is the 89th sura in the Quran; *El Nass* is also a sura in the Quran and a clear legal injunction. *Kumshlam* is a mal-literation of the answer to *salam aleikum*: *aleikum salam*; *Paradis* refers to the same imagined place as *Al Montāz*, which is derived from the Persian word *farduz*, 'paradise'.

2.6.8 Personal, Family and Company Names

Mubarak and *Mabruka* have already been mentioned; female brand names include *Yasmina*, derived from *yasmin*, a singular flower of the shrub jasmine. *Raissa* means 'the female leader'; the Iranian female name *Nihal* means the 'little plant' or 'the thirsty one'; *Amgro* is a personal name in Yemen. *Maiga* is the name of an influential extended family based in Djenné but also found in other Malian towns. Other brand names are family names of tea importers, which often form part of their company designation: examples are *Koutam* and *Lah*. AAA are the initials of Ahmed Abderahmane Abdi, concommitantly conveying the connotation of the high quality of his imported tea through the use of the A's. *Hassane Ousmane* is named after the importer's late father; *Ousmane Oumar* also alludes to being the name of a family head; *Lobo* is the personal name of the importer; *Amar* is the personal name of a deceased Saharan importer; *Haidara* is the name of the well-known Muslim preacher Serif Ousmane Haidara, and *Wilibali* is a title name for the same preacher; *Oumar ben Tawile* was an Arab poet. *Agouni Salam* is the name of a company selling tea, but also of a travel agency, which is on Facebook with its recent tea packages of the same name. *Chunli* and *Konfo* are Chinese company and brand names.

2.6.9 Historical and Contemporary Personalities

Le Patron is a word that comes from Arabic *al patrūn*, the patron; the image on its package portrays a person, possibly a family ancestor of the importer; *Baobab* is a tree in West Africa, but in Arabic it is spelled *baowāb*, meaning 'the one who guards the door', or the guardian of the house; *Sancho* is named after Fernando Sancho, a character of a Western feature film.

Al Farouk was the last King of Egypt (reign 1936–1952); it is also a male Arabic name, meaning 'the one who is able to differentiate between right and wrong'. Farouk is the epithet for the second khalif after Mohamed and for someone who is ready to do his utmost. *Adoua* was the name of a Moroccan from Taroudant, the leader of the resistance movement Polisario.

Arafat is not only the Muslim pilgrimage site on the route to Mecca but also refers to the late Palestinian politician and Nobel Peace Prize winner (1994), Jassir Arafat. The Malian importer explained that he rather liked this double meaning of the name and had thought of including a photograph of Arafat on the package but then decided for an earthenware teapot. *Mubarak*, registered in the same year as *Arafat*, is owned by another Malian trader and likewise has a double meaning, being a Muslim greeting and a personal name, and is the name of the former Egyptian president, Hosni Mubarak.

2.6.10 Political, Social and Military Events

Mali was very proud to host the Africa Cup in 2002 and the event was commemorated in the design of several tea packages (*La Main en Main*, *Askia*, *Cheval*) that depict footballs. In 2010, Mali celebrated the fiftieth anniversary of its political independence from France (Leyh 2011) and commemorating the event that year, *Cinquantenaire* appeared on the market.

One of the earliest branded tea packages, *Thé Saddam la Force* was created in reference to the waging by the USA of war against Saddam Hussein, the now deceased former president of Iraq, in 1998. Following this, several other brands adopted Saddam in their brand design.

Gaza Super, created in 2006, commemorates the political conflict between Israel and Palestine. The importer explained that they decided to name their brand after the conflict as it was evocative for Malians and especially concerning for the country's Muslims.

Obama emerged in 2008, the year in which Barack Obama was elected American president. The brand was created to celebrate this unique historical election; it is also to be understood as a comment on an international political event. The brand is owned by a Malian, a Djokoramé; the first package design depicts a Chinese tea plantation and the abstracted wooden box imagery; the second version portrays part of an American flag.

In response to the territorial gains won by rebel Muslim groups following the 2012 coup, with the approval of the UN, France, between January 2013 and August 2014, allied with the Malian military and launched a campaign called Opération Serval that had as its objective to liberate the north from the rebels (chapter 1). This military campaign is commemorated by two tea importers who in 2013 created the brands *Serval* and *François Hollande* (the French president at the time). Other recent tea brands such as *Tabankort* also recall conflicts in the north of Mali.

2.6.11 Technical Innovations and Media Channels

Created following the launch of the television channel Canal+ and Multicanal,[3] the tea brand *Canal* was registered in 2003. The Malian partner of the Chinese brand owner explained: 'All people liked the name Canal, which sounded good and modern in their ears'. *Thé Canal* extends the chatting of friends during the tea ritual, emphasising its role as a facilitator of communication, to electronic media, thereby relating a local ritual to global connectivity.

Registered in 2005, the tea brand *Africable* was created by a Malian importer to honour the independent Malian television station established in Bamako in 2004. Africable broadcasts in large parts of Francophone Africa and also broadcasts commercials on behalf of the brand, ensuring both the brand and the television channel create added value through mutual advertising. *Wel Taré*, a term in Fulfulde, is the name of a programme broadcast by Africable at the time. The *Wel Taré* brand was registered in 2009.

There was also *Ikathé portable*, a tea brand registered in 2007; in Bámanankan Ikathé means 'your tea', but the addition 'portable' is in reference to Ikatel, 'your mobile phone provider'. In the same year, when *Ikathé* was created, Ikatel was eventually purchased by the French provider Orange.

These brands connect in various ways the tea ritual to electronic media, and thus the local to the global and vice versa, which is a characteristic feature of successful branding and advertisement (Malefyt and Moeran 2003). The association between the beverage, the brand name and the media serves to add value to each.

2.7 *Company Logos*

Some packages display a company logo in addition to images and brand names. A company logo appears on the packages when a company wishes to promote several different products under one brand name. As the company expands,

3 In 2003, Télé Klédu and Multicanal SA merged as Canal Satellite Horizons and were placed on a new satellite channel (Dioh 2009: 137–143).

the logo may be created from the central image on the tea package, either as a diminished photo or as a stylised image. For example, the logo of Punjabi is an abstracted image of a horse, seen on all packages of *Thé Cheval* and other products of the company. The logo of the company Ousmane Lah et Frères is an oval encompassing an image of a tiger's head with the company's name below it. The tiger figured prominently for the first time on the package of *Hassane Ousmane* and was subsequently employed in small size as the company logo.

Other company logos are more abstract. The package of *Thé Mona* carries a logo consisting of a yellow slice, surrounded by red and blue circles and a grey square or circle in which the company name is written. The package of *Thé François Hollande* depicts the logo of the company – PC, rendered in red – next to the company name 'Prix Casse', which appears in small font.

The company logo is a stable element in the changing world of tea brands. It connects the various products owned by a company and ensures the brands are recognisable as belonging to the same individual importer. However, most tea packages lack any identifiable logo and carry only a brand name in large letters and/or an image, prominently displayed on the packet. From a western economic perspective this would be viewed as short-sighted, working against the idea of establishing the company brand and using it to build up a long-lasting reputation (Mertha 2005). Some importers are indeed unaware of the value of a logo whilst others rather prefer the anonymity that not having a logo confers.

3 Tea Brands, (Multi)Referentiality and Commemoration

The previous sections described the various components that appear in the designs printed on the tea packets. In this section I will consider the entire ensemble of the brand designs, their images, their combinations and their meanings, and how some of them are interpreted by consumers and importers. More specifically, I examine the extent to which the individual elements of design correspond to each other; or whether the name, the images and the design are rather more a bricolage of different ideas than a unit; and how this ensemble may be understood (for further examples of such tea packages, see Figures 59 and 60).

3.1 *Relationship between Picture and Brand Name*

The various elements on a package design – background colours, decorations, logos and pictures – are brought together with the brand name to comprise the brand (Okediji 2006; Packard 2010: 159). This combination should make the brand unique. Analysis of the various tea brands will show that in some the name and associated images correspond well but in many other cases the match is less easy to spot or not obvious at all. Only about a third of the tea packages in my collection show strong correlation between picture and name.

Among the brands demonstrating such strong correlation is *Thé Niger,* which sports a medallion at its centre, upon which is depicted the River Niger, an important waterway on which tea was transported to the villages in the inner Niger Delta in Mali. Other brand names have a far less obvious relationship with the picture emblazoned on the package, although some connection may be established. Consumers generally associated strong animals being depicted on the tea packets with their vigour and resilience of surviving the parched climate, a trait supposedly conveyed upon the consumers. For example, one consumer noted that 'you consume the tea, and you gain the strength of a horse, you will be full of energy' (interview, Bamako, 2007). Then upon being shown the *Ciwara* tea package, portraying a horse-rider with a spear, the same consumer remarked: 'The horse is a royal symbol. It is fed with millet and salt, but you do not think about a warrior with a spear when you see a horse'. Some consumers criticised associating a horse with tea. Referring to a commercial for *Thé Cheval,* one of the senior staff of AMAP explained:

> The choice of a horse for this commercial was totally bizarre. The horse connotes strength and power (*la force*), this does not go together with tea but it can go with milk. Those people who made the commercial have seemingly not understood that the horse is about strength. The product, which gives strength is the milk. But tea does not provide strength, it is a stimulant. Hence, the commercial is difficult to understand. INTERVIEW, BAMAKO, 2009

He criticised the Chinese brand owner's commercial, which he felt did not resonate well with Malian cultural connotations.

The brand name *Elosra* ('family' in Arabic) refers to family values, the picture renders tea glasses on a tray surrounding an oriental teapot. It inspires the assumption that the family drinks tea together, but Malians generally would not associate tea consumption with family values nor would the entire family consume tea together; moreover, the meaning of the Arabic word is also unfamiliar to Malians. They would only understand the tea equipment, which conveys the impression of belonging to a wealthy household.

Some brands offer even fewer opportunities for linkages between product, brand name and design elements. The brand name *Capitaine* refers to the fish of the same name. There is one brand with that name that has a picture of fish, but there is also another brand called *Capitaine,* the packet of which depicts a family of elephants. Similarly, *Piano* displays a dromedary on the package. Only the dromedary has some connection with tea, being used to transport it across the desert.

Whilst the images used on some packages – gazelles, camels, caravans, desert landscapes, plantations, tea glasses, waterfalls, footballs, mosques – will be fully understood by many people they may have further connotations that require a closer look, cultural background knowledge and the willingness to delve into local cultural imagination. One needs to know that *Taoudeni* is a salt mine in northern Mali to appreciate its importance as a centre for commerce on the trans-Saharan trade route.

Brand names and the associated designs may each comprise several layers of meaning that are not, at first, very obvious. Some package designs evoke meanings related to the name, to the image, or the colours, which may again evoke further interpretations. For example, *Gazelle* refers to the animal, dainty, elegant and agile; young women are attributed these same positive characteristics and are also frequently – in their absence – the topic of conversations in the men's tea *grins;* gazelle is a sobriquet for a beautiful woman, often flatteringly called 'ma gazelle'. *Ghriim al baraka* refers to a white gazelle – a blessed animal among Muslims. *Super Lion* not only alludes to the big cat as a powerful animal of the savannah but also recalls it as the 'totemic animal' of the Keïta royal family, the founders of the former Empire of Mali.

Both *Arafat* and *Mubarak* embody the double reference to the Arabian politician and Muslim religion but the packages show a Chinese teapot, or a person riding a dromedary in the desert.[4] Similarly, *Canal* combines connotations of tea as a facilitator of sociability and global connectedness through media but the package design depicts a tea plantation in China. *Zamane* also conveys several meanings: in Arabic the word means 'age'; the term also refers to a daily newspaper and a Malian radio channel, whilst its image reminds of the earlier *Flecha* design. *Askia* was registered in 2004, sometime after Mali had hosted the Africa Cup, by a broker selling tea of the Chinese company Dapeng. The packet appeared in several variations that all depict a football, with an eagle – the symbol of the Malian national football team; the images on its reverse include a waterfall in China, a rose, or a tea plantation. The name Askia is a direct reference to the Songhay Empire's ruling dynasty during the fifteenth and sixteenth centuries before its conquest by Morocco; thus, three separate meanings are assembled in one package design: Malian history, national sports and Chinese imagery.

4 The rider on the dromedary actually rather looks like a tourist with a photo camera hanging around his shoulder, an image probably just downloaded from the internet for the purpose.

These multi-faceted designs could be explained by the cooperation between different actors in creating tea brands, but they may also be understood as an exercise in bricolage, reflecting how in everyday practice people experience that not everything is coherent, or in fact, devoid of contradiction but may be rather multi-referential. This opens a door into a new way of considering the iconography of tea packages against the backdrop of local cultural worlds and discourses about tea. Forming part of a transcultural art of creating designs and marketing green tea brands that include local imagery and partly incomprehensible foreign elements that may raise curiosity and become meaningful to local consumers by combining, as mentioned earlier, local references and themes that connect consumers to global life (Moeran 1996; Mazarella 2003). In this sense of fusing local and global ideas they could be termed glocal – glocalisation being understood either as individuals making sense of the interaction between local and global or as the creation of products or services intended for the global market, but customised to suit the local cultures (Habibul Khondker 2005). Regarding the second meaning, the tea brands are not glocal because they are only meant for a local market that only gradually globalises with the migrants from this region. Many designs, however, although containing a global product, remain decidedly local.

3.2 *Tea Brands and the Culture of Commemoration*

A surprise is the discovery that many brand names and images on the tea packets have nothing to do with the product that they contain and promote. A link is only obvious in brand names and images that make direct reference to tea equipment, drinking groups, tea leaves and plantations; perhaps also oblique references to its country of origin, the trade route along which it travelled, and the camel caravans which transported it. A commonality of meanings might also be established by employing symbols referring to the properties of tea, for example, as an energiser, and perhaps also where the brand name refers to a well-known tea trader.

The names of these tea brands whose package design have little or nothing to do with tea rather reflect a lively culture of commemoration and referencing. They illustrate the broad range of connections and disparities ranging from unfamiliar tea equipment to social events, from technological innovations to international politics. This resonates with tea being Mali's national beverage, meaning whilst it is embraced as a means of communication, a medicine, an energiser, a facilitator of socialising, at the same time its critics may also project onto the beverage the problem of youth unemployment, frictional social relationships and corruption (Röschenthaler forthc.). Hence, tea may represent many different themes at the same time, even when they appear contradictory and ambiguous. In so doing, a variety of different interpretations, or otherwise condensing multiple references may be assembled and make a beverage such as tea a complex, multi-referential or multi-vocal symbol (Malefyt and Morais 2012: 37). The tea package design seems to follow such an approach.

From the start, tea brands offered a spectrum of meanings and references, a practice that continued with subsequent brand creations. *Thé Saddam La Force* was an important trend setter in that it made direct reference to a significant world event. Registered in 1998 in Dakar, but also sold in Mali, this tea reflects Saddam Hussein's particular qualities – not without some irony – of personal strength, although perhaps he was too stubborn. The same was said about the tea: it was not very good but strong. For several years, *Thé Saddam La Force* reminded consumers of the Iraq war, and *Gaza Super* and *Nuovo Gaza* of the hostile relationship between Israelis and Palestinians in the Gaza region. *Thé Canal* commemorated the advent of the television channel Canal+ and Canal Horizon in 2003, and *Africable* the creation of the independent television station by a Malian in Bamako in 2004 (Diakon and Röschenthaler 2017). *Thé Haidara* recalls the influential religious leader Serif Ousmane Haidara in 2005. The footballs on tea packages recall, even years after the event, the excitement created in Mali when the country hosted the Africa Cup in 2002. *Ikathé* celebrated the opportunities that the mobile telephone brought to Malians, *Thé Obama* the election of Barack Obama as American president in 2008, and *Cinquantenaire* the fiftieth anniversary of Mali's independence in 2010. Thé *Tabankort*, *Serval* and *François Hollande* remind people of the complications brought by the conflict and the military mobilisation in the northern part of Mali. All except of *Askia* and *Canal* are owned by local importers.

The tea brands employ either stylised portrayals, or otherwise photographic images of landscapes, architecture or other items, although not normally photographs of people for their package designs. The exceptions have already been mentioned: *Le Patron* and *Wilibali*. However, placing a portrait of a prominent living personality on the tea package like that of *François Hollande* is a new idea. *Obama* and *Haidara* also refer to contemporary personalities but portraits are not employed to represent them on tea packages. A great number of items that displayed the portrait of the American politician and the religious leader, however, were seen on the market, including fancy fabrics in Mali (Röschenthaler 2015). Obama's image was reproduced on numerous items all over Africa.[5] All the event-related tea package designs like *François Hollande* – as well as many others – obviously have nothing directly to do with tea. Past

5 See Mutongi Kenda (2017), for Obama images on public transport vehicles in Kenya.

problems in the northern part of the country do collide with the concept of people from the north being the earliest acknowledged tea consumers and the recognised connoisseurs of tea in Mali; they are among the most successful importers. Green tea however, was never politicised in the way that other drinks were – beer for example, in Cameroon and in Ethiopia (Getachew Senishaw and Röschenthaler 2021) or food stuffs such as rice in Mali – because the drink is embedded in different political and social constellation in the country, i.e. the politicians are not involved in the importation or price regulation of tea (for a comparison, see Röschenthaler 2019).

Many of the brand names resonate with people's experience or rather imagination of savannah and desert animals, trading places, Bamana moral values, social events and the importance of the media. Brand names of trading places refer to the towns along the trade routes to the north, but only some have been selected – Timbuktu, Arawane, Tilimsi, Taoudeni – there is no tea named Djenné, Mopti, Gao, Bamako or Tindouf and none of the names of trading places in the southern part of the country have been chosen at all. Place names are chosen for two reasons: either because of their prominence in the tea trade (also known to Chinese traders) or because their owner hails from the place.

Despite the current methods of conveying imports aboard container ships, the imagery of camel caravans winding their way across the sand dunes of the Sahara is sustained by both Chinese and Malian traders whose tea brand names evoke the history and the ancient grandeur and glamour as well as the adventure and risks associated with trans-Saharan trade. By evoking memories of historic salt caravans, they add value to their teas using names such as *Azalai* (salt caravans), *Taoudeni* (the salt mines), *Azawad* (the region through which these caravans travelled), *Arawane*, the camel watering place, and *Tombouctou*, the trading hub and centre of Muslim scholarship as well as *Le Nord*, referring to the geographical direction from which green tea arrived and from which Islam came, too – also a very popular reference for tea brands.

Other brand names refer to places, animals, things or ideas that are less familiar to Malian consumers. *Kangourou*, for example, was employed by its Malian owner because the animal is virtually unknown in Mali. The readings of the imagery employed in the tea packets also illustrates how complex can be the meanings ascribed by consumers to the brands and also the disparate ways in which they can be interpreted by consumers and importers coming from different cultural contexts.

The names given to tea brands reach far into the past (*Askia*) and also deep into the social life and values of Malian people (*Dambé*, *Dawla*) as well as delving into distant political events and conflicts that have international implications (*Gaza, Obama, Saddam La Force*). Tea brands have been created and sold shortly after the respective event commemorated by their name. Malian consumers were fully aware of the connection of brand creation with an event and confirmed it. When referring to tea brands recalling social and political events, the importer of *Thé Cinquantenaire* used the expression *thés evennementielles*, 'event-related teas', that has also been used in the context of fabrics printed for specific events and depicting important personalities (interview, Bamako, 2013; Röschenthaler 2015; Spencer 1982).[6]

The creation of the tea packet designs stands for an active examination of events of social, cultural and political relevance. The tea brands arouse an event-related kaleidoscopic imaginary framework which encompasses references to military action, social and political tournaments, local values, cultural references, history and religion. Different from its ambiguous meanings as a national drink, the brand names of tea are not subject to local political controversies but events and connotations that are of relevance for daily life and thinking. It provides an unsystematic and eclectic overall view employing bricolages and assemblages of themes that are partly local and partly cosmopolitan, by combining geographically and temporally diverse ideas, for example, a tea plantation, with football and Malian royal history, words in Chinese, Arabic, French and English. Thus, the tea brands consist to different proportions of African, Chinese and global design elements and combining Malian and Chinese input through co-creation. Some of them keep to local and regional references (*Gazelle, Koutam, Taoudeni*), others form a hybrid or bricolage of Sino-Malian references (*Askia, Arawane, Arafat*) and still others can be termed glocalised designs (Robertson 1995; Habibul Khondker 2005: 191; Hannerz 1992). These are symbols of cosmopolitan reflection fusing local and global images and experiences (*Canal, Ikathé, Obama, Gaza, François Hollande*).

4 Trends in the Tea Package Design

The references to wooden boxes on the package design and the floral decorations that have been frequent in the 2000s are no longer seen on recent tea packages. They have lost their meaning with the fading memory of wooden boxes among consumers and were abandoned in favour of landscapes and other singular features referring to historical trade routes or more topical themes. Also, tea is no longer simultaneously offered in several qualities, each

6 More well-known is the term 'commemorative fabrics' for such textiles (Spencer 1982).

indicated by a different colour; now the predominant colours used at any given time rather follow those employed by popular tea brands as they emerge every few years.

Another recent trend is the deletion of all dispensable information, even including indications of the quality of the tea. Some importers go so far as to refrain from promoting a brand name, or even indicating that the package contains Chinese green tea. This is not necessarily an indication of low quality, for even some high-quality metal tea boxes may not carry a brand name, only displaying an image and designating the quality. The registration of a brand with OAPI does not require a brand name; this will become clear in chapter 7. As mentioned earlier, green tea brands are relatively colourful – compared to most other brands registered in BOPI – and intuitively recognisable by conveying an ambiance also evoked by the tea ritual. Oriental ornaments, sand-inspired colours, images of dunes, camel caravans, tea equipment, fresh leaves and the pouring of tea into glasses contribute to such an ambiance, in combination with the arrangement of a central image and brand name.

Interesting again is how such designs are created through a process of negotiation and collaboration between Malian importers and Chinese brokers and suppliers, or between Malian and Chinese trading partners. Others are generated by individual Chinese tea brokers on their own. As mentioned earlier, many Chinese brokers have developed their own ideas about appropriate imagery and names for use in brand designs for the African market. They combine images and names from a wide range of potentially appealing African, oriental and Asian themes. Doing this, they do use a kind of research methodology compared by Malefyt and Morais (2012) to the work of anthropologists in their studies of advertising companies seeking to find what advertisement would be appealing to potential consumers.

The early brand names include references to diverse cultural contexts, the Arabic cultural space, through references to Islam and also the earlier experiences of Chinese traders selling in Arabic markets. Such findings corroborate the impression that Chinese traders have been pushing into the Malian market after 1991 but that Malian importers have found ways and means to dominate in the long run and this is reflected in the tendencies and trends seen in their brand names. This revelation obviously stands in contradiction to the widespread opinion that China is the sole economic actor in the export business and swamps African markets with cheap products, an impression underscored by official statistics (cf. Alden 2008; Broadman 2007; Shinn and Eisenman 2012). It is rather more that Chinese brokers offer elements from their tool box but Malian importers, provided they are themselves creative and entrepreneurial, propose their images and make the final decisions about the style and content of the design that will appear on their tea packets. After the earliest brand names for green tea were created by Chinese suppliers, except for *Baro* and *Saddam La Force* and a few others, some time elapsed before more Malians themselves began to proffer their own brand names.

With few exceptions, only the Chinese-owned brands display Chinese imagery such as waterfalls, Chinese architecture and tea plantations, and the carrying of such imagery usually indicates Chinese ownership; otherwise, it may suggest a Malian importer with little specific idea as to the style of a brand he preferred. Animal emblems, especially those that live in the desert or on the savannah and also historical locations is shared by both, but event-related tea brand names are almost exclusively applied by Malian and Saharan importers and do not form part of the Chinese repertoire.

The later development of tea branding is characterised by mutual influencing, learning and imitating trends, if not the copying of brand names and images (chapter 8). It is interesting to note that despite mutual influence, co-creation and imitation, there are differences between the approaches to the creation of the tea package design of Chinese and Malian traders. The most unusual and more curious brand designs – those having the greatest variety of images and the highest bricolage character – are of Chinese origin, especially *Askia*.

Whereas many Chinese brands comprise a bricolage of various elements, Malian importers prefer singular images such as the salt of Taoudeni, a volcano, the River Niger, a tiger, or another attractive animal. These images are timeless and usually harmonise well with people's ideas of drinking tea at a tea ritual. Examples of brand designs that reduce the detailing included on a packet to a minimum of important information, whilst providing a clear message are *Achoura, Rocki, Dawla, Mabruka* and *François Hollande*. Some importers applied this strategy from the outset, in the first half of the 2000s; these include *Mona, Le Nord* and *Diamant*. All these brands are owned by Malians, but also the popular Chinese-owned *Simida* adopted such a design in 2016. In short, most of the big Malian importers pursue images not yet included in the Chinese brokers' brand construction kit. Durable trademarks are only gradually becoming more widespread among tea importers, some of whom developed their company logo from the central image of their tea package design. They only begin to do this when they have several brands, or products under the same brand name.

Different from the tea package design, Malian tea advertisement has refrained from working with the exciting range of themes and images addressed in the designs (chapter 3). Malian importers did not employ the combination of local and global references displayed on so many tea packages that according to

Malefyt and Moeran (2003) characterise a compelling advertisement. In their commercial tea advertisement, Malian merchants almost exclusively focused on the product itself and the consumption of green tea by ordinary people in the local tea ritual.

As this and the previous chapters have shown, brand names, company logos, and specific typography are designed to distinguish the products of one producer from those of another and guide consumers in their purchasing decisions. Advertisement, packaging and graphic design also add value to the brand and enable it to communicate its message (chapter 3). The investment in design and marketing the brand entitle brand owners to claim it their exclusive intellectual property which others may only use with their permission. The next chapter discusses how these ideas have been implemented and received in Mali.

CHAPTER 7

Tea Brands as Intellectual Property and the Challenge of Piracy

The purchase of a brand-named product involves traders and consumers acquire ownership of the material components of a product – the package and its contents – but not the immaterial aspects – the package design, brand name and trademark. Legally, they own only a part of the bundle of rights connected with the product. They may consume the contents or even sell them but they would not be permitted to sell different tea in a package of the same design, since with its purchase they did not acquire the rights associated with the commodity's immaterial aspects as represented by the design on the package.

Whilst tea was sold loose from wooden boxes, the idea that one could possess the rights to the immaterial aspects of it, occurred to no-one. The added value tea held, nevertheless depended on its rarity, it being a curiosity, and the prestige associated with its consumption as part of an impressive and exclusive ritual (Röschenthaler forthc.). As presented in chapter 2, there were different appellations, qualities and types of tea but as yet, there were no brands. Tea leaves were just considered *ataya* (tea). Over the course of the twentieth century, consumers and traders were exposed to industrially produced brands of various products, most of which were owned by foreign companies, such as instant coffee and black tea. A few Malian wholesalers acquired exclusive rights to sell such products in the country but without owning the brands. This changed in the 1990s, shortly after the creation of the trademark office.

In Mali, the Centre Malien de Promotion de la Propriété Industrielle (CEMAPI), responsible for registering trademarks, was created in 1983. Intellectual property rights only acquired importance, after the 1990s, in the context of the growing neoliberal market economy and its pervasive commercialisation, mediatisation and judicialisation. This process began as a consequence of technological improvements, the liberalisation of the market and media reforms (Röschenthaler and Diawara 2016). This was when tea brands began to proliferate with such names as *Saddam La Force*, *Chameau*, *Baro*, *Cheval* and *Askia*. From then on, Malian merchants understood they could claim a package design and brand name their exclusive property. From the outset, as has been documented in the BOPI and outlined in chapter 2, most of the registered brands were owned by foreign companies, but soon Malian merchants

 | DOI:10.1163/9789004505698_009

began to gradually register their own brands. A brand owner is most usually the producer, or patron, who commissions the design, however, with regards to Chinese green tea, they are, almost exclusively, either (Chinese) brokers or (Malian) importers.

Intellectual property law and brand registration enables importers to lay claim to a brand as their property. This ensures that each brand name becomes connected to specific importers. Registration of tea brands impact on the use of design elements and names, denying free availability to others because they have exclusive ownership. Intellectual property law thus prevents traders from profiting from the creative work of other traders because the latter have presumably invested in developing the brand. It is in principle possible to purchase permission to acquire the right to use the brand name belonging to another trader, as a senior staff member of CEMAPI told us:

> What justifies this ownership of brands is that someone has invested in the brand creation, but the other person has only seen the finished product and wants to work with it. To do this legally, the commercial law provides the possibility of making a licencing contract that allows another party to exploit the brand without previous investment.
> INTERVIEW, BAMAKO, 2016

But I have not heard of any Malian importer ever making use of this option.

In this chapter, I first examine how international trademark protection gained relevance in Mali and consider how trademark protection organisations and the national offices of member states emerged in Africa. I also look at the tasks they perform and the various brand registration requirements that exist. Then I continue to discuss the geographical reach out of brand protection, China's approach to intellectual property and how Chinese and Malian partnerships work together within this framework. Finally, with relevance to Mali, I look at the various possibilities with regard to the management of intellectual property in brands and in particular how it relates to Islam, given that the majority of Malians are Muslims.

The chapter shows that different ideas prevail in Francophone Africa and in China about what exactly trademark law protects. Malian agency emerges when importers invest trust in their Chinese partners to share ownership in brands in order to bridge the diverging rights regimes. Mali with a large Muslim population and post-colonial socialist experience is an interesting field for reflecting about alternative ways of conceptualising intellectual property. These reflections provide the background on which to understand Malian importers' considerate dealing with pirates (chapter 8).

1 Trademark Law and the Working of OAPI and CEMAPI

This first section examines the history behind the concept of intellectual property regarding trademarks and brand names, the means by which they acquired importance in Mali (and other Francophone West African countries). These issues form part of a more general discussion about the ways people cope with regulations imposed upon them by their governments (Diawara and Röschenthaler 2016).

1.1 *The Beginnings of Trademark Law*

More generally, notions about local rights in immaterial cultural goods were already widespread long before the introduction of international intellectual property law (Hirsch and Strathern 2004; Röschenthaler 2011; Röschenthaler and Diawara 2016) and also there were means to indicate a producer and owner of certain valuable products. Trademarks have existed as seals (Wengrow 2010) and marks of individual potters on ancient Greek and Roman pottery (Rogers 1910) as well as on cloth in medieval Europe (Packard 2010: 162; Richardson 2008). A first trademark law was passed by the English Parliament in 1398, requiring bakers to mark the bread they produced with their sign (Schechter 1925: 49). More recent trademark laws were introduced with the advent of industrial mass production in the nineteenth century. Trademarks were created in order to distinguish between the products of industrialists and from them, the idea that value was added by the marks in relation to other brands, emerged. Subsequently, ownership in the immaterial aspects of products became of national importance in Europe. France kicked off national trademark legislation in 1857, and was followed in 1862 by Britain – registration of trademarks only began in Britain in 1875 – and the USA in 1870.

In African countries trademark protection was introduced during colonial times although at the time, it was intended to protect European interests, rather than those of Africans who were excluded under the pretext that they were in a state of poverty and had neither protectable brands, nor relevant inventions (Peukert 2016a). The present registration and publication system, as it is practiced by the Organisation Africaine de la Propriété Intellectuelle (OAPI), was set up first in Britain in 1938, and is based on the intent-to-use concept with an examination-based application and publication system. Under this system, trademarks could become subject to licencing, which became the model for other trademark registration systems (Bently 2008). Most countries require formal registration in order to legally pursue its violation. OAPI adopted this system of protection by registration, as had France. Trademarks are also protected under authors' rights, however, without the possibility of bringing a case to court.

The precise functioning of the trademark law in Mali is based on the French model, introduced during colonial times. Following independence, most African governments merely adopted the colonial model. African countries signed the 1962 agreement of Libreville (with 12 members, including Madagascar) and the Bangui agreement of 1977. Based on colonial legacies, the African Regional Intellectual Property Organisation (ARIPO),[1] created by the 1976 Lusaka Agreement, is the organisation that protects industrial designs, patents and trademarks in most Anglophone countries. The Francophone countries first united under the auspices of the Office africain et malgache de la propriété africaine (OAMPI, with Madagascar as a member), subsequently replaced by the creation of OAPI, following the 1977 Bangui Agreement. OAPI has 17 member countries, with headquarters in Yaounde, Cameroon (for a history of the establishment of intellectual property in Africa, see Peukert 2016a).[2] Each member state has a national office which collects and manages the local registrations.

As a Francophone country, Mali is a member of OAPI and the responsible national institution, created in 1983, is called Centre Malien de Promotion de la Propriété Industrielle (CEMAPI). Between the years 1983–2002, CEMAPI was part of the ministry of commerce, however, from 2002, it became an autonomous institution. Another institution is responsible for the rights of authors over music, arts and literature, which in Mali is called Bureau malien du droit d'auteur (BUMDA) and has existed since 1986. The offices for authors' rights are not united in an overall organisation such as OAPI and ARIPO and they only adhere to the 1886 Berne convention, following its agreements (Peukert 2016a; Röschenthaler and Diawara 2016). A similar organisation to OAPI has been created in North Africa, which also registers green tea brands of companies based in Morocco, for example.[3]

1 The headquarters of ARIPO is in Harare, Zimbabwe. Member countries of ARIPO are Botswana, Gambia, Ghana, Kenya, Lesotho, Liberia, Malawi, Mozambique, Namibia, Rwanda, Sao Thomé and Principe, Sierra Leone, Somalia, Sudan, Swaziland, Tanzania, Uganda, Zambia, and Zimbabwe. Nigeria, Libya, Egypt and Tunisia have observer status. Of these countries, only Gambia and Ghana are situated in West Africa. At first, the name of this organisation was African Regional Industrial Property Organisation. In 2005, it was renamed African Regional Intellectual Property Organisation. In 2003, the Banjul agreement on trademarks was issued (Ncube and Laltaika 2013).

2 The OAPI member states are Benin, Burkina Faso, Cameroon, Central African Republic, Comores, Congo-Brazzaville, Côte d'Ivoire, Equatorial Guinea, Gabon, Guinea, Guinea Bissau, Mali, Mauritania, Niger, Senegal, Togo, Tchad (www.oapi.int, accessed April 2020).

3 Each of the member countries of the Maghreb has its own national office. In Morocco it is called Office marocain de la propriété industrielle et commerciale (OMPIC), created in 1982; In Tunisia: Institut national de la normalisation de la propriété industrielle (INNPI), created in 1982; and in Algeria: Institut national Algérien de la propriété industrielle (INAPI), created

Whilst intellectual property was validated in 1962, in most African countries it acquired relevance for authors' rights in the 1980s, and a short while later for industrial inventions and trademarks. Encouraged by the World Bank on the grounds that it was essential for a country's economic development the implementation of intellectual property law was established to reduce informal economic activity and give African governments a system of control, order, secure product quality and ensure the health of consumers, because national laws were considered insufficient (OAPI 2018).

According to this approach, the investment in trademarks (creation of the design, advertisement, registration with CEMAPI) justified exclusive ownership of the brand and secured for proprietors the monopoly wherever the law applied. This approach follows a logic that is based on the assumptions of the capitalist market economy (Okediji 2006). This means that 'if signs are protected, profit falls to a few' (Hulme 2015: 18). It also means that ultimately consumers pay for benefits accrued by more hygienic packaging, proofed quality, the inclusion of correct quantities and trust in the integrity of brand owners; and, most important, it provides government with additional tax revenues. Concomitantly, introduction of the law requires an increased control effort and brings about the busying of the commercial court because the industry of brands creates an industry of fake brands (Chang 2004, Röschenthaler and Diawara 2016; Sundaram 2010). With the growing accessibility of digital technology, the copying of art forms and designs has become easier and with the upsurge in trademark infringements the discourse on piracy – the inevitable twin of intellectual property (Sundaram 2010) – came to be established.

1.2 *The Role of OAPI and CEMAPI*

As defined on the OAPI website (www.oapi.int), the organisation is responsible for the registration and protection of industrial design, patents (inventions) and trademarks. For example, green tea brand protection falls beneath trademarks, which more generally concern creations with ornamental and aesthetic character, but not the technical characteristics of the product to which the trademark is attached. It is about the two- or three-dimensional surface of an object, i.e. the lines, forms and colours, not its inner functioning, or its physical

in 1998. It protects the brands for ten years with an option of extension. Morocco and Algeria signed the protocol of Madrid in 1891 and Tunisia in 1892, but no longer in 1988. The Maghreb countries apply the 1957 Nice classification of products. The designs are registered in OMPIC without names as in Mali. See the website of the OMPIC: www.ompic.org.ma, accessed April 2020.

form. The technical aspects may be protected as a patent (invention) and the outer form of the product as industrial design.

A trademark can be protected for a period of five years, with the option of extending protection twice, each for five more years. The website states that trademarks and industrial designs are of a two-fold nature (*une nature hybride*) as they fall under the remit of both art and industry. They do not belong to one precise judicial field but are situated between the authors' rights and industrial property law. Creators of a design or mark can register it with OAPI and benefit from the protection granted by industrial property law, as issued by the revised annex IV of the Bangui agreement. The protection can be extended to a maximum 15 years (less than the 25 years applicable in France). They can alternatively, or additionally, refer to authors' rights for which in principle no registration is necessary as it protects from the beginning of creation. In Mali, the authors' rights protect for 50 years after the death of the creator (in France it is 75 years). Creators who have not registered their trademark are still protected by their authors' rights or intellectual property law (OAPI 2018; Peukert 2016a).

OAPI follows the procedure prescribed for international trademark registration by the Madrid protocol of 1989, which is based on article 6 of the Paris convention of 1967 (a union of all member states) and provides a trademark with a renewable five-year protection. It prohibits the use of imitation trademarks which could create confusion for consumers. Should an imitation be discovered, a request for cancellation must be submitted within five years. Additionally, OAPI supports CEMAPI in its work by providing materials for the promotion of intellectual property (advertising, stalls at trade fairs, flyers, information materials, and regular training in France for staff in responsible positions) (interview, Bamako, 2009).

Registration grants brand owners the right to exclusive ownership to their design and its use for their commercial purposes. No other trader may use a given registered design without the express permission of its owner. Some importers register brands because they consider doing so represents a worthwhile investment, others, less certain of its value, do so without expecting much benefit from it. Many Malian tea importers register their brands, even though it reduces their profits slightly, to acquire – at least in theory – access to legal support in the event that they need to consider commercial court (*tribunal commerciale*) action against copiers. One importer remarked that 'at the beginning, you do not need to register, but when you notice that it is selling, you will register your brand with OAPI, so that no other person is allowed to use it', whereas another importer immediately registered his brand before travelling to China for the first time (interviews, Bamako, 2013). Of 163 brands, collected between 2007 and 2016, 72 are registered, compared with 91 unregistered brands; my photographic collection includes further 20 unregistered brands. An explanation as to why this is so, will be provided over the course of this and following chapters.

2 Requirements for Registering a Brand

CEMAPI manages the registrations of brands submitted by businesspeople in Mali. In 2009, CEMAPI had fifteen employees, whose salaries were paid by the state. They check the applications for completeness and then forward them to the headquarters of OAPI, at Yaounde. CEMAPI provides this service free of charge, but OAPI charges fees for the registration. To avoid corruption, the registration fees are directly sent to OAPI and don't go through the hands of CEMAPI's employees.

An application for the registration of a brand must include the following documents: the name and address of the applicant, the place (town, country) of commercial activity, the name of a licenced lawyer (who can represent a case at court), a sample (image) of the trademark or brand, the colours that the brand depicts, the products or classes of foods to be traded (Nice classification) and a receipt from a bank showing that the registration fees have been paid to OAPI. OAPI follows the Nice international worldwide classification system of goods and services, which groups marketable products and services into 45 classes. Classes 1 to 34 refer to goods and classes 35 to 45 to services. Tea, other beverages and foods are in class 30 (OAPI 2018). Importers are left to decide whether to register their brand for tea only, or to include a variety of class 30 products. They may limit their trademark to a single class or extend it to include two more classes. The different *Canal*, *Lawal* and *Hayat* products, for example, covered several product classes which included tea, coffee, grain products and oils. This classification system is designed to limit the extension of the trademark to defined products. Thus, another trader may use the same trademark but for a different product class for which it has not previously been registered by the initial trader. As milk and tea belong to different product classes, for example, *Lait Sahel* and *Thé Sahel* can be legally registered by two different importers.

CEMAPI will confirm the documentation and the design meet its official requirements before dispatching the application to OAPI in Yaounde. OAPI will consider the application, either accepting it, rejecting it or it may request modifications. On acceptance, the brand is published in the BOPI, where all the attendant details are noted. The registration is valid in all the seventeen member countries of OAPI and hence the brand is granted protection in those countries. Before and after 2010, there were an average of fifteen applications per year from Mali (interview, Bamako, 2009), ten years later there were as many as 30 applications for green tea alone.

Registration fees are 400,000 francs CFA, but should the brand be published in colour, an additional fee of 50,000 francs CFA must be paid to OAPI. After successfully registering their brand, importers will receive several documents, all under OAPI's seal: the certificate of registration, the certificate of non-forfeiture (*non-déchéance*) and the certificate of non-deletion (*non-radiation*). No-one else can legally use the registered brand. The documents are essential in the event that an importer decides that the copied products should be seized by the police and the pirate sued in court.

3 The Work of CEMAPI and OAPI

The receipt of applications for registration, including confirmation of their satisfactory completion, or alternatively the indication of errors or inconsistencies contained within, is the main task of CEMAPI, before it dispatches them to Yaounde. Compliance with legal requirements is also inspected, so for example, article 6 of the Paris convention states that a brand image cannot depict the national flag of a country. Applicants may choose whether to register the visual representation of a name or an image or a product package, together with an indication of the colours applied.

Tea importers had differing opinions about the responsibilities of OAPI. One argued that OAPI should check whether a brand name already existed in Africa, or Europe (interview, Bamako, 2009); another felt that the registration of *Gazelle et ses petites* should have been rejected by OAPI because it amounted to unfair competition (interview, Bamako, 2013; the case will be explained in chapter 9). Only a senior CEMAPI staff member was able to explain that it was not within the remit of OAPI to check whether a brand name already existed. OAPI's sole duty was to examine applications against the formal criteria. He also stated that a foreign trader who wished to import products to Mali was recommended to register his brand in the country (interview, Bamako, 2013, 2016). He also outlined that the trader who registered a brand first possessed the exclusive right to sell under that brand name. In the event of several similar applications to use the same brand name, OAPI would accept both applications and wait whether the importer who registered first, noticed that another importer had also registered the brand, and decided to sue the trader. A plaintiff has six months to file an opposition. One of the importers was aware that 'if a brand on the market is not registered, then any other trader can register this brand and sell the product under that name, and if one's Chinese business partner has registered it then it is not possible for the Malian partner to register it as well' (interview, Bamako, 2013). Nevertheless, there were many brands on the Malian market that were neither registered in Mali nor in China.

The principle that it is the task of claimants to claim their right in a brand name or another name or design before a court becomes active, produces many legal uncertainties and delegates the responsibility from the law makers away to members of the society. For example, regarding *François Hollande*, I was informed by the importer that he had requested permission to use the name as his tea brand but it is most unlikely that the owners of *Tombouctou, Touareg, Ayoune*, or *Haidara* similarly sought permission. Having a tea brand named after you may be considered an honour – as it is generally meant – a recognition, or even advertisement for one's name and town (chapter 6) but it may be seen as an illegitimate exploitation of someone else's immaterial property, or aspect of their personality from which someone else is earning an income.[4] Some names or terms are part of the commons and may be freely used, but once registered they can no longer be used freely, whereas other names must remain within the commons. There are rules concerning this issue, but their application in daily practice is complex.

Registration of a product involves all the design components appearing on the package, including the colours specified in the application. The number of colours is unlimited and depends on the complexity of the image. The registered colours can be applied on the design in various combinations. The design may be protected in these colours, however, the situation is rather uncertain, should the image be sold in different colours by someone else. Many importers register brands with the image of a tea package on which is written 'Thé vert de Chine' but they also register this image for other products. Of course, this tea image is not appropriate for another product without adaptation. For example, pasta cannot be sold in a package displaying the legend 'green tea'. Very few importers register merely their company logo or trademark, most believing that doing so would not be sufficient to protect their brand. That the importers of *Canal* and *Lawal* have registered their brands several times, once for tea, once for the typeface of the name, and once for several product classes but all still employ the tea design, serves to highlight these uncertainties. It indicates that a measure of confusion exists as to what registering of a brand actually means, which method is best employed to protect the brand and what exactly ought to be protected.

---

4 The Tuareg clans received indeed a share in the profits of Volkswagen, which named one of its cars *Touareg* (pers. comm. Georg Klute, Bayreuth, 2013).

After the first five-year phase of protection had elapsed, the Malian partner of the Chinese importer of the *Canal* brands registered the design and the typeface under his own name, but did so at a time when the brand was no longer selling. *Gazelle* has also been registered several times, at first with the written name, then again without the written name, and finally again with the name appearing in Arabic letters. As mentioned earlier in the context of *Thé Sahel* and *Lait Sahel*, when a brand is registered for a certain class of products but not for another, then it is legitimate for another importer to register that brand name for a different class of products, and there are many products sold by various importers under the name *Gazelle*. Some importers will thus register their brands under as many classes of products as they can to prevent this, of course doing so increases registration fees. CEMAPI provides importers with advice but ultimately it is a matter for the importers themselves to decide upon.

4 Intellectual Property in China and the Geographical Reach out of the Brand Protection

OAPI protection covers all the seventeen member states but in how far it also coveres the ARIPO member states and Europe, North America and China, who are all members of the Berne and Paris conventions, is less clear. There are mutual agreements signed, but in principle, outside the OAPI region, the brands would merely be protected under the authors' rights legislation, as trademark protection was limited to the region in which it was protected (Packard 2010: 161). Malian importers were convinced that if they wanted their brands to be protected in the ARIPO region, they had to register them there as well. One of them said:

> At present, my brand is *Achoura* [say Asura]. I protect it at CEMAPI. If I would sell it in Cameroon, OAPI would protect it there. But in Mozambique and Gambia, it is ARIPO. These are different zones, in which you have to protect your brand again. If you do not protect your brand in the ARIPO zone, someone else, an African or even your Chinese supplier, can register your product and import it there'. INTERVIEW, BAMAKO, 2013

Hence, for importers it is vital to decide the relevant markets for their products. In the case of Chinese green tea brands, the market lies in sub-Saharan Africa, particularly Francophone West Africa and only to a small extent in the Anglophone countries and Central and East Africa.

Most importers considered it not worthwhile registering a brand with ARIPO because the only relevant country in the ARIPO zone was Gambia and that country was very small. In Europe and North America there is no market for the West African type of Chinese green tea, thus there is little need to protect brands there. Similarly, there is no substantial market in China even though China is the country where the Malian green tea is produced. But circumstances differ in China because there, different ideas about intellectual property and the subject of registration prevail. Brands are registered in China but by the Chinese partner of the Malian importer to prevent other Chinese traders from exploiting the brand by selling it in Africa. The Malian importer has no objections to his partner's registration of the brand because both traders cannot sell the tea in China but only in Africa. If a Malian importer would obtain his tea from Korea or Japan, he could employ the same brand, because these countries fall outside the remit of China's intellectual property regime.[5]

China was one of the last countries (after the USA and the former Soviet Union) to sign up to the international convention for the protection of intellectual property. A large part of China's trade revenues are accrued through the sale of small, cheap, rapidly changing commodities (Cissé 2015; Plietz 2012), rendering the consideration of brands obsolete, for in many cases, the process of registering brands would take longer than the duration of their shelf lives (Huang 2008; Hulme 2015; Röschenthaler 2020c). After becoming a member of the WTO, China created an office for trademark protection on the understanding it would help protect its own interests. On the website of the State Commerce and Trademark Bureau[6] can be found a list of all trademarks registered in China (provided one can read Chinese).

In principle there are agreements between the different organisations and conventions on copyright and trademark protection and OAPI as a signatory to the Madrid Agreement Concerning the International Registration of Marks and the Berne Convention of the Protection of Literary and Artistic Works is a member and thus connected to all of them. That means a trader in Gambia, in Europe or even in China could be made liable for using an OAPI registered trademark. In practice, of course, taking legal action against someone operating within the jurisdiction of another regional organisation would be too challenging for most importers – particularly as this merely concerns the

5 These findings are based on statements from both tea importers in Mali in 2016 and Chinese brokers at the Canton Trade Fair in 2018.

6 China has offices for trademark law, patent law and copyright law, see the website of the State Commerce and Trademark Bureau at www.chinatrademarkoffice.com.

non-registered version of copyright or authors' rights law – requiring as it would having to bring a transgressor to a court on the next judicial level.

In both Mali and China, the concept of international trademark protection is relatively new and both are experimenting with the opportunities it offers for products that had until two to three decades ago been sold largely without privately-owned brand names. Foreigners may register their brand in China, but for Malians this has not been an option. Moreover, in the collaboration between Chinese and Malian traders, various ideas about what should be protected by this law collide when green tea brands are to be protected, as will be shown in the next section.

5 Collaboration between Chinese Suppliers and Malian Brand Owners

Whilst Malian importers were aware that foreigners could register brands in Mali, they considered it impossible to register their own brands in China. Collaboration offered a mutually beneficial solution to this issue. Many Malian importers were unsure about how this collaboration would work in China but they recognised the importance of registering their brands in Mali. One of the importers suggested that he had to register all his brands with OAPI, because

> If you do not register, then a Chinese will come here and register your brand and there is nothing you can do about it. This is important because often you will find your brand pirated in another country. A Chinese [trader], however, will register his brand in Mali and in China. INTERVIEW, BAMAKO, 2013

He provided no further comment on what he thought happened to his brand in China. Another importer explained that all four of his brands were registered with OAPI. On being asked whether they were also registered in China, he answered:

> No, the Chinese have nothing to do with this. I can register this here, and the Chinese [trader] does it in China under their own name. Yes, because the law does not talk about this. OAPI is for the Francophone African countries only. The Chinese also have their own brands, just as they can also register the global brands here in Africa. INTERVIEW, BAMAKO, 2013

When I asked whether his brands were also registered in China, one of the biggest tea importers answered: 'Yes, I register them with the factories with whom I work in China [he corrected himself], in cooperation with them' (interview, Bamako, 2013).

Another importer makes this a bit clearer: 'Look, this is the new design of *Thé Niger* [he showed me the design on his computer], it is already submitted. It is registered in Africa and in China. Here it is registered in our company name with OAPI'. I asked whether he himself registered it in China, he hesitated, then explained:

> Yes, in principle, but in China we are in partnership with a Chinese company. So, to assure them you trust them, you ask them to register the colours there in their name. By this means they possess a hundred percent monopoly on the products of the brand in China. If I give you this [pointing at a tea package], and I also give this to another person who produces this, too [this is not good]. But if I allow only you to produce this tea, you make more money and it is a more serious [partnership] at that time ... because only you have the right to produce the product. However, if I give it to three or four different people [in China] to produce, and a problem emerges, it will be difficult to know who is the one to blame. INTERVIEW, BAMAKO, 2013

This importer emphasised the significance of trust between himself and his Chinese partner in his acceptance of the partner registering his brand in China. Concomitantly, this he thought better protected the brand when only his partner possessed the right to produce the brand-named tea in China; however, only the Malian merchant's company had the right to sell it in Mali. No other Chinese trader could sell the brand in Mali or the OAPI zone but they could sell it in the ARIPO zone. The Malian trader might consider registering his brand there as well, but the market was probably too small to justify the effort. The Chinese trader might consider selling it in North Africa but the market would not be that inviting, at least in Morocco, where Gunpowder was more popular than Chunmee.

One importer explained the brand registration in China further:

> You register your brand here and the Chinese will register your brand in China under their name. This means you will have to continue purchasing your tea with that supplier. You will change your supplier only upon creating a new brand. INTERVIEW, BAMAKO, 2016

This procedure obliges Chinese and Malian partners to establish a solid partnership. It has an impact on the philosophy of branding, and explains the reason Malian importers create new brands once in a while, which serves to reduce their dependency on one Chinese supplier. Seen from this perspective, new brands represent new opportunities.

In a way, this is a form of 'shared brand ownership' (Aguilar 2018; Belderbos et al. 2014, for patents), but in different geographical and property rights settings. The arrangement also protects Malian importers against other African traders who may ask a Chinese factory to produce the same brand as that being sold by another African merchant. If a Malian importer refuses to allow his Chinese supplier to register the Malian brand, they will not produce the tea because they will fear another Chinese company will step in and register the brand under its name, arguing that as the first Chinese company has not registered the brand, they no longer have a right to produce and sell it. At the Canton Import and Export Fair in 2016, I overheard a conversation, in which one Chinese broker refused to produce a copy of the *Flecha* brand for a Libyan customer. The Chinese broker knew doing this would reduce the value of the brand which was not yet registered and instead considered registering it himself in China (interview, Guangzhou, 2016).

One of the big Malian importers knew that his Chinese supplier could just type a name into the website of the Chinese trademark office to check whether this or a similar brand name already existed in China. From this he can be sure that a new name he wants to register does not already exist. The importer explained: 'There are too many rights and wrongs in this matter, because if you have your tea, then you have possibilities to make it work on the market' (interview, Bamako, 2013). Chinese suppliers registering a Malian trader's brands in China should not be interpreted appropriating the Malians' intellectual property; rather it is intended to protect the interests of both partners. Indeed, Chinese brokers appeared somewhat irritated when I asked them whether they thought I should register, just in case, my tea brand in China. They said 'oh this is not necessary, don't worry about that. We can do that for you' (interviews, Guangzhou, 2018). This reaction only makes sense against the background of this logic; furthermore, there is no market for the African tea brands in China itself.

Thus, what appears conclusive at first sight actually includes some interesting complications, because Chinese and Malian intellectual property procedures register different aspects of branding. Intellectual property law in Mali and the other OAPI member states protects the design and the brand name integrated in the brand image, but seemingly only the name matters in China. Thus, Chinese suppliers encourage their African customers who do not wish to create their brand themselves to adopt an existing design but choose another brand name for their product. There are many examples of designs mimicking those belonging to another importer with only the brand name being different. The Chinese brokers have no problem with this in China but in Mali this causes the issue of trademark infringement. The incongruence of the two intellectual property regimes creates the problem; moreover, Malian customers tend to look less for the name but more for the design and the colour (see also Van den Bersselaar 2005 for gin in Nigeria). Some African importers may adopt such a design unintentionally, being unaware that there is one or even several tea brands with the same design already on the market; others do it quite intentionally following their Chinese supplier's suggestion, adopting the design of a popular brand merely using a new name, and then selling it in adjacent countries, especially where the brand owner does not have a trade representative. The Malian commercial court considers these cases trademark infringements arguing they create confusion among consumers (for examples, see chapter 8).

Upon examining brand names and images, it is interesting to note that some specific images and names appear again and again. *Khaima*, the tent image, is registered by an importer whose company headquarters are in Paris; he also registered the typeface of *Khaima*; then there is *Rass al Khaima* with the same tent image. This image was also registered in Nouakchott in the same year (2003) by a Chinese trader and distributed by a Malian trader within Mali. The brand *El Kiyam* (OBS Alimentation, Nouakchott) has the same design as *Rass al Khaima*. There are many other examples (chapter 8). Thus, the same design with the use of a different name was proposed to several African importers by a Chinese trader, corroborating the fact that only the name is of legal importance in China and that the design is not an exclusive intellectual property, whereas in Mali – and probably also in Morocco – the design and the associated name form an entity that belongs to the original importer.

At first sight what might appear to be a trademark infringement may, however, be quite different. The brands *Couronne* and *Taaj* provide an example. *Couronne* depicted with the name *Couronne* and carrying an image of a bird with a large feather crown was supplanted by another tea with the same design on its packet but with a different name – *Taaj*. One importer explained this was not a case of trademark infringement because the owner of *Couronne* had himself changed the name to *Taaj* (pronounced Taash) and registered the new brand with CEMAPI. This change followed the replacement of his tea supplier with a new partner and therefore he also had to create a new brand name. He continued: I will explain to you, in China, the colour [i.e. the design] is of no importance. Over there, only the name is important'. This means, the owner of *La Couronne* wished to end his relationship with his original Chinese supplier who had, of course, registered the name *Couronne* in China. The new Chinese supplier then registered the new name, *Taaj*, there too, and the Malian importer re-registered the design with its new name with CEMAPI (interview, Bamako, 2013).

In the event that a Malian importer changes his Chinese supplier for whatever reason, he must then also change his brand name. This provides a motivation for not changing one's supplier too often. But if a change is necessary, then one should also develop a new design lest consumers fear the tea has been pirated and cease buying it. Many importers own several brands, from different Chinese suppliers.

Unlike China's intellectual property organisation, OAPI does not provide a list of all the registered brand names. This is possible in China, because there the name is registered, but with OAPI it is the entire image. With OAPI, the brand names do not form part of the application nor are they noted separately. The names are simply integrated parts of the entire design and some registered brands do not even have a brand name but merely a design. This means a Chinese broker cannot register them in China. Some Chinese brokers have resorted to registering their entire tea package design with OAPI in Malian style and then also the typeface for their brand name only (*Canal, Askia, Hayat*). Most Malian importers have not registered the typeface of their brand name but only the entire packet design. This conceptual differentiation in the two brand registration practices raises questions about variety in the concepts behind managing intellectual property and whether possession of exclusive rights in intellectual property is considered legitimate or not.

6 Managing Intellectual Property: Islam and the Monopoly on Signs and Symbols

There are convincing reasons for implementing international copyright and trademark laws. As previously mentioned, these laws are based on Western European developments since the invention of the printing press and industrial mass production. The reasons for implementing these laws are often presented as if they were the only means to guarantee a healthy economy, however, it should be asked whether there are no other possible ways to manage immaterial economic assets. Also, as previously mentioned, prior to the introduction of international intellectual property regulations, various societies had their own ideas and measures to handle the immaterial aspects of cultural production and they valued immaterial cultural goods at least as much as material objects. Valuable immaterial goods were neither owned by all in the same way, nor communally by an ethnic group, but often by specific groups of people who had acquired the rights (Röschenthaler 2011). They could also be understood not in terms of ownership but of stewardship (Hirsch and Strathern 2004).

The Paris Convention for the Protection of Industrial Property (1883) was introduced several decades after the implementation of copyright laws (Röschenthaler and Diawara 2016). Formerly, the idea of an exclusive property being held by a single individual in such goods was however comparably rare (Hirsch and Strathern 2004; Röschenthaler and Diawara 2016) but local protection of rights in immaterial cultural goods is known from all continents. These rights were concerned with the use rights of such goods and the distribution of wealth (Röschenthaler 2011). In Mali, this has become particularly obvious in the domain of privileges in music genres that were held by particular families and social groups (Diawara 2016). Rights in the immaterial aspects of economic productions and knowledge have also been reported and successfully defended in lawsuits (Comaroff and Comaroff 2009).

In Mali, various concepts about the management of rights in intellectual property collide: firstly, the French-inspired intellectual property legislation, which portrays an individual or a legal entity as the exclusive owner of a 'work' or a brand; secondly, the socialist idea, which does not endow an individual with exclusive rights in creations but ensures that these belong to the entire populace and are managed for them by the state (Altbach 1986); this concept has been influential in Mali (and in Morocco) since 1960s and continues to a large extent to be practiced in China, although there, private companies and international law are gradually gaining in importance, albeit with divergent interpretations. Thirdly, informed by Islamic law, although trademarks are not mentioned in the Quran, scholars have developed different interpretations based on the Sharia as to how laws should be devised and applied to trademarks. Islamic law emphasises that all creation, including immaterial products, is accomplished by God – an idea also found in the Old Testament (Theisohn 2009) – which means no human being should have a monopoly over such creations. Islamic law advocates for the equal distribution of economic assets and does not accept exploitation at the expense of others, nevertheless, some scholars claim that Islamic law was compatible with international trademark law, as will be discussed below. Finally, there are local concepts of rights in immaterial cultural expressions that are held by particular families. These notions are more prevalent in crafts, music and performance than for industrial intangible property but they, different from the international intellectual property law, acknowledge that no creation is completely novel but owes a large part of its existence and 'originality' to previous generations (Barthes 1977; Diawara 2016; Foucault 1984; Röschenthaler and Diawara 2016).

Some importers mentioned preferring a friendly approach towards dealing with pirates, not just because of the familiar atmosphere within the Malian tea trading community – consisting of Muslims, I am unaware of any exception – and they all knew each other but also because they adhered to the Muslim principle of rejecting excessive punishment, which tends to foster revenge. A few also questioned the legitimacy of claiming as one's exclusive property an image, design, name and logo, because it contradicted the Islamic notion that things had been created by God in order that human beings could freely make use of them. One importer explained when we looked at images of imitation tea packages from my collection:

> This is one hundred percent piracy, but in Islam this does not exist. … You cannot create something for yourself alone. It creates complications. Islam does not allow monopoly. … At the same time, just copying your brand is what in Europe is called unfair competition. I have spent much money, so someone else ought not to make the same [image].
> INTERVIEW, BAMAKO, 2013

This importer saw both sides, a complication within Islamic perception, also resonating with local concepts of artistic creativity, and his own investment in a brand. It all depended on how property and brands were conceptualised.

Claiming immaterial cultural goods as exclusive property has often raised concern and has been criticised as a product of capitalist market economy preventing the free use of a common good. The importer explained: 'The problem is: monopolising something without creating proficient laws is unhealthy because it permits some to take advantage and prosper at the expense of others' (interview, Bamako, 2013). With this, he criticised the idea that capitalist logic encouraged making money from everything, i.e. the growing commercialisation and judicialisation of all social domains (see also Röschenthaler and Diawara 2016; Smiers 1999). He added that it was the government's role to establish laws creating a just social order and delimiting monopolising tendencies. Mali's economic actors would need clear rules to follow.

Other traders were aware of Islamic attitudes towards monopoly but claimed there was no inherent contradiction, and considered intellectual property law to be compatible with Islam (interviews, Bamako, 2013, 2016). Merchants merely had to agree among each other, draw up rules regarding the handling of the rights in their brands and avoid copying brands. Discussing this issue in the popular wholesale boutique – as usual full of customers – belonging to a family of strict Wahabis, our questions aroused huge debate with many opinions on the topic being enunciated. The conversation revealed that traders lacked clarity on the difference between a brand and marks of quality in terms of possible ownership and most were also unaware that authors' rights in brands existed independently of registration. The boutique owner suggested I consult texts of Muslim scholars of which he was aware because he often consulted Islamic websites.

Muslim scholars have formulated opinions on the issue regarding the relationship between trademarks and Islam. Some maintain intellectual property law and Islam were fully compatible (Azmi et al. 1997; Jamar 1992; Khan and Lone 2013); some underpin this assertion by reference to the existence of antique forms of the recognition, marking and protection of intellectual property (Khoury 2003). They enumerate reasons favouring intellectual property law: trademarks were protected under Islamic law, but did not permit the rights holder to carry out illegal activities; trademark law only protected legitimate goods and services (no alcoholic beverages for example); the fruits of one's labour should be reserved for the owner; Islamic law prohibited unfair competition and was supposed to protect traders and consumers; it also aspired to prevent confusion about a brand's origin. Applied to trademarks, this implied copying another's work, selling it under one's own name and enjoying the profit, should not be tolerated.

Other scholars were more critical, arguing that the concepts of *halal* and *haram* would be inappropriate in describing transgressions of intellectual property law (Mahafsah, Melhem and Haloosh 2009). Beltrametti (2010), Elmahjub (2015) and Bayoumi and Rosman (2018) raise further critical issues about whether Islamic law could be interpreted in support of intellectual property law, given that intellectual property was not actually regulated in the Quran. They took the view that the extant intellectual property framework failed to meet the needs and aspirations of Islamic countries because it followed a utilitarian approach in contradiction to Islamic Sharia, prioritising only the interests of developed countries (see also Okediji 2006 more generally). Whilst Islamic law and intellectual property law were not totally contradictory, there were principles that did not mesh: Islamic law promoted work and productivity but it strongly considered public interest; intellectual property law did that too, but only rhetorically (Elmahjub 2015). Intellectual property law was intended to foster development, but this was not development as required by Islamic law.

These are some of the details that have been studied. They explain potential tensions and problematise the monopoly of ownership. For example, trademarks with obscene contents cannot be protected and Islamic law also discourages harmful inventions. This is however also true for international intellectual property law, although the criteria may differ. Islamic law also protects human life and wealth, the right to health care, educational resources and a decent level of income which would encourage development. Bayoumi and Rosman (2018), however, criticise that most educational resources, for example, were under the intellectual property regime of the developed world, which prevented copying and free dissemination. Creations – and this has significance for tea trademarks – should be under the stewardship of their owner but ultimately ownership of resources and end products were the prerequisite of Allah, the creator of both the resources and the human beings who worked with them. Human beings were mere trustees whom Allah permitted to enjoy the fruits of these assets. They should spend them in the public interest as if they were not their own but another person's wealth and thereby fulfil their responsibility towards society. This then explains the prohibition against the concentration of wealth in the hands of a few and the encouragement of circulating resources (Bayoumi and Rosman 2018: 32).

The idea of the circulation of resources for the benefit of society is not totally dissimilar to ideas conveyed by capitalism. Capitalism, however, employs these ideas about benefit as economic tools for the justification of wielding those resources, which ultimately works at the expense of society. Hence, the capitalist system has been criticised for focussing on the owners' exclusive rights, which leads to the concentration of wealth and power in the hands of a few. Bayoumi and Rosman (2018) rather suggest that spiritual values, the ideas of amiability and cooperation should be woven into the law. Monopoly was prohibited by the Sharia because it undermined the public interest in favour of individual interests. Rather a proper balance of both types of interest were required, but public interest should come first (Elmahjub 2015). Malian importers would agree to all that, and some of these ideas also emerge in the following discussion about dealing with brand pirates. They also accepted that having come to terms with the idea that each of them could have their brand registered, when they wished to do so, and, as they had all agreed on that, there was no problem with the concept of brand ownership. They were aware that the court was working following the French legal model that was based on international conventions and understood it as a useful instrument to keep pirates in their place and remind them of their responsibility, but the merchants' ethical principles also obliged them not to punish pirates excessively. The next chapter examines these issues further in the light of conceptual complications inherent in the concept of intellectual property.

CHAPTER 8

Tea Brands and the Conceptual Complexities of Intellectual Property

This chapter focusses on copying of popular tea brands from the perspective of the conceptual challenges of intellectual property, which are related to questions of similarity and singularity, originality or uniqueness of a brand image. It demonstrates that within the tea brand spectrum some successful designs served as models for numerous other imitations which renders it conceptually difficult to discern between their similarities and their singularities. It is a question of how different the designs and names need to be in order to be considered new and singular creations and when a brand design might rather be declared a copy, deserving of prosecution as a trademark infringement and a case of unfair competition. This quandary, having legal implications, calls for a more nuanced reflection rather than an either-or answer. The chapter begins by reflecting on the various types of brand piracy and continues with two examples illustrating the 'social life' of particularly successful tea brands that have been frequently copied and counterfeited. It discusses the complexities in the registration policy of OAPI and whether these copies might be better understood as collage and montage, rather than either legal or pirated, thus paying homage to local concepts of the immaterial qualities that acknowledge the fragmented character of creation.

1 Piracy: Trademark Infringement and Counterfeiting

This section looks at some implications arising from the pervasive copying of brands and the varieties seen in these activities. Marketing theory and other narratives that assume the pre-given intelligibility, coherence and stability of the brand, overlook the ongoing dialectic between brand and surfeit or excess. Nakassis in his study on these issues noted that 'there is a complex interaction between brand and surfeit' (2013: 120), as was shown regarding the tea crisis in chapter 5. When a brand becomes so popular that there is a surfeit, brands are copied most often. This is what Kavita Phillip (2005) meant when he emphasised that popular brands create excessive demand, which eventually leads to the difficulty distinguishing between original and copy.

 | DOI:10.1163/9789004505698_010

The term 'piracy' forms part of a polarizing vocabulary that emphasises the benefits of intellectual property law and denounces its transgression as piracy. Piracy is closely associated with a lack of good quality tea, or rather with the shortage of a particular brand, encouraging counterfeits with often lower quality than the original brands, which are abandoned when consumers note the reduced quality. One of the importers observed that

> Those who produce the counterfeiting of all these well-going tea brands, leave for China and, in addition to ordering their own product, they go to the other factories and ask there to make them another tea brand, and the Chinese will not refuse. If you do not write the address on the package, and you are not discovered, then nothing happens; but if you are discovered as the one who brought the pirated tea, and if he [the owner of the original] knows who you are, then you will be pursued. INTERVIEW, BAMAKO, 2013

Without the assistance from Chinese suppliers, Malians could not produce counterfeits. The counterfeits are fabricated in China but it is the Malians (and some Chinese brokers) who inspire their production. The same importer added: 'If the Chinese did not do this, the Malian traders could not bring it [counterfeited tea] here'.

Interestingly, the Malian importers gave the impression that they knew how to distinguish an original from a counterfeit and identify trademark infringement. But maybe they only became aware when they noticed such a brand, or discovered a drop in demand for their brand. One of the wholesalers explained how pirated tea can be discovered. He said the pirated package closely resembles the original but little differences would be discernible. Firstly, small signatures of difference in design might be seen in the letters, the name, the form of the logo and image; also a different address and phone number might appear; secondly, the packet size may differ; thirdly, there may be differences in the material employed or in the size of the tea sachets, or they may not be closed; fourthly, the quality of the tea might differ. To be detected, the latter two indications require the opening of the package (interview, Bamako, 2013).

Actually, the distinction noted by this wholesaler between the small differences detectable from the exterior and those of the interior that are hidden resonate with legal terminology. The differences that can be seen are the trademark infringement, whilst those hidden within the packet are the result of counterfeiting (Mertha 2005: 167–168). When Malians discuss this issue, they do not differentiate between the two types but use the French words *pirater* and *contrefaçon* interchangeably. These terms are part of legal discourse, having clear connotations of illegality, or at least illegitimacy.

Frequently trademark infringements modify the name, or the image, in other words they copy the original design but employ a different name or use the same name alongside a variation of design. A few examples will suffice to illustrate such infringements of trademark law.

Arawane, a well-known tea brand, has been pirated several times (chapter 4). I discovered one such package in Bobo Dioulasso in 2012. Instead of *Arawane* the name appeared as *Araouane* and the package carried no name, or address of an importer (Figures 50 a,b). The importer was surprised and upset upon being shown the packet and decided he would follow it up and, if possible, extract damages from the offender, as all his brands were registered. He also recalled a similar case where pirates had exchanged a few letters in the name, printing *Anawara* on their package whilst using exactly the same design. A wholesaler in Bamako told us about the same trademark infringement but explained the issue was about sachets, rather than packages (interview, Bamako, 2013). I captured a photograph of one of these sachets, but interestingly, the wholesaler refused to sell one, because he claimed the pirate no longer wished his product to be visible on the market. I also found in Ghana an *Arawane* packet on which the ornamental band was much broader than on the original and which unlike the original displayed an expiry period of as long as eight years. A similar trademark infringement happened to *Thé Azawad* that was misspelled as *Azawan* (Figures 51a, b).

FIGURES 50A, B Trademark infringement of *Arawane* (original) by *Araouane*

FIGURES 51A, B Trademark infringement of *Azawad* (original) by *Azawan*

Between 2007 and 2009, *Sonikara* was sold in a package sporting a Chinese-style house against a golden background, with a 'window' set into the package so the customer could see the tea leaves; the numbers 555 indicated its quality (Figure 26b). The brand was registered in 2007 by a Djokoramé importer although he did not print his address on the package. The same design was also sold in Morocco under a different name in a 250g carton, as mentioned earlier. In 2009, a media specialist told us that *Sonikara* tea had been pirated, proven by small errors on the portrayal of the house and the letters; the pirated package had no address either. *Sonikara* was not even a best-selling tea (interview, Bamako, 2009). The importer, it was said, then intended to exchange the Chinese house image with that of a mosque but if he did, I have never seen it, however, a mosque is depicted on his next tea brand *Chaban*. *Rakim* and *Dambé* are further examples where just the name is exchanged (Figures 52a, b).

In 2012, in Ouagadougou, we discovered a pirated package of *Lobo*. In that case, parts of the image in the square on the package have been exchanged, although the name is printed correctly (Figures 53a, b). The original design depicts two tea-drinking men in northern Malian dress, whereas the design on the pirated package displays an image of the Great Wall of China instead. The writing indicated the tea was distributed by the Bamako-based importer, as on his original. The importer was surprised and denied having ever printed this image on their tea package.

In Yaounde, I found several packages of *Temple du Ciel* that were there called *Palais du Ciel*. Further examples on which the name has been exchanged are *Touareg*, of which the entire consignment was confiscated by the police. *Achoura* and *Hamza* were pirated in the same way, too (Figures 54a, b). *Taoudeni* was pirated by the first version of the brand *Yasmina*, sold by a Chinese trader in Burkina Faso in 2010.

FIGURES 52A, B Same design but different names: *Rakim* and *Dambé*

FIGURES 53A, B Trademark infringement of *Thé Lobo*: the picture of the Tuareg tea group was replaced with the Chinese Wall

Such trademark infringements of this nature are much easier to expose than counterfeited products, where package designs are rather faithful to the original design. That something might be wrong is discovered by opening the package and checking the sachet and the tea leaves.

FIGURES 54A, B *Charifa* pirated the design of *Achoura*, photograph taken from the mobile phone of the owner, Bamako, 2016

For example, the sachets of the *Gazelle* packages that arrived from Mauritania in Bamako, had a darker colour than the original. One of the wholesalers said, they were not sealed and the tea tasted different too. He explained the problem was in such cases that

> Often the consumers do not know how to differentiate between the true (*le vrai*) and the pirated (*contrefait*) packages. Consumers do not understand. They think the importer has lowered the quality, whereas the true *Gazelle* has not at all changed its taste. INTERVIEW, BAMAKO, 2013

He added that pirated tea might be imported as often by African as by Chinese traders; they would just copy a brand, modify it a little and sell it in Mali. In 2012, in Accra, I found a package on which was indicated the importer of *Gazelle* was based in Nouakchott. On another *Gazelle* package there was no indication of an importer at all. Original *Gazelle* packages always display the name of the importer and his address in Bamako. The importer of *Gazelle* showed me an entire collection of counterfeited tea packages (Figure 56). Some counterfeiters even supplied their name and telephone numbers on the packages; one of them imported to Gambia and sold in Dakar, not far from the Region of Kayes in Mali from where the tea can easily take the road to Bamako. Other *Gazelle* pirates even came from Bamako itself. Their product was confiscated and they were sued in court. When the importer discovers pirated packages abroad, Interpol is called in to investigate. Recently, the controls have increased but of course the market is vast.

2 'Biographies' of Popular Tea Brands: the Examples of *Gazelle* and *Flecha*

In order to understand how some trademark infringements are connected and form part of the 'social lives' (Kopytoff 1986) or 'cultural lives' (Coombe 1998) of trademarks and their importers, I will offer the two most prominent examples: *Gazelle* and *Flecha*. These biographies will shed further light on the background to branding, the creation, counterfeiting and trademark infringement as well as on the relationship between importers. All importers with whom I spoke were careful in their avoidance of discussing issues that might antagonise a fellow importer and more than one importer was the source of these two stories. What follows is my understanding – no doubt incomplete – derived from what I have pieced together from the snippets of information gathered during many years of research.

2.1 *Gazelle*

Around 2003, the Chinese owner of *Thé Gazelle* was planning to sell his tea in Africa. The tea came in a white package with the name *Gazelle* emblazoned on it. The Chinese trader had registered the brand name *Gazelle* – because this is what counts in China – in Geneva, base of the World Intellectual Property Organisation (WIPO), where his headquarters were located. One day, he met the Saharan trader, named Amar Taleb, in Geneva and they decided that he would sell *Gazelle* for him (chapter 4). Amar Taleb decided to improve the appearance of the package suggesting the placement of the image of a gazelle with thinly striped light green-yellow colours on the packet and also packaging a good quality Chunmee tea; he also wanted his name as a distributor to be included.

When the Chinese trader – who worked for Hui-Hong International – became aware that this tea was becoming popular in Mali and the Saharan trader was making a considerable amount of money from the brand, he asked for a higher share of the proceeds from the sales. The Saharan trader claimed it was not he who was selling most of it and therefore he had nothing to give. Subsequently, each time he ordered more *Gazelle*, the Chinese trader reminded him that he had to give him more money (interview, Bamako, 2009). Another version of the story reports that when the contract elapsed, the Saharan trader refused the Chinese trader's request for money for using his brand name *Gazelle*. The Chinese trader then insisted that the Saharan trader could no longer use the name *Gazelle*. In order to pre-empt retaliation by the Chinese trader, Amar Taleb had the idea to remove the name from the package (interview, Bamako, 2009). This was around 2010.

We saw the change appear on the packages displayed at the Grand Marché. In 2011, both versions of the packages were still available, although the one with the name was getting rarer and we were told by most wholesalers and retailers that there were none left. Consumers were also trying to obtain a package of what they called '*Gazelle premier*' (the first *Gazelle*) which created some problems for traders now selling *Gazelle* without the printed name because consumers feared it was a pirated version. Some friendly retailers were offering packages sporting similar gazelle motifs – and there were many, as will be shown below (Figures 55a–k) – insisting that these were *Gazelle premier*, as they used to do for other customers. We eventually found a wholesaler who sold *Gazelle premier* (*Gazelle* with the name written on the package) from a carton hidden beneath his desk at a higher price, but only to the most persisting customers.

The tea wholesalers told us that the Saharan trader had removed the writing because the Chinese trader had repeatedly asked for money, reminding him of his ownership of the brand. The Saharan merchant had attempted to circumvent this, firstly by registering the brand design in his own name and secondly by deleting the name *Gazelle* from the package altogether, leaving the design intact but without the letters. One wholesaler explained that for most of his customers and consumers it made little difference whether there was a written name on the package or not, as they were anyway unable to read. Many people in Mali were illiterate and did not read the brand names. They would recognise the image and just say 'give me the yellow with the animal' (interview, Bamako, 2013). In this case, the commercial tribunal could not do anything to assist the Chinese trader and the Saharan trader simply continued importing his tea from the same supplier, Hui Hong International.

The Chinese trader, having registered only the name rather than the brand, but not even with OAPI, provided an opportunity for his erstwhile partner who took advantage of the situation in August 2007, by registering the entire brand design, including the name and the gazelle image in his own name in Bamako. In December 2009, he then also registered the *Gazelle* typeface and a second brand, with the picture of a sitting gazelle but devoid of a name. Then in May 2010, due to the persistent complaints of the Chinese supplier, he re-registered the *Gazelle* design without the written name. He also registered the design with the name gazelle written in Arabic. Some years later, we also found packages with the written name *Gazelle Premier* on the market.

Around 2007, the first trademark infringements of *Gazelle* were seen in the market. Packages carrying an almost mirror image of the same gazelle with the same yellow-green colours and letter types appeared. One had the name *Gaza Super*, the other *Antilope No.1*. These brands were registered with OAPI in 2007 and 2009. In 2009, *Gazelle* had a representative in Bamako. He said that Mohamed Amar Taleb was a major and widely respected trader who ran many foundations, among them was the Fondation Amar Taleb (chapter 4). He confirmed that the headquarters of *Gazelle* was in Geneva (probably referring to the Chinese owner of the name) and he said that the owners of both *Gaza Super* and *Antilope* would be persecuted by law. But this did not actually happen, because, as will be explained below, the infringements came 'from within the same family'. We soon noticed that the owners of both *Antilope* and *Gaza Super* had created several variations of their brands in order to smooth out the problem.

The owner of *Gaza Super* then replaced the gazelle with a camel, keeping the general design and renaming the brand *Super*. But in 2013, he returned to employing the image of the gazelle animal with a brand called *Nuovo Gaza*. The owner of *Antilope No.1* replaced the yellow-green colours and the fine stripes with a somewhat darker green with broader stripes and using blue in the letters of a different font. Obviously, these changes had been insufficient because around 2010 when he registered a new design with OAPI, it had been changed once again to yellow without any blue or any stripes, although the animal persisted. In 2011, he confirmed that the first iteration of *Antilope* sold well, and that at least one year separated the two new designs. Some retailers thought the changes resulted from piracy, but clearly in this case, the changes were made by the owner, probably because he was obliged to do so. He added, that the court proceedings had taken a lot of time and money. There was no published final decision available. So, in this case, it seems very likely that a lawsuit was lodged and, at some point thereafter, withdrawn, as will be discussed in the next chapter.

In the course of the next few years, further trademark infringements afflicted *Gazelle*. There was *La Biche*, sporting in its packet the green-yellow stripes but a different gazelle. It was registered in 2011 and available in Bamako and in Guinea, but lacked the popularity of *Gazelle*, *Gaza Super* and *Antilope No.1*. In 2010, there was *Gazelle et ses petites*, with the original gazelle and the two identical small gazelles below. When we met the owner, a Wahabi, in his office the following year, this was shortly after the lawsuit and he was not at all pleased to see us, refusing to say anything about the history of his brand, except to state that he was also trading other products from Germany. Some may say those who have nothing to hide are the more willing to talk about their companies.

In short, *Gazelle* was first registered in 2007 with the name, and in 2010 without the name, and also with Arabic script, as these letters functioned as a different 'design'; BOPI also reveals further copies of *Gazelle*. *Gazelle et ses Petites* was not only registered by the Wahabi trader in 2010, but in the same year again, with the same design and name, by another company in Nouakchott. In 2011, yet another trader in Nouakchott registered the design of *Gazelle* with the name in Latin script, and in 2012, a Senegalese trader registered the *Gazelle* design in Dakar. I found *Gazelle* packages from Mauritania as far afield as Accra, but there I also obtained both *Gazelle* and the packet showing the lying gazelle, carrying an inscription reporting they were imported by Amar Taleb.

BOPI also holds details on similar other brands carrying designs of horned animals resembling deer that are named *Daim*, or *ghraim,* in Arabic, another word for gazelle – as mentioned earlier (chapters 2 and 6) – and registered in Dakar in 2012. There is also *Edami*, a brand with a different type of gazelle in red, and *Village* with a similar animal, both registered in Dakar in 2011, before Amar Taleb decided to change the colour his brand *Gazelle* to a red package in 2013. An image of a deer also figures prominently in the brand *Al Baraka*, and *Thé N.B*, which I found in Bobo Dioulasso in 2012, had the same design but without any animal. In Guangzhou, I also purchased a package with the gazelle design and the name *Century-El Ghazala* and in Cameroon there was a variation called *Chazel*, with green-yellow stripes and a gazelle image with long horns.

Reflecting on all these examples, one wholesaler suggested the reason for so many copies of *Gazelle* was that its first owner, the Chinese trader, had failed to register it in the OAPI region. When the brand had become popular, this was the moment when copying began, i.e. when *Antilope*, *Super Gaza*, *La Biche* and *Gazelle et ses Petites* arrived. When he had eventually registered *Gazelle*, Amar Taleb began to sue the copiers. The wholesaler quickly added that today pirating *Gazelle* had declined: 'the pirates have become tired because of the many court cases. They are afraid now' (interview, Bamako, 2013). *Gazelle* had strong trade agents in Bamako but, nevertheless, copies were still often sold in rural Mali and neighbouring countries. Eventually, Amar Taleb made another brand, *Le vrai gazelle* in the original design, urging consumers to buy this brand and ignore the imitations (Figures 55a–k).

A sales manager of *Gazelle* in Bamako confirmed that 'there were too many imitations of the brand, too many' (interview, Bamako, 2013) and he showed us his collection of imitations. These consisted all of counterfeits that were at first

FIGURES 55A–K Original *Gazelle* packages and trademark infringements

sight not easily recognisable as such. The packages looked the same, but small details like an address and a phone number and above all the sachets inside and the quality of the leaves were different. Some of these pirates had even copied the name Amar Taleb on the package. Others placed their own name and phone number as did someone from Gambia and there was a *Gazelle* package from Abidjan with the name of a Chinese company (different from the supplier) (Figure 56). The trade agent whom we met earlier said: 'The Chinese do not actually cheat people, its rather Malians who do this'. He referred to

FIGURE 56 Counterfeits of *Gazelle*, the second to the left is the original

Antilope and *Super Gaza* who would 'only confuse those consumers who cannot read' (interview, Bamako, 2009). His colleague commented: 'This is pure counterfeiting, all these copiers, they just want to profit from other people'. And he also complained that the consumers did not care to study the packages, they would just ask for the gazelle design and nothing more.

Probably no tea was copied and pirated as often as *Gazelle*, beginning with *Gaza Super* and *Antilope No.1* and all those who just placed another animal on the package or even used the same animal, alongside another name, and including lower quality tea. Some did this in a very offensive way, both African and Chinese importers, even registering these brands; most were active in other countries which they thought beyond the brand owner's reach out. Hence, *Gazelle* gradually lost value, continuing to be purchased only in the rural areas and neighbouring countries. Following the trend of superior qualities, the last *Gazelle* that the owner launched under this brand name was the *Gazelle* on the red packet with superior 41022 quality. This was after his daughter had taken over the company in 2013 following his death in old age (chapter 4). This package, still recognisable as a variation of the original, depicted a gazelle but of another type, its colour also set it apart from the earlier *Gazelle* design. With these modifications, the owner achieved what was necessary for the evolution of brands: make them similar but different or how Brian Moeran (2014: 47) put it: 'recognisable but not quite recognisable'.

The senior member of staff at CEMAPI agreed that what had happened to *Gazelle* was 'unfair competition' and all the different gazelles were 'made to confuse people'. But he also made it clear that it was not the obligation of OAPI to do something against the registration of these clearly very similar brands. OAPI only had to check the correctness of the application and it was the task of the brand owners to check whether there were other brands too similar to theirs within a six months' time frame (interview, Bamako, 2013). Hence, OAPI is clearly a market economy institution and a bureaucratic apparatus to provide the commercial court with cases and the institution with fees for managing the brands. It was simply managing the trademark registrations, made ownership of trademarks official and provided the necessary documents for the filing of lawsuits in matters of trademark infringement and counterfeiting.

More background to the history of the *Gazelle* brand will make its story more comprehensible. That *Gazelle* was copied so often was also the result of divergent registration practices pertaining in China and Mali, i.e. that the Chinese trader had in accordance with practices in China only registered the name *Gazelle* in Geneva before giving the brand to Amar Taleb, the businessman of Saharan origin in Niger, for sale. Taleb then convinced his Chinese supplier to accept the new design with the gazelle picture. This design was later copied in many different ways, firstly by fellow Malian importers of Saharan origin and then also by other West African and Chinese traders as well. One representative of *Gazelle* said that the importer of *Antilope No.1* was an agent of Taleb at the time and he sold tea Gazelle for him and, after some time, he [the owner of *Antilope*] thought he could make his own tea. He created *Antilope* with the same design, and also made other things of which the representative did not want to give the details, but he added that maybe the selling of tea was to cover his other businesses (interview, Bamako, 2000). Another importer added that:

> These two, *Antilope* and *Super Gaza*, they were working for Taleb. They were part of the company. They received tea from him to sell in Bamako. They were collaborating, they were partners, and at a certain point, they decided to have their own brands, and these brands were so similar [to *Gazelle*]. *Antilope* had grown up in the family. But then both became independent and even competitors of *Gazelle* on the market. Amar Taleb was of course unhappy and wanted to take them to the commercial court.
> INTERVIEW, BAMAKO, 2013

He added that the importer of *Gaza Super* began with creating the similar designs, and he looked at me saying, 'but you cannot [take him to court]' – and I heard several people saying this – 'because this is the family, this is complicated, [lowering the voice] very complicated'. But there was some pressure so that these two importers, of *Gaza Super* and *Antilope No.1*, had to modify their brands to continue to remain on the market. In some way, these tea importers were from one big extended family: those of *Gazelle, Super Gaza, Antilope No.1.*

The importer of *Gaza Super* continued to sell his *Super* teas before following the trend and importing superior Chunmee 41022 tea upon which they became among the most successful tea importers with a new brand named *Koutam*. In contrast, the importer of *Antilope* encountered various problems due to his dubious business practices and the rebellion in the northern part of the country, following the 2012 coup, caused him to go into hiding, as mentioned in chapter 4. Other people (his remote family) continued selling *Antilope No.1*, henceforth only available in 250g packages without the gazelle depicted.

After the *Antilope* and *Gaza Super* importers ceased working with Amar Taleb around 2006 or 2007, he employed another young man to sell *Gazelle*. He had just completed his studies at university, was new to the tea business and fascinated by his work as trade agent in Bamako. As did his predecessors, he travelled to China, visited plantations and factories, and supervised the quality and packaging of *Gazelle* tea. His involvement increased the popularity of *Gazelle* more than ever before. Then there was a disagreement and he broke company with Taleb to begin his own career as importer. He had acquired enough experience in the tea business and the 'work of tea' and lacked only the capital to import. To overcome this problem, he worked in cooperation with his cousin, under whose name he imported his own tea brand *Taoudeni* (chapter 4)

Its design was different from that of *Gazelle*. He employed sandy and blue colours, name and image corresponded to each other, and the packet depicts salt bars that are extracted in the northern Malian desert. At variance from his predecessors, he owned his singular brand right from the outset and no one could reproach him for jumping on the success of another importer. In a very short time, *Taoudeni* became one of the best-selling teas. It contained the same good quality as *Gazelle* – good but not too good – so he made sufficient profit from selling it; it became a success in Bamako and in Mali's countryside as well as in neighbouring countries.

At the very moment, when the 41022 Super Chunmees became popular, this newcomer had assembled enough profit to establish company under his own name, created and registered a new brand, *Achoura*. In a short time, it became the most popular brand in Mali and beyond. *Achoura* was pirated by another brand *Charifa*, which hijacked the packet design but applied a different name. Soon after, in 2016, *Achoura* was pirated again by yet another trader in Timbuktu (not of Saharan or Djokoramé origin) who exchanged the name *Diam Welle* for *Achoura*. The tea was confiscated and the trader sentenced to six months in prison with a fine of 3 million francs CFA (Coulibaly 2017).

It seems most likely that the importer cancelled the lawsuit (chapter 9). Its owner decided to show both the original and the pirated copy of *Achoura* in ORTM to assist consumers in distinguishing between the two rather than just assuming the quality had been reduced.

This story of *Gazelle* illustrates how an African trader appropriated a Chinese brand in a way that did not conflict with the law. *Gazelle* was successful because its quality remained constant over time despite frequently being copied. At first, the copying involved competition within an extended family, before the surfeit extended to the region. In the end, however, the numerous copies destroyed its reputation at the time when the good quality Chunmee was replaced by the Super Chunmees. The importers of *Antilope* and *Gaza Super*, as well as many other pirates, had jumped on *Gazelle's* success imitating its design. The importer of *Taoudeni*, however, showed that it was not just the brand name and design that were the selling point. He demonstrated that success could be repeated with a brand whose design did not at all resemble *Gazelle*. He insisted on being different and thereby also avoided trouble. His success was due to his knowing 'the work of tea' well. In contrast to the other copiers of *Gazelle*, the importer of *Gaza Super* obviously also understood the 'work of tea' for he continued with a brand – *Koutam* – that also became one of the best-selling Super Chunmee variations. In 2016, both *Koutam* and *Achoura* had become much more popular than *Gazelle*, all its imitations, and even its modification as a Super Chunmee in the red package.

2.2 *Flecha*

In the footsteps of *Gazelle* followed *Flecha*, a 4011 Chunmee that I noticed for the first time in 2007 when its brown-yellow striped packages of 250g appeared on the market, even before people began to talk about it. It might be argued that, as with *Gazelle*, stripes were an important background feature but these stripes were broader and more visible, and also the *Flecha* brand had a very distinct logo, the bow and arrow. This brand was owned by a Chinese company, Zhejiang Highten, which as indicated on the package, supplied it to a wholesaler, Rambazo Moussa in Tahoua, Niger. Two years later, *Flecha* had become one of the best-selling teas in Mali.

Around the same time, a second company, Senico Sarl from Dakar, owned by a Senegalese Wolof merchant, also began to sell *Flecha*. This company had earlier sold *Thé Saddam La Force* in 1998.[1] Senico obviously also received *Fle-*

1 Senico, the short form of the company name Senegalaise d'industries et de commerce, was created by a Senegalese, named Abdoulaye Dia, in 1989. Abdoulaye Dia is among the top Senegalese billionaires and his import-export company a member of the Club des

cha from Zhejiang Highten and in the same brown-yellow striped package. Whilst Rambazo Moussa did not employ a trade agent in Mali, therefore obliging Malian traders to travel to Niger to obtain *Flecha* from him, Senico worked with trade agents.

Senico's trade agent had temporarily an office in Bamako and delivered *Flecha* to wholesalers, one of which recalled purchasing *Flecha* from this trader and that it sold well. He remembered ordering more tea from the trader, paying for it immediately but then facing a delay of six to eight months, a time during which *Flecha* was in great demand. When the tea finally arrived, Senico's trade agent suggested that the wholesaler could become the exclusive *Flecha* trader in Bamako to which the wholesaler readily agreed and a price was negotiated. However, the wholesaler soon noticed that some other traders were also obtaining *Flecha* from the Senico representative and at a better price. Concluding that the representative had failed to honour the deal simply to make money, the wholesaler issued court proceedings (interview, Bamako, 2013). Since then, this representative only sells milk powder.[2]

Following this incident, the *Flecha* representation in Bamako was closed and another ambulant trade agent took over the distribution of *Flecha* from Senegal to the aforementioned wholesaler in Bamako. The trader insisted that his tea came via Dakar directly from the supplier in China and was not pirated. Then the wholesaler advised in future he bring the more popular 25g packages rather than 250g packages and he did so. Initially, Senico sold the 250g packages, as did Rambazo Moussa, but soon after began selling 25g packages, which were probably, after some time, distributed both from Niger and from Dakar. Then, as did the first Senico trade agent, this second individual also proposed that the wholesaler become his exclusive *Flecha* customer. At the arrival at Bamako of the container, however, the representative only supplied a tenth of the contents to the wholesaler, although he had paid in cash, and he distributed the rest to other wholesalers. They remain in contact, but the representative no longer personally supplies tea to the wholesaler, giving it all to *coxeurs* to sell for him. The *coxeurs* visit the wholesaler who pays them to buy *Flecha*.

---

investisseurs Senegal agro-industrie. At first, two brothers began as Dia & Frères in the Keur Massar suburb of Dakar to sell tea. They distributed the brand called *La Force* [*Saddam la Force*]. Meanwhile the company has become big and produces and sells many products. It has representations in Senegal, Mauritania, Mali, Niger, Burkina Faso, Gambia, Guinea Bissau, Sierra Leone, Gabon, Congo and Equatorial Guinea. In 2019, their most prominent brands were *Flecha* (green tea), *Jadida* and *Halib* (mayonnaise, milk etc.) (as indicated on their website: www.senico-sn.com, accessed 20 November 2019).

2 He sells the *Jadida* brand, for which there were commercials in ORTM with the well-known griotte Nafi Diabate dit Marimar.

The wholesaler trusts the *coxeurs* more than he does the agent. By this means, great quantities of *Flecha* were sold in Bamako, creating such a shortage of it in Senegal that traders from there came to the wholesaler to obtain *Flecha*.

At the time, both types of 4011 Flecha – from Niger and Senegal – were sold in Mali and countries further east. Demand for it created another tea crisis and several trademark infringements emerged on the market. There were, for example, *Thé Sahara* (registered 2009) and *Thé Zamane* (registered 2012) whose packets exactly imitated those of *Flecha*, replacing only the name, visible only on closer examination. A Cameroonian importer then created *Flechena*, clearly based on the same design but was unregistered (Figures 57a–d). There is no proof but it is possible the 25g packages containing this tea were – according to the package inscription – distributed from Niger, also counterfeits, One Malian importer was certain that Rambazo Moussa was, at least initially, only selling 250g packages (interview, Bamako, 2013).

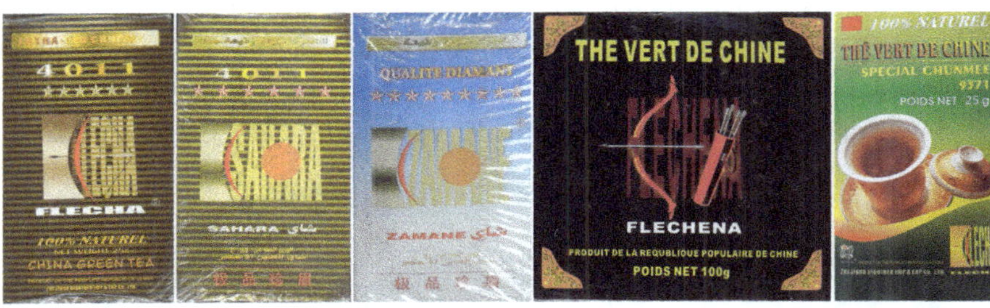

FIGURES 57A–E Trademark infringements of the early *Flecha* brand: *Flecha* (original), *Sahara*, *Zamane*, *Flechena*, *Flecha* (*Cameroon*)

In 2009, a new *Flecha* design was created: pale green at the bottom, with silver-coloured waves; the *Flecha* logo, writ large, occupied the upper section, on a white background, beneath a small cup with a Chinese dragon and the quality number 41022. In one corner was another small *Flecha* logo. With this new design, *Flecha* set the trend for the superior quality 41022 Chunmee teas. Rambazo Moussa was again the first to sell this new *Flecha* in the 250g packages. The itinerant Senico trade agent soon also brought the new *Flecha* packages to Bamako.

It was not long before this design became subject to numerous trademark infringements. One importer explained: 'Almost the same thing [as with *Gazelle*] happened to *Flecha*' (interview, Bamako, 2016) and *Flecha* was not registered either. This was one of the reasons why it was so often pirated. There was an entire series of copied packages, some with exactly the same design, but instead of the name *Flecha*, they placed their own name (*Hayat*, *Lawal*, etc.) in the same letter type, which was hardly distinguishable from the original.

Others also borrowed from this design but modified it sufficiently so that the imitation was less obvious. The design was in actual fact different but the colours were the same. There was *Koutam* with a larger tea cup with handle, *Super Thé*, and *Hassane Ousmane* with the tiger; there was a deer without a name, and in Cameroon, there was *Flechena*, now also in the lighter colours. The imitations by *Lawal* and *Koutam* were even registered with OAPI (Figures 58a–i).

At first, a difference between the *Flecha* from Niger and that from Senegal was visible: the former had the 41022 in the small dragon cup, but Senico did not show that number, although they added the number in later versions. Then there was a third provider of *Flecha* in Mauritania, which was also not registered. The Mauritanian *Flecha colis* came in two larger cartons, while the *Flecha colis* from Niger and Senegal came in the usual four rectangular cartons of 5kg. Then there was another *Flecha* variation in green, yellow and red, whose design was very different but it still carried the *Flecha* logo with the bow and arrow. This type of *Flecha* was found by one of my assistants in Cameroon (Figure 57e). Retailers developed their own ideas about the *Flecha* brand, as one of the owners of a *butiki súraka* told me in 2013: 'There are three qualities of tea *Flecha*, from Niger was the best, then came that

FIGURES 58A–I Trademark infringements of the Super Chunmee *Flecha*

from Senegal and finally that from Mauritania', which he would not sell in his shop.

One importer commented on trademark infringement practices: 'there are a lot of people who do not know how to "work" [properly]; they only want to harvest from those who work hard'. This importer recalled that when he began to trade, *Flecha* – sold by Rambazo Moussa and in 250g packages only – was considered the best-selling, most expensive quality tea in Mali. He continued that

> Then all these small packages came, and they just place their name, this makes me crazy and sad, they just want to profit from the work of other people. You will not even want to taste this tea. This is not good. It hurts me. Someone who worked hard who is tired from his work, he made a lot of effort, he has ideas, he invested a lot of money, you cannot just make whatever you want with this. And what is even worse, they put low quality tea inside what looks like your tea [packets]. INTERVIEW, BAMAKO, 2016

That some of these teas are of poor quality is confirmed by the fact that a set of ten is often less expensive than the original *Flecha*.

We tried to contact both the Niger- and the Senegal-based *Flecha* traders on the phone, but neither wished to say much other than to confirm that their tea came directly from China and was provided by the same supplier and that their tea was not pirated. We managed to meet Senico's ambulant trade agent once, but he was only prepared to meet us in a quiet street, giving the impression he was nervous and wished to end our conversation sooner rather than later (chapter 4). One wholesaler was sure that first on the market was the tea from Niger and that it was better quality than that which arrived later from Senegal, one just needed to taste it. He said that *Flecha* first arrived with Malian traders from Niger via Gao (interview, Bamako, 2013). The wholesaler said the reason why so many copies appeared on the market was that *Flecha* did not have a trade agent in Mali but only sold the tea from Niger. And – talking about the 41022 version of *Flecha* – from among all the copies such as *Lawal, Hayat, Koutam, Super Thé, Hassane Ousmane*, etc., *Flecha* from Niger had the best quality. And then came the other company in Senegal that brought *Flecha* to Mali. Only from 2017, the Senegalese *Flecha* had proper representation in Bamako with a permanent office and from then onwards, they managed expensive publicity campaigns on television and billboards, as my assistant established (Figure 33).

Whereas in the case of *Gazelle*, importers and wholesalers were rather of the opinion that the imitations were trademark infringements and not legitimate, in the case of *Flecha*, the discussion became more diverse. There were different opinions, all including some good points. A senior member of staff at CEMAPI stated that the first person to register a brand possesses the exclusive right to exploit it. If the importer in Niger had registered *Flecha*, he would possess the right to sell it in the OAPI zone, and the Senegalese trader would only be able to do so with the permission of its Nigerien owner. If the Chinese trader had registered *Flecha* with OAPI, he or she would have been free to give it to the Nigerien to sell in Niger and also for him to supply other trade agents, for example, in Senegal, to sell it for him and receive part of the profit (interview, Bamako, 2016). But *Flecha* – the cup with the dragon – was not registered until 2018 and in 2019 also the typeface was registered by Zhejiang Highten, with an address in China, not the entire design.

It is possible that the Chinese company told the importer in Niger that he was the only customer but they then also sold it to the Senegalese company in slightly lower quality. Or, alternatively but less probable, the Senegalese company might have received its tea from another Chinese supplier. Indeed, a major wholesaler said the quality of *Flecha* from Niger was better compared to that from Senegal and another wholesaler also considered the Niger version to possess excellent quality and that this was sold in 250g packages. As he sold only a limited quantity of tea, it was not he who created the surfeit but the Senegalese company and that resulted in the *Flecha* crisis (interview, Bamako, 2013). The wholesaler reasoned that if the Senegalese had the tea from the same Chinese supplier than the Nigerien then there was no piracy between the two, but if the Senegalese trader was obtaining it from another supplier, this would be fraud. But on being asked whether he thought that the many copies of the *Flecha* design were piracy, too, he disputed the suggestion arguing that their design only resembled the original and there was another brand name on the packages and that they were also registered (interview, Bamako, 2013). Maybe he did not want me to think that he sold pirated tea.

Some of these tea brands had indeed been registered but in court they would certainly have been declared trademark infringements. Indeed, another importer insisted that

> *Flecha* is the tea that is sold more often than any other and it has been copied so often. It is the best tea on the market but there are people who infringe it because the owner is a Chinese and he is not here in Bamako. … Therefore, it is easy to modify and import it. Brands such as *Flecha* are most often counterfeited. Normally, we importers among ourselves do not counterfeit our brands. We all know each other and normally, we do not copy each other's brands. The Chinese register their brands in China.

> But as they are not often here, we do not know them and when they come here, they generally do not have the time to sue a copier. But many Chinese producers refuse now to supply Africans with such counterfeited brands. INTERVIEW, BAMAKO, 2013

Importers considered it far less objectionable to copy the brands of foreign traders than those of fellow Malian traders (for similar observations in the Nigerian music and video business, see Gani 2020: 80 and Jedlowski 2016: 300). As has been explained earlier, to avoid such irritations, Malian importers and their Chinese partners are increasingly practicing a kind of shared trademark ownership whereby the Chinese broker registers it in China and the Malian importer in Mali (chapter 7). Hence, in order to keep their African trading relationships, the Chinese brokers increasingly refrain from providing importers with counterfeited tea, thus developing a Sino-Malian solution to the problem of piracy that does not involve the commercial court.

These two tea brand biographies are as yet unfinished, *Flecha* even more than *Gazelle*. They represent the most prominent examples of trademark infringement on the Malian tea market of the 2010s, illustrating how African importers have managed to appropriate a brand – especially in the case of *Gazelle* – from their Chinese suppliers who failed to register it with OAPI in time. Due to their popularity, the brands created a crisis on the Malian market during which there was insufficient good tea and trademark infringement practices flourished. Counterfeit tea, concerning the tea quality in the packages, are more difficult to detect than the easily recognised trademark infringements seen in the designs on the tea packages. There has been only one published lawsuit that I know of dealing with these two brands, i.e. between *Gazelle* and *Gazelle et ses petites* (see chapter 9). Both brands have survived the crisis, *Gazelle* rather less well than *Flecha*, which arriving somewhat later, benefitted from being adapted to the shift from 4011 to 41022 Super Chunmee. Whilst the importer of *Gazelle* placed her hopes in a new brand, *Raissa*, the Senegalese company has made huge efforts to ensure *Flecha* survived the crisis and the trademark infringements through managing major publicity campaigns.

3 Conceptual Challenges of Intellectual Property

Obviously, many importers expected to profit from their brand being similar to an existing popular tea brand. Others, in contrast, tried to create a singular design that stood out against existing brands (*Taoudeni, Achoura, Sancho, Ayoune*). With increasing popularity, these might become the models for new similar creations (such as happened to the variations of *Gazelle* and *Flecha*). Because many consumers could not or did not bother to inspect the packets, relying instead on their first impressions ('give me the yellow with the animal') this copying worked well for some of these brands. Because the colours employed in brands are a defining element with OAPI and not the letters, i.e. the brand name, principally all the different coloured versions of a brand needed to be registered except the same colours are just exchanged or reversed (background blue, image yellow and vice versa).

This raises the question as to what it is that signifies a brand: is it the name, the image, the logo, the colour or the entire design? I will look in more detail at some of these peculiarities not providing definite answers but rather further questions, and return to my characterisation of the green tea brands as montage and bricolage (chapter 6). Then I will examine again how importers modify their brands, discuss the identity of the individuals committing the piracy and consider the role of tea crisis in this.

3.1 *Particularities of the Tea Package Design and the OAPI Registration Policy*

Chinese green tea packages in West Africa follow particular design styles that, with a little practice, are easily recognised in BOPI, as mentioned earlier. Most tea packages thus rather resemble each other when compared to the designs employed by most other products such as cloth, rice, pasta, and even other beverages. One reason for this is that the designs are playful and atmospheric and another is that the entire package is depicted in BOPI. By contrast, most other brands are more sober and depict only the typeface of the brand name, or the trademark but not the product itself, unless the company specialises in one product, such as wax cloth or rice. However, if tea brands depicted only the importer's company logo, they could no longer be identifiable as a tea brand in BOPI, especially when the company also sells other products under the same logo. Thus, the depiction of the entire package design enables easy identification of a copied package even when the name or the logo has been changed. This is impossible if only the name or the logo is registered. The main disadvantage is that the registered brand can only function for the product depicted on the design, especially when the design states that the product is *Thé vert de Chine* and tea equipment, or tea leaves are depicted.

There are several options by which an intellectual property organisation may progress with a registration: it can register the name, the typeface, the company logo or trademark, the whole design, or the entire package, including the front and backsides (i.e. the unfolded carton). Many tea importers include the entire package in their application. By this approach, it is easier to identify and define trademark infringements than it is in China where only the name is registered. The Chinese company Zhejiang Highten, for example, eventually registered the typeface of *Flecha* with OAPI in 2019. According to the Chinese model, the entire series of *Flecha* imitations cannot be legally challenged because the name *Flecha* does not actually appear on the packages. Illiterate consumers may perhaps recognise the brand name typeface but may not read it. Consumers in Mali, as a senior member of staff of CEMAPI stated, 'people recognise the brand by signs … hence, some traders work with colours to confuse consumers' (interview, Bamako, 2013). They use the same colours as those by a popular brand at a certain time for their own package designs.

What some describe as 'creating confusion among consumers', others do not consider illegitimate, arguing that 'camouflage is not understood as piracy' (interview, Bamako, 2013). Even I took a while to uncover some of the *Flecha* imitations as such. However, as colours comprise an important part of the registration procedure, one should consider these imitations a legal issue. However, is the brand name *Pasta Roma* – owned by the importer of *Kangourou* – also creating confusion among consumers being produced in Bamako rather than in Italy? The entrepreneur explained his reasons saying 'because people think that the original pasta comes from Italy. The pasta is Malian-made but it sounds better with that name'. The name is meant to evocate the idea of the pasta having a taste like that made in Italy (interview, Bamako, 2013). But whether it is considered a legitimate practice would surely depend, in this case, on the existence of a law regulating regional appellations, i.e. restricting free naming.

3.2 *The Green Tea Brands as Bricolage and Montage*

As mentioned earlier (chapter 6), package designs consist, to various degrees, of elements provided by a Chinese broker with whom the Malian importer cooperates. Among these, the Chinese broker will ensure the selected name is distinct, whereas other elements of the design are freely combined and rearranged. Following Marcus Boon (2010: 142–146), the Chinese brokers create a collage – a two-dimensional reconfiguration of materials – for their Malian business partners. It is also a montage – a term used in the film industry meanwhile also applied to non-moving pictures. The montage is composed using a set of design elements stored on the Chinese partner's computer. African importers may or may not be aware of this recycling and reorganising of existing images but if they like a design, they often simply consent to its use on their tea packages.

From the Chinese perspective, only the name needs to be distinctive but this can create future problems for Malian importers operating in the OAPI zone where the design counts and the name as such is most often not registered separately. Moreover, Chinese traders are usually more interested in selling the product than the brand because they assume economic conditions change so fast that it becomes superfluous to care for brand development (Hulme 2015: 48; Röschenthaler 2020c). This seems to have been the case with *Gazelle* and *Flecha*, at least at first. OAPI, in turn, registers what the customer asks it to register, only checking for inconsistencies and other errors. The name not being mentioned in the registration papers makes it difficult for importers to search for existing brand names. Such a tea package design, assuming it is not completely recycled, combines existing and new elements, partly acquired from the Chinese trader's ensemble and partly found, or created, by the Malian importers themselves. Perhaps explaining why one Mauritanian importer used hand-drawn images for his tea package design rather than pre-existing pictorial elements. Most of the other designs consist of collages and montages using various fragments taken from the internet and also recycled in ongoing combinations, which is reminiscent of Lévi-Strauss' (1962) concept of bricolage. The bricolage or montage supposedly figures as new and distinctive, design that becomes the exclusive intellectual property of the importer.

Many designs – such as that of *Rakim* used in at least two other brands – are freely found on the internet. The brand *Sonikara*, mentioned earlier, has not only been pirated but its design has also been used in Morocco for Gunpowder tea. The design of *Bonya* and *Golden* has also been used several times. A version of *Bonya's* design was also sold in Cameroon. The *Golden* brand was registered in 2008 by a Chinese trader (Wang Xiao Fang) in Mali but *Bonya* belongs to a Djokoramé, in Bamako. The oriental-style decorated arch motif depicting a man in front of a blue pear-shaped teapot and samovar first used in a design for *Moul Atay Al Atik*, in Morocco, and imported by Maedis, was also used for *Thé du Sahara* but rather than portraying the man pouring tea, it incorporated a camel and a palm tree. The same arch later appeared on a version of *Thé Rakim*. The brand *Al Nekhil* – registered in Nouakchott – has the same design as *Palmier* – registered in Abidjan by a Malian. The design of *Golden* was recycled with *Tamanrasset*. Similarly, the tent motiv used in *Al Khaima* was applied to a number of different tea packages (chapter 7)

It seems likely, that there are no genuine originals when it comes to these tea package designs. They are out-of-context copies, cut-out from photographs, or electronically created, recombined in unique ways and transferred from various media, assembling oriental motifs, floral designs, signs and symbols, photographs, letters from different writing systems. These montages and remediations (Jedlowski et al. 2015) are further disseminated into other product categories when they become company logos or used in advertisement. An importer may then use them for their various product portfolios, and trade them to other countries and across different property regimes. Even though tea brands are not actually unique except perhaps for the combination of the elements, they can still become the intellectual property of the person who registered them first.

It is the duty of brand owners to keep themselves informed about developments in the market and the OAPI registrations. The commercial court only acts upon a person initiating court proceedings upon feeling their rights in their brand have been violated and the investments ignored. Importers 'creating' a brand that resembles the brand of another importer are considered 'pirates', whether they are aware of the resemblance or not. Admittedly many knew and set about creating the similarity intentionally. But certainly, there are some who were not aware the same design was already in use, particularly if it is in another country.

4 Singularity and Similarity of the Package Designs

With counterfeiting, intentional deception can be clearly defined as an attempt by one individual to appropriate the image, as closely as possible, generated by its legitimate owner and placed on his product package. With trademark infringement, however, whilst it may be based on similar intentions, the question of similarity cannot be defined as easily as with counterfeiting. This is because the question what is similar and what is unique or singular is a philosophical one. Both may confuse consumers and promote unfair competition for importers. Philosophers have noted similarity is an 'undefined concept' (Hubig 1990: 138). The extent to which one brand is similar to another is a matter of subjective interpretation: brands cannot be protected against mere associations resulting from the perception of some similarities. Despite this approach, legal institutions seem to extend trademark protection increasingly towards such associations that might lead consumers to infer a similarity of quality (Assaf 2015). These ideas would apply to examples like *Kontak* instead of *Koutam* (in Bamako) (Figure 56i) and *Azawan* instead of *Azawad* (found in Yaounde, 2014) (Figure 51b).

Consumers in Mali are familiar with items that appear similar but are not actually the same. They would say there is real tea and fake tea (*té fànà bè,* which literally means 'there is tea and there is tea'), or they talk about imitation and pretending: *ka'la dégé,* which means 'to appear as' (*dégé* means 'to pretend' and *ka ala* 'to imitate'). But normally such ideas are expressed more elegantly such as with a proverb. For example, in an advertisement when showing a particular tea is the real thing rather than a fake, one would say 'the rabbit is not the child of the donkey', meaning they have similarities but are not the same or from the same family.

One of the importers reflected that 'the package designs can be similar to a certain degree, but you have to make a different design'. Such was the case with *Koutam*, in which the *Flecha* design was changed to an extent that its importer considered it sufficiently different to be recognisable as a new singular brand. But about some of the other *Flecha* imitations he said,

> All these are just copies ... here in Mali, we have this problem of distinction. They say, people do not know what is written on the package, they just see that it is blue. They say, give me the blue, they do not say what is written on the package. They don't say: 'Give me *Thé Koutam*'. Here, with *Flecha*, they just put another name, and consumers see, ah, that is white and green, give me the white; they do not distinguish, but there are so many white packages. ... People have a problem to say the names of the tea brands. INTERVIEW, BAMAKO, 2016

Whilst consumers do not read the name and inspect the package, anything may be sold under the label of a 'white package' and if consumers have no awareness of copying, then differences that might otherwise be noticed have a greater influence and may easily confuse consumers. Here is where the power of the wholesaler comes who can decide to prioritise which of the many different 'white packages' he will distribute to his customers and which he leaves on the shelves.

If consumers are only vaguely aware of the details emblazoned on a package, the question is raised as to whether they would even recognise company logos, especially when the logo is the only consistent element in the design and colours, names and pictures might change with each type of tea, package size, or product. However, they might still recognise logos. The earlier mentioned senior member of staff at CEMAPI said that consumers in Mali did look out for symbols that they recognised such as the football and the eagle on *Askia*, the horse on *Cheval*, the tea plantation on *Arawane*, the tiger on *Hassane Ousmane* or the animal on *Gazelle*. When the owner of *Gazelle* just eradicated the name from the package, this obviously did not change much for the consumers and the legal framework in Mali. It only changed something for the Chinese trader and his understanding of his brand ownership. A package design can be modified to various extents, but the question remains how much must be changed to become a unique singular brand that would be recognised as distinct by law, by consumers and by other importers. The montage or bricolage can principally be modified until it becomes a unique brand.

Importers were unsure, however, whether retailers and consumers were completely ignorant about the details printed on their tea packages and many importers refrained from amending package designs because for fear that this might lead to them being interpreted as pirated. As mentioned earlier, when importers did change some elements of their designs, rumours detrimental to brands circulated among traders. It is indeed often difficult to decide whether modifications to designs are the consequences of copying, decisions of the brand owners, or are an incidental result of the printing process. Importers themselves sometimes found it difficult to account for such variances (Figures 51a, b).

The similarities between tea brands have so far been discussed within the parameters of copying and the creation of consumer confusion thereby. But it could also be understood in a different way, for example, that the 'pirate importers' would quote and comment each other's brands and with each slightly modified design develop the image and package design further. Otherwise, they may 'play games', challenging their former boss or 'testing' for a reaction from a competitor, even to the point where they perhaps inadvertently ruin the competitor's brand and then find themselves confronted with a lawsuit. The histories of *Gazelle* and *Flecha* might imply something like that. That consumers specify colours and images rather than ask for brands and brand names, as noted by importers and wholesalers, recalls an observation by Dmitri van den Bersselaar (2005) about gin in Nigeria: 'Trademarks were thus very important, not to distinguish the goods of one producer or seller from that of others, but as an indication of specific characteristics of the product itself' (2005: 53). Consumers made sense of brand-named products following a local logic. Once products were widely accepted, they acquired a local 'market name': The reference 'yellow package with the animal' or the 'white package' could represent such a market name and indicate a particularly appreciated quality of tea.

There are various ways by which to understand these similar package designs. Brands may be used to challenge and provoke other importers – as Nigerian writers anonymously quoted each other's texts in early newspapers (Barber 2016) – not necessarily solely to make profits at another's intellectual expense. Someone may register another importer's brand simply to test the ground to discover whether the disadvantaged brand owner has the money to launch a legal case. An importer might legitimately register an importer's brand name for another product or product class. The image and colours of this brand might remain the same, be modified, or amended with the addition or exchange of other elements. Whether it is trademark infringement depends on the product class and the legal system. All of this amounts to the legal framework has difficulties providing for the challenges and complexities posed in daily practice (Röschenthaler and Diawara 2016), is open to various manipulations and points to the 'striking misfit between the academic theory and its use in the real world' (Parchimovsky and Siegelman 2002: 1457). The interpretation, however, is the responsibility of the importers who must present themselves as plaintifs at the commercial court when they require its assistance in resolving a case. How this is done is the topic of the next chapter.

CHAPTER 9

Bureaucracy: The Commercial Tribunal, Statistics and Border Controls

Generally, popular brands are subject to copying, as brand piracy is rewarding only when the tea can be sold quickly. There are few well-known green tea brands that have not been pirated at some point in their history. Pirates tend to target unregistered brands whose owners have little or no local representation thereby reducing the likelihood of early discovery and confiscation by the police. On the other hand, unregistered brands are often of poor quality and less attractive for pirates.

As explained in the previous chapter, *Gazelle* and *Flecha* were lucrative candidates for piracy, experienced counterfeiting and trademark infringements, as they were of good quality and not, at least initially, registered, popular among consumers and owned by Chinese traders who lacked a presence in West Africa. They were targeted both from within 'the family' of the distributor, in the case of *Gazelle*, as well as from 'non-related' African and Chinese importers. Eventually the *Gazelle* brand was appropriated by a Saharan importer – a notable case of African agency.

This final chapter examines tea brands as the importers' intellectual property and their perspectives on the usefulness of the available institutions for protecting their brand names and designs. It looks at the context within which importers understand that claiming brand ownership is of benefit to them and explores the point at which they resort to the commercial courts on encountering piracy. As will be shown, whilst importers register their brands as their own intellectual property, their conviction in the benefits of doing so is only partial. They possess a good sense of the value of their brands but they tend to hesitate before bringing other importers to court for copying a brand, preferring to clarify issues between themselves. The chapter examines three brand piracy lawsuits before discussing further undocumented practices and concerns regarding tax and customs officials, which influence the validity of official statistics and complicate the connection between intellectual property law, piracy and the working of the state.

 | DOI:10.1163/9789004505698_011

1 Judgements of the Commercial Court

Tea importers frequently worried about brand piracy and talked about legal measures such as lawsuits, prosecution, confiscation of pirated products, 'teaching them a lesson', inflicting high financial damage claims upon them, and if necessary, calling upon Interpol to apprehend culprits based in neighbouring countries. A trade agent of *Gazelle* confirmed: 'We can control the market here in Bamako, but we cannot control the market in the wider countryside', by which he meant the rest of Mali and adjacent countries (interview, Bamako, 2011). Another importer explained: 'It is difficult to control our brands in China. China is completely outside of the orbit of OAPI. But if brand imitations leave China and arrive here in Mali or another country that is covered by OAPI, we can actively go ahead. We can try to protect our Malian market [by being alert and fight copies]' (interview, Bamako, 2016).

In comparison to the number of tea brands that have experienced infringement and counterfeiting, however, the number of documented court cases concerning piracy is surprisingly low. Whilst ongoing cases are not public, court decisions are and we obtained reports of some of these determinations. Given the few published cases – they are published by OAPI – many lawsuits must certainly have been withdrawn by the plaintiff and will therefore never be accessible to the public.

Of the three lawsuits presented here, one was between two Chinese companies, a second involved an importer of Saharan origin and a Djokoramé trader and the third was between an importer of Saharan origin and a Soninke trader. Except for the first case, the parties were not of the same ethnic identity. The parties involved in the second case, initially sought an extra-judicial/out-of-court settlement but it was not respected. As will be shown later, there are cases of importers of the same ethnic identity but these have been largely resolved by other means.

The first lawsuit from 2005 involved the owner of *Canal* (Canal Mali Sarl) and that of *Askia* (Usine de Thé Dapeng). Canal Mali Sarl stated they created the brand *Canal*, registered it in December 2003 and it was published by OAPI in Yaounde, in December 2004 under the number 50175. The Chinese owner discovered his trademark had been infringed by the *Askia* brand which reproduced its design under their own brand name and created confusion among the consumers. Canal Mali Sarl pleaded to the tribunal that Dapeng cease selling this type of *Askia* and pay damages to the sum of 150 million francs CFA. Dapeng argued that as they were the only company to register the brand *Askia*, it was their property, according to the Bangui agreement, and thus the two brands were completely different. They counter-claimed demanding that the plaintiff pay them 160 million francs CFA for damaging their reputation. The court responded that they protected Malian interests against foreign interests, that Canal Mali Sarl was regularly registered in Mali and that they had registered all aspects of their brand with the different colours (blue, red, yellow, black, white, grey and green), and that Dapeng had not defended itself well. *Askia* was registered under the broker's name Wang Xiao Fang in 2004, but *Canal* had been registered before *Askia*. The court insisted on the similarity of the blue design on the *Canal* package with that of *Askia* but that the football on the *Askia* package would not figure in the registration. Finally, the court decided that *Canal* had been counterfeited, that Dapeng was no longer allowed to sell this *Askia* product and that Dapeng had to pay 100,000,000 francs CFA to *Canal*. It is clear from this case that the confusion stems from differing ideas about what constitutes a brand. Dapeng believed it was all about the name, whereas *Canal* which worked more closely with a Malian partner, understood that OAPI registration concerned the entire brand design.

The second lawsuit, a case about counterfeiting, in October 2005, involved *Thé Azawad* (Alfata Ould Mohamed) against a Djokoramé importer (whose name I refrain from mentioning here). Alfata stated he was the owner of the popular brand *Azawad*, registered under his name with OAPI in December 2004, and that he obtained his tea from a Chinese company. He was in the possession of all the necessary related legal documentation. He had observed his trade in Mali, Niger and Algeria had declined without any known reason and following investigation he discovered fraudulent importation of his brand by the Djokoramé trader with the complicity of his Chinese supplier. He had subsequently contacted the Djokoramé and signed a contract with him. The latter accepted their fault, promised reparation, agreed to cease importing the brand and sell the remaining tea in the three months from September 2004. However, they failed to keep the agreement: three months later they had not yet paid all the reparation and had furthermore continued importing *Azawad* tea [of lower quality]. This had created a catastrophic economic situation for Alfata who sold more than 20,000 cartons but nevertheless had lost several hundred million francs. He argued that he had registered his brand and that according to the Bangui agreement, counterfeit was theft and unfair competition, and that he had made considerable intellectual and financial investment in creating the brand and the design.

Alfata stated, however, that the confiscated tea could be handed back to its owner, but that the court should agree to the suit demanding that the Djokoramé pay 280 million francs CFA for his financial losses and 125 million for the loss of value to his brand to compensate for the risk that consumers may no longer trust the product sufficiently to continue purchasing it. He also demanded they pay 50 million for his direct investments in the creation and design of the brand. These accumulated sums amounted to 455 million francs CFA. Alfata further demanded that, if they continued selling the brand, their company should be shut down. The Djokoramé answered that the plaintiff was of Nigerien nationality for which reason other rules would apply and that his request was unacceptable. The court waited for Alfata to show his Malian identity card. But whether he had Malian identity or not, as the case of *Canal* and *Askia* has shown, the law applies as much to foreigners as it does to Malians. The court concluded that with the agreement they had signed with Alfata in 2004, the Djokoramé had accepted that they had counterfeited the brand, and could not now argue Alfata's claim was unfounded. Accordingly, they had not fulfilled their obligations and therefore the court condemned the Djokoramé to pay 10 million francs CFA to Alfatah. This case of counterfeiting confirms that an importer who has no representatives in the country or a region of it, easily becomes the victim of counterfeiting or trademark infringement. It also demonstrates how a capricious pirate can be taught a lesson but that the court can still be mindful not to ruin an importer completely.

The third example of a lawsuit was filed in 2012 by the owner of *Gazelle* (Amar Taleb) against the owner of *Gazelle et ses petites*, a Soninke trader. *Gazelle* was registered under the number 57854 in June 2007 and *Gazelle et ses petites* was registered with the number 62089 in July 2009. The owner of *Gazelle* formulated a complaint against this registration, saying the brand (*la marque*) was too similar to his own and that it would create confusion because it was used for a similar or identical product. The *Gazelle* package depicted the animal on a yellow-greenish background with small stripes. *Gazelle et ses petites* had the same package design but instead of one gazelle there were three, a larger one and two small ones, which were diminished and mirrored versions of the original gazelle (Figure 55). The owner of *Gazelle et ses petites* argued that there was no risk of confusion and additionally, the revised Bangui agreement stated that anyone who wanted to oppose the registration of a brand had to do this within six months of the publication of the brand in BOPI, whereas Amar Taleb only opposed it in 2012.

Amar Taleb formulated a second complaint, resulting in the OAPI director deciding to rescind the registration of *Gazelle et ses petites*. The owner, however, continued to argue that there was no confusion because his brand had three gazelles and the name on the package clearly indicated that it was a mother gazelle and two offspring, whereas in contrast Amar Taleb had just one gazelle and no name on his package – Taleb had already removed the name from the package at that time. Taleb responded that he was the first to register the brand and that it was in opposition to the Bangui agreement that the defendant had registered another brand with a similar name. Eventually, in November 2013, the court's final judgement decreed there was a risk of confusion for consumers phonetically as well as visually, and in spite of the fact that Amar Taleb had not formulated a complaint within six months of publication, he had registered the brand first. This lawsuit again highlights the difficulty in deciding upon questions about the similarity and singularity of brands.

One may conclude from the judgements that the damages plaintiffs calculated are considerable, including as they did both financial penalties and imprisonment. After the hearing, the judge might lower the payments but these may still be exorbitant for less well-off importers. The Malian (or Saharan) plaintiffs were aware of this and attempted to mitigate the consequences.

2 'Mali's Law is the Law of the Street' or How to Sue Pirates

In 2011, on several occasions, we visited the commercial court to inquire about cases of tea brand piracy. The chief clerk explained that in the case of trademark infringements and counterfeits the court only began its work after a plaintiff filed a lawsuit claiming his or her trademark had been pirated. The importer involved his or her lawyer and following the conclusion of the court case, in the event piracy was proven, the court decided the amount of compensation to be paid to the plaintiff and any pirated products would be destroyed. The cases of which he was aware mostly concerned infringement of logos and designs (interview, Bamako, 2011). How exactly the court works and how the judges decide about the question of similarity of brands needs further research. Here I rely mostly on what importers told me and also call upon some of the protocols followed in public court sessions.

Upon becoming aware that their brands have been pirated, importers whose brands are registered can ask the police to confiscate the pirated products. To accomplish this, the complainant has to present the documents issued by OAPI confirming their ownership and proof that the brand is still registered, to his lawyer and to the court, who may then give permission to confiscate the products. If the pirate is from outside Africa, he is obliged to pay the fine but if from Mali or another African country, the fine may be subject to negotiation. The plaintiff will say it is 'someone from the family' who he feels should not have to pay the compensation. Only the packages are confiscated and destroyed but the tea may be returned and sold again. Only rarely the product will be also destroyed. The aforementioned senior member of staff at CEMAPI explained:

> This is serious, it is what the law recommends, but you can make it in an amiable manner, because not every copied product is of bad quality. … If the quality is good, he [the plaintiff] says, okay, I will sign a contract with you, and you leave me that part with which I started and also I will pay you something. This happened once with [pirated packages of] *Canal* in Kayes. This possibility exists since about 2008. INTERVIEW, BAMAKO, 2016

If the pirate has registered his pirated brand with OAPI, then the brand can be cancelled. This can be done by an application to OAPI, who verifies the correct owner of the brand and informs the pirate that he no longer owns it.

Some importers have enjoyed good experiences with the commercial tribunal but not always. The sales manager of *Gazelle* complained that

> The court often takes too long, but often also they agree with us, we are anyway right. We cannot just leave someone or a Chinese whom we discover inflagranti [without a lawsuit] … because generally, these people have less good quality than the quality we sell. … If we want to get in touch with them [the court], we know how to make them work. And we know that *Gazelle* is a strong brand on the market and that we have to defend it. Scam is never legal … counterfeiting can kill a brand. But if you look after your rights, you take them to court, but if we insist on our rights, this can bring us even more difficulties. INTERVIEW, BAMAKO, 2016

Many importers think the same way; they consider the trademark law useful and effective but they are hesitant about the virtues of the lawsuits. They also feel the court could operate with more transparency and many believe that only wealthy importers could use the court to assert their rights. One of them said: 'If you do not have enough money, you do not even need to go there'. He said, he gave 2 million francs CFA to his lawyer but he did nothing and he added that perhaps the pirate gave him even more money. He continued that less prosperous importers would not even need to register their trademarks, but they do because they never know whether this might prove beneficial one day (interview, Bamako, 2013). Reflecting upon these statements, my assistant remarked: '*La loi du Mali, c'est la loi de la rue* (Mali's law is the law of the street)' (Bamako, 2013). With this he wanted to say that 'the law of the street is the law of men who are popular and who can make a crowd of people move in the street and frighten you by this power. And it can be a wealthy man who has the means to bribe the judges and the Malian forces of order'. This strongly reminds of the power with which Big Men in many parts of the world create influence (Sahlins 1972; Godelier and Strathern 1991).

2.1 *Tea Importers' Opinions on Trademark Registration*

Generally, importers believed ownership of brands and their registration with OAPI made sense because this allowed them to prosecute those who sought to profit from their work. One of the importers explained why he had established his own brands, saying that when he worked as a representative of a producer or supplier, he would work for that company and sell their products on the Malian market; if he successfully sold 'five or ten shipping containers of the product, it would be in the [foreign] company's name and for its profit'. But if he had his own brand, he could negotiate much better conditions with his supplier: 'he would then not be able to produce my brand and sell it himself' (interview, Bamako, 2013).

This importer clearly emphasised that he had invested time, effort and money into his brand, and if his packages did not contain good quality tea then the reputation of his brand – for which he had worked many years – was destroyed. Registering his brand provided the means to defend it:

> If you have your own brand, and you do not represent the brand of someone else, then you register it. You advertise it and make it known and you can also prevent others from using your name. If someone else wants to make your tea and travels to China to bring tea with your brand name, then it can happen that you do not have the means to prevent him. But if I make my tea and I see you selling my tea and you are not in my distribution network I will catch you. INTERVIEW, BAMAKO, 2013

Another importer also considered brand registration useful but added some critical comments, saying

> When my brand begins to sell, I register it, but you are not obliged to register your brand. The fees are high. It is not my supplier who created my brands, it is me and therefore I have to register them. It helps against piracy; then nobody else can use your brand. But you see … there have been problems because here in Mali, people do not understand the opportunities of a business, they think everything is permitted. There are people who think they can import and just take what is available. INTERVIEW, BAMAKO, 2013

He continued that some people might consider that everything, i.e. the designs and brand names, were free for anybody to use. This is actually what the critics of copyright are asking for (Röschenthaler and Diawara 2016), but from a different perspective and against government guidelines and large multinational business contexts.

Many importers found brand protection in theory quite useful but understood that in practice it could often be complicated to use it in defence of their brand. One of them looked rather sceptical at it when he remarked that 'even if this [brand registration] is of no use, today, I do this and I keep a copy of each package, in ten years I can still look at it' (interview, Bamako, 2013). Asked for the reasons for this complication, another importer stated that intellectual property was

> A good idea but it is difficult to apply in Africa because the court does not play its role of protector. What is important here is the informal sector, which is very difficult to see through. You do not know who is who. And even if you know, it is very difficult. It is a society full of social relations. This makes it very difficult to protect your brand. INTERVIEW, BAMAKO, 2016

He said, his brands were copied several times but he could not go to Dabanani on the tea market where the importers were and confiscate their tea. He would not dare do that. It was too difficult to compete with these 'informal traders' who would not declare anything or only a little or do this with the complicity of the forces of law and order. It was not possible to fight against such practices.

Even the biggest importers who had fought some law suits questioned the benefits of registration, saying

> In Mali, in West Africa, you pay a certain amount of money to protect your brand, but when you pay this money, you do not know yet whether your brand will be selling, but you throw your money like this. There are many importers who made no profit at all and could not even continue. And others do not register their brand because they know that it will not work. They only want to sell some tea. ... There are still others who imitate us, they take your colours, a bit of your name or logo, but they will not gain much, because if you call Interpol or the commercial court [then they have a problem], this is everywhere the same thing in Africa, it is a bit difficult. INTERVIEW, BAMAKO, 2016

The terms 'difficult' and 'complicated' always came up when it was about social relations, when people cheated or copied brands belonging to their relatives.

Some importers have suggested that the best strategy would be for all importers to unite behind an agreement that they show no tolerance towards brand pirates.

Piracy has been in all societies at all times (Jones 1994) but more precisely it is everywhere where immaterial aspects of things have value and private individuals can make money selling them. There was no piracy in the tea trade whilst the state had the import-export monopoly. Brand piracy arrived with the advent of a market economy in which private importers began to invest in brands, in advertisement and were able to claim rights in intellectual property. This then is the context within which piracy proliferates as the 'twin of intellectual property' in a neoliberal economy (Sundaram 2010). One of the Malian specialists noted that as long as Malians and other Africans did not possess the means to manufacture copies of products themselves, there was little necessity for Western industrialists to register their brands in African countries. This insight corroborates the assessment that intellectual property rights were initially made for their European and North American inventors or creators in the context of capitalist market economies (for a discussion see Röschenthaler and Diawara 2016) but now with increasing Sino-African trade had become a significant issue in Africa as well.

2.2 *'Le Social Prime au Mali': How Importers Deal with Pirates*

Those few cases recording legal action against tea pirates demonstrate just how much money may be made with tea and also through copying successful brands. However, no public judgements are available for most instances of tea piracy. This is because many tea importers prefer to avoid pursuing legal action not just because they are convinced that only those with money can successfully prosecute through the courts but also because they consider it important to maintain good social relationships. My assistant suggested Malians preferred to avoid the courts because suing someone would bring to an end any further social involvement with their family, and therefore, legal action would be undertaken, if at all, only as a last resort. Malians preferred to avoid the police and the court and regulate things among themselves because, as one specialist told me, 'social relationships are of primary importance (*le social prime au Mali*)' and 'you do not have a right over your father (*on a pas le droit sur son père*)', which means you have to respect your forefathers and your older relatives. It also means that you have to obey them more than the law (interview, Bamako, 2016).

One of the importers told me that his cousin, who makes *Thé Obama* once counterfeited his tea brand, the blue *Hamza*. The importer showed me the package and the modified image at the back. 'It was my cousin, *Obama*. He pirated me, but I said nothing. He did not sell this tea for long. He only had a 20-foot container with 500 *colis*. He was not successful selling it, so he stopped it'. The importer explained that he could have phoned his cousin but did not even do this, 'but, you know, it is my cousin, whatever, he is my cousin' (interview, Bamako, 2013). We also had tried to contact the importer of *Obama* to discuss with him his wonderful creation of *Thé Obama*, but he always gave reasons why he could not meet us. As the example of *Gazelle* showed, there was a lot of social disagreement but only one published lawsuit, because, I was told several times, 'you know, it is too complicated (*c'est trop compliqué*)'. Lawsuits that were not withdrawn at some point were fought with pirates not of the same extended family and who refused to cooperate such as with *Gazelle* and *Gazelle et ses petites*. Another importer explained to me that

> If a brand is pirated and you discover it, often here in Mali, and in the other African countries it is the same, because here, you are in a family. If there is counterfeiting, normally, we discuss this among ourselves, and the issue ends on this level. But in other countries [like in Europe, you cannot do this, discussing in the family, because] you don't know the people. INTERVIEW, BAMAKO, 2013

Once the tea brand *Touareg* was pirated by a Djokoramé who copied the design, replacing the name with his own. It was not exactly the same design, but you could easily mistake it for *Touareg* whose owner explained:

> You see, it is not only about the name, it is about all that which can create confusion in the head of the consumer. This is not correct. This has happened so often also with other brands, with *Arawane* and *Gazelle*. INTERVIEW, BAMAKO, 2016

When he learnt his brand had been pirated, he went to the commercial court with his own and an example of the copied packages along with his registration papers:

> Once you discover such counterfeiting, you present yourself at the commercial court of your commune and present your case. You take a lawyer, and then the police will confiscate the tea in the warehouse. The commercial court will consider the case and determine whether this is counterfeiting, creating confusion among consumers. If it is decided that it is piracy, then the tribunal can sue the pirate to pay a fine plus one year and four months of prison. You are asked to assess what damages you

> had, and how many months of profit margins you have lost due to that. The court fined the pirate the equivalent of four months' worth of profit and sentenced him to six months in prison. But I did not want him to go to prison and I did not want his money. I just wanted to make him understand. But I took the tea cartons and destroyed them and put all the tea in big bags which I gave back to him. I told him: 'I do not want your money, you are a trader like me, but you will have to pluck up the courage to make your own brand or sell someone else's. I don't want to see again a trader who burns the spirit of someone's brand who has worked for ten years to create it'. I made him promise that this is the last time that he pirated another traders' tea. INTERVIEW, BAMAKO, 2016

He continued reflecting 'you have to create your own brand, and you have to fight, if you can stay on the market, it's good, it's your chance. And if you are on the market, people will say, he makes tea, look, he is well dressed, he has a beautiful car, a nice house, he sells tea, there is profit [to make]'.

What to me appeared to raise difficult philosophical questions, for these tea importers, they proved much easier to resolve. They possessed a relatively clear idea as to when a tea brand was rather too similar to their own and merited consideration as outright piracy. One importer said, some of the *Flecha* imitations were sufficiently dissimilar to be considered a singular brand, with only the colours being similar. He may have said so because he also owned such a *Flecha* imitation. But then, he showed me examples of what he considered trademark infringements. The design was the same but the name was changed from *Koutam* into *Kontak* and it appeared obvious that the name had been intentionally changed in order to deceive consumers. He knew the pirate, a Malinke, who had travelled to China to obtain tea from a small company that, however, collaborated with the larger company from whom the owner of *Koutam* procured his tea. Initially, the pirate had intended to just copy the design, but the factory broker suggested it would be better to also change the name a little (interview, Bamako, 2016).

The larger Chinese tea factory learnt about the copy and tipped off the owner of *Koutam*. The container holding the pirated tea was confiscated at the port of Dakar and the commercial court fined the pirate 110 million francs CFA. The owner of *Koutam* destroyed the packages but not the tea. He told the pirate that he did not want his money because he knew his family nor did he want to damage them. Reflecting on this, he said: 'We were very nice to them'. But he also knew that other importers had destroyed tea in the packages. The owner of another best-selling brand had reacted in a similar way. He did not want the 80 million francs CFA that the commercial court had fined the pirate for trademark infringement. He explained: 'But I was not in need of the money. I said, I do not touch your money but I will destroy your tea'. He destroyed everything, the packages and their contents.

Hence, one importer explained that whenever someone discovered piracy it was important to have the registration documents and the documents from the Direction nationale de commerce et de la concurrence:

> When we import a product, we pay for the brand, we register it. But we are in a country where it is not easy to anticipate fraudulent people, and there are many. Counterfeiting is violation and we bring them to court. If we feel that we were cheated, we inform Interpol when it is international fraud. INTERVIEW, BAMAKO, 2013

Most of the time the court will decide trademark infringement is a matter of deceiving consumers and unfair competition. Most often Malian importers refrain from accepting the financial penalities inflicted on the pirate and most also refrain from destroying the product, partly because of the social relationships and partly because Islam does not encourage the destruction of value.

For Malian importers, cases of piracy involving their brands beyond Mali is more difficult to identify. Therefore, it is essential to have a properly functioning distribution network with representatives (chapters 1 and 5). When the brand *Taoudeni* was pirated by the Chinese brand *Yasmina*, a representative of *Taoudeni* informed the owner that he saw it in a town near the border to Burkina Faso and sent him a photo of the pirated tea by his mobile phone. The owner contacted the officer at the border to establish from where the tea arrived. The owner then called his trade agent in Ouagadougou to verify in a certain shop whether he could discover there the pirated tea. Next Interpol was asked to confiscate the tea. The Chinese shop owner escaped with most of the tea, although 10 *colis* were confiscated. The Chinese pirate called the owner of *Taoudeni*, pleading with him not to bring the case to the commercial court and asking whether there was another solution. They came to an agreement and the importer added:

> It is not nice to confiscate the tea of someone, especially the retailers who have already paid the money to get the tea. It is not their fault because they did not intend to get pirated tea, and you never know how it can turn back on you again because you destroy money. If it would have been a Burkinabé, it would have been even more complicated.

The Chinese pirate agreed to change the colour of the package from blue to green and remove the image of the salt bars, characteristic for *Taoudeni*, and replaced them by jasmine flowers.

When *Achoura* was pirated by *Charifa*, the pirate left the design and the colour almost the same, only the name *Achoura* was substituted by *Charifa*. Several importers knew about it and commented that this was a perfect imitation (*c'est une imitation parfait*) (interviews, Bamako, 2016). In 2016, the owner of *Achoura* confiscated all the pirated packages at the port of Abidjan. Again the packages were destroyed but the tea was returned to the pirate, but of course such a tea does not sell well. The owner of *Achoura* explained:

> You are winning the court case but the winner has to forgive the pirate. Mali is a small country. There is a lot of humanism. All these traders pray to God to help them in their business. They pray that I will not ruin them. They come and want to negotiate about the money, but I say your money is not interesting to me. They only had a 20-foot container of 30 million francs, I will only burn the packages in front of them to make them understand that it is not about [their] money'. He continued that 'you will forgive him before the judgement is made. You bring him to court, but there is no judgement. You will take back the dossier and cancel the complaint and stop the process. All this is because of social concerns.
> INTERVIEW, BAMAKO, 2016

The pirate was of Saharan origin, whose son resided in Abidjan and was an in-law to the owner of the brand. He had purchased the tea from a company in China who knew the brand owner and informed him. All this 'forms part of a long complicated story' (*c'est trop compliqué*). Many of the tea importers, especially those of Saharan origin, are related to each other, have married into each other's families or have worked together at one time. They will say, 'we are from the same family (*nous sommes de la même famille*)'. In the same way but to a lesser extent, the Djokoramé families cooperate in many ways, and often also with the traders of Saharan origin. They cooperate on the one hand and on the other hand, they are in competition with each other as each of them has his or her own business and account. Social considerations play a huge role; not so much because of altruism but more because of caution and wisdom. This also means not giving up easily but ensuring that you teach your competitors a salutary lesson; it is necessary to fight to hold your place in the market (*il faut se battre*); and the examples show that an importer also needs the help of a large network of collaborators widely scattered in different places.

Taken together, the commercial court is only called upon to teach a culprit a lesson, if other means failed to achieve the desired resolution. After the confiscation of the pirated tea and the decision of the court, the lawsuit is withdrawn and the plaintiff waives the money, destroys the packaging materials and most often returns the tea. They would rather not ruin the pirate and allow him to sell the product. Destroying food and another's existence would be contrary to the Muslim ethics. That the 'naked tea' is difficult to sell, corroborates the idea that branding enhances the product's value and demonstrates that despite people's thoughts on the matter it is not really all about the taste and quality of the tea but at least in part it is also about the attractive brand design on the packaging. Tea importers are convinced that managing one's brand and controlling its distribution enables them to identify pirated products and even perhaps obstructs pirates in their work. Conversely, when a brand is often pirated, it suggests the importer is unable to exert control over their products. Hence, importers often wavered between being annoyed by pirates and hesitating to admit their brand had been pirated for this conveyed the impression that their mastery in business was less than perfect. Importers had however not only to get along well with their pirates but also with the authorities.

3 How Importers Protect their Tea Brands

Tea arrives in Mali from China via the West African ports. Some traders held the opinion that the shipping containers should be inspected at the port in order to confiscate pirated tea directly there. However, this is not feasible because customs officials check the conformity of products and documents but are unaware as to the legitimacy of a particular brand, unless they are tipped off by a brand owner who has himself been warned and alerted about piracy of their product. From the ports, tea is transported to its respective importer's warehouses. From there, it is distributed to the representatives and wholesalers, often with the help of a *coxeur* (chapter 4). It is possible that *coxeurs*, retailers and wholesalers all have a stake in the distribution of pirated tea, just as they obviously do with legitimate brands. Some people suspect them of being accomplices of the pirates (interview, Bamako, 2011). At least they were the ones who were most reticent about responding to my questions. Serious wholesalers generally preferred to work with the major importers whom they trust not to sell them copied tea. The importer also relied on trust that wholesalers would refrain from stocking pirated versions of their brands accepted from another importer, which they could acquire cheaper (interview, Bamako, 2013). Selling pirated tea could place the wholesaler in some difficulty, as it might damage their reputation, nevertheless, there is a strong temptation, particularly for smaller traders who still need to acquire the necessary capital to make their trade grow.

Small orders of tea entail printing short runs of cartons that would prove costly for the supplier, so Chinese companies accept minimum orders of no less than a 20-foot container; thus, importing tea is expensive and only those traders with substantial capital can afford to participate in the trade (chapter 3). Thus, lesser traders are not the copiers, as one wholesaler noted: 'The small traders do not have the means to pirate" (interview, Bamako, 2011).

Consumers generally considered Chinese traders to be the pirates, stating they mixed good tea with teas of lesser quality before selling their tea in the copied packages (interview, Bamako, 2011). These opinions reflect the generally bad reputation Chinese traders have in Mali. A senior staff at AMAP said: 'People say the Chinese came here to develop themselves with piracy. [But it is] Malians [who] want to live like Europeans and when others [the Chinese] are not as mediocre as they themselves, they cannot accept this' (interview, Bamako, 2007).

Other importers observed the Chinese walking around in the market, taking photographs and studying the products on display, and concluded that they imported products resembling existing ones, but sold them cheaper:

> They take a photo, send it to their factory in China, change the name a bit and then they bring the cargo here. If you discover it, you can take them to court. We work ten years with our brands, we make promotion and publicity, we put a lot of money in our brands. INTERVIEW, BAMAKO, 2013

My assistant suggested that some of the pirates were *coxeurs,* retailers, or even wholesalers who asked a Chinese trader wandering around in the market to order tea on their behalf and explaining whilst they did not yet have the necessary capital, they knew how to sell tea and that if they worked together, they both would profit from the deal. Tea packages that were produced under such arrangements would not disclose names and addresses of the importers thus obscuring their origin (interview, Bamako, 2013). Whilst containers are accompanied with all relevant documentation, once the tea is in the country, it cannot easily be ascertained who imported it. As my examples have elucidated, if an importer does not receive information about the piracy of his brand by his Chinese supplier, he must discover it himself, oblige the seller to disclose the identity of the person who supplied it to them and ask the authorities to confiscate the tea.

Tea importers suggested there were several tea pirates among the Chinese traders but most were certainly other Africans. One suggested, 'it is the Mauritanians who devalue the tea names. They take money from the bank, go to China, find some tea that has not been sold because it was bad quality, put it in a package [with a well-known name] and sell it here' (interview, Bamako, 2013). Others however insisted that the Mauritanians had high quality tea. Both can be true, as traders had the tendency to refer to one example and generalise from this (interview, Bamako, 2011). Another importer saw the reason for the proliferation of piracy in the lack of creativity seen in other Malian importers:

> You see, in Mali, people often are too lazy to search well, to fabricate, to make innovations. They no longer look for what is good and don't put energy in creating. There are already so many creations on the market. They just look around, they see a tea, it has good quality, it sells, they want to copy their carton, and then their quality is not good. INTERVIEW, BAMAKO, 2016

Another importer corroborated this impression:

> There are so many people [importers], they do not know how to work, because there are others who work hard, and they just want to harvest from the work of other people. This is not normal. They don't make an effort, and often they bring bad quality and that creates the problem because people [consumers] can no longer distinguish good from bad, and then the people no longer pay [your tea]. This is bad luck, but also for the copiers because they destroy themselves, because they cannot provide quality, and then it is over. INTERVIEW, BAMAKO, 2013

Even when the quality is acceptable, pirates trick consumers into believing they have purchased the legitimate brand. If quality and taste diverge from what they are used to, the pirate undermines the market value of the tea brand, nullifying the owners' previous efforts in building their brand's popularity. Even if consumers followed local criteria of product classifications, the impact for the brand was the same, because they would evaluate the taste of the copied brand in relation to that of the original.

Both the Malian government and OAPI were aware of rampant piracy. OAPI organised awareness workshops to raise consciousness about intellectual property rights and 'salons de thé' against piracy. The national newspaper *Essor* reports regularly on the activities of OAPI and in 2008, for example, noted that piracy had to be fought worldwide and represented 5 to 9% of global markets and thus was not just a Malian problem (*Essor* 2008). Additionally, to pursuing pirates through the courts, importers might also announce incidents of piracy involving their brands in the media and issue advice to consumers as to how they may distinguish between the legitimate and pirated brand designs. This might make pirates aware their activity has been discovered and perhaps encourage them to desist.

Most efficient in protecting a brand, however, is a network of reliable representatives in all regions where an importer intends to sell tea. These representatives will distribute the tea only to reliable wholesalers and ensure they will not accept the same tea brand from other sources. There will also be employees who receive the tea containers, take the tea to the warehouse, organise the documents and check whether there is more of their brand of tea on the market than they have distributed to the wholesalers. These employees are paid monthly, have no experience in selling tea and do not sell it themselves. Their task is solely the management and surveillance of the brand. Knowledgeable importers have employees and trade agents checking the market everywhere. Tea importers who are poorly represented easily fall prey to piracy from local importers, as the example of *Flecha* illustrated.

4 Statistics, Border Controls and Tax Collection

This last section examines the transportation of tea around West Africa, its interface with customs at border crossings and importers' attitudes towards paying tax, all of which renders it difficult to establish exactly, how much tea enters Mali. Here, also the idea prevails about social relationships being more important than adhering to the demands of bureaucratic rules.

4.1 *The Import Statistics of Tea*

Demand for green tea is constantly growing in Mali (and not only there), raising questions as to whether China is able to produce the large quantities of tea at a consistent quality. The production has challenges, with seasonal and annual variation, among other issues so that when a brand becomes popular, the appropriate tea leaves become scarcer and leaves from other regions must be blended in an attempt to reproduce the taste of the original (chapter 5). One of those importers who had very popular tea brands knew that this was a problem for China:

> All those tea factories I know [in China], they cannot produce more than a container every three month. … If you tell me that you sell more than one or two containers of a tea of the *Flecha* quality than I have to assume that you are lying and that it is not of that same good quality, because you cannot produce and market that much good tea. INTERVIEW, BAMAKO, 2013

But he did not elaborate on the implications for his business which sold at least about 20 containers of tea each month in Mali. He did explain that his tea was a slightly lower quality than *Flecha* and that his Chinese supplier had to blend leaves.

Another importer suggested: 'they blend the tea as long as it assumes the taste that Malians like' (interview, Bamako, 2013). It is also possible that China blends the tea with imports from other countries such as India and Sri Lanka.[1] Still another importer suspected that China exported

> Four or five times more tea than it was possible to produce on its territory. ... The higher qualities of buds and small leaves are consumed in China. They consume most of their high-priced tea themselves. They blend the tea [for export], they put some good tea, some mediocre tea and some other tea whatever it is. And then they offer you a price. INTERVIEW, BAMAKO, 2013

He even suggested that 'red tea', i.e. black tea, or a colouring agent was possibly mixed in to make the liquid darker and perhaps even something to make it foam more might be added. But at what point can this activity be considered blending and when does adulteration begin? This question requires further research. Uncertainties continue with import statistics.

Mali provides no regular and coherent tea import statistics concerning tea. Irregularities probably arise at the borders and the customs control points. The UN Comtrade (2021) database indicates that in 2013, China exported 7,500 tons of tea with a value of USD 31 million to Mali, but in 2018, only 5,500 tons. UN Comtrade (2021) statistics also reveal that in 2018, Morocco had imported 74,000 tons of green tea, Algeria 14,300, Libya 7,200, Mauritania 14,000 and Niger 1,900 tons.[2] When Mali's figures are compared with those from some other West African countries, it is surprising to learn that Senegal's tea imports in 2018 were 17,800, Ghana's 14,800 and Togo – a small country – 14,000 tons. These import figures far exceed those credited to Mali. Among them, Senegal has the highest green tea consumption, but here, drinking tea not as widespread as it is in Mali. According to the statistics these countries have higher

1 In 2018, China imported 10,044 tons of black tea from India and from Sri Lanka each, but less than 400 tons of green tea from Vietnam and neglectable quantities from Kenya, Turkey and Japan each, much less than the tea it exports to these countries (UN Comtrade 2021).

2 In 2019, Morocco was chosen to open China's first tea company in Africa, signalling China's growing presence in the continent (https://www.statista.com/statistics/1033746/china-tea-export-volume-by-destination/, accessed 28 April 2021).

tea imports, but especially Togo and Ghana consume less green tea because only migrants from the Sahel and the Mande-speaking minority drink it. This is reflected in the rare offer of tea packages in city shops and markets, and its complete absence in southern rural areas. Only in Bobo Dioulasso in Burkina Faso near the Malian border is Chinese green tea to be found in larger quantities.

My observations of the Malian tea market imply considerably higher tea consumption in the country. A hypothetical calculation makes this seem obvious. In 2013, for example, I counted 74 tea brands on Bamako's Grand Marché. There are certainly many more because it is unlikely that I saw all of those available at one moment in time. If just fifty of these brand owners import one 20-foot container containing 10 tons in 2013, then that would represent 500 tons. If 10 importers sold at least one 40-foot container per month, that would amount to an additional 2,400 tons and if in addition to this, 15 big tea importers sold at least five 40-foot containers per month, then these would be 18,000 tons, which makes altogether 20,900 tons, this is just very lowly-calculated estimate because of the big importers some import considerably more than 5 containers of 20 tons per month. One journalist estimated that alone of *Gazelle* were sold 50,000 tons in 2007 (Fall 2007).

My interviewees confirmed they also held the impression that the official figures for Mali were far too low. According to their estimates, Mali might even import more Chinese green tea than Morocco. One reason for an incomplete statistic could be that the tea always arrived in landlocked Mali through the port of another West African country in which it might be recorded. In addition to this, much of the tea is not registered. One importer complained that many other importers would not fully itemise their products and therefore it was difficult to compete with them in the tea trade. The statistics also do not reveal anything about the identity and nationality of the importers, i.e. they veil importers' agency, who are, as was discussed in chapter 2, to a large extent Malians.

4.2 *Tax Collection, Border Crossing and Corruption*

Many tea importers pay their taxes, but others try to circumvent the tax payments to a certain extent. One of the importers who was successfully selling tea told us that it would not be very wise to pay all taxes at once because 'you can never pay enough tax'. When the tax collector came, he would pay them a little 'to make him leave you in peace for a while' (interview, Bamako, 2007). When we came to talk to him again two years later, he was angry with us because he suspected that we were the reason that the tax collector had come more regularly. He told us that during the first three or so years, they did not have to pay much tax. But after our last visit, the tax authorities had visited them several times requiring more money and that we might have been behind this (interview, Bamako, 2009). We managed to convince him that we had nothing to do with the authorities. On our next visit, we noticed that he had created another company and after some more years he owned a few more companies, probably to profit from the tax reductions. Malian law indeed encourages the creation of enterprises, offering young companies reduced tax rates during their first three years of operation, after which the normal tax rate has to be paid (République du Mali 2012; chapter 3).

As outlined in chapter 3, importers, although ready to invest some of their profits in placing billboards and commercials, also hesitated to advertise their products because they feared unnecessarily attracting the attention of tax collectors. Merchants suspected that commissioning advertising billboards in town, encouraged people to automatically assume they were as rich as the multinational companies. Similarly, the ORTM actor who performed in the *Canal* tea advertisement, told us that people came to his house assuming he was advertising his own tea brand (chapter 3). These visitors seemed to believe that the billboards in town were his and that he was wealthy: they wanted to claim their share.

The perceived threat of attracting the tax authorities probably explains why many importers refrain from placing their names and addresses on their brand-named tea packages. Some importers argued traders would prefer to avoid providing not only their own names but also those of their Chinese suppliers both because they feared competition from fellow traders. One Malian trader in Shanghai noted that it would make a lot of sense not to supply name and phone number details on packages because of issues around transport, customs and tax, and alternatively that some importers printed fake names and numbers on their packages for that reason (interview, Shanghai, 2014). Having the phone number on the package enabled potential customers to convey their interest in the product to its owner, however, most importers dismissed this as unnecessary because their distribution network satisfied this role. Wholesalers and *coxeurs* knew whom to contact in the value chain (chapter 4). Other traders were aware that consumers who purchased poor quality tea and experienced health issues could not even direct their complaints to the importer.

A pertinent explanation for some of these irregularities was a lack of capital. Setting up in business, with all the attendant costs – registration fees, assembling the money to purchase and import the tea, paying customs and tax dues – is not an easy matter. Capital could be obtained with credit from a bank, an option few traders considered a good idea; they preferred the lower risk option of asking relatives to lend them money, or to work, at least initially, with a Chinese trader who sufficient cash of his own to import tea himself and was prepared to share the profits with the Malian trader responsible for distributing and selling their product. My assistant suggested that if none of these options was available, a trader would

> first make fraud on the back of those who were already successful and with the profit subsequently create their own company and thereafter import goods legally; some even [manage to] create factories and employ their children who [in that way] do not have the same problem of getting into business. This procedure has the appearance of a form of money-laundering (*blanchir de l'argent*). INTERVIEW, BAMAKO, 2013

He suggested that many traders had probably initially acquired their capital fraudulently through tax and customs evasion. This resonates with Mary Gani's (2020: 85; see also Röschenthaler 2017) finding in Nigeria that after having made money with piracy, 'pirates' invested their profits in legal business. Others instead tried to become tax and customs officers for the same reason of creating capital. My assistant told me that in earlier years parents would rather prefer their children did not become customs or tax officers because the money they earned did not come from honest hard work with their hands. Parents were convinced that the child 'would have to face hell' as a consequence. He explained that during the socialist era, all people worked for the well-being of the country and before colonial rule for the wellbeing of the king. When the king mentioned that a horse was beautiful, it was an honour to give him the horse as a gift. The horse figured as a kind of a pawn that guaranteed the king's blessing. People made efforts and worked for the nation as a whole. My assistant thought corruption was a new phenomenon, not something that went back to established African patrimonial practices (Bayart 2009). These days, nobody would care any longer whether the money they earned was 'good' or 'bad' (see also Bloch and Parry 1989) and they would even risk getting imprisoned.

This attitude had begun during the rule of Moussa Traoré (1968–1991) but had greatly increased during democratisation. People only thought about themselves and their own profit, fraud was encouraged because more money than ever was required to send children to school and also have them get good marks. The media debated how to prevent this behaviour, suggesting individuals should explain how they acquired their money, but the government rejected this idea as dishonourable. My assistant complained that everything had to go by *prendre le pot de vin*, which means by 'giving money under the table'. In terms of tea, probably only half of the money for a container that has to pass customs goes to the government and the other half to the customs official. People were aware that customs officials all had big cars and houses.

Copying, fraud and smuggling have been practiced everywhere, and at all times, when things gained in value and certain people made claims on them (Jones 1994). Such practices have to be evaluated not as natural phenomena and mere bad behaviour but in conjunction with particular legislations. In Mali, illegal copying considerably increased with the advent of neoliberal politics in the 1990s, with private importing, brand creation and the promotion of intellectual property. In the post-colonial era (1960–1991) when Mali had closed its borders for private import-export trade, tea and sugar were smuggled from neighbouring countries and probably products were also adulterated. However, no trademark infringements occured as yet there were hardly any tea brands and no legal private importation. During that time, the state was the strongest agent in the trade, and muted the agency of other traders. Nevertheless, some of them managed to bring some variety of tea into the market by smuggling it across the border. Individuals of considerable religious standing could even get the government to overlook it. Thus, rather than studying agency as peoples' capacity to change their fate in a binary against obstructive culturally embodied practices and/or structural constraints imposed by governments, it will be more rewarding to examine agency as the capacity of various individuals in an arena of stakeholders who pursue different interests and achieve their projects to varying degrees.

Conclusion

This study set out to examine the complexity behind economic processes often presented in highly abstract fashions. It has highlighted the agency of individual economic actors, their creativity in the manner they organise this trade and promote their products, as well as the social and cultural context in which they conduct their work. Through this approach, the study aimed to contribute an improved understanding of present-day South-South trade and globalisation processes without minimalising the agency of economic actors or locating their activities in the realm of the informal as a form of othering African economies.

The first three chapters considered the development of the popularity of green tea in Mali, beginning in chapter 1 with an examination of the link between regional awareness of the country's tea plantation and Mali becoming a centre of tea distribution. The ritualised consumption of tea had a special attraction and ambiance that eventually led to the beverage becoming the country's national drink. It explained how the tea ritual was disseminated with migrants from the Mande World to other regions, encouraging other people previously unaware of ritualised tea consumption to try the beverage and local merchants to import the product. Chapters 2 and 3 explored the way that green tea is promoted to Malian consumers, the tea standards, the quantitative increase in brands and the values attached to green tea through the local concept of quality, the exigencies of trade and advertisement and through its popularity among consumers.

Chapters 4 to 6 introduced the economic actors who play the leading roles in the tea trade between China and West Africa. Here I have discussed the means by which they finance their businesses, how this highly competitive economic sector was established and also, I described how Malian importers were effective in holding their own on the African markets against otherwise very successful Chinese and European traders. Chapter 6 analysed the brand designs printed on the tea packaging, including the materiality, arrangement and meanings conveyed by them, co-created between Malian merchants and their Chinese business partners. The importers' intentions were to promote popularity and therefore success for their brands but there were hidden threats that could arise from success for great popularity could easily create demand that could not be satisfied and in such cases ruin the brand.

Chapters 7 to 9 considered the intellectual property component of tea brands and the experiences of the Malian traders with this law, with the organisations for registering trademarks and with the state bureaucracy concerned

 | DOI:10.1163/9789004505698_012

with trade. The three chapters elaborated the ideas Malian importers held regarding the protection of their brands and discussed the solutions that they pursued when dealing with those who copied their brands. Also considered were the various challenges and uncertainties aroused by intellectual property law, particularly in relation to concepts of similarity and uniqueness in brand presentation.

My conclusions are arranged in four sections: the first discusses the interconnectedness between the different economic actors and the organisation of their trade; the second emphasises the innovative and original creation and the commemorative referencing of the green tea brands in Mali; the third section summarises the experiences of African importers with the intellectual property system; and the final section brings out what can be learned from this study about the agency of economic actors and the South-South trade in a globalising world.

1 Merchant-Entrepreneurs: The Green Tea Traders and the Organisation of Trade

When Chinese green tea arrived in northern Mali in the nineteenth century, it did so with the equipment for its preparation, the ritualised manner of consumption and some of its meanings that remain attached to it until today. Further meanings relate to the historical circumstances surrounding its introduction and the socio-political contexts at the time it became a popular beverage. Its status as Mali's national drink entails a deeply felt ambivalence that includes beneficial attributes as an energiser, a medicine and a means of sociability as well as fears about the decline of social values, unemployment, laziness and corruption. The tea importers became a focus for these considerations as they brought the beloved beverage to Mali and were easily attributed with being the heralds of the vices associated with it. By uniting in an association and contributing funds for the re-launching of the country's tea plantation, the major tea importers employed collective agency to divert accusations away from their profession.

This study has examined the importers' complex organisation of the tea trade and their distribution of the product from storage in warehouses to the small retail outlets where consumers buy their tea leaves on a daily basis. It also described how via trade and migration the tea ritual was disseminated to neighbouring West African countries, to the port cities on the Atlantic coast, to Central and even East Africa (Mozambique) and ultimately back to China. Once a sufficient number of Mande World migrants, capable of consuming at least one shipping container of tea a month, settled in a country, importers conveyed tea to there. Preferably they shipped to these places the most popular package size (25g), created specifically for the Malian market and which contained exactly the quantity of tea required for conducting one tea ritual. Thus, Malian traders extended their networks into these new regions and competed with Chinese and local traders who would also attempt to establish a foothold in the same market. Thanks to their own tea consumption and their on-street sales of the beverage, such migrants have introduced local African populations to green tea drinking and, as I have observed in Cameroon, this has further encouraged local importers who had not previously sold green tea, to import their own tea brands, beginning with tea qualities that no longer sold in Mali itself.

Coupled with these trading activities are two interconnected movements: African importers seek to close the distance between themselves and the locale of tea production, whilst Chinese traders seek closer proximity to consumers in Africa as part of their efforts to expand their markets. These trends began with Chinese brokers establishing trading posts in various Asian countries and West African Atlantic ports where Malian traders discovered them latest in the 1990s. Subsequently, Malian traders began travelling to Hong Kong and thence to the tea factories in China. Conversely, more recently, Chinese tea brokers have also increasingly moved to Bamako and other West African cities with the intention of more directly selling to consumers. Malian importers apply several strategies in the tea trade, carefully considering which strategy in which place would be the most rewarding: for the procurement of green tea, Malian importers prefer to work on their own, negotiating directly with the tea factory brokers and involving as few intermediaries as possible. For the actual distribution of their products, however, they commonly make use of intermediaries, namely the *coxeurs* who mediate between them, or their trade agents and the wholesalers. Chinese brokers also attempt to work with as few intermediaries as possible, but in Mali their approach has been met with resistance by local traders. These instead sought to submit them to their own established trade regime and successfully prevented them from selling tea at wholesale prices to street vendors – another instance of Malian tea importers' collective agency. These activities may be understood as manifestations of competition between Malian, other local African and Chinese traders but also as interconnecting teascape networks that extend from China to Mali and other African countries and back to China.

Tea was not disseminated via following a diffusion model but rather through the agency of individual traders and migrants, their strategies and trading activities. Entrepreneurial traders selected the tea qualities in China and advised the Chinese brokers as to how to create teas that appealed to Malian consumers. This entailed complex processes of negotiation in which language barriers and culturally specific ideas about how trade was carried out had to be overcome, at least to some extent. Dissemination of tea along the tea trail and increasing demand in Africa have spurred both the manufacture of tea equipment at various locations along the historical trade route and more recently within China as well as the establishment of new industries supporting tea production, processing and packaging. Together these industrial offshoots from tea consumption have offered numerous employment opportunities for people on the tea trail, in West Africa, and especially for many Chinese workers now busy fulfilling the wishes of their companies' African clients.

In order to show the importance of the leading players in the trade, chapters 2 to 5 described the various categories of actors, how the tea trade developed in Mali, the amount of tea that the major traders import, the number of brands they have, their education, their ethnic identity and how they collaborate with their Chinese business partners. On the tea market in Bamako, which offers hundreds of tea brands, the most popular and long-lasting of which are owned by some fifteen major importers, mostly of Saharan and Dyula origin but including a few Chinese. Both Malian importers and Chinese brokers' know-how were combined in this endeavour, despite frequent initial mistrust. Trust is essential in such a venture, both parties recognised this and wanted to work with each other but sometimes had conflicting ideas about conduct. Reasonable traders were able to establish trust between themselves and with experience also found ways to reduce the piratisation of their tea brands, stabilise their partnerships and protect their investments (chapters 5, 7).

As the evaluation in chapter 2 illustrates, the number of Chinese traders with registered tea brands (and of Chinese tea traders in Mali in general) is far less than that of Malians. Among the latter, the importers of Saharan and Dyula origin were the most successful. Access to distribution networks was decisive in selling larger quantities of tea and in this respect, traders of Saharan and Dyula origin definitely had an advantage having grown up with an intimate awareness of the importance of such networks and the knowledge of where to look for them. Bamana newcomers who had not 'been born with tea (*nés dans le thé*)' and whose parents had not been traders lacked this capacity. Chinese traders were also deficient in appreciating how distribution networks functioned in Mali and were additionally disadvantaged by being stereotyped as the purveyors of cheap products in contrast with traders of Saharan origin seen as connoisseurs and experts in selling good tea.

Chapter 5 explained the various strategies employed by tea importers to enlarge their business. Some strove to increase the quantity of tea they sold, others added new products to their sales portfolios by becoming representatives of a foreign company, and still others established their own supermarkets. In their business ventures, Malian importers combine several economic roles: travelling traders when they journey to China and to international trade fairs; merchants when procuring trade goods, which they distribute to wholesalers but they do not sell to consumers themselves; entrepreneurs when reinvesting their profits in more and diversified trade goods, in acquiring the means of transport and store their products, investing in property and occasionally in production (food products, animal farming). Importers had to decide when would be the right time to diversify their brands and commodities. Whilst some took such steps early on, others of the major importers preferred to initially focus on one or two brands – and to reduce risks – adding more only when these were successful and higher qualities were required. They also considered it wise to control as much as possible of the value chain. This highlights an overlap of economic roles that the successful tea importers combine in their profession and the wise employment of strategies adapted to the local social environment.

The barrier for importing green tea to Africa is that the minimum order is always one shipping container. This contrasts with the importation of other commodities from China that can be acquired in smaller quantities and conveyed in suitcases, by air cargo, or in shared containers. This is due to the requirement to produce large runs of printed tea cartons; shorter runs would be uneconomic. Thus, the acquisition of sufficient initial capital was the greatest obstacle for newcomers to new entrants into the trade. Whenever possible these entrepreneurs did not employ bank loans, rather preferring to use their own money or obtain loans from relatives. As Amselle (1987) outlined, the traditional route to obtaining starting capital was via an apprenticeship through which a young trader was assisted by his patron to test whether he was capable of success in his own venture. This route, which most of the importers to whom I spoke had followed, provides a more secure way to experiment as a trader; in the event of failure, bank loans may leave the unlucky trader with crippling debts.

Descendants of Saharan and Dyula traders learn in their role as a member of the family business, as outlined above. Newcomers may come from *koroboro* families whose members might save and enlarge their businesses until they become retailers and wholesalers. This also applies to the *coxeurs* who are also newcomers. A third group of newcomers are Bamana traders, usually wholesalers working in another sector, who try to become tea importers. However, this group often has difficulties getting a foot into the trade. This was partly a consequence of their inexperience, lack of knowledge of the 'work of tea' and inability to create distribution networks, and also partly due to the efforts of major traders to maintain their position by reducing competition. Thus, agency is not equally distributed among tea traders; and it becomes stronger with experience and the size of their ventures.

The evolution and modification of trade have historical, geographical, technological and socio-historical dimensions. During the past century, the means by which trade and travel were undertaken have greatly changed. The present-day tea traders overcome time constraints and large distances by airplane and get inspiration by novel trade goods available on a global scale. They are the new 'vernacular cosmopolitans' (Bhabha 1996; Werbner 2006). Their parents rarely boarded an airplane; they mainly travelled inside Africa on foot or by car and many received no formal schooling. Their grandparents traded on foot, moving their goods across the Sahara, the Sahel and the savannah by means of porting animals. Today's young merchants travel around the globe and organise their trade with computers and electronic gadgets. Often supplemented by university studies, the system of apprenticeship, however, remained important. Years of training precede a young trader being sent as a broker to reside with a landlord-broker relative in another town, where he would organise business for itinerant traders from his home place, save his profits and then start a business. He would later marry, begin a family once he returned home and after he had others working for him. With similar ideas in mind, many Malians ventured to China to work as brokers for itinerant African traders (Cissé 2015; Haugen 2018; Marfaing and Thiel 2015; Mathews 2015; Röschenthaler 2021).

All Malian tea importers have travelled to China, visited tea plantations and factories and negotiated with the factory brokers. The Chinese brokers are freelance workers, fluent in several languages, paid a commission on their sales by the tea factories. The Malian traders adapted their geographic and sociocultural knowledge to meet the requirements of their new trading sphere and learned how to negotiate with their Chinese partners. Both were interested in business – in selling, or buying tea – but they held quite diverging opinions about how trade should be handled, which, should they not be reconciled, might easily result in allegations of untrustworthiness.

The large variety of tea brands sold on the Malian market and the substantial amounts of money that can be made from their sale illustrate the importance of this trade. However, most Malian importers favoured 'hidden capitalism' to ostentatious displays of wealth. Awareness of the precarious position of traders being deviant actors from the farming norm (Simmel 1950 [1908]) has caused them to present themselves more as generous and philanthropic individuals, especially in times of crisis (Röschenthaler 2020b). Historical social stratification still continues to shape ideas about social life in present-day Mali.

This has set traders and artisans apart from access to political office (Hoffman 2000, Diawara 2003, Schulz 2001). Therefore, entrepreneurial individuals are less strongly perceived as political rivals by Malian government than those in other African countries where such strong social stratification did not exist (Grégoire and Labazée 1993: 28–29; Socpa 2016). Nevertheless, political crisis can easily acquire existential consequences for merchants and entrepreneurs (Jalloh 2002). A crisis that is existential for some, however, may provide a source of profit for others (Röschenthaler 2020b). All importers expressed their wish for greater political appreciation of their work and more support for entrepreneurship.

2 Tea Quality, Co-Creation of Designs and the Commemoration of Events

Chapters 1 to 3 detail the evolution of green tea branding focusing particularly on the several, partly parallel, developments seen in Mali, including the technical innovations and more direct trade routes, which served to reduce travel time between China and West Africa, from several years in the nineteenth century to 45 days in addition to transport from the ports of arrival to Mali itself. Tea supply and importation by caravan trade of the nineteenth and early twentieth centuries was replaced by the socialist state monopoly and, following the economic reforms in the 1990s, opening up opportunities for private trade; tea supply was changed from lose to packaged tea and from large wooden boxes to the small 25g packages; tea names changed from the general terms *ataya* or *duté,* via tea qualities such as *Quatre-mille-once* to brand-named tea such as *Baro, Cheval, Canal, Gazelle, Achoura*; the types of tea available also changed from Hyson – popular during the caravan trade – to Farako plantation tea mixed with Chunmee – during the post-colonial era – to Gunpowder in the 1990s and back to Chunmee in the 2000s and to Super Chunmee in the 2010s. These developments reflect consumers' changing tastes and are only topped by the most expensive teas sold in decorated metal boxes; brand design was adapted from the earlier more playful, multi-referential images to those conveying a more straightforward, clearer message.

Tea importers moved from selling teas of several qualities, indicated by colours carried on the packets to selling one good quality of tea popular at a given time; they also shifted from package design incorporating diverse printed information to designs conveying the barest minimum. Tea advertising evolved from mere product information to little stories about tea *grins* and women serving tea to (important) men, and included billboards highlighting catchphrases. During these developments, Malian traders gradually assumed mastery over large parts of the green tea value chain, which in the nineteenth century was shared between many intermediate traders and brokers along the trade route. With their increasing control, Malian importers' capacity to influence the market also increased.

Some aspects of these developments will be highlighted here: The tea package designs sell much more than tea itself, as many of them do not directly refer to the product. They commemorate trading contexts, historical references, social events of national and international importance. Many of the tea package designs reference past and present concerns and convey local values and images of the good life to be had by drinking tea. The names and designs refer to production in China, the historical journey through the desert, to trading places and personalities. In short, they represent a lively practice of commemoration when they take up not only historical and religious references but also political and social events of national and international importance with their names and designs. Similar naming practices have also been observed with textiles in West Africa (Bauer 2007).

In contrast to brands in the Western market economy, tea brands do not sell a particular lifestyle but rather portray connotations and images, combining and conveying feelings of local values and global connectivity (Malefyt and Moeran 2003). Tea package designs connect into the imaginations of consumers, influencing how they perceive their beverage, their belonging and place in society. In many cases, these designs and brand names have nothing to do with tea as a product. The tea packages with their multi-referential bricolage of meanings become a medium with which topical events and happenings are thematised and commemorated, thus representing a form of 'vernacular cosmopolitanism' (Bhabha 1996; Werbner 2006). In doing this, Malian tea brands differ from those found in many other parts of the world.

The package designs and brand names raise the awareness of participants in the tea *grins* for certain topics, when they sit together and converse. Whilst the young men might not gather specifically to discuss the brand names, nevertheless, the packages inspire conversation about daily concerns, political issues and military conflicts. Of course, the young men also discuss women but this topic, although some tea commercials make reference to the subject, is not explicitly addressed in the tea package designs (with the exception, perhaps, of *Gazelle*). Whilst multinational companies tailor black tea advertisement at the middle classes, the commercials of local importers rather speak to the large majority of Malians employing local themes. More generally, tea advertisements promote different themes from those of the brand designs and names which they promote. Commercials and billboards firstly inform but increasingly also pick up the context of consumption in the tea *grin*. The vibrant culture of commemoration and bricolage, seen in the printed designs on tea packets is not reflected in the publicity which tends to focus on themes more directly related to the consumption of tea.

Consumers say they ignore adverts, especially those on billboards, regarding them as suspicious because they believe people should not promote their own achievements; praising rather is a job fulfilled for their patrons by griots and advertising rather reminds people of post-colonial propaganda. Whilst consumers insist, irrespective of the image on the packets and the praise of advertising, only the taste and quality of the tea are relevant for them, they nevertheless note advertising is a useful source information about novelties on the market. They will purchase a new brand, check its quality by tasting it, purchase it again or not, as they see fit, before sharing opinions among their friends. News of this nature travels across entire neighbourhoods very quickly and importers consider it the most effective and inexpensive form of advertisement. It works in a similarly effective way as do media reports of brand-named products and consumers displaying the brand names of products they wear and use.

Package size, brand name and design impact on consumers' perceptions about tea. A tea product offered without a name in thin transparent 250g plastic bags, lacking any written information, is indicative of a cheap tea from China, or pirated and confiscated tea and both are difficult to sell. Conversely, displaying a properly branded trendy tea brand bolsters the self-respect and prestige of a tea *grin* and declares its connoisseurship. Thus, the branded tea packages are important non-verbal mediums of communication. By consuming the popular, good quality brands, a tea *grin* demonstrates its appreciation of refined taste and promotes its ability to gain respect among the other tea *grins* within a neighbourhood. By additionally commemorating historical and current events, however, tea brands are also mediums of communication in a more encompassing sense than Mary Douglas and others imagined (1992; see also Burke 1996b; Trentmann and Otero-Cleves 2017).

The economic reforms allowing private trade were a decisive factor in the development of the tea trade in its current form. Whilst this initially reduced the quality of the tea available for some time, it did lead to increased competition among importers, lowered the prices of the product and saw a multiplication in the number of tea brands. There were several reasons for this, including the feeling among wholesalers that there was a lack of tea on the market – even though this was not the case, there was merely a shortage of popular tea brands – which spurred them importing it themselves. Some wholesalers also took advantage of opportunities to purchase cheap tea from

China in addition to that which they regularly imported. Another even more decisive factor was the example set by major tea importers whose success enabled them to acquire property, freight transport and build office complexes after only a few years, which in turn inspired others to emulate their success.

By their efforts, tea importers democratised tea drinking, making available high-quality tea at affordable prices. Furthermore, they improved the quality of the tea to be found in Mali and thus influenced the tastes of Malian consumers. As long as tea was sold from larger boxes, consumers could purchase the amount of tea they required for a certain price; whilst the price was set, they could negotiate the quantity, as has been observed in other market transactions in Africa (Valenciano-Mañé 2019). Packaging tea in 25g packets also democratised tea sales because retailers needed not purchase entire wooden boxes of tea but only smaller quantities (sets of ten packets). Traders influenced the price and the quality by selling 25g packages of tea at a set price (100 francs CFA), regardless of quality – price being always fictitious (Guyer 2009) – enabling consumers to afford good quality should they choose to do so; they only needed to establish what constituted good quality. This in turn contributed to a positive perception among consumers of the importers owning these brands.

Tea having to be sold at just 100 francs CFA required careful assessment during the purchasing process. The importer needed to make his profit while buying (see also Vierke 2005: 439 for Tanzania) and he also had to be cognisant of the need to price *colis* of tea such that it permitted intermediate traders to also make their own profits. Thus, the quality of the tea purchased in China (which is dependent on price) had to be good but not so good that it cost too much to buy. This was at the same time a strategy the Malian importers employed to reduce competition with local newcomers and Chinese traders who tended to sell lower qualities because of conviction or lack of capital. The major importers were able to sell sufficiently good quality and dominate the market because of the sheer quantity of tea passing through their hands. What was probably an unintended side-effect, the strategy negatively affected the sale of Farako plantation tea which led to the accusations levelled by officials that private importers were threatening the plantation project (chapter 1). As an attempt to demonstrate their support for the Farako plantation, a group of private importers established the Association des Investisseurs du Thé Farako.

Most literature on moral economy reflects on tensions between producers and consumers, between peasants and the state, or between consumers and traders (Valenciano-Mañé 2019); in the case of tea, the notion of moral economy is played out between the various local hierarchies of traders, whom importers – unlike Chinese brokers – included in their considerations of pricing. This is reminiscent of the discussion about 'just price' which concerns one of the key debates in moral economy (Bloch and Parry 1989; Guyer 2009; Valenciano-Mañé 2019). In contrast to Valenciano-Mañé's example of packaged food in Equatorial Guinea and the creation of differing prices for various categories of consumers – one for the ordinary people and one for the more affluent – in the Malian tea trade the differentials seen in purchasing power are not applied to the 25g packages but do exist for the larger packet sizes.

Tea importers observed each other's work closely, learning from their experiences and improvements and they also monitored changing fashions in brand designs and choice of lead colours, which resulted in the changing appearance of brands approximately every four to five years. Malian wholesalers – especially their more educated children – adopted each other's ideas, and developing them further. The experience began with the 25g sachets, their placement within printed cartons, the creation of tea brands and their association with ideas imagined to be meaningful to Malian consumers. Chinese brokers were eventually persuaded to supply them the tea in folding carton in the small packet size, which not only increased costs but also had environmental implications as it produced more waste. However, at the same time prices fell and consumers gained the impression that the tea became more affordable and therefore attractive. The 25g packages were specifically created in Mali and soon became much more popular than any of the larger packets – despite its comparably higher price – because they were ideal for the conduct of a single Malian tea ritual. Tea in this type of package was distributed from urban centres to the countryside and followed the Mande migrants abroad.

Tea importers developed a variety of strategies in relation to the management of their tea brands: some maintained only a few, others created a new brand every other year; some managed one or two brands but several qualities in different colours; others sold each of their tea qualities under a different brand name, and still others gave different brand names to their various package sizes. Whilst the shelf life of many brands has been rather short, importers attempted to build their brands and sustain them for years; some managed several brands, selling smaller quantities of each and protecting themselves from risks, others felt it was more rewarding to sell larger quantities of fewer brands. Brands tended to be successful provided their quality remained consistent, their price affordable and consumers appreciated their taste.

Importers built their reputations upon ideas about the quality of their brands and – although these mostly contained the same type of tea – making them distinct from those of other importers. Additionally, their identities could influence their success. Consumers regarded the information appearing on packaging as less important and trustworthy – for example, its absence could mean either high or low quality – than the image of the tea seller himself; both consumers and retailers preferred to buy tea from a Malian, especially one from the northern part of the country. This was the case, even if a Chinese trader was selling good quality tea, for Malians tended to stereotype Chinese as purveyors of cheap, low quality goods much as Chinese traders stereotyped Malians as being poor and only interested in buying cheap items.

Notwithstanding, the tea brands are designed collaboratively, between Malian importers and their Chinese brokers (chapter 6) in similar fashion to that described for the Sino-Mozambican textile trade by Von Pezold and Driessen (2021; see also Vilarinho 2019). Which of the two parties involved has the larger share in this co-creation depends upon the creative capacities of the Malian importers who are the Chinese brokers' clients. Whilst Malians are the patrons of the trade, and their Chinese partners supply the products and the final brand design, they do follow their clients' suggestions, the collaboration exercised over package design may result from the equal or unequal contribution of both partners (see also Habibul Khondker 2005: 184). Depending upon whose influence prevails, the final product might consist of local, global and foreign (Chinese, Arabic) elements and conform to what has been termed as 'glocal', 'culturally hybrid' or 'creolised' (Hannerz 1992), a 'bricolage' image (Lévi Strauss 1962), or otherwise remain in some cases decidedly local.[1] Roland Robertson (1995: 28) first employed the concept of glocalisation to understand the interaction between the local and the global in processes of globalisation which becomes meaningful only when examined in local contexts. Both the word and the idea were first employed by Japanese marketing experts to describe products of Japanese origin that should be localised somewhere else and suited to local taste and interests (Habibul Khondker 2005: 184). It seems that glocalisation prioritises the perspective of producers whereas looked at from the perspective of the consumers this process has been termed 'local appropriation of global goods' (Hahn 2012; Rao and Ziff 1997; Silverstone, Hirsch and Morley 1992). The outcome of globalisation depends on what the historical actors make of it (Habibul Khondker 2005: 182), or otherwise, as Kate Meagher (2010: 169) formulated about Igbo industrialists' networks and which resonates well with the tea importers' strategies to maintain their place in the market: they 'reveal a genius for combining pre-colonial legacies with new institutional forms in response to the changing economic and political context'.

1 Glocalisation involves blending, mixing adapting of two or more processes one of which must be local; a hybrid version does not necessarily involve local elements (Habibul Khondker 2005: 191).

3 The Value of Tea Brands, Intellectual Property and the Impact of Copying

In addition to their social and economic impact, the tea package design is also of judicial relevance. The popularity of particular tea brands is closely related to the problem of the surfeit that creates a crisis on the tea market (chapter 5), followed by the pervasive copying of popular brands (chapters 7–9), which leads to questions about how importers understand the intellectual property law, deal with the copiers, protect their brands, make sense of the working of the commercial tribunal and relate it to the primacy of social relationships in Mali. Chapter 9 illustrated the great importance that traders attributed to properly functioning social relationships which in the long run were considered more beneficial than obeying the bureaucratic regulations. Import statistics and the small number of published court cases do not provide a comprehensive picture of commercial activities and efforts to combat piracy.

Undocumented practices of customs officials and importers' concerns about tax collectors appear to impact on the validity of the statistics which clearly do not capture the 'real economy' (MacGaffey 1991), veiling the agency of African traders and projecting an impression of China being the agent of the tea trade. Fears that an extensive presence in the media might unnecessarily attract the attention of the authorities also contributes to the evident reluctance of some Malian tea importers to place advertisements and expand the visible and audible reach in their agency into the public space. This is also reflected in their comportment, many preferring 'hidden accumulation' rather that ostentatious display of wealth.

Considerable values of different kinds were implicated in the tea trade. Added value was created by transferring the loose tea leaves from boxes into sachets, contained within printed folding cartons (chapter 2). From then on, people no longer merely drank *ataya* or *duté* but *Azawad, Gazelle, Achoura* and *François Hollande*. This added value helped Malian (and Chinese) tea importers understand they had created an asset, which needed to be protected and entitled them to claim it their intellectual property. Being part of OAPI, CEMAPI's establishment was an outcome of the structural adjustment programmes of the 1980s. However, it became of importance for local traders only after the 1991 reforms, when markets were opened for private trade. Sometime after they began importing, they created brands and protected them as their exclusive intellectual property by registration (chapter 7).

The histories of *Gazelle* and *Flecha* demonstrate that at the point of success, when a brand crisis strikes, most brand piracy occurs. They also highlight to the complexity involved interpreting the similarity and uniqueness of tea brands (chapter 8). The copies of both brands encompass a whole range of identical, similar and even less similar brand designs. This raises conceptual problems around similarity and singularity or uniqueness, which are up to the importers to claim and commercial court judges to decide. Concerning these conceptual challenges, it remains unclear upon which conceptual basis they are made, i.e. on a clear concept of similarity, or the assumed intentions of the pirates (chapters 8, 9). Looked at from a philosophical perspective, their similarity is not simply a question of 'yes' or 'no' but rather a matter of degree.

The copying of package designs – officially called piracy – is an intrinsic consequence of the application of intellectual property law to product branding. It supposedly leads to the destruction of brand value and undermines the owners' investment in the creation and building of their brands. In this context, most scholarly literature on the subject concerns the brands of producers, whereas in respect of Chinese green tea, brand owners are only rarely the producers (cultivators, the tea factory) but are either Chinese brokers or private Malian importers. Also dissimilar from some scholars' statements, brands as such do not create trust (Fanselow 2009), as this study shows, rather they demand trust from consumers, who can no longer inspect the tea leaves themselves, nor check their quality before purchase (chapter 5).

Discussion of the price of tea illustrates the substantial capital required in order to import it. Brand value was created partly due to the desire of consumers to engage in tea rituals and partly through the particular quality required of the tea leaves at a given time, through their packaging, the publicity and above all through the appreciation of particular brands by consumers (chapter 3). The role of wholesalers in disseminating tea to retailers was important in the success of specific brands because some retailers and many consumers rarely asked for particular named brands but rather, having memorised colour and design on the packet – asking aspects of it, such 'the yellow [packet] with the animal' (chapters 4, 7 and 8). This finding resonates well with Van den Bersselaar's (2005) observation that more important than the brand itself are often local classifications of products, i.e. having a local 'market name'. Similar practices have been observed for fabrics (Sylvanus 2016) and other commodities (Röschenthaler 2020c).

The intellectual property law speaks of 'misleading consumers', however, it should also be asked how consumers 'read' the brands and what are the relevant criteria for them. Van den Bersselaar (2005: 53) observed that trademarks were important not so much to distinguish the products of one producer or trader from those of another (Hellmann 2003) but as 'an indicator of specific characteristics of the product itself'. In the case of tea merchants, they were aware of local product classifications but having understood the value of brands, they then had to grapple with the interpretation of local consumers, Chinese tea standards and the international instruments of brand protection. Whilst for consumers this might not present a problem because they adhered to the local perspective on regimes of value (Guyer 2004), for importers much more was at stake. They had to navigate between these various regimes and come to terms with what has been identified as the 'striking misfit between the academic theory and its use in the real world' (Parchimovsky and Siegelman 2002: 1457). Notwithstanding these issues, the major importers emerged as the main actors and patrons exercising control over the Malian tea market.

Tea importers had differing experiences with those institutions established to protect their intellectual property. Not all of them were convinced as to how worthwhile it was to seek support from the commercial tribunal when their brands had been pirated but, nevertheless, many and not only the major importers, accepted the bureaucratic measures and registered their brands despite CEMAPI and OAPI being only responsible for registering. Observing the market was left to the importers who were obliged to identify instances of piracy and if they felt so inclined, to file a lawsuit. All this was of course, an added expense but cost was not the primary reason why importers preferred to regulate piracy privately among themselves. Importers were reluctant to drag other tea importers before the courts because it was felt that maintaining amicable social relationships was more important than justice obtained from a bureaucratic institution. Employing the services of the commercial court was generally considered only as a last resort when all other private options had come to nothing or they felt the pirate deserved to be taught a lesson. In such cases they would allow the court to go so far as to announce the level of compensation to be paid and at that point withdraw the lawsuit. This explains why a number of cases are known of but so few judgements have been published. The latter cases involved foreigners, importers of distant 'family relationship' (unrelated newcomers) or where attempts at amiable negotiation proved fruitless.

Despite the existence of international agreements, brands have to be registered in each zone in which they are to be protected. In the OAPI zone, foreigners such as Chinese importers can register their brands, but for Malians doing so in China is made difficult because of language problems and they would need representation in the country. Thus, in order to prevent Chinese traders from producing a Malian-owned brand and piracy by African competitors, Malian importers and Chinese suppliers began to collaborate for their mutual benefit. Each partner registers the brand in their own country which suffices to prevent competitors from producing and selling it. This is a procedure that can be understood as a variation of 'shared ownership' (Aguilar 2018;

Belderbos et al. 2014). The solution requires the establishment of long-term and more stable relationships between both parties. It has also led to some Malian importers creating several brands in order to ensure they are not too dependent on one supplier. However, there are also differences in China and with OAPI over the aspects of brands – only the name or the entire design – that are to be protected. This can lead to complications for those Malian importers who have failed to conduct sufficient research into existing brand designs. Such research is much easier for traders in China who merely type their chosen brand name into the registration database of the Chinese trademark protection organisation, whereas with OAPI, as the names form part of the design, they are not separately noted which thus complicates obtaining an overview of existing brands. Shared brand ownership is not due to the co-creation of the brand design but is practiced as a means of dealing with the intellectual property regimes which otherwise, in tackling cases of copying, would be difficult to navigate.

Furthermore, the Western or international model of intellectual property which considers brand ownership as exclusive property, is not the only useful or possible way to manage brands or trademarks and other artistic creations. Malians were also familiar with two other alternative models of understanding the immaterial aspects of trade goods: the socialist model that considers immaterial cultural goods the people's property which is managed by the state and which is still practiced to some extent in China and explains why Chinese traders often attribute less significance to brands; and the Muslim concept that relegates all creations to God, also discouraging monopolies such as exclusive property and the unequal distribution of wealth, at least in theory (chapter 7). Malians have however arranged themselves with the international model, although it is embraced with some hesitation.

4 The Agency of Malian Importers in the Tea Trade between China and West Africa

In its entirety, this study highlights the important role of the economic actors – people largely responsible for the popularity of Chinese green tea drinking in this region – trading tea between China and Africa along intricate trade networks. In the global context, these economic actors excel in trade – a dis-embedding and de-territorialising practice (Appadurai 1990; Giddens 1990: 21) – and transfer products across vast distances, encouraging cultural mobility along the trade route where commodities are re-imbedded and appropriated once again. In the example of green tea, over the course of some 200 years,

Malian consumers have gradually come to identify with the beverage and adopted it as their national drink (Röschenthaler forthc.; see also Fromer 2008 for Britain).

Despite 'local adjustments' and 'assertions' (Robertson 1995) and the essentialising idea of a national tea culture, there are connections and interlinkages between the various tea cultures that may be grasped with the concept of a 'teascape' – a spatial and cultural concept which counterbalances and unites what the various tea cultures – connected and entangled with each other through cultural mobility that trade and social networks entail – may have in common (Röschenthaler 2020a). In these trade ventures and their networks, mostly Africans and some Chinese are the leading economic actors, ordering, paying for, distributing and consuming Chinese green tea. The Chinese suppliers receive the orders, produce, process and package the tea and orient production towards the African market, thus African importers have become the patrons of tea production and packaging in distant China. In Africa itself, the more popular Malian tea brands acquired further dissemination via migrants from the country who carried the 'previously unknown product' (Mintz 1985) abroad with them, establishing themselves as models for new local consumers in their host countries to gradually adopt the beverage themselves.

The process of acceptance and interpretation of products introduced from Europe in the colonial context has been studied from the perspective of African consumers (Prestholdt 2008) who through their selection and preferences shaped the supply of such commodities on the market (Burke 1996a, 1996b; Van den Bersselaar 2005, 2007). In the current global context and through the perspective of traders, researching these tea importers helps enrich the scope of these earlier studies. Having the advantage of possessing a greater understanding of the tastes and attitudes of their consumers – better than that of their European predecessors and their Chinese competitors – these tea importers have democratised tea drinking and shaped their customers' tastes by improving the quality of the tea sold by offering high quality tea at affordable prices. Thus, it makes much more sense to explain the large-scale importation of the product to the Sahel countries and beyond by the agency of African importers rather than through metaphors of the swamping of African markets by Chinese products.

Unlike most studies of agency which are concerned with the efforts of common people to seize control of their lives (Brettel 2002; Ortner 2006), this one, although considering inhabitants of a country in the Global South, concerns more influential people. It highlights that merchants profit from their established local knowledge about consumption preferences and tastes of their customers which should, in any case, not be seen as a cultural constraint

(Archer 2000) but as an asset (Rapport and Overing 2000; see also Meagher 2010) essential for success. It is also important to note that agency should not be understood as a capacity that one has or does not have; it can appear in various forms and to different degrees; it can be weak or strong (Clough 2020; Evens 2008), individual or collective (Archer 2000, Bork-Hüffer et al. 2016); it can be present and also lost again.

The tea traders employ implicit knowledge that they acquired through experience, or their apprenticeship in the family business. They subscribe to the national legal framework by registering their companies and tea brands, paying tax and customs fees; they have formal businesses but, where possible, prefer to prioritise social relationships over legal regulations. Their situation is not so much one of individual agency versus structural or cultural constraints but situating themselves within various other agencies: that of other traders and importers, of consumers, and of the representatives of the state. Weak ties and stronger ones exhibited in their various social relationships with individuals (Stovel and Shaw 2012) are managed via delicate acts of counterbalancing, for example, by employing *coxeurs* (Röschenthaler 2021) but nevertheless prepare consumers to be interested in their brand-named tea.

Malian importers and Chinese brokers, able to forge sustainable relationships with their business partners and resolving the issue around mutual trust, may be attributed strong agency. Those merchants retaining their stereotypes are less likely to overcome their mutual mistrust, and thus display rather weak agency; they will be less prosperous and successful in their business ventures. Whilst each merchant works independently, in competition with their peers, when the need arises, they will combine forces and impose their 'collective agency' (Archer 1995; Bork-Hüffer et al. 2016) on those who endanger their businesses. Collective agency of tea merchants was observed in several instances: the creation of the Association des Investisseurs du Thé Farako to divert accusations of causing negative impacts of tea consumption; the decision to sell tea for 100 francs CFA in an endeavour to assert themselves in the competition with Chinese traders; by raising the quality of the tea which permitted all the traders throughout the network to earn a living; and by cooperating with their Chinese suppliers and co-sharing brand ownership to reduce piracy.

The new generation of tea importers began their work during the time of economic and media reforms, when publicity, brand creation and the registration of trademarks were encouraged and when exclusive intellectual property and brand piracy became an issue of legal importance. Together with their Chinese suppliers, they experimented with the new possibilities and opportunities offered by these developments and the trade itself. They created new packaging systems, tea brands and modes of cooperation, sought to understand whether and in which way the intellectual property law could be of use to them and how compatible it was with their own experiences, local knowledge and wisdom about managing the trade and the associated social relationships.

Chinese and Malian merchants, although in competition with each other, were also obliged to cooperate in order to ensure the success of their brands. Some importers lost all their investments, others were more successful, making a great deal of money. They developed an entrepreneurial spirit, investing their profits in trade, property, production and social relationships. Malian and Chinese merchants positioned themselves in an 'arena' (Bierschenk 2008) of competitors in which the extent of the visibility of their tea brands on the market defined their place. The colourful designs of the tea brands testify to the ubiquitous tea consumption in Mali and also reference the past and the present, the local and the global, and important events. Such brand creations are only possible as long as the inhabitants of Timbuktu, Arawane or Taoudeni as towns, Azawad as a region, Haidara as a personality and the Tuareg and Dogon as an ethnic group refrain from suing tea importers for making money on the backs of their identities but continue to see this as an honour or as positive publicity.

Trade between countries of the South has often been termed 'globalisation from below'. This term builds a binary opposition to 'globalisation from above' or high-end globalisation (Mathews and Vega 2012), which refers to big transnational business and official trade sanctioned by (Western) governments. Globalisation from below rather means all the activities of small traders who contribute to the democratisation of consumption, especially in the countries of the South, as outlined in the introduction to this study, but mostly with informal, illegitimate or illegal means situated in the shadow economy (Mathews and Vega 2012; Van Schendel and Abraham 2005). An example are small unregistered businesses who carry out trade in a petty commodity chain, transporting trade goods in suitcases or shared containers and where trust is difficult to establish between suppliers and traders (Haugen 2017; Lyons, Brown and Li 2013).

The green tea trade does not easily sit on either side of this binary. Malian tea importers submit to extensive and expensive bureaucratic measures (company creation, import licences, transport documents for each container, brand registration) which enable them to import the product (chapter 7). The quantities imported are not particularly small seeing as the minimal quantity an entire container. The small quantities of tea carried in their suitcases from Mali to China by Malian traders which enable Malians in China to drink tea favoured at home may certainly be termed 'globalisation from below'. That some informality plays a role in this is reflected in the refusal in China of Chinese sellers to say anything about this. China aids such informality by preventing Africans from selling such 'African' products themselves and hence the complications arise they later on complain about (Haugen 2012; Röschenthaler 2017).

The advantages and disadvantages of such laws and their capacity to reduce underdevelopment, injustice, the unequal distribution of wealth and the recovery of investments have to be evaluated. It must also be spelled out, for whose benefit these laws are made and whether the increasing commodification and judicialisation of all aspects of life (Röschenthaler and Diawara 2016) help to make the world a better place. Where the respective laws are not existing, there is also no transgression, corruption and piracy and this does not necessarily mean existence of greater disorder (Sundaram 2010).

The trading in green tea with China does not form part of the North-South exploitative plantation economy, to which the tea trade between India and Britain clearly belongs; it is part of South-South, or rather South-East trade but not therefore necessarily 'globalisation from below'. The documentation of the border crossings of the product are not fully transparent, but in the end, the tea importers – as do big global businesses as well – use loop holes in the legal framework (Ribeiro 2012). They rely on social relationships to bring their product to its consumers. Thus, it is important to get beyond such dichotomies and examine why economic actors work in the way they do, and through the research that informs this study, it was intended to take a step in this direction.

The study intended to carve out some of the contradictions in which tea importers find themselves entangled: on the one hand they participate in the neoliberal system of trade and intellectual property with its bureaucratic apparatus, they advertise and register their brands and employ the commercial court to deal with piracy. These measures inflate the costs of those importers affluent enough to bear them but who may hesitate to embrace them for other reasons. Intellectual property law inflames animosities, which most importers seek instead to defuse by refraining from suing their colleagues, in favour of forgiving them, supporting the equal distribution of wealth and good social relationships which, in the long run, are generally more rewarding than punishment and demanding the payment of compensation. These considerations bind to a moral economy of social relationships in more socially responsible but not necessarily less stressful handling of economic goods. Other complexities emerge from the different interpretations and practices of protecting brands. Finally, most remarkable is the inventive creation of tea brands as a collage and montage that emerged from the Sino-Malian cooperation in this South-South/East tea trade, which encouraged the farsighted among the Malians and Chinese traders to overcome mistrust and mutual stereotyping for the benefit of both parties.

FIGURE 59 Examples of tea package design

FIGURE 60 Further examples of tea package design

References

Aguilar, Ananay. 2018. 'Distributed ownership in music: between authorship and performance'. *Social & Legal Studies* 27, 6: 776–798.

Akinyoade, Akinyinka, Ton Dietz and Chibuike Uche (eds). 2017. *Entrepreneurship in Africa*. Leiden: Brill.

Alden, Chris. 2008. *China Returns to Africa*. London: C.Hurst & Co.

Alozie, Emmanuel. 2005. *Cultural Reflections and the Role of Advertising in the Socioeconomic and National Development of Nigeria*. Lewiston: Edwin Mellen Press.

Altbach, Philip. 1986. 'Knowledge enigma: copyright in the Third World'. *Economic and Political Weekly* 21 (37), 13 September: 1643–1650.

Amselle, Jean-Loup. 1987. 'Fonctionnaires et hommes d'affaires au Mali'. *Politique africaine* 26: 63–72.

Amselle, Jean-Loup. 1977. *Les négociants de la savane*. Paris: éditions anthropos.

Anon. 1970. 'La plantation de thé de Farako'. *Bulletin de Liaison* (Abidjan: CURD) 2: 49–56.

Appadurai, Arjun. 1986. 'Introduction: commodities and the politics of value'. In: Arjun Appadurai (ed.). *The Social Life of Things*. Cambridge: Cambridge University Press, 3–63.

Appadurai, Arjun. 1990. 'Disjuncture and difference in the global cultural economy'. *Public Culture* 2, 2: 1–24.

Appadurai, Arjun. 1996. 'Here and now'. In: Arjun Appadurai (ed.). *Modernity at Large: Cultural Dimensions of Globalization*. Minneapolis: University of Minnesota Press, 1–23.

Applbaum, Kalman. 2005. 'The anthropology of markets'. In: James Carrier (ed.). *A Handbook of Economic Anthropology*. Cheltenham: Edward Elgar, 275–289.

Archer, Margaret. 1995. *Realist Social Theory: The Morphogenetic Approach*. Cambridge: Cambridge University Press.

Archer, Margaret. 2000. *Being Human: The Problem of Agency*. Cambridge: Cambridge University Press.

Arsan, Andrew. 2014. *Interlopers of Empire: The Lebanese Diaspora in Colonial French West Africa*. Oxford: Oxford University Press.

Arvidsson, Adam. 2005. 'Brands: a critical perspective'. *Journal of Consumer Culture* 5, 2: 235–258.

Assaf, Katya. 2015. 'Der Zauber der Marke: Ein anthropologischer Blick auf das Markenrecht'. *GRUR International*: 426–438. Available at SSRN: https://ssrn.com.

Axelsson, Linn. 2012. *Making Borders: Engaging the Threat of Chinese Textiles in Ghana*. Stockholm: Acta Universitatis Stockholmiensis (Stockholm Studies in Human Geography) No. 22.

Azarya, Victor. 1980. 'Traders and the center in Massina, Kong, and Samori's state'. *The International Journal of African Historical Studies* 13, 3: 420–456.

Azmi, Ida Madieha, Spyros Maniatti and Bankole Sodipo. 1997. 'Distinctive signs and early markets: Europe, Africa and Islam'. In: Alison Firth (ed.). *Perspectives on Intellectual Property*. London: Sweet & Maxwell, 123–158.

Bamba Kiabou. 1992. 'Mali: Opération thé, mission accomplie'. 1 May. www.syfia.info/index.php5 ?view=articles&action=voir&idArticle=1771 (6 May 2012).

Barber, Karin. 2016. 'Authorship, copyright and quotation in oral and print spheres in early colonial Yorubaland'. In: Ute Röschenthaler and Mamadou Diarawa (eds). *Copyright Africa: How Intellectual Property, Media and Markets Transform Immaterial Cultural Goods*. Canon Pyon: Sean Kingston Publishing, 105–127.

Barnard, Alan. 2000. *History and Theory in Anthropology*. Cambridge: Cambridge University Press.

Barth, Heinrich. 1965. *Travels and Discoveries in North and Central Africa, being a journal of an expedition undertaken under the auspices of H.B.M.'s Government, in the years 1849–1855*. London: Frank Cass, 5 vols (reprint of the 1857–1858 edition, London: Longman).

Barthes, Roland. 1977 [1967]. 'The death of the author'. In his: *Image – Music – Text* (translated from French by Stephen Heath). London: Fontana, 142–148.

Bauer, Kerstin. 2007. *Kleidung und Kleidungspraktiken im Norden der Côte d'Ivoire*. Münster: Lit.

Bayart, Jean-François. 2009. *Politics of the Belly: The State in Africa*. Michigan: Wiley.

Bayoumi, Kawthar Abdalla and Arieff Salleh Rosman. 2018. 'Framing an Islamic vision of intellectual property: Maqasid-based approach'. *International Journal of Islamic and Civilizational Studies* 3: 25–40.

Beckert, Sven. 2014. *Empire of Cotton: A Global History*. New York: Alfred Knopf.

Belderbos, René, Bruno Cassiman, Dries Faems, Bart van Looy. 2014. 'Co-ownership of intellectual property: exploring the value-appropriation and value-creation implications of co-patenting with different partners'. *Research Policy* 43, 5: 841–852.

Beltrametti, Silvia. 2010. 'The legality of intellectual property rights under Islamic Law'. In: T. Mach et al. (eds). *The Prague Yearbook of Comparative Law*. Prague, 55–94.

Bently, Lionel. 2008. 'The making of modern trademarks law'. In: Lionel Bently, Jane Ginsburg and Jennifer Davis (eds). *Trade Marks and Brands*. Cambridge: Cambridge University Press, 3–42.

Bertoncello, Brigitte and Sylvie Bredeloup. 2007. 'De Hong Kong à Guangzhou, de nouveaux "comptoirs" africains s'organisent'. *Perspectives chinoise* 1: 98–110.

Bhabha, Homi. 1996. 'Unsatisfied: notes on vernacular cosmopolitanism'. In: Laura Garcia-Morena and Peter Pfeifer (eds). *Text and Nation*. London: Camden House, 191–207.

Bierschenk, Thomas. 2008. 'Development projects as arenas of negotiation for strategic groups: a case study from Benin'. *Sociologia Ruralis* 28, 2–3: 146–160.

Bloch, Maurice and Jonathan Parry. 1989. 'Introduction: money and the morality of exchange'. In: Maurice Bloch and Jonathan Parry (eds). *Money and the Morality of Exchange*. Cambridge: Cambridge University Press, 1–32.

Boateng, Boatema. 2011. *The Copyright Thing Doesn't Work Here: Adinkra and Kente Cloth and Intellectual Property in Ghana*. Minneapolis and London: University of Minnesota Press.

Bodomo, Adams and Caroline Pajancic. 2015. 'Counting beans: some empirical and methodological problems for calibrating the African presence in Greater China'. *The Journal of Pan African Studies* 7, 10: 126–143.

Bondaz, Julien. 2013. 'Le thé des hommes. Sociabilités masculines et culture de la rue au Mali'. *Cahiers d'Études africaines* LIII (209–210), 1–2: 61–85.

Boon, Marcus. 2010. *In Praise of Copying*. Cambridge, MA: Harvard University Press.

Bork-Hüffer, Tabea, Birte Rafflenbeul, Zhigang Li, Frauke Kraas and Desheng Xue. 2016. 'Mobility and the transciency of social spaces: African entrepreneurs in China'. *Population, Space and Place* 22, 199–211.

Bourdarias, Françoise. 2009. 'Migrants chinois au Mali. Une pluralité de mondes sociaux'. *Revue Européenne des migrations internationales* 25, 1: 7–24.

Bourdieu, Pierre. 1977. *Outline of a Theory of Practice*. Cambridge: Cambridge University Press.

Bräuchler, Birgit, Kathrin Knodel and Ute Röschenthaler. 2021. 'Brokerage from within: a conceptual framework'. *Cultural Dynamics* 33, 4: 281–297.

Brecher, Jeremy, John Child and Jill Cutler. 1993. *Global Visions: Beyond the New World Order*. Montreal: Black Rose Books.

Bredeloup, Sylvie. 2012. 'African trading post in Guangzhou: emergent or recurrent commercial form?' *African Diaspora* 5: 27–50.

Brégand, Denise. 1998. *Commerce caravanier et relations sociales au Bénin. Les Wangara du Borgou*. Paris: L'Harmattan.

Brettel, Caroline. 2002. 'The individual/agent and culture/structure in the history of social sciences'. *Social Science History* 26, 3: 429–445.

Broadman, Harry. 2007. *Africa's Silk Road: China and India's New Economic Frontier*. Washington: The World Bank.

Brooks, George. 1972. *The Kru Mariner in the Nineteenth Century: A Historical Compendium*. Newark: Liberian Studies Association in America.

Brush, Stephen and Doreen Stabisky (eds). 1996. *Valuing Local Knowledge: Indigenous People and Intellectual Property Rights*. Washington: Island Press.

Burke, Timothy. 1996a. *Lifebuoy Men, Lux Women: Commodification, Consumption, and Cleanliness in Modern Zimbabwe*. Durham: Duke University Press.

Burke, Timothy. 1996b. '"Fork up and smile": marketing, colonial knowledge and the female subject in Zimbabwe'. *Gender 8. History* 8, 3: 440–456.

Butel, Paul. 2007. *Histoire du thé*. Paris: Desjonquères.

Caillé, René. 1996 (1830). *Journal d'un voyage à Tombouctou*. Paris: Imprimerie Royale, vol. 2. (reprint: Paris: La découverte poche).

Calkins, Tim. 2005. 'The challenge of branding'. In: Tim Calkins and Alice Tybout (eds). *Kellogg on Branding*. New Jersey: John Wiley & Sons.

Caratini, Sophie. 1989. *Les Rgaybat (1610–1934)*. 2 vols. Paris: L'Harmattan.

Castells, Manuel. 1996. *The Information Age: The Rise of the Network Society*. Oxford: Blackwell.

Castillo, Roberto. 2015. '"Homing" Guangzhou: emplacement, belonging and precarity among Africans in China'. *International Journal of Cultural Studies* 19, 3: 1–20.

Chang, Hsiao-Hung. 2004. 'Fake logos, fake theory, fake globalisation'. *Inter-Asia Cultural Studies* 5, 2: 222–236.

Charry, Eric. 2000. *Mande Music: Traditional and Modern Music of the Maninka and Mandinka of Western Africa*. Chicago: University of Chicago Press.

Chatterjee, Piya. 2001. *A Time for Tea: Women, Labour, and Post-colonial Politics on an Indian Plantation*. Durham: Duke University Press.

Cissé, Daouda. 2015. 'African traders in Yiwu: their trade networks and their role in the distribution of 'Made in China' products in Africa'. *The Journal of Pan African Studies* 7, 10: 44–64.

Clarke, Gracia. 1994. *Onions are my Husband: Survival and Accumulation by West African Market Women*. Chicago: University of Chicago Press.

Clough, Paul. 2020. 'Agency, time and morality: an argument from social and economic anthropology'. In: Peter Róna and Lázló Zsolnai (eds). *Agency and Causal Explanation in Economics*. Cham: Springer, 115–124.

Cohen, Abner. 1971. 'Cultural strategies in the organisation of trading diasporas'. In: Claude Meillassoux (ed.). *The Development of Indigenous Trade and Markets in West Africa*. Oxford: Oxford University Press, 166–281.

Comaroff, John and Jean Comaroff. 2009. *Ethnicity, Inc.* Chicago: University of Chicago Press.

Coombe, Rosemary. 1997. 'The demonic place of the nowhere: trademark rumours in the postindustrial imaginary'. In: James Ferguson and Akhil Gupta (eds). *Culture, Power, Place: Explorations in Critical Anthropology*. Durham: Duke University Press, 249–274.

Coombe, Rosemary. 1998. 'Objects of property and subjects of politics'. In Rosemary Coombe (ed.). *The Cultural Life of Intellectual Properties*. Durham: Duke University Press, 41–87.

Coulibaly, Abdoulay. 2017. 'Parasitisme commerciale. La DNCC incinère onze tonnes de thé'. *Malijet*, 23 February. http://malijet.co/economie/parasitisme-commercial-la-dncc-incinere-onze-tonnes-de-the (accessed 21 April 2020).

Creyaufmüller, Wolfgang. 1983. *Nomadenkultur in der Westsahara*. Stuttgart: Burgfried.

Curtin, Philip. 1984. *Cross-Cultural Trade in World History*. Cambridge: Cambridge University Press.

Damani, Ahmed Elbachir. 2013. *Aschay as-sahrāoui: Dars at-tarīkh wa siyaqāt at-taghāyur alīkhtimāyi* (Tea of the Sahraouis: Lessons in History and the Framework of Social Change, written in Arabic). Casablanca: Al marqiz athaqāfi al a'arabi (Centre of Arabic Culture).

Daxueconsulting 2020. The Tea market in China: analysis of the largest tea market in the world. www.daxueconsulting.com, accessed 25 May 2021.

Diakon, Birama and Ute Röschenthaler. 2017. 'The Chinese presence in the Malian mediascape'. *Journal of African Cultural Studies* 29, 1: 96–113.

Diawara, Mamadou. 2003. *L'empire du verbe – L'éloquence du silence: Vers une anthropologie du discours dans les groupes dits dominés au Sahel*. Köln: Rüdiger Köppe.

Diawara, Mamadou. 2016. 'Breaking the contract? Handling intangible cultural goods among different generations in Mali'. In: Ute Röschenthaler and Mamadou Diarawa (eds). *Copyright Africa: How Intellectual Property, Media and Markets Transform Immaterial Cultural Goods*. Canon Pyon: Sean Kingston Publishing, 246–269.

Diawara, Mamadou and Ute Röschenthaler. 2012. 'Green tea in the Sahel: the social history of an itinerant consumer good'. *The Canadian Journal of African Studies* 46, 1: 39–63.

Diawara, Mamadou and Ute Röschenthaler. 2013. 'Mediationen: Normenwandel und die Macht der Medien im subsaharischen Afrika'. In: Andreas Fahrmeir and Anette Imhausen (eds). *Die Vielfalt normativer Ordnungen. Konflikte und Dynamik in historischer und ethnologischer Perspektive*. Frankfurt: Campus, 129–164.

Diawara, Mamadou and Ute Röschenthaler (eds). 2016. *Competing Norms: State Regulations and Local Praxis in sub-Saharan Africa*. Frankfurt: Campus.

Dioh, Tidiane. 2009. *Histoire de la télévision en Afrique noire francophone, des origines à nos jours*. Paris: Karthala.

Douglas, Mary. 1992. 'Why do people want goods?' In: Shaun Hargreaves Heap and Angus Ross (eds). *Understanding Enterprise Culture: Themes in the Work of Mary Douglas*. Edinburgh: Edinburgh University Press, 19–31.

Douglas, Mary and Baron Isherwood. 1978. *The World of Goods: Towards an Anthropology of Consumption*. Harmondsworth: Penguin Books.

Dougoutigi [alias Seydou Traoré]. 2010. 'Groupe AMI: une saga familiale face au défi de l'industrialisation'. *Journal Du Mali*, 27 January. http://www.journaldumali.com/article.php?aid=996 (accessed 10 March 2016).

Drewal, Henry (ed.). 2008. *Sacred Waters: Arts for Mami Wata and Other Divinities in Africa and the Diaspora*. Bloomington and Indianapolis: Indiana University Press.

Du Bois, Mikhalien. 2018. 'Justificatory theories for intellectual property viewed through the constitutional prism'. *PER / PELJ (Pioneer in peer reviewed, open access online law publications*) 21: 1–38. DOI http://dx.doi.org/10.17159/1727-3781/2018/v21i0a2004.

Ellis, Markman, Richard Coulton and Matthew Mauger. 2015. *Empire of Tea: The Asian Leaf that Conquered the World*. London: Reaktion Books.

Ellis, Stephen and Yves-A. Fauré. 1995. *Entreprises et entrepreneurs africains*. Paris: Karthala-Orstom.

Elmahjub, Ezieddin. (2015). 'An Islamic perspective on the theories of intellectual property'. In: Brian Fitzgerald and John Gilchrist (eds). *Copyright Perspectives*. Cham: Springer, 51–84.

Essor. 2008. 'Mali. Contrefaçon et piraterie. Effets destructeurs'. *Essor*, 15 August. http:/www.essor.gov.ml/cqi-bin/view/article16486, accessed 15 September 2008.

Evens, T.M.S. 2008. *Anthropology as Ethics: Nondualism and the Conduct of Sacrifice*. New York and Oxford: Berghahn.

Fanselow, Frank. 2009. 'The bazaar economy or how bizarre is the bazaar really?' *Man* 25: 250–265.

Fall, Birama. 2010. 'Commercialisation du thé vert au Mali: L'État affiche son favoritisme pour la société Achcar & Fils'. *Le Républicain*, 6 September. http://www.maliweb.net/economie/commercialisation-du-the-vert-au-mali-l%E2%80%99etat-affiche-son-favoritisme-pour-la-societe-achcar-fils-4465.html (accessed 10 March 2016).

Fieldhouse, David. 1994. *Merchant Capital and Economic Decolonization: The United Africa Company 1929–1987*. Oxford: Clarendon Press.

Finsterhölzl, Regina. 2015. *Die kommerzielle Werbung in Westafrika. Die Werbebranche und der politische Wandel in Ghana 1930–1970*. Köln: Böhlau.

Fofana, Modibo. 2014. 'Le Groupe AMI aujourd'hui'. *Journal du Mali*, 14 March. http://www.journaldumali.com/article.php?aid=8025 (accessed 10 March 2016).

Forde, Daryll (ed.). 1956. *Efik Traders of Old Calabar*. Oxford: Oxford University Press.

Foster, Robert. 2007. 'The work of the "New Economy": consumers, brands and value'. *Cultural Anthropology* 22, 4: 707–731.

Foster, Robert. 2008. 'Commodities, brands, love and kula: comparative notes on value creation'. *Anthropological Theory* 8, 1: 9–25.

Foucault, Michel. 1984 [1969]. 'What is an author'. In: Paul Rabinow (ed.). *The Foucault Reader*. New York: Pantheon, 101–120.

Frith, Simon. 1993. *Music and Copyright*. Edinburgh: Edinburgh University Press.

Fromer, Julie. 2008. "Deeply indebted to the tea-plant": representations of English national identity in Victorian histories of tea'. *Victorian Literature and Culture* 36, 2: 531–547.

Gani, Mary. 2020. *Creative Autonomy, Copyright and Popular Music in Nigeria*. New York: Palgrave Macmillan.

Gardella, Robert. 1994. *Harvesting Mountains: Fujian and the China Tea Trade, 1757–1937*. Berkeley: University of California Press.

Gardi, Bernhard. 1985. *Ein Markt wie Mopti. Handwerkerkasten und traditionelle Techniken in Mali.* Basel: Ethnologisches Seminar der Universität und Museum für Völkerkunde.

Geertz, Clifford. 1963. *Peddlers and Princes: Social and Economic Development in Two Indonesian Towns*. Chicago: Chicago University Press.

Gereffi, Gary. 2018. *Global Value Chains and Development.* Cambridge: Cambridge University Press.

Gereffi, Gary, J. Humphrey and T. Sturgeon. 2005. 'The governance of global value chains'. *Review of International Political Economy* 12, 1: 78–104. doi: 10.1080/09692290500049805.

Getachew Senishaw and Ute Röschenthaler. 2021. 'The politicisation of beer in Ethiopia'. *Brewery History* 185: 19–40.

Giddens, Anthony. 1984. *The Constitution of Society: Outline of the Theory of Structuration*. Cambridge: Polity.

Giddens, Anthony. 1990. *The consequences of modernity*. Oxford: Blackwell.

Giddens, Anthony. 2002. *Runaway World: How Globalisation is Reshaping Our Lives.* London: Profile Books.

Giersch, Patterson. 2010. 'Across Zomia with merchants, monks, and musk: process geographies, trade networks, and the Inner-East-Southeast Asian borderlands'. *Journal of Global History* 5: 215–239.

Giese, Karsten and Laurence Marfaing (eds). 2018. *Chinese and African Entrepreneurs: Social Impacts of Interpersonal Encounters*. Leiden: Brill.

Girier, Christian. 1996. *Parlons Soninké.* Paris: L'Harmattan.

Giulianotti, Richard and Roland Robertson. 2006. 'Glocalization, globalization and migration: the case of Scottish football supporters in North America'. *International Sociology* 21, 2: 171–198.

Godelier, Maurice and Marilyn Strathern. 1991. *Big Men and Great Men: Personifications of Power in Melanesia.* Cambridge: Cambridge University Press.

Graeber, David. 2001. *Towards an Anthropological Theory of Value.* New York: Palgrave.

Grégoire, Emmanuel. 1999. *Touaregs du Niger. Destin d'un mythe.* Paris: Karthala.

Grégoire, Emmanuel and Pascal Labazée. 1993. 'Introduction. Approche comparative des réseaux marchands ouest-africains contemporains'. In: Emmanuel Grégoire and Pascal Labazée (eds). *Grands commerçants d'Afrique de l'ouest.* Paris: Karthala, 9–36.

Gusterson, Hugh. 1997. 'Studying up revisited'. *Political and Legal Anthropology Review* 20, 1: 114–119.

Guyer, Jane. 2004. *Marginal Gains: Monetary Transactions in Atlantic Africa.* Chicago: University of Chicago Press.

Guyer, Jane. 2009. 'Composites, fictions and risk: toward an ethnography of price'. In Chris Hann and Keith Hart (eds). *Market and Society: The Great Transformation Today*. Cambridge: Cambridge University Press, 203–220.

Habibul Khondker. 2005. 'Globalisation to glocalisation: a conceptual exploration'. *Intellectual Discourse* 13, 2: 181–199.

Hagberg, Sten and Gabriella Körling. 2012. 'Socio-political turmoil in Mali: The public debate following the coup d'État on 22 March 2012'. *Africa Spectrum* 47, 2/3: 111–25.

Hahn, Hans-Peter. 2012. 'Consumption, identities, and agency in Africa: an overview'. In: Hartmut Berghoff and Uwe Spiekermann (eds). *Decoding Modern Consumer Societies*. New York: Palgrave Macmillan, 69–86.

Hannerz, Ulf. 1992. *Cultural Complexity: Studies in the Social Organization of Meaning*. New York: Columbia University Press.

Harrison, Simon. 1993. 'Commerce in cultures in Melanesia'. *Man* (ns) 28: 139–158.

Hart, Keith. 2006. 'Bureaucratic form and the Informal Economy'. In: Basudep Guha-Kasanobis, Ravi Kanbur and Elinor Ostrom (eds). *Linking the Formal and Informal Economy: Concepts and Policies*. Oxford: Oxford University Press.

Haugen, Heidi. 2012. 'Nigerians in China: a second state of immobility'. *International Migration* 50, 2: 65–80.

Haugen, Heidi. 2017. 'Petty commodities, serious business: the governance of fashion jewellery chains between China and Ghana'. *Global Networks* 18, 2: 307–325 (Version of Record online: 23 MAY 2017 / DOI: 10.1111/glob.12164).

Haugen, Heidi. 2018. 'From pioneers to professionals: African brokers in a maturing Chinese marketplace'. *African Studies Quarterly* 17, 4: 45–62.

Held, David (ed.). 2004. *A Globalizing World? Culture, Economics, Politics*. London: Routledge.

Hellmann, Kai-Uwe. 2003. *Soziologie der Marke*. Frankfurt: Suhrkamp.

Hémadinquer, Jean-Jacques. 1962. 'Le thé à la conquête de l'occident. Le cas marocain'. *Annales. Économies, Sociétés, Civilisations* 17, 6: 1145–1151.

Hinsch, Bret. 2016. *The Rise of Tea Culture in China: The Invention of the Individual*. Lanham: Rowman & Littlefield.

Hirsch, Eric and Marilyn Strathern (eds). 2004. *Transactions and Creations: Property Debates and the Stimulus in Melanesia*. New York: Berghahn.

Hodacs, Hanna. 2016. *Silk and Tea in the North: Scandinavian Trade and the Market for Asian Goods in Eighteenth-century Europe*. London: Palgrave Macmillan.

Hoffman, Barbara. 2000. *Griots at War: Conflict, Conciliation, and the Caste in Mande*. Bloomington IN: Indiana University Press.

Hopkins, Anthony. 1988. 'African entrepreneurship: an essay on the relevance of history to development economics'. *Genève-Afrique* 26, 2: 9–28.

Houtkamp, John and Laurens van der Laan. 1993. *Commodity Auctions in Tropical Africa*. Leiden: African Studies Centre.

Huang, Yasheng. 2008. *Capitalism with Chinese Characteristics*. Cambridge, MA: CUP.

Hubig, Christoph. 1990. 'Analogie und Ähnlichkeit. Probleme einer theoretischen Begründung vergleichenden Denkens'. In: Gerd Jütermann (ed.). *Komparative Kasuistik*. Weinheim: Beltz, 133–142.

Huetz de Lemps, Alain. 2001. *Boissons et civilisations en Afrique*. Pessac: Presses universitaires de Bordeaux.

Hulme, Alison. 2015. *On the Commodity Trail: The Journey of a Bargain Store Product from East to West*. London: Bloomsbury.

Imperato, Pascal. 1970. 'The dance of the Tyi wara'. *African Arts* 4, 1: 8–13, 71–80.

Jalloh, Alusine. 2002. 'African Muslim business in post-colonial West Africa'. In: Alusine Jalloh and Toyin Falola (eds). *Black Business and Economic Power*. Rochester: Rochester Press, 311–330.

Jamar, Steven D. (1992). 'Protection of intellectual property under Islamic law'. *Capital University Law Review* 21: 1079.

Jedlowski, Alessandro. 2016. 'Regulating mobility, reshaping accessibility: Nollywood and the piracy scapegoat'. In: Ute Röschenthaler and Mamadou Diarawa (eds). *Copyright Africa: How Intellectual Property, Media and Markets Transform Immaterial Cultural Goods*. Canon Pyon: Sean Kingston Publishing, 292–310.

Jedlowski, Alessandro, Patrick Oloko, Ute Röschenthaler and Ibrahima Wane. 2015. 'Across media: mobility and transformation of cultural materials in the digital age'. *Journal of African Media Studies* 7, 1: 3–9.

Johns, Adrian. 2009. *Piracy: Intellectual Property Wars from Gutenberg to Gates*. Chicago: The University of Chicago Press.

Jones, Mark. 1994. 'Why fakes?' In: Susan Pearce (ed.). *Interpreting Objects and Collections*. London: Routledge, 92–97.

Kalusa, Walima and Bizeck Phiri. 2013. 'Advertising, consuming manufactured goods and contracting colonial hegemony on the Zambian copperbelt, 1945–1964'. In: Robert Ross, Marja Hinfelaar and Iva Peša (eds). *Objects of Life: The History of Consumption and Social Change, 1840–1980*. Leiden: Brill, 167–185.

Kamian, Bakari. 2006. Fondation Emile Achcar (1904–1994). Unpublished document in honour of Emile Achcar. Bamako.

Khan, Javaid Iqbal and Naveed Ahmad Lone. 2013. 'Intellectual property rights in Islam: a perspective'. *International Journal of Research in Social Sciences* 3, 1: 153–162.

Khoury, Amir. 2003. 'Ancient and Islamic sources of intellectual property protection in the Middle East: a focus on trademarks'. *IDEA: The Journal of Law and Technology* 43: 151–206.

Kieffer, Julien. 2006. 'Les jeunes des "grins" du thé et la campagne électorale à Ouagadougou'. *Politique africaine* 101: 63–82.

Knowles, Caroline. 2014. *Flip-Flop: A Journey through Globalisation's Backroads*. London: Pluto Press.

Kopytoff, Igor. 1986. 'The cultural biography of things: commoditization as process'. In Arjun Appadurai (ed.). *The Social Life of Things: Commodities in Cultural Perspective*. Cambridge: Cambridge University Press, 64–91.

Krieger, Martin. 2009. *Tee. Eine Kulturgeschichte*. Köln: Böhlau.

Lakhdar, Omar. 2002. *Mogador. Judaïca. Dernière génération d'une histoire millénaire*. Essaouira: Géographique.

Lakhsassi, Abderrahmane and Abdelahad Sebti: 2012 (2.ed.). *Min aschay ila el Atay: Al adar wa at-tarikh* (in Arabic: From Aschay to Atay: Tradition and History). Rabat: College of Literary and Human Sciences.

Le Bail, Hélène. 2008. 'Les Chinois en Afrique de l'Ouest: au-delà des mythes (Chinese in West Africa: beyond the myths)'. *Africa Spectrum* 43, 3: 439–441.

Leriche, Albert. 1953. 'De l'origine du thé au Maroc et au Sahara'. *Bulletin de l'IFAN* 15, 2: 731–736.

Lévy, Armand. 1995. *Il était une fois les juifs marocains: témoignage et histoire de la vie quotidienne*. Paris: L'Harmattan.

Lévy-Strauss, Claude. 1962. *La pensée sauvage*. Paris: Plon.

Levtzion, Nehemia. 1968. *Muslims and Chiefs in West Africa*. New York: Oxford University Press.

Leyh, Elena. 2011. 'Die Inszenierung von Geschichte. Das Cinquantenaire in Mali'. In: Carola Lentz and Godwin Kornes (eds). *Staatsinszenierung, Erinnerungsmarathon und Volksfest. Afrika feiert 50 Jahre Unabhängigkeit*. Frankfurt: Brandes & Apsel, 158–174.

Lindell, Ilda. 2010. 'Introduction: the changing politics of informality – collective organizing, alliances and scales of engagement'. In: Ilda Lindell (ed.). *Africa's Informal Workers: Collective Agencies and Transnational Organizing in Urban Africa*. London: Zed Books, 1–30.

Liu, Yong. 2007. *The Dutch East India Company's Tea Trade with China, 1757–1781*. Leiden: Brill.

Lovejoy, Paul. 1978. 'The role of the Wangara in the economic transformation of the Central Sudan in the fifteenth and sixteenth centuries'. *The Journal of African History* 19, 2: 173–193.

Lovejoy, Paul. 1980. *Caravans of Kola: The Hausa Kola Trade 1700–1900*. Zaria: Amadou Bello University Press.

Lovejoy, Paul. 1986. *Salt of the Desert Sun: A History of Salt Production and Trade in the Central Sudan*. Cambridge: Cambridge University Press.

Lowie, Robert. 1928. 'Incorporeal property in primitive society'. *Yale Law Journal* 37, 5: 551–563.

Lydon, Ghislaine. 2009. *On Trans-Saharan Trails: Islamic Law, Trade Networks, and Cross-Cultural Exchange in Nineteenth-Century Western Africa*. Cambridge: Cambridge University Press.

Lyons, Michal, Allison Brown and Li Zhighang. 2013. 'The China-Africa value chain: can Africa's small-scale entrepreneurs engage successfully in global trade?' *African Studies Review* 56: 77–100. doi:10.1017/asr.2013.80.

Mahafsah, Qais Ali, Basem M. Melhem and Hitham A. Haloosh. 2009. 'The perspective of moral and financial rights of intellectual property in Islam'. *Arab Law Quarterly* 23, 4: 457–468.

Macfarlane, Alan and Iris Macfarlane. 2003. *Green Gold, the Empire of Tea: A Remarkable History of the Plant that Took Over the World*. London: Ebury.

MacGaffey, Janet. 1987. *Entrepreneurs and Parasites: The Struggle for Indigenous Capitalism in Zaire*. Cambridge and New York: Cambridge University Press.

MacGaffey, Janet. 1991. *The Real Economy of Zaire*. Oxford: James Currey.

Malefyt, Timothy de Waal and Brian Moeran (eds). 2003. *Advertising Cultures*. Oxford: Berg.

Malefyt, Timothy de Waal and Robert Morais (eds). 2012. *Advertising and Anthropology: Ethnographic Practice and Cultural Perspectives*. Oxford: Berg.

Manchuelle, François. 1997. *Willing Migrants: Soninke Labor Diasporas, 1848–1960*. Athens: Ohio University Press.

Mann, Susan. 1984. 'Brokers as entrepreneurs in pre-socialist China'. *Comparative Studies in Society and History* 26, 4: 614–636.

Manning, Paul. 2010. 'The semiotics of brand'. *Annual Review of Anthropology* 39: 33–49.

Marfaing, Laurence. 2012. 'Living together and living apart in Nouakchott'. In: James McDougall and Judith Scheele (eds). *Saharan Frontiers: Space and Mobility in Northwest Africa*. Bloomington and Indianapolis: Indiana University Press, 185–199.

Marfaing, Laurence and Alena Thiel. 2015. 'Networks, spheres of influence and the mediation of opportunity: the case of West African trade agents in China'. *The Journal of Pan African Studies* 7, 10: 65–84.

Marfaing, Laurence and Alena Thiel. 2017. 'African entrepreneurs in China: true actors of globalization'. In: Ute Röschenthaler and Alessandro Jedlowski (eds). *Mobility between Africa, Asia and Latin America*. London: Zed Books, 200–218.

Masquelier, Adeline. 2013. 'Teatime: boredom and the temporalities of young men in Niger'. *Africa* 83, 3: 470–491.

Massing, Andreas. 2000. 'The Wangara, an old Soninke diaspora in West Africa?' *Cahiers d'Études Africaines* 40 (158): 281–308.

Mathews, Gordon. 2011. *Ghetto at the Center of the World: Chungking Mansions, Hong Kong*. Chicago: Chicago University Press.

Mathews, Gordon. 2015. 'African logistics agents and middlemen as culture brokers in Guangzhou'. *Journal of Current Chinese Affairs* 44, 4: 117–144.

Mathews, Gordon and Alba Vega. 2012. 'Introduction'. In: Gordon Mathews, Gustavo Lins Ribeiro and Carlos Alba Vega (eds). *Globalization from Below: The World's Other Economy*. London: Routledge, 1–15.

Mazarella, William. 2003. *Shoveling Smoke: Advertising and Globalization in Contemporary India*. Durham: Duke University Press.

Mazarella, William. 2004. 'Culture, globalization, mediation'. *Annual Review of Anthropology* 33: 345–367.

McLeod, Kembrew. 2005. *Freedom of Expression: Overzealous Copyright Bozos and Other Enemies of Creativity*. New York: Doubleday.

Meagher, Kate. 2010. *Identity Economics: Social Networks & the Informal Economy in Nigeria*. Woodbridge: James Currey.

Meillassoux, Claude. 1963. 'Histoire et institution du *kafo* de Bamako d'après la tradition des Niare'. *Cahiers d'études africaines* 4, 14: 186–227.

Meillassoux, Claude. 1964. 'The "Koteba" of Bamako'. *Présence africaine* (English edition) 24 (51): 28–62.

Mertha, Andrew. 2005. *The Politics of Piracy: Intellectual Property in Contemporary China*. Ithaca and London: Cornell University Press.

Middleton, John. 2001. 'Merchants: an essay in historical ethnography'. *Journal of the Royal Anthropological Institute* (N.S.) 9: 509–526.

Miège, Jean-Louis. 1957. 'Origine et développement de la consommation du thé au Maroc'. *Bulletin économique et social du Maroc* 20 (71): 377–398.

Miège, Jean-Louis. 1961. *Le Maroc et l'Europe (1830–1894)*. Vol 2. Paris: Presses universitaires de France.

Miège, Jean-Louis. 1981. 'Le commerce transsaharien au XIXe siècle'. *Revue de l'Occident Musulman et de la Méditerranée* 32: 93–119.

Miller, Daniel. 1987. *Material Culture and Mass Consumption*. Oxford: Basil Blackwell.

Miller, Daniel. 2005. 'Materiality: an introduction'. In: Daniel Miller (ed.). *Materiality*. Durham: Duke University Press, 1–50.

Mintz, Sidney. 1985. *Sweetness and Power: The Place of Sugar in Modern History*. New York: Viking.

Moeran, Brian. 1996. *A Japanese Advertising Agency: An Anthropology of Media and Markets*. Richmond: Curzon.

Moeran, Brian. 2014. *The Business of Creativity: Toward an Anthropology of Worth*. London: Routledge.

Moeran, Brian and Christina Garsten. 2013. 'Business anthropology: towards an anthropology of worth'. *Journal of Business Anthropology* 2, 1: 1–8.

Müller, Angelo and Rainer Wehrhahn. 2013. 'Transnational business networks of African intermediaries in China: practices of networking and the role of experiential knowledge'. *Die Erde* 144, 1: 82–97.

Muniz, Albert and Thomas O'Guinn. 2001. 'Brand community'. *Journal of Consumer Research* 27, 4: 412–432.

Murillo, Bianca. 2017. *Market Encounters: Consumer Cultures in Twentieth-century Ghana*. Athens: Ohio University Press.

Mutongi Kenda. 2017. *Matatu: A History of Popular Transportation in Nairobi*. Chicago: University of Chicago Press.

Nakassis, Constantine. 2013. 'Brands and their surfeits'. *Cultural Anthropology* 28, 1: 111–126.

Narotzky, Susana and Niko Besnier. 2014. 'Crisis, value, and hope: rethinking the economy: an introduction to supplement 9'. *Current Anthropology* 55, Suppl. 9: 4–16.

Ncube, Caroline and Eliamani Laltaika. 2013. 'A new intellectual property organization for Africa?' *Journal of Intellectual Property Law & Practice* 8, 2: 114–117.

Nordström, Carolyn. 2007. *Global Outlaws: Crime, Money, and Power in the Contemporary World.* Berkeley: University of California Press.

Nwankwo, Nkechi. 2019. 'Spatial politics and gendered strategies: women traders and institutions in Oke Arin market, Lagos'. *Africa* 89, 1: 61–78.

OAPI. 2018. Official website of OAPI. www.oapi.int/index.php.fr (last accessed April 2019).

Okediji, Ruth. 2006. 'Africa and the global intellectual property model beyond agency'. *African Yearbook of International Law*, 207–251.

Oonk, Gijsbert. 2013. *Settled Strangers: Asian Business Elites in East Africa (1800–2000).* London: Sage.

Oonk, Gijsbert. 2017. 'Karimjee Jivanjee & Co in Tanzania, 1860–2000: a case for "diasporic family firms"'. In: Ute Röschenthaler and Alessandro Jedlowski (eds). *Mobility between Africa, Asia and Latin America.* London: Zed Books, 49–71.

Ortner, Sherry. 2006. *Anthropolgy and Social Theory: Culture, Power, and the Acting Subject.* Durham, NC: Duke University Press.

Ouma, Marisella. 2006. 'Optimal enforcement of music copyright in sub-Saharan Africa: reality or a myth?' *The Journal of World Intellectual Property* 9, 5: 592–627.

Packard, Ashley. 2010. 'Intellectual property: patents, trademarks, and trade secrets'. In his: *Digital Media Law.* Chichester: John Wiley & Sons, 156–178.

Parchimovsky, Gideon and Peter Siegelman. 2002. 'Towards an integrated theory of intellectual property'. *Virginia Law Review* 88, 7: 1455–1528.

Perinbam, Marie. 1973. 'Social Relations in the Trans-Saharan and Western Sudanese Trade: An Overview'. *Comparative Studies in Society and History* 15, 4: 416–436.

Peukert, Alexander. 2016a. 'The colonial legacy of the international copyright system'. In: Ute Röschenthaler and Mamadou Diarawa (eds). *Copyright Africa: How Intellectual Property, Media and Markets Transform Immaterial Cultural Goods.* Canon Pyon: Sean Kingston Publishing, 37–68.

Peukert, Alexander. 2016b. 'Vom Warenzeichen zum Markeneigentum. Ein Polanyischer Erklärungsversuch'. In: Wolfgang Büscher et al. (eds). *Markenkommunikation zwischen geistigem Eigentum und Verbraucherschutz*, 405–426. Available at SSRN: https://ssrn.com/abstract=2858769.

Peynaud, Emile. 2005. 'Tasting problems and errors of perception'. In: Karolyn Korsmeyer (ed.). *The Taste Culture Reader: Experiencing Food and Drink.* Oxford: Berg, 272–278.

Pezard, Stephanie and Michael Shurkin. 2015. 'A brief history of Mali's rebellions and the implementation of peace accords'. In their: *Achieving Peace in Northern Mali: Past Agreements, Local Conflicts, and the Prospects for a Durable Settlement.* Santa Monica: Rand Corporation, 5–22.

Philip, Kavita. 2005. 'What is a technological author? The pirate function and intellectual property'. *Postcolonial Studies* 8, 2: 199–218.

Piel, Simon and Joan Tilouine. 2015. 'SwissLeaks: les millions à Genève de Gérard Achcar, "l'intouchable" de Bamako'. *Le Monde,* 19 February. http://www.lemonde.fr/evasion-fiscale/article/2015/02/19/swissleaks-les-millions-a-geneve-de-gerard-achcar-l-intouchable-de-bamako_4579709_4862750.html (accessed 10 March 2016).

Pieterse, Jan Nederveen. 1995. 'Globalization as Hybridization'. In: Mike Featherstone, Scott Lash and Roland Robertson (eds). *Global Modernities.* London: Sage, 45–68.

Plietz, Olivier. 2012. 'Following the new Silk Road between Yiwu and Cairo'. In: Gordon Mathews, Gustavo Lins Ribeiro and Carlos Alba Vega (eds). *Globalization from Below: The World's Other Economy.* London: Routledge, 19–35.

Prestholdt, Jeremy. 2008. *Domesticating the World: African Consumerism and the Genealogies of Globalization.* Berkeley: University of California Press.

Racaud, Sylvain. 2018. 'Ramifications discrètes de routes marchandes transnationales: circulation de la pacotille chinoise entre marchés ruraux et villes secondaires au Cameroun'. *Les Cahiers d'Outre-Mer* 71 (278): 433–464.

Raji, Noufissa Kessar. 2003. *L'art du thé au Maroc.* Paris: ACR Édition Internationale.

Rao, Pratima and Bruce Ziff (eds). 1997. *Borrowed Power: Essays on Cultural Appropriation.* Brunswick, NJ: Rutgers University Press.

Rapport, Nigel and Joanna Overing. 2000. *Social and Cultural Anthropology: The Key Concepts.* New York: Routledge

République du Mali 2012. Loi no 2012–016 du 27 Fev 2012 portant code des investissements. http://www.droit-afrique.com/upload/doc/mali/Mali-Code-2012-investissements.pdf (accessed 20 April 2021).

Ribeiro, Gustavo Lins. 2012. 'Conclusion: globalization from below and the non-hegemonic world system'. In: Gordon Mathews, Gustavo Lins Ribeiro and Carlos Alba Vega (eds). *Globalization from Below: The World's Other Economy.* London: Routledge, 221–235.

Richardson, Gary. 2008. 'Brand names before the industrial revolution'. *NBER Working paper* 13930.

Robertson, Roland. 1995. 'Glocalization: time-space and homogeneity – heterogeneity'. In: Mike Featherstone, Roland Robertson and Scott Lash (eds). *Global Modernities.* London: Sage, 25–44.

Robinson, David. 2004. *Sociétés musulmanes et pouvoir colonial français au Sénégal et en Mauritanie, 1880–1920.* Paris: Karthala.

Rogers, Edward. 1910. 'Some historical matter concerning trade-marks'. *Michigan Law Review* 9, 1: 29–43.

Röschenthaler, Ute. 2009. 'Werbung im Kontext: Perspektiven auf ein neues ethnologisches Forschungsfeld'. *Zeitschrift für Ethnologie* 134: 213–251.

Röschenthaler, Ute. 2011. *Purchasing Culture: The Dissemination of Associations in the Cross River Region of Cameroon and Nigeria.* Trenton: Africa World Press.

Röschenthaler, Ute. 2015. 'Dressed in photographs: between uniformization, self-enhancement and the promotion of stars and leaders in Bamako'. *Africa* 85, 4: 696–720.

Röschenthaler, Ute. 2016. 'Good quality or low price? Competition between Cameroonian and Chinese traders'. *African East-Asian Affairs* 1–2: 32–65.

Röschenthaler, Ute. 2017. 'In constant search of money to survive: African youth in Malaysia'. In: Arndt Graf and Azirah Hashim (eds). *African-Asian Encounters.* Amsterdam: Amsterdam University Press, 17–45.

Röschenthaler, Ute. 2019. 'Liquid traditions: worlds of drink-taking in Africa'. In: Jan Beek, Konstanze N'Guessan and Mareike Späth (eds). *Zugehörigkeiten. Erforschen, Verhandeln, Aufführen im Sinne von Carola Lentz.* Festschrift für Carola Lentz. Köln: Rüdiger Köppe, 167–184.

Röschenthaler, Ute. 2020a. 'Chinese green tea in Mali, cultural mobility and African agency in the Global South'. *African and Asian Studies* 19, 1–2: 133–156.

Röschenthaler, Ute. 2020b. 'Crisis and credit: social and political challenges on the Malian tea market'. *African Identities* 18, 3: 253–262.

Röschenthaler, Ute. 2020c. 'Original and fake, fake originals or multiple degrees of quality? Chinese manufactured consumer goods on Cameroonian markets'. In: Ruth Achenbach, Rirhandu Barthels, Jan Beek, John Karugia and Frank Schulze-Engler (eds). *Afrasian Transformations.* Leiden: Brill, 280–300.

Röschenthaler, Ute. 2021. Brokers in the tea trade between China and West Africa. *Cultural Dynamics* 33, 4: 401–417.

Röschenthaler, Ute. Forthc. *A History of Mal's National Drink: Following the Tea Ritual from China to West Africa.*

Röschenthaler, Ute and Mamadou Diarawa (eds) 2016. *Copyright Africa: How Intellectual Property, Media and Markets Transform Immaterial Cultural Goods.* Canon Pyon: Sean Kingston Publishing.

Röschenthaler, Ute and Dorothea Schulz (eds). 2016. 'Introduction: forging fortunes: new perspectives on entrepreneurial activities in Africa'. In: Ute Röschenthaler and Dorothea Schulz (eds). *Cultural Entrepreneurship in Africa.* London: Routledge, 1–15.

Röschenthaler, Ute and Alessandro Jedlowski. 2017. 'Introduction: landscapes of opportunity, mobility and entrepreneurial perspectives'. In: Ute Röschenthaler and Alessandro Jedlowski (eds). *Mobility between Africa, Asia and Latin America.* London: Zed Books, 1–27.

Rowlands, Michael. 2004. 'Cultural rights and wrongs: uses of the concept of property'. In: Caroline Humphrey and Katherine Verdery (eds). *Property in Question: Value Transformation in the Global Economy.* Oxford: Berg, 207–225.

Rubbers, Benjamin. 2009. '"We, the Congolese, we cannot trust each other": trust, norms and relations among traders in Katanga, Democratic Republic of Congo'. *British Journal of Sociology* 60, 3: 623–642.

Sahlins, Marshall. 1972. *Stone Age Economics*. Chicago: Aldine de Gruyter.

Salmons, Jill. 1977. 'Mammy Wata'. *African Arts* 10, 3: 8–15, 87–88.

Sassen, Saskia. 2007. *A Sociology of Globalization*. New York: W.W.Norton.

Schechter, Franc Isaac. 1925. *The Historical Foundations of the Law Relating to Trademarks*. New York: Columbia University Press.

Scheele, Judith. 2012a. *Smugglers and Saints of the Sahara: Regional Connectivity in the Twentieth Century*. Cambridge: Cambridge University Press.

Scheele, Judith. 2012b. 'Garage or Caravanserail?'. In: James McDougall and Judith Scheele (eds). *Saharan Frontiers: Space and Mobility in Northwest Africa*. Bloomington and Indianapolis: Indiana University Press, 222–237.

Scheld, Suzanne. 2010. 'The "China challenge": the global dimensions of activism and the informal economy in Dakar'. In: Ilda Lindell (ed.). *Africa's Informal Workers: Collective Agencies and Transnational Organizing in Urban Africa*. London: Zed Books, 153–169.

Schroeter, Daniel. 1988. *The Merchants of Essaouira: Urban Society and Imperialism in Southwestern Morocco, 1844–1886*. Cambridge: Cambridge University Press.

Schroeter, Daniel. 2002. *The Sultan's Jews: Morocco and the Sephardi World*. Stanford: Stanford University Press.

Schulz, Dorothea. 2001. *Perpetuating the Politics of Praise: Jeli Singers, Radios, and Political Mediation in Mali*. Cologne: Rüdiger Köppe Verlag.

Schumpeter, Josef. 1934 [1912]. *The Theory of Economic Development*. Cambridge: Harvard University Press.

Schwimmer, Brian. 1979. 'Market structure and social organization in a Ghanaian marketing system'. *American Ethnologist* 6: 682–701.

Sebti, Abdelahad. 1999. 'Itinéraires du thé à la menthe'. In: Crédit communal (ed.). *Tea for Two. Les rituels du thé dans le monde*. Brussels: Crédit communal, 141–153.

Sharma, Jayeeta. 2011. *Empire's Garden: Assam and the Making of India*. Durham and London: Duke University Press.

Shinn, David H. and Joshua Eisenman. 2012. *China and Africa: A Century of Engagement*. Philadelphia: University of Pennsylvania Press.

Shore, Cris and Susan Durão. 2010. 'From a political anthropology to an anthropology of policy: interview with Cris Shore'. *Ethnográfica* 14, 3: 595–614.

Silverstone, Roger, Eric Hirsch and David Morley. 1992. 'Information and communication technologies and the moral economy of the household'. In: Roger Silverstone and Eric Hirsch (eds). *Consuming Technologies: Media and Information in Domestic Spaces*. London: Routledge, 15–31.

Simmel, Georg. 1950 [1908]. 'The stranger'. In: *The Sociology of Georg Simmel*. Transl. and ed. by K.H. Wolff. New York: Free Press, 402–408.

Smiers, Joost. 1999. 'Copyrights: a choice of no choice for artists and Third World countries'. *Iwalewa Forum* 3: 5–38.

Socpa, Antoine. 2016. 'Political entrepreneurship in Cameroon'. In: Ute Röschenthaler and Dorothea Schulz (eds). *Cultural Entrepreneurship in Africa*. London: Routledge, 99–118.

Spencer, Anne. 1982. *In Praise of Heroes: Contemporary African Commemorative Cloth*. Newark NJ: Newark Museum.

Steiner, Chris. 1985. 'Another image of Africa: toward an ethnohistory of European cloth marketed in West Africa, 1873–1960'. *Ethnohistory* 32, 2: 91–110.

Stovel, Katherine and Lynette Shaw. 2012. 'Brokerage'. *Annual Review of Sociology* 38: 139–158.

Sundaram, Ravi. 2010. *Pirate Modernity: Dehli's Media Urbanism*. London: Routledge.

Sylvanus, Nina. 2008. 'Rethinking "free-trade" practices in contemporary Togo: women entrepreneurs in the global textile trade'. In: Ulrike Schuerkens (ed.). *Globalization and Transformations of Local Socio-Economic Practices*. London: Routledge, 174–191.

Sylvanus, Nina. 2016. *Patterns in Circulation: Cloth, Gender and Materiality in West Africa*. Chicago: University of Chicago Press.

Tan, David. 2010. 'Differentiating between brand and trade mark'. *Singapore Journal of Legal Studies*, July, 202–210.

Taylor, Scott. 2012. *Globalization and the Cultures of Business in Africa: From Patrimonialism to Profit*. Bloomington: Indiana University Press.

Theisohn, Philipp. 2009. *Plagiat: Eine unoriginelle Literaturgeschichte*. Stuttgart: Alfred Kröner.

Trager, Lilian. 1981. 'Customers and creditors: variations in economic personalism in a Nigerian marketing system'. *Ethnology* 20: 133–146.

Trentmann, Frank and Ana María Otero-Cleves. 2017. 'Presentation. Paths, detours, and connections: consumption and its contribution to Latin American history'. *Historia Crítica* 65: 13–28.

Trubek, Amy. 2005. 'Place matters'. In: Karolyn Korsmeyer (ed.). *The Taste Culture Reader: Experiencing Food and Drink*. Oxford: Berg, 260–271.

Ukers, William. 1935. *All about Tea*. New York: The Tea and Coffee Trade Journal Company, 2 vols.

UN Comtrade. 2021. 'International trade statistics database', online resource, available at: https://comtrade.un.org/.

Valenciano-Mañé, Alba. 2019. 'When the big ones abandon the marketplace: morals and politics of price in Equatorial Guinea'. *Research in Economic Anthropology* 39: 49–70.

Van den Bersselaar, Dmitri. 2005. "'Keeps you fit and healthy": marketing and consumption of imported gin in twentieth-century West Africa'. Paper prepared for the EBHA Annual Conference, Frankfurt, 2 September. www.ebha.org (accessed 20 April 2021).

Van den Bersselaar, Dmitri. 2007. *The King of Drinks: Schnapps Gin from Modernity to Tradition*. Leiden: Brill.

Van Driem, George. 2019. *The Tale of Tea*. Leiden: Brill.

Van Dyke, Paul Arthur. 2005. *The Canton Trade: Life and Enterprise on the China Coast, 1700–1845*. Hong Kong: Hong Kong University Press.

Van Schendel, Willem and Itty Abraham (eds). 2005. *Illicit Flows and Criminal Things: States, Borders and the Other Side of Globalization.* Bloomington: Indiana University Press.

Vierke, Ulf. 2006. Die Spur der Glasperlen – Akteure, Strukturen und Wandel im europäisch-ostafrikanischen Handel mit Glasperlen. Bayreuth African Studies Online No. 4.

Vilarinho, S. 2019. Capulana in a D4S Perspective: Identity, Tradition and Fashion-able Challenges in the 21st Century. PhD dissertation, University of Lisbon.

Von Pezold, Johanna and Miriam Driessen. 2021. 'Made in China, fashioned in Africa: ethnic dress in Ethiopia and Mozambique'. *Africa* 91, 2: 317–336.

Vries, Peer. 2009. *Zur politischen Ökonomie des Tees*. Wien: Böhlau.

Wadle, Elmar. 1997. 'Markenschutz für Konsumartikel. Entwicklungsstufen des modernen Markenrechts'. In: *Europäische Konsumgeschichte. Zur Gesellschafts- und Kulturgeschichte des Konsums (18.-20.Jh)*. Frankfurt and New York: Campus, 549–670.

Waterbury, John. 1972. *North for the Trade: The Life and Times of a Berber Merchant.* University of California Press.

Wendl, Tobias. 2002. *Afrikanische Reklamekunst*. Wuppertal: Peter Hammer.

Wengrow, David. 2010. 'Introduction: commodity branding in archaeological and anthropological perspectives'. In: Andrew Bevan and David Wengrow (eds). *Cultures of Commodity Branding*. Walnut Creek: Left Coast Press, 11–33.

Werbner, Pnina. 2006. 'Vernacular cosmopolitanism'. *Theory, Culture & Society* 23, 2–3: 496–498.

WIPO. 1999. African Intellectual Property Organization (OAPI), Agreement Revising the Bangui Agreement of March 2, 1977, on the Creation of an African Intellectual Property Organization, Bangui (Central African Republic), 24 February 1999. https://wipo.int (accessed 25 April 2021).

Wooten, Stephen. 2000. 'Antelope headdresses and champion farmers: negotiating meaning and identity through the Bamana Ciwara complex'. *African Arts* 32, 2: 18–33.

Zhang, Jinghong. 2014. *Puer Tea: Ancient Caravans and Urban Chic.* Seattle and London: University of Washington Press.

Index